Social Dimensions
of Moral Responsibility

Social Dimensions
of Moral Responsibility

EDITED BY KATRINA HUTCHISON,
CATRIONA MACKENZIE,
and
MARINA OSHANA

OXFORD
UNIVERSITY PRESS

OXFORD
UNIVERSITY PRESS

Oxford University Press is a department of the University of Oxford. It furthers
the University's objective of excellence in research, scholarship, and education
by publishing worldwide. Oxford is a registered trade mark of Oxford University
Press in the UK and certain other countries.

Published in the United States of America by Oxford University Press
198 Madison Avenue, New York, NY 10016, United States of America.

© Oxford University Press 2018

CIP data is on file at the Library of Congress
ISBN 978–0–19–060961–0

1 3 5 7 9 8 6 4 2

Printed by Sheridan Books, Inc., United States of America

CONTENTS

ACKNOWLEDGMENTS

We want to thank all the contributors of this volume for the care and effort they put into this project. We know the book is much stronger because of their dedication and patience. We owe a huge debt to Wendy Carlton for her excellent editorial assistance on the volume in its entirety. Her work on behalf of the project has been invaluable. We have been fortunate to work with Lucy Randall, our editor at Oxford University Press. Lucy has responded with enthusiasm and encouragement to our labors, for which we are most appreciative. We also thank the capable and efficient team involved in the book's production. The idea for this volume arose originally from a workshop on the Social Dimensions of Moral Responsibility at Macquarie University in late 2014. We are grateful to the Centre for Agency, Values and Ethics, and the Faculty of Arts at Macquarie University for organizing and funding the workshop, and for funding Marina's visit to Sydney and Catriona's subsequent visit to Davis. We also owe thanks to the workshop participants, especially Jules Holroyd and Natalie Stoljar, for the excellent discussion their work produced and for lending further incentive to pursue the ideas generated at the workshop. Finally, we would like to thank one another for each contributing in full measure her talents and time to this project. It has been a labor of love and of learning, one that has demanded much in terms of coordination of effort and managerial skills. We have learnt much from one another and we hope the final project reflects this.

Katrina Hutchison, Macquarie University, Sydney
Catriona Mackenzie, Macquarie University, Sydney
Marina Oshana, University of California, Davis
May 2017

CONTRIBUTORS

BENNETT W. HELM is Elijah E. Kresge Professor of Philosophy at Franklin & Marshall College. His work focuses on understanding what it is to be a person and, in particular, the role the emotions and various forms of caring play in our being moral creatures. He has received fellowships and grants from the ACLS, NEH, NSF, Templeton Foundation, and Princeton's Center for Human Values. He is the author of *Emotional Reason: Deliberation, Motivation, and the Nature of Value* (Cambridge University Press, 2001); *Love, Friendship, and the Self: Intimacy, Identification, and the Social Nature of Persons* (Oxford University Press, 2010); and *Communities of Respect: Grounding Responsibility, Authority, and Dignity* (Oxford University Press, 2017).

JULES HOLROYD is a Vice-Chancellor's Fellow in Philosophy at the University of Sheffield. Her research focuses on the ways our cognitions may be shaped by and complicit in sustaining broader patterns of injustice. She has published work on implicit bias, on feminist philosophy and the moral emotions, and has recently concluded a three-year interdisciplinary project that investigates the impact of moral interactions on implicit racial bias and explicit attitudes toward combating them.

KATRINA HUTCHISON is a research fellow in philosophy at Macquarie University. She works mainly in bioethics and moral psychology. Her research draws on feminist scholarship and is unified by concern about the way social disadvantage, underrepresentation, and powerlessness arise in specific contexts. Her current research project focuses on gender in surgery, examining biases that affect women surgeons and patients. She makes use of empirical methods alongside the more traditional methods of analytic philosophy, and often collaborates with surgeons, lawyers, and policymakers on applied projects.

NEIL LEVY is Professor of Philosophy at Macquarie University, Sydney and a senior researcher at the Uehiro Centre for Practical Ethics, University of Oxford.

CATRIONA MACKENZIE is Professor of Philosophy and Associate Dean (Research) in the Faculty of Arts at Macquarie University, Sydney. She has published widely in moral psychology, ethics, applied ethics, and feminist philosophy in a variety of edited collections and journals. She is coeditor of several volumes, including (with Natalie Stoljar) *Relational Autonomy: Feminist Perspectives on Autonomy, Agency, and the Social Self* (Oxford University Press, 2000), and *Vulnerability: New Essays in Ethics and Feminist Philosophy* (Oxford University Press, 2014).

ELINOR MASON is a Senior Lecturer in philosophy at the University of Edinburgh. Her research focuses on ethics, moral responsibility, and feminism.

MICHAEL MCKENNA is Keith Lehrer Chair and a Professor of Philosophy in the Department of Philosophy and in the Center for the Philosophy of Freedom at the University of Arizona. He is the author of *Conversation and Responsibility* (Oxford University Press, 2012); *Free Will: A Contemporary Introduction* (Routledge, 2016), coauthored with Derk Pereboom; and numerous articles on free will and moral responsibility. McKenna has held appointments at Ithaca College and Florida State University. He received his PhD in Philosophy from University of Virginia in 1993.

MARINA OSHANA is Professor of Philosophy at the University of California, Davis. Her research reflects her evolving interest in three broadly connected areas in ethics and moral psychology. These are the nature of personal autonomy and the conditions for autonomous agency, the meaning of moral responsibility and the conditions for responsible agency, and the nature of the self and of self-identity. She has extended her research to encompass feminist analyses of responsibility. Her teaching centers in these areas as well as in philosophy of law.

MAUREEN SIE is Professor of Philosophy of Moral Agency, TILPS, Department of Philosophy, University of Tilburg. Prior to that, she was Professor of Philosophical Anthropology on behalf of the Socrates Foundation, at the Institute of Philosophy, Leiden University and Professor of Metaethics and Moral Psychology at the Department of Philosophy, Erasmus University in Rotterdam. From 2009 to 2014, she led a small research group funded by a personal grant of the Dutch Organization of Scientific Research, exploring the implications of the developments in behavioral, cognitive, and neurosciences for our concepts of moral agency, reasons responsiveness (free will), and personal responsibility.

NATALIE STOLJAR is an Associate Professor in the Department of Philosophy and the Institute for Health and Social Policy, McGill University. She received her PhD in Philosophy from Princeton University after having studied Philosophy and Law at the University of Sydney. She held positions at the Australian National University, Monash University, and the University of Melbourne before coming to McGill in 2006. Her research is in feminist philosophy, social and political philosophy, and the philosophy of law. In feminist philosophy, she has written on feminist metaphysics, including the notions of essentialism, realism, and nominalism. In social and political philosophy, her work focuses on autonomy and other aspects of moral psychology. She is coeditor (with Catriona Mackenzie) of *Relational Autonomy: Feminist Perspectives on Autonomy, Agency, and the Social Self* (Oxford University Press, 2000). In the philosophy of law, she has published on legal interpretation, constitutional interpretation and judicial review, and the methodology of law.

MANUEL R. VARGAS is Professor of Philosophy at the University of California, San Diego. He is the author of *Building Better Beings: A Theory of Moral Responsibility* (Oxford University Press, 2013); coauthor (with John Martin Fischer, Robert Kane, and Derk Pereboom) of *Four Views on Free Will* (Blackwell, 2007); and the author of numerous articles on agency, moral psychology, philosophy of law, and Latin American philosophy.

ANDREA C. WESTLUND is an Associate Professor of Philosophy and Women's and Gender Studies at the University of Wisconsin–Milwaukee. She works primarily in ethics, moral psychology, and related areas of feminist philosophy. Her current research projects are focused on blame and responsibility, the ethics of forgiveness, and the moral uses of autobiographical storytelling.

Social Dimensions
of Moral Responsibility

Introduction

Moral Responsibility in Contexts of Structural Injustice

KATRINA HUTCHISON, CATRIONA MACKENZIE, AND MARINA OSHANA

1 Introduction

The impetus for this volume is to initiate a dialogue between three recent philosophical developments of relevance to theories of moral responsibility. One is
the emergence of approaches to moral responsibility that focus attention onto
the interpersonal and social dimensions of our agential capacities and responsibility practices. A second is theories of relational autonomy, which seek to
explicate the socio-relational dimensions of autonomous agency and to analyze
the ways that social oppression and structural inequality can impair personal
autonomy. A third is work in social epistemology and feminist epistemology on
oppression, epistemic injustice, and the role of stereotyping and implicit bias in
perpetuating structural inequalities, such as those of gender and race.

Moral responsibility theorists may wonder why there is a need to initiate a
dialogue between these literatures. Collectively, the contributions to this volume provide an answer to this question. In brief, however, our answer is that
if we take seriously the idea that moral responsibility is an interpersonal and
social practice, then we must also acknowledge that many of our moral responsibility practices are not reciprocal exchanges between equally empowered and
situated agents. These exchanges all too often occur in contexts characterized by
structural injustice of various kinds. While the past two decades have witnessed
the emergence of an increasingly sophisticated literature on the interpersonal
and social dimensions of moral responsibility, this literature assumes an overly
idealized conception of agents and of our practices. The situational features of
those holding and being held responsible have been underanalyzed. Moreover,
insufficient attention has been given to the impacts and implications for moral
responsibility practices of social and environmental factors such as oppression,

structural injustice, hierarchies of power, and socially constructed identities inflected by markers of race, gender, or class. This inattention is no doubt due to the way the recent literature has emerged from mainstream philosophical scholarship, particularly the compatibilism of P. F. Strawson (1962), and from metaphysical preoccupations with free will and determinism that characterize much of the philosophical debate about moral responsibility. While the essays collected here do engage with this mainstream scholarship, one of the central aims of the volume is to demonstrate why philosophers should attend to the non-ideal social contexts in which our moral responsibility exchanges occur. In this respect, we propose, philosophical theorizing about moral responsibility has much to learn from the insights of feminist work in moral psychology and epistemology, which attends to the way oppression and social power infiltrate our interpersonal practices.

This introductory chapter summarizes the state of play in the three areas of inquiry that inform this book: moral responsibility, relational conceptions of autonomy, and feminist theories of oppression and social epistemology. In section 2, we provide an overview of the emergence of social theories of moral responsibility, from P. F. Strawson's influential "Freedom and Resentment" to recent theories inspired by his work. In section 3, we summarize developments in relational autonomy theory and highlight their connections to social theories of moral responsibility. In section 4, we summarize developments in feminist social epistemology that are directly relevant to this topic due to the epistemic conditions of moral responsibility. Finally, in section 5, we provide an overview of the chapters in the volume and discuss how they bring theoretical work on relational autonomy, oppression, and social epistemology to bear on our understanding of moral responsibility in a range of new ways.

2 Strawsonian Social Theories of Moral Responsibility

Most (if not all) of the recent social approaches to moral responsibility—directly or indirectly—owe a debt to P. F. Strawson's influential 1962 paper "Freedom and Resentment." In this paper, Strawson argues not only that moral responsibility practices are social, but more importantly that philosophers should look to these practices, rather than the metaphysics of free will and determinism or individual moral psychology, to discover the necessary and sufficient conditions for moral responsibility.[1]

Despite the influence of "Freedom and Resentment," Strawson never developed a comprehensive account of moral responsibility—almost all he wrote on the topic is in the one paper.[2] The approach that he recommends, while highly suggestive, lacks detail and precision. Both proponents and critics of his view have needed to flesh out various details, and as a result there are a variety of very different views in the secondary literature that are referred to as "Strawsonian." Many of these views are "social" in some sense, but they are not all social in the same way. In order to understand these different views, and the different social dimensions of moral responsibility they invoke, it is worth identifying some of the key features of Strawson's approach.

Perhaps most importantly, Strawson reoriented the focus of philosophical concern about the underpinnings of moral responsibility. Previously, the emphasis had been on metaphysical conditions, such as whether moral responsibility is compatible with physical determinism (or indeterminism). In contrast, Strawson emphasized the nature of our moral responsibility practices and the significance of these practices in the context of our lives, especially our interpersonal relationships. We care how others treat us in all our different sorts of relationships and interactions with them, from the most significant to the most trivial—"as members of the same family; as colleagues; as friends; as lovers; as chance parties to an enormous range of transactions and encounters" (Strawson 1962, 191–192). Gary Watson refers to this as "the basic concern," which gives rise to an expectation, "the basic demand": in all our interactions, we expect others to show good will and a degree of regard for us (2014, 17).[3] When this expectation is not met, or when it is exceeded, we tend to respond in a way that is both emotional and morally loaded—that is, with what Strawson calls "reactive attitudes" (Strawson 1962, 192) such as resentment and gratitude.

However, Strawson argues, both our expectations of others and the corresponding reactive attitudes are tempered in response to excusing and exempting conditions. Excuses function to modify our reactive attitudes toward the actions of an agent who is typically eligible for these responses. For example, if we discover that the agent's action was accidental, we do not react to the agent as we would were the demand for good will and regard to have been flouted. The agent is not blameworthy on this occasion, even if the behavior is of a type that typically invites blame. Exemptions function to modify our ordinary social practices in interacting with those we view as "psychologically abnormal—or as morally undeveloped" (Strawson 1962, 194). With such agents, we do not form the same sorts of relationships, and we do not interpret their behavior in the same way. Specifically, we do not take it personally when they fail to treat us with basic regard.

Alongside the reactive emotions of resentment and gratitude are our practices of praising and blaming one another. Strawson mentions praise and blame as practices that are intimately connected with moral responsibility, but he does not give a detailed account of what praise and blame are. While it is widely agreed that moral responsibility is a necessary condition for justified moral blame, it has been observed that we do not always blame those we judge to be morally responsible for wrong actions, and we sometimes blame those who are not responsible (e.g., Pickard 2013). Strawson is widely associated with the view that blame is best understood as a sort of reactive emotion, an approach that has been developed more recently by R. Jay Wallace (1994, 2011). However, philosophers such as Sher, Scanlon, and Smith have argued that while moral blame often has an emotional aspect, this is not best captured by regarding blame as a reactive attitude (Sher 2005; Scanlon 2008; Smith 2012b).[4]

Most philosophers accept that Strawson has identified real and important features of our responsibility practices. It is in his *use* of these observations that the approach is distinctive. According to Strawson, we can identify the real underpinnings of moral responsibility from paradigm examples of such interactions.[5] That is, we identify what it means for an agent to be responsible by examining the practices under which we hold agents responsible. At the center of these practices are the reactive attitudes and attendant practices of praising and blaming. Likewise, our actual practices of excusing or exempting are the very places we should look to identify when it is appropriate to modify our responsibility ascriptions and which agents should be exempted from those ascriptions. Strawson therefore develops a *practice-dependent* theory of moral responsibility. Our social status as it relates to moral responsibility—i.e., whether or not others in our moral community treat us as moral agents—is the key to whether or not we are, in fact, moral agents. Social practices (partly or wholly) determine moral responsibility status.

Three aspects of Strawson's social approach to moral responsibility that have been the focus of recent analysis are of particular relevance to this volume. The first is the centrality of interpersonal relationships in Strawson's account of moral responsibility. The second is the interlocutive or conversational properties of the morally reactive exchange. The third is the role of our moral responsibility practices and the broader moral environment in scaffolding the development of the capacities for moral responsibility. It is important to stress that these three themes are not exclusive, and overlap in the work of the authors we discuss below. Nevertheless, they help to elicit different senses in which a theory of moral responsibility might be social.

2.1 The Importance of Interpersonal Relationships for Moral Responsibility

A number of philosophers, such as Gary Watson (1996, 2014), T. M. Scanlon (2008, 2012), David Shoemaker (2011), and Stephen Darwall (2006), have emphasized how the involvement of individuals in interpersonal relationships gives rise to expectations, obligations, and demands. They argue that moral responsibility cannot be understood in the absence of these relationship-dependent features. For example, Gary Watson argues that a core idea unifying several elements of Strawson's approach is that moral responsibility requires "the realized capacity for standing in reciprocal interpersonal relations" (2014, 21). If Watson is right that a capacity for reciprocal interpersonal relations with others is a necessary condition of moral responsibility, then this would help explain the nature of Strawson's concerns about the "gains and losses to human life, its enrichment or impoverishment" that would ensue were we to radically alter our responsibility practices (1962, 199). The losses and impoverishment he is thinking of involve profound changes to the nature of our closest relationships.

Several other philosophers have also emphasized the role of relationships in grounding aspects of our moral responsibility practices. Stephen Darwall (2006) describes this in terms of the importance of the second-personal standpoint: the stance we adopt whenever we address demands to one another as persons. Central to this view is the idea of a relationship of mutual respect and openness to the demands of one another. T. M. Scanlon's (2008, 2012) influential account of blame also emphasizes the importance of relationships for moral responsibility. According to Scanlon, justified blame occurs when the blamer modifies her relationship with the blamed due to a violation of the demands of their relationship. David Shoemaker, too, associates relationships with one aspect of responsibility: accountability. In his view, an individual is only accountable (and apt for certain forms of blame) when she is acting under a demand for good will that is central to all our moral relationships. Accountability judgments assess the extent to which "relationship-defining norms" (2011, 631) are met by parties to a moral relationship. Shoemaker says that "one is susceptible for being held to account just in case one has the capacity to recognize and appreciate the demands defining the various relationships as reason-giving" (631).

2.2 Conversation and Moral Responsibility

Several recent theories, for example Michael McKenna's conversational view (2012) and Marina Oshana's moral interlocution view (1997, 2004), are social in their focus on the interlocutive or conversational properties of the morally reactive exchange. These views hold that the capacity to participate in interpersonal conversations (with others) about our actions and their moral significance is a necessary condition of being a morally responsible agent. These approaches can be contrasted with related views that invoke the idea of being able to give reasons of a certain sort—usually justificatory reasons—by speaking only hypothetically of agents' capacities to respond to such a demand. Many views of moral responsibility include a condition that the agent would in principle be able to "answer" a demand for an explanation of her behavior were that demand made. Angela Smith, for example, says,

> [T]o say that an agent is morally responsible for something is to say that it would be *intelligible* to ask her to "answer for" that thing—to give her (justificatory) reasons for thinking, feeling, or acting in the way she has—and that she is *eligible for* certain moral responses based on the nature of the thing in question and the quality of the justificatory reasons she is able to offer in support of it. (2015, 103)

Despite the dependence of Smith's account on the idea of agents being asked for reasons, her notion of answerability does not focus much at all on the social aspects of communication. The capacity in question is hypothetical rather than actual, and the demands are mainly demands of the agent as a *reasoner*, not as an interlocutor with others.

In contrast, in his "conversational view," McKenna (2012) develops a parallel between moral responsibility practices and conversations between competent speakers of natural languages. In some respects, the argument proceeds by analogy—moral responsibility practices, particularly as exemplified in Strawsonian morally reactive exchanges, have similar dynamics to conversations in natural languages. McKenna draws attention to the respects in which the actions, reactions, and responses involved in our moral responsibility practices are a form of conversation. Suppose an offense is committed. For McKenna, the first contribution to the "conversation" is the offensive behavior. Whether or not the agent intends it, this behavior communicates something to its victim about the perpetrator's regard for her. When the victim responds with anger or resentment, she thereby reveals her interpretation of the offender's behavior. In turn, the offender has the opportunity to correct this interpretation if it is incorrect by offering a plea or excuse. One role of the moral responsibility "conversation" is for the parties to reconcile their different understandings of the initial action. For McKenna, the ability to participate in the conversation is essentially interpersonal. It depends on the agent having been "inculcated into the practices of adult interpersonal life, able to appreciate others' demands, able to appreciate what would be liable to elicit blame from others, and so on" (2012, 215). In this respect, the communicative dimensions are much more substantial than the hypothetical role that being asked to answer for behavior plays in Smith's account.

Marina Oshana, too, has developed an interpersonal account of the conditions of moral responsibility that invokes the notion of a conversation (1997, 2004). For Oshana, a morally responsible agent "must be constituted in a way that makes it possible for her to grasp certain reasons for action as interpersonally salient, where this is manifest in her ability, if not her willingness, to have a conversation with persons other than herself about the moral merit of her actions" (2004, 256). This ability does not only require conversational skills. It also involves an ability to understand and be responsive to the standards that others are likely to find acceptable. This includes a particular sort of epistemic competence, which "sustains a capacity for moral reasoning and dialogue that can only transpire among persons who are in a position to participate in interpersonal moral relationships" (258). Furthermore, agents are not passive with respect to these standards; they must be able to evaluate and discuss their normative value. Oshana's approach is therefore social in at least two respects: it requires the ability to converse with others and the ability to be sensitive to which standards others are likely to find acceptable.

Oshana and McKenna are not the only philosophers who develop approaches that emphasize communicative dimensions of moral responsibility. Indeed, both Victoria McGeer's (2012) co-reactive account of moral responsibility and Watson's (1987) expressivist interpretation of Strawson's compatibilism, discussed below, could be classified in this category.

2.3 The Social Scaffolding of Moral Responsibility

Until recently, most discussions of the influence of social situations on moral responsibility have focused on the negative impact of pernicious social factors on agents' capacities. In a well-known discussion of the moral agency of the murderer Robert Harris, for example, Gary Watson discusses the weight that should be attributed to Harris's difficult formative circumstances in ascribing to him responsibility for his cold-hearted acts. Watson notes that although Harris appears to be "an 'archetypal candidate' for blame" (1987, 271) due to his heartlessness and viciousness, familiarity with his formative circumstances challenges this assessment. In fact, due to the neglect and abuse he suffered as a child, Harris "is incapacitated for [ordinary interpersonal] relationships—for example, for friendship, for sympathy, for being affected by moral considerations" (1987, 274). While Watson remains ambivalent about whether Harris is a moral agent, he shares the widely accepted view that upbringing can negatively impact an agent's moral responsibility capacities and status.[6]

Recently, some theorists have offered a more positive face to the potential of social circumstances to enable or scaffold agency. Manuel Vargas (2013) develops an account of moral responsibility that highlights the interaction between agents' rational capacities and the features of their social context that influence the development or exercise of these capacities. For example, he considers how different cultural contexts can influence moral agency with respect to racism: "Being raised in an anti-racist context presumably plays a role in enhancing sensitivity to moral considerations tied to anti-racist concerns. Similarly, being raised in a sexist, fascist, or classist culture will often shape a person's dispositions to ignore egalitarian concerns" (2013, 247). Vargas refers to the features of our environment that shape our moral sensitivities and capacities as our "moral ecology." He argues that since our moral ecology influences moral agency, we can foster the moral agency of individuals in a society through "moral architecture"— the conscious shaping of the moral ecology to foster agents' sensitivity to moral considerations and their capacities to act on these considerations. Whether and how to do this, he says, is "arguably a question in political philosophy" (248).

Another philosopher who has recently focused on social factors as potential enablers of moral agency is Victoria McGeer (2012, 2013; McGeer and Pettit 2015), who interprets Strawsonian reactive attitudes as morally reactive exchanges—an idealized version of the "conversation" that sometimes takes place between a wrongdoer and victim. In such conversations (at least in their idealized form), the victim expresses resentment and seeks a response from the offender. The conversations take place within a moral community, and (again, ideally) bystanders or representatives of the community as a whole are also involved in expressing reactive attitudes (such as moral disapprobation) that echo those of the victim.

A feature of these exchanges is that they proceed on the basis that both parties have the capacity to recognize and respond appropriately to the sort of moral demands involved—we do not make morally reactive demands of those with severe cognitive impairments who will not be able to understand. It is the capacity to take part in this sort of exchange that is the primary capacity relevant to moral responsibility, according to McGeer. And the exchange plays a role in scaffolding the agencies of those involved in two ways. First, because making the demand—initiating a co-reactive exchange with someone—means we ascribe them the relevant capacity and thus express a sort of "faith" in their moral agency. Second, because the exchange itself affects the status of parties in the moral community. It (ideally) draws offenders back into the moral community once the co-reactive exchange yields a shared understanding of the moral significance of the action.

Just as Vargas's approach seems to require us to become architects of our moral ecology in order to promote the moral agency of members of the community, McGeer's approach also has practical implications. In particular, some of the scaffolding features of her account seem to depend on agents participating in actual co-reactive exchanges. McGeer highlights the potential of specific processes, such as restorative justice processes, to facilitate morally reactive exchanges between offenders and their victims (2012, 316–318).

What the varieties of social approach to moral responsibility discussed above seem to take for granted is that there is an uncomplicated relationship between an agent's moral capacities and an agent's moral responsibility status. For the views that focus on the impact of social factors on agents' capacities, it is taken for granted that if agents do have the relevant capacities, or can be brought to have them through alterations to the moral ecology or through social scaffolding, then the *recognition* of their capacities will be unproblematic. For the views that work backwards from facts about agents' social status or relationships to facts about their moral agency, it is similarly assumed that there is an unproblematic connection between the status agents are ascribed in our actual practices and other factors relevant to their being responsible.[7] None of the views we have hitherto discussed raise the concern that a wedge may be driven between an agent's capacities for moral agency, and the status they are ascribed by others in their community. Yet it is far from obvious that this complacency is well founded. Moral responsibility is a status we attribute to one another, but it is not necessarily transparent to us which agents have the relevant capacities. As such, it is possible for moral responsibility ascriptions to *fail to track* the relevant capacities and instead track irrelevant characteristics of the agent. This suggests a different, but related social dimension of moral responsibility ascriptions that has received almost no consideration in the literature: that individuals whose capacities are intact may be (incorrectly) *judged* to lack the relevant capacities due to their social situation. Others' assessments of the moral agency of an individual might track social identity rather than capacity.

In contrast to the moral responsibility literature, which typically assumes an overly idealized conception of our practices and social relationships, the literature on relational autonomy takes seriously both the importance of social scaffolding in the development and exercise of our agential capacities, and the fact that agents develop and exercise these capacities in social contexts that are often far from ideal. In other words, relational autonomy theorists aim to explicate both the social dimensions of autonomous agency and the ways in which individual autonomy, understood as both capacity and status, can be thwarted or impaired by social oppression, structural injustice, and social identity markers, including class, race, or gender. A sustained development of the social dimensions of moral responsibility would therefore be wise to turn to the (now well-established) exchanges on relational autonomy for insight into the issues at the center of socially constrained, interpersonal agential practices.

3 Relational Autonomy and Social Oppression

Relational autonomy is an "umbrella term," referring to approaches to autonomy that take seriously the fact that "persons are embodied, and socially, historically and culturally embedded, and their identities are constituted in relation to these factors in complex ways" (Mackenzie 2014, 21).[8] Relational theories seek to counter the individualistic assumptions about agency and identity that are prevalent in much of the philosophical literature on autonomy. Further, in line with their attention to the social constitution of identity, these theories seek to analyze the effects of social oppression on agents' autonomy.

Autonomy is both a capacity and a status concept. To have the capacity for autonomy is to satisfy the conditions for self-governing agency—however self-governance is defined. To enjoy the status marker of autonomy is to be socially and politically *recognized* as having both authority over choices of practical import to one's life, and the power to act on that authority. Ideally, status and capacity are closely linked, such that status tracks capacity. However, relational autonomy theorists have drawn attention to how, in oppressive or inegalitarian social contexts, this relationship is often subject to distortion. Agents who possess the relevant capacities may be deprived of the status markers of autonomy, or, more insidiously, the withholding of status may impair the development or exercise of the relevant capacities. In what follows, we briefly outline the different proposals developed by relational autonomy theorists to explain the autonomy-impairing effects of social inequality and social oppression. Where relevant, we also link these proposals to the literature on moral responsibility.

The recent literature on relational autonomy typically distinguishes two broad conditions for self-governing agency—authenticity and competence (Meyers 1989; Christman 2009). Authenticity conditions specify that to be self-governing is to be able to act on the basis of preferences, motives, commitments, or values that are genuinely one's own. Competence conditions specify the requisite capacities and competences for self-governance.

Debates about *authenticity* in the mainstream philosophical literature on autonomy have been strongly influenced by Harry Frankfurt's (1971) hierarchical analysis of freedom of the will as reflective (second-order) identification with one's first-order motives, and by Gary Watson's (1975) critical emendation to this analysis, which characterizes freedom of the will in terms of harmony between one's motivational and valuational systems. Frankfurt's and Watson's theories have also been highly influential in the development of contemporary compatibilist theories of free will, specifically so-called Real Self Theories. Proponents of "Real Self" or "True Self" views of autonomy (Neely 1974; Taylor 1976; Dworkin 1976, 1988) and of responsible agency (Frankfurt 1971) argue that in order to be an autonomous, or a morally responsible agent, one's actions must be governed by one's desires or controlled by one's will *and* one's will must be governed by one's "deepest" self, that is, by those of one's desires that survive critical reflection and endorsement or that express one's values. The "Real Self" is the self with which we identify and in virtue of which we are self-governing, morally responsible agents.[9] The recent literatures on autonomy and moral responsibility therefore share a common ancestry. Indeed, some theorists (e.g., Arpaly 2004; Mele 1995, 2002) tend to use the concepts interchangeably. Given this common ancestry, it is surprising that moral responsibility theorists have paid scant attention to relational autonomy theorists' critiques of hierarchical theories of freedom of the will, since these critiques also have implications for theories of moral responsibility.

Hierarchical theories are procedural. According to procedural theories, an agent's motives, choices, or values are authentically her own, whatever their content, just so long as these are endorsed via an appropriate critical reflection procedure. Hierarchical theories explain authenticity in terms of structural features of the agent's will at the time of reflection and action, specifically second-order endorsement of one's first-order motives—for Frankfurt, having the will one wants to have (1971, 15). Relational autonomy theorists argue, however, that second-order reflective endorsement is not sufficient to distinguish autonomous from non-autonomous reflection. In oppressive and inegalitarian social contexts, second-order reflection upon first-order elements of one's motivational or valuational structure may simply reinforce internalized oppressive stereotypes and norms, or adaptive preferences.[10] Why then assume that second-order reflection is authentic and authoritative? In other words, relational theorists argue that hierarchical theories overlook the historical processes of identity formation— the way a person acquired her preferences, commitments, and values. Attention to these historical processes is crucial, however, for understanding how agents' psychologies may have been shaped by internalized oppression.[11]

The relational critique of hierarchical theories has led to the development of a range of alternative accounts of the conditions for self-governing agency. Some theorists, such as Marilyn Friedman (1986, 2003) and John Christman (1991, 2009), remain committed to a procedural approach, while offering alternative accounts of what constitutes authentic, autonomy-conferring critical reflection. Friedman's *integration* test, for example, responds to the concerns outlined above about the authority of higher-order desires. She points out that in oppressive social contexts a person's second-order preferences may be more likely to conform to oppressive stereotypes and norms. In contrast, feelings of internal conflict at the first-order level (apparently "wayward" first-order desires) may help prompt critical reflection on higher-order desires and values. The *integration* test therefore specifies that reflective endorsement is autonomous only when lower-order preferences and higher-order normative commitments are integrated in a person's motivational structure as a result of two-way processes of bottom-up and top-down reflection. Christman's *nonalienation* test responds to concerns about the importance of historical processes of identity, desire, and value formation for autonomy. The test is historical and counterfactual, specifying that an element of a person's motivational set is authentically her own if, were she

counterfactually to engage in reflection on the historical processes of its formation, she would not repudiate or feel alienated from that element.[12]

Other theorists, such as Diana Meyers (1989), link authenticity to *competence*. Meyers argues that authentic self-governance requires a complex repertoire or suite of reflective skills, which may be developed and exercised to
varying degrees and in different domains. These include emotional skills, such
as the capacity to interpret and regulate one's own emotions; imaginative skills,
required for understanding the implications of one's decisions and envisaging
alternative possible courses of action; and capacities to reflect critically on social
norms and values. According to Meyers, a person is autonomous, and her choices
are authentically her own, to the degree that she has developed these skills and
can exercise them in understanding herself (self-discovery), defining her values and commitments (self-definition), and directing her life (self-direction).
Oppressive socialization can impair autonomy by truncating the development
or stunting the exercise of these skills.

The theories of Friedman, Christman, and Meyers are "causally relational."
These theories emphasize the crucial causal role of social relationships and
institutions in shaping our preferences, commitments, and values—for better
or for worse—and in scaffolding the development and exercise of autonomy
competence. In this respect, these relational theories prefigure both McGeer's
and Vargas's recent attention to the way that social factors scaffold our agential
capacities, and the role of the broader moral ecology in shaping our agency (e.g.,
McGeer 2012; McGeer and Pettit 2015; Vargas 2013).

Another group of relational theorists charge that procedural analyses of the
conditions for self-governance do not adequately explain the autonomy-impairing effects of social oppression. These theorists propose a range of more substantive conditions for agential self-governance. Marina Oshana, for example, argues
that a person's socio-relational status is the crucial determinant of her autonomy
(1998, 2006). She argues that to be autonomous is to have both de jure and de
facto authority and power to exercise effective practical control over important
aspects of one's life. In her view, social relations of subordination, subservience,
deference, or economic or psychological dependence undermine autonomy,
because they deny agents effective practical control over significant domains of
their life. This is the case even if the agents in question satisfy the procedural
conditions for autonomy specified, for example, by Friedman or Christman.
Autonomy, in her view, is both causally and constitutively social, because a person's ability to be a self-governing agent is a function of that person's socio-relational status.

Oshana's view has been criticized for conflating autonomy with substantive
independence, for being overly prescriptive in dictating to people the kind of
lives they should lead, and for disrespecting the agency of people who manage

to lead self-governing lives despite being subject to crushing forms of oppression (Christman 2004; Khader 2011). Such critics point to people like Martin Luther King Jr. as counter-examples to Oshana's view. In response, Oshana acknowledges that King, and others like him who struggled against racial oppression and injustice, managed to exercise some degree of autonomy despite the oppression and domination to which they were subject. However, rather than demonstrating the implausibility of the socio-relational account, she suggests that such heroism "should rather serve as an example of an *exception* to the socio-relational account" (2015, 11).

Other substantive theorists, such as Paul Benson in his earlier work (1991) and Natalie Stoljar (2000), object to procedural theories on different grounds. Their strong substantive theories hold that only preferences, values, or commitments that meet specific *normative competence* constraints count as autonomous. To be autonomous, agents must be able to critically discern the difference between true and false norms, and their preferences, choices, and actions must be guided by true norms.[13] Agents whose preferences, choices, and actions are guided by false norms or stereotypes cannot be autonomous. It is important to note that neither Benson nor Stoljar are making global claims about the autonomy of agents who fail the normative competence test. Their claim is rather that these agents' autonomy is impaired with respect to the specific norms in question and the choices and actions that flow from them. Despite this caveat, the normative competence view has been criticized for failing to recognize the range of reasons that people might have for complying with oppressive norms (Narayan 2002; Khader 2011; Sperry 2013), thereby encouraging condescending attitudes toward persons who are subject to oppression, impugning their agency, and opening the door to objectionably paternalistic and coercive forms of intervention in their lives.

A different criticism of the normative competence view is that it seems to blur the difference between self-governing and morally responsible agency. For example, Oshana argues that moral responsibility, but not autonomy, "requires the ability to recognize moral norms evaluative of one's reasons for action as well as the ability to respond to these evaluations" (2002, 267). Further, while individuals can remain morally responsible agents even when their ability to control the external forces that shape their lives are severely compromised, such agents are not autonomous.

This criticism might also be leveled at other substantive theories. Benson's more recent (2005, 2014) weak substantive view, for example, characterizes autonomy in terms of ownership of one's choices and actions: regarding oneself as positioned, and as having the appropriate authority, to speak for oneself and to answer others' critical perspectives. Andrea Westlund proposes a related view of autonomy as taking responsibility for oneself, which requires a disposition for "dialogical answerability" or "the disposition to hold oneself answerable to external critical perspectives" (2009, 28). Both views seem to understand self-governance as involving the kind of capacities for second-personal answerability that have been the focus of attention in the recent literature on moral responsibility. Despite some differences between their accounts, Watson (1996), Shoemaker (2011, 2015), and Smith (2007, 2008b, 2012a, 2015), for example, all understand answerability as a condition of morally responsible agency and as focused primarily on the agent's justificatory reasons for action. An agent is answerable if she has (in principle) the capacity to respond to others' demands to provide justificatory, evaluative reasons for her actions and attitudes.

The question of whether Benson and Westlund's views blur the differences between autonomy and moral responsibility is complex and no doubt arises partly from disagreements about the conditions for both autonomy and moral responsibility. Autonomy is typically understood as equivalent to agential self-governance. However, Mackenzie (2014) argues that autonomy is a multidimensional concept and that this multidimensionality accounts for some of our conflicting intuitions about autonomy. She identifies three distinct but overlapping dimensions of autonomy: self-determination, self-governance, and self-authorization. To be self-determining is to be able to exercise control over important domains of one's life and to make and enact decisions of practical import to one's life. The *self-determination* axis is thus conceptually allied to freedom from domination, and identifies the kind of external, structural socio-relational conditions for autonomy on which Oshana's account focuses. To be self-governing is to have the skills and capacities necessary to make and enact decisions that express or cohere with one's deeply held values and commitments. The *self-governance* axis therefore identifies internal conditions for autonomy, specifically authenticity and competence, as explicated by procedural theorists, such as Christman, Friedman, and Meyers. To be self-authorizing is to regard oneself as normatively authorized to take responsibility for one's life, one's values, and one's decisions, and as able to account for oneself to others. Self-authorization is a central concern of Oshana's socio-relational view, which holds that autonomous persons have a "characteristic type of social standing" (2015, 159). It is also central to the concerns of Benson and Westlund, who highlight the importance for autonomy of taking ownership of one's actions and holding oneself answerable to others.

Similarly, some theorists have proposed that moral responsibility is a multidimensional concept. Watson (1996) distinguishes two "faces" of responsibility: attributability and accountability. Attributability is the "aretaic face" of moral responsibility—connected with character assessments. For Watson, the attributability face of responsibility always involves being able to provide justificatory reasons for one's behavior—that is, it always involves answerability.

Accountability focuses on the quality of an agent's regard for others and is connected to practices of praise, blame, and holding to account. Shoemaker (2011, 2015) distinguishes three distinct dimensions of moral responsibility: attributability, answerability, and accountability. His aim is to account for conflicting intuitions about moral responsibility in cases of "marginal agency." Shoemaker argues that an agent is responsible in the attributability sense if the action can be attributed to her character, even if, contra Watson, she cannot give an account of how she came to have the values and dispositions she has. Answerability focuses on the quality of an agent's judgments and justificatory reasons. Accountability, as for Watson, emphasizes the quality of an agent's concern for others and is linked to practices of praise and blame. However, Shoemaker argues that an agent cannot be held accountable for her actions if she is unable to grasp moral norms, even if her actions are attributable to her.[14]

These multidimensional analyses of autonomy and responsibility offer a clearer understanding of which dimensions of autonomy and moral responsibility overlap. For example, the self-governance dimension of autonomy and the attributability dimension of moral responsibility both focus on authenticity: the extent to which the agent's attitudes, choices, and actions are the ones she wants to have. This, in turn, can help explain why some philosophers draw a sharper distinction between autonomy and moral responsibility than others. It is not surprising that Mele, who emphasizes authenticity, does not distinguish autonomy and responsibility. It also helps explain why Oshana, who emphasizes the accountability dimension of moral responsibility and the self-determination dimension of autonomy, sees the two concepts as quite distinct. Beyond this, the multi-dimensional analyses of both concepts can help reveal which of the insights from the relational autonomy literature are also relevant to moral responsibility. Although the task of investigating the complex relationship between the different dimensions of these concepts remains to be done, we hope that this volume will spur further work on this topic.

4 Oppression, Injustice, Stereotypes, and Implicit Bias

The extent to which morally responsible agency is vulnerable to asymmetrical practices of answerability and accountability in contexts of social oppression and structural injustice is a recurring theme in this volume. In engaging with this theme, a number of contributors draw on recent research in philosophy and psychology on oppression, structural and epistemic injustice, stereotypes, and implicit bias. In this section, we provide a brief overview of some of this research and its relevance for theories of moral responsibility.

Ann Cudd (2006) has developed the most detailed, recent philosophical theory of social oppression, drawing on both modern economic and game theory and psychological research on social cognition. She defines oppression as "an institutionally structured, unjust harm perpetrated on groups by other groups using direct and indirect material and psychological forces" (2006, 51). This definition highlights three central features of oppression: first, it is made possible and perpetuated by unjust institutional structures; second, it is a form of group harm that affects individuals through their classification as members of stigmatized social groups; and third, it is internalized in individuals' psychologies through a variety of mechanisms, such as stereotyping, explicit and implicit bias, objectification, and cultural domination.

Institutions, on Cudd's analysis, include formal structures, such as economic, legal, and political structures, and informal social structures and constraints, such as norms, conventions, and practices (2006, 20). Institutional structures and constraints are unjust if they institutionalize relations of domination and subordination between different social groups, systematically harming and disadvantaging members of some groups while conferring unfair power, advantage, and privilege on members of other groups. Cudd's analysis of social groups is externalist: social group membership is determined not by the intentions of individuals but "by the actions, beliefs, and attitudes of others, both in the group and out, that constrain their choices in patterned and socially significant ways" (44). While some social groups are voluntary, it is nonvoluntary social groups that are of primary interest to Cudd and other theorists of oppression. These are groups, such as those based on gender, race, class, or sexual orientation, whose members face common, nonchosen, institutionally structured constraints that subject them to unjust harms, inequality, social stigma, and disadvantage (51).

Among the various social forces that perpetuate social oppression and disadvantage, Cudd identifies as a central cause systematic violence directed toward members of target social groups (including but not limited to state-sponsored or sanctioned violence), or the social threat of violence. Another central cause is the economic oppression of members of target social groups, for example through job segregation, exploitation, wage gaps, employment discrimination, group-based harassment, and opportunity inequalities, all of which result in economic inequality and deprivation. These causes, especially violence, typically give rise to direct psychological harms, which can include terror, trauma, humiliation, degradation, and objectification.

Important as these material causes are, Cudd argues that oppression is also maintained via psychological mechanisms, specifically social group stereotyping. Drawing on a vast body of empirical literature on stereotyping in social cognition theory, she proposes that social group stereotypes perpetuate oppression in three main ways. First, stereotypes are generalizations that associate social groups with specific attributes. These generalizations are learnt through the social environment and function as cognitive schemas that guide perceptions, beliefs, and attitudes about social groups and the behavior of individual members of those groups—regardless of whether the stereotypes fit the individuals in question. The social entrenchment and reinforcement of these schemas mean that "stereotypes that bias some groups positively and others negatively will tend to remain that way even in the face of contrary data" (2006, 79). Second, individuals form their self-identities and engage with the social world within the constraints imposed by social group membership and attendant stereotypes. The internalization of pernicious stereotypes that stigmatize, humiliate, or degrade members of target social groups can lead to feelings of shame, self-doubt, and social inferiority, which can then function to confirm the stereotype (80). One way this can occur is through the phenomenon of "stereotype threat." The psychological literature on stereotype threat has focused predominantly on its effects on academic task performance (Steele 1997, 2010).[15] In these contexts, when an individual is made aware (directly or indirectly) of a widely held stereotype about his or her social group, the individual's anxiety about conforming to the stereotype interferes with the person's focus on the task at hand, leading to underperformance. However, Cudd and other philosophers urge the need for a wider understanding of stereotype threat that connects it with the way negative stereotypes are embedded in structures of social inequality and injustice, and internalized by members of stigmatized social groups.[16] Third, members of oppressed groups are "typically motivated to acquiesce in and assimilate these oppressive stereotypes" (Cudd 2006, 81) through social and psychological incentives (social group identification) and economic constraints and incentives that shape individuals' preferences and choices. The gender wage gap combined with social norms regarding the gendered division of labor, for example, can make it rational for women to make individual choices about their careers and domestic arrangements that collectively disadvantage all women and often, if not always, disadvantage the individual women concerned (2006, 147–153).

The work of Cudd and others, such as Elizabeth Anderson (2010), has greatly enriched our theoretical understanding of how social oppression, stereotyping, and structural injustice function as unjust constraints on the agency of target social groups and individual members of those groups. In a different but related vein, Miranda Fricker's (2007) work on epistemic injustice has drawn attention to how stereotyping and social identity prejudice constrain the epistemic agency of individual social group members, impugning their credibility and status as knowers. The notion of epistemic injustice refers to the phenomenon of being subject to prejudicial exclusion from knowledge practices on the basis of one's social group membership. Fricker distinguishes two broad kinds of epistemic injustice: testimonial injustice and hermeneutical injustice.

Testimonial injustices focus on judgments we make about others' credibility. Often we rely on indicators or stereotypes to inform these judgments: for example, professional qualifications are usually a reliable indicator of a doctor's or lawyer's professional credibility. However, our judgments are sometimes mistaken, and when they are mistaken, the person whose credibility is on the line suffers a credibility deficit or enjoys a credibility excess, depending on whether the person is attributed with more or less knowledge than she actually has.[17] Credibility deficits are not always unjust—sometimes they are the result of a nonculpable mistake. However, sometimes they result from what Fricker calls "negative identity-prejudicial stereotypes": widely held disparaging associations between a social group and one or more attributes, which are resistant to counterevidence (2007, 35). In such cases, the person's testimony is ignored due to features that mark her as a member of a stigmatized social group—her accent denoting (low) social class, for example. This is *unjust* because the credibility deficit is due to her position in an unjust social hierarchy. It is an *epistemic* injustice because she is wronged in her capacity as a knower.

Hermeneutical injustice focuses on the influence of social hierarchies on shared conceptual resources and the determination of social meanings. A distinction can be made between a hermeneutical *deficit*—when a society does not have the conceptual resources to talk about a particular kind of experience—and hermeneutical *injustice*, which occurs when such a deficit is a consequence of unjust social arrangements. The emergence of a previously unknown medical syndrome can involve hermeneutical deficits—there is no name or agreed-upon understanding of the syndrome, its symptoms, or the broader experiences of the patient group. This can add to the suffering of patients as well as limiting the ability of medical professionals to offer satisfactory treatments. However, such cases do not involve *injustice*. Rather, in these cases, the hermeneutical deficit results from a genuine (nonculpable) lack of conceptual resources to adequately understand or interpret the syndrome or experiences of the patient group. In contrast, when a social group is marginalized within a society, such that their experiences are systematically absent from the discourse that shapes shared social understandings, the lack of hermeneutical resources to identify and discuss these experiences can involve an injustice. In particular, such hermeneutical deficits are unjust when they involve experiences that are harmful to members of the marginalized group while being neutral or even beneficial to members of the dominant group.

An example discussed by Fricker that illuminates some of the key features of hermeneutical injustice is sexual harassment. The experience of being sexually harassed at work, while unwelcome and unpleasant, could not be rendered intelligible until a term was coined in the 1970s to name the experience and define the nature of the wrong. In addition to involving harm to members of a marginalized social group—women—sexual harassment involved no parallel harm to the dominant group—men. Furthermore, it can be regarded as what Fricker calls a "systematic" hermeneutical injustice because of its tendency to be self-perpetuating: negative workplace experiences such as sexual harassment can render unattractive roles that would allow women greater power over society's shared hermeneutic resources—careers in journalism and politics, for example (Fricker 2007, 155–156). Hermeneutical injustice can also be compounded by testimonial injustice, manifesting in "the speaker struggling to make herself intelligible in the testimonial exchange" (159), as is the case when women's complaints about sexist jokes in the workplace are dismissed with ridicule.

Earlier, we suggested that recent work on the social dimensions of moral responsibility has overlooked the way that moral responsibility ascriptions may *fail to track* the relevant capacities and instead track irrelevant characteristics of agents arising from their social identities. The theoretical ideas outlined in the previous paragraphs—on the material forces of social oppression, the psychological mechanisms of stereotyping and stereotype threat, and their effects on the epistemic agency of target social groups and individuals—provides useful resources for analyzing how this can happen; that is, how our moral responsibility ascriptions and practices may be caught up in the dynamics of social power. A number of contributors draw on these ideas to explicate these dynamics. Work on epistemic injustice also makes salient the importance of attending to the broader social dimensions of the epistemic conditions on moral responsibility, such as the character of the agent's epistemic environment, and whether an agent's epistemic agency is recognized and respected by others.

In addition to the empirical research in cognitive social psychology on stereotyping, philosophical reflection on social identity-based forms of prejudice and injustice has also been influenced by a significant body of psychological research on the phenomenon of implicit bias.[18] In contrast to explicit bias, which manifests in explicitly (and often consciously articulated) prejudiced attitudes and behaviors, implicit bias refers to negative social group evaluations that operate largely outside conscious awareness or control, and often in direct conflict with a person's avowed egalitarian beliefs, values, and attitudes. Implicit biases are therefore "introspectively opaque" to the person who holds them, and recalcitrant, in the sense that they are not easily amenable to reflective correction and control (Washington and Kelly 2016, 18). The empirical research has shown that it is not only members of dominant social groups who hold implicitly biased attitudes toward members of subordinate or disadvantaged social groups. Widely used tests for implicit bias, such as the Implicit Association Test (IAT), provide evidence that members of groups targeted by these biases commonly also hold the same biases toward their own social group.[19]

In the recent literature, there has been considerable debate about whether or not agents can be held morally responsible for implicit biases. This debate is an extension of debates between voluntarists and nonvoluntarists concerning control conditions for moral responsibility. According to voluntarists, an agent can be held morally responsible only for actions and attitudes that are within her control (either directly or indirectly). Many excuses function by appealing to this condition—for example, by showing that the *action* was accidental, coerced, or unavoidable. But how plausible is the control condition when it comes to agents' *attitudes*? Nonvoluntarists question the assumption that we are not responsible and blameworthy for attitudes that may not be under our voluntary control, citing a range of examples involving emotions (e.g., sudden outbursts of anger), omissions (e.g., forgetting a friend's birthday), and attitudes (e.g., being amused by something morally offensive), where blame seems appropriate.[20]

The nonvoluntarist challenge extends to cases involving implicit bias. Is it reasonable to excuse someone for implicitly racist or sexist attitudes, given the impact these attitudes can have on a person's judgments and behavior? Voluntarists (e.g., Levy 2013, 2014) argue that implicit attitudes, of which an agent is not consciously aware, are not deeply attributable to that agent because these attitudes are not available for reflective deliberation and endorsement, and hence do not reflect the agent's "evaluative stance." In addition, conscious awareness is crucial for satisfying the epistemic and control conditions on moral responsibility; thus we cannot be blameworthy for attitudes of which we are not conscious. Those who find the implications of this position troubling have suggested a range of responses. Zheng, for example, draws on the distinction between attributability and accountability to explain some of the conflicting intuitions on this issue, and proposes that "we ought to hold people morally accountable, but not attributively responsible, for actions caused by implicit bias" (2016, 76). Glasgow focuses on the implications of implicit bias for Real Self Theories and connects these implications to the broader issue of responsibility for actions and attitudes from which one is alienated. He argues that whether or not alienation, including from one's implicit biases, "can exculpate depends on whether the act or attitude in question is sufficiently *harmful*" (2016, 57). Washington and Kelly (2016) highlight the importance of the wider epistemic environment and the person's situation in determining degrees of responsibility for implicit biases: if knowledge about implicit biases and their effects on judgment is available in one's epistemic environment, and one occupies a social position in which this knowledge is relevant, then one should be held responsible for one's biases.

As the foregoing discussion indicates, questions concerning responsibility for implicit bias are of direct relevance to the challenge of theorizing moral responsibility in non-ideal social contexts. A number of the contributors to this volume make use of cases of implicit bias to illustrate how structural injustice and social oppression can corrupt moral responsibility practices, distorting our assessments of who counts as an agent or an equal participant in morally reactive exchanges, and what forms of reproach individuals are liable for. Others raise concerns about the impact of implicit bias on the moral standards or expectations to which we hold one another. Although the influence of implicit biases can be seen in the actions of individuals, these biases are properly understood as arising out of a social context. This has prompted several contributors to this volume to expand the focus of attention from individual responsibility for implicit bias to broader social concerns about how practices of holding agents to account for implicit bias can play a role in effecting moral change. In the final section of the introduction, we provide an overview of these and other contributions to the volume, and explain how they investigate and propose new ways to respond to some the issues discussed in the preceding sections of this introduction.

5 Chapter Overview

In the first chapter of the volume, Michael McKenna explores the implications for his theory of moral responsibility of a social context marked by imbalances of power. McKenna examines the idea operating at the center of his theory—and of Strawsonian theories more generally—that the propriety of our responsibility practices rests on the demand that persons who stand in various relationships to us display some amount of respect or good will. A key element of McKenna's conversational theory is the idea that an agent's actions are potential bearers of meaning. Actions that are deemed praiseworthy or blameworthy, and that elicit like responses, convey meaning representative of the agent's quality of will. When we hold an agent morally responsible by demonstrations of sentiments such as resentment, indignation, or gratitude, we do so having judged the agent's actions as conveying a level of regard that falls short of (or rises to) standards established by the moral community. But McKenna worries that Strawsonian accounts have overlooked a crucial fact. This is that the social contexts within which morally responsible agents engage in the interpretive and communicative enterprise of signaling what qualifies as appropriate regard are shaped by cultural practices that include asymmetrical dynamics of power. Social inequality means that "those who make the demands for a reasonable degree of good will and those prepared to react to departures from those demands are not all equally empowered" (McKenna, chapter 1, this volume). Persons who wield disproportionate control are better positioned to set the terms for what counts as the requisite quality of good will in a particular conversational exchange. Conversely, persons who have less social power must exert greater effort in negotiating potentially coercive demands upon them, and in coming to recognize themselves as equally entitled to expect good will and regard from other, more powerful persons. In addition, disparities of social power infiltrate and compromise both the control and the epistemic conditions for responsible agency. A competent moral agent must be alert to and responsive to the interpretive framework of conventions against which the moral community ascribes significance to types of behavior. Persons whose social position diminishes their access to the social resources that make effective communication possible are disadvantaged in setting the terms of expected meaning. The upshot is that, given social inequity, "many agents who are morally responsible for their conduct . . . operate in contexts that are morally unfair to them as agents" (McKenna, chapter 1, this volume).

Catriona Mackenzie's chapter aims to show why moral responsibility theorists who take seriously the socio-relational scaffolding of agency and the interpersonal dynamics at the heart of our practices need to pay more sustained attention to the ways in which the social context, and especially dynamics of power and oppression, can distort moral responsibility exchanges and practices. In developing her argument, Mackenzie adopts Shoemaker's (2011, 2015) tripartite distinction between attributability, answerability, and accountability. Shoemaker's aim, in distinguishing these three dimensions of moral responsibility, is to tease out how impairments of *capacity* with respect to one or more of these dimensions affect agents' eligibility for moral responsibility ascriptions. Mackenzie, however, uses the distinction to tease out how moral responsibility ascriptions and practices are entangled with social dynamics of power, thereby affecting persons' *statuses* as morally responsible agents. Drawing on recent feminist analyses of social oppression (e.g., Cudd 2006) and epistemic injustice (e.g., Fricker 2007), she shows that although attributability responses are deeply enmeshed in the fabric of our social interactions, these responses are often shaped by unjust social stereotypes and social role schemas, for example of race, gender, or class. With respect to answerability and accountability, she suggests that Shoemaker and other moral responsibility theorists, such as McKenna (2012) and McGeer (2012; McGeer and Pettit 2015), present answerability and accountability practices as symmetrically and reciprocally structured. Using a number of different examples, Mackenzie shows that this idealization overlooks the extent to which these practices are also deeply enmeshed in social hierarchies of authority and power that determine who has the standing to hold answerable and accountable. In concluding, she suggests that her analysis might lead in two radically divergent directions. In one direction, it might be taken to lend strong support to a deep skepticism and critique of Strawsonian theories and justifications. If our moral responsibility practices and reactive attitudes are indeed so entwined with dynamics of power and oppression, then how can these practices and attitudes provide any kind of justification for moral responsibility ascriptions? In the other direction, this analysis might be thought to lend support to a Strawsonian account of the social scaffolding of responsible agency. Because we only become agents in the first place by being socialized into moral responsibility practices, our agential status and capacities are inescapably vulnerable to the dynamics of social interaction. We must therefore be vigilant in subjecting these interactions to ongoing scrutiny, critique, and reform.

Marina Oshana's contribution expands the analysis of moral responsibility as a form of accountability to attend to dynamics of social and political status that frame the background against which assessments of responsibility occur. The focus of Oshana's analysis is on the status of the party positioned to hold another responsible relative to that of the party from whom an account is expected. She examines two scenarios in which the power of interlocutors and those held accountable is relativized to their gendered, economic, and ethnic social status, and is frequently rendered asymmetric because of gender, class, and ethnicity. The contexts are the university classroom and the situation of persons of color interacting with law enforcement officials. Oshana discusses two different ways in which the various power differentials that track social identity can corrupt the legitimate hierarchies involved in holding persons responsible. In the context of academic life, Oshana investigates how the appropriate power relationship between professor and students can be disrupted when the professor's gender or race are socially marginalized. In these cases, the professor is, unfairly and inappropriately, unable to hold students to account for their academic performance or disruptive behavior despite the legitimacy of her doing so. In the law enforcement context, while the individuals held to account are conventionally and appropriately the less powerful party in the relationship, they often are unfairly disadvantaged because of their social identity. The legitimate power advantage of those involved in law enforcement can be abused where the social identities of those being called to account are devalued. Those in positions of dominance may defy (and are sometimes legally authorized to defy) the norms and practices of the reciprocal holding to account that Oshana takes to be central to an adequate account of moral responsibility. The result is that, too often, the less powerful constituents are denied the opportunity to offer an account of themselves in response to the demands made of them by officers of the law. In both types of exchange—academia and law enforcement—those marginalized by prevailing arrangements of authority, expectations about credibility, and conventional assumptions about one's proper "place" lack an opportunity to contribute to the interpersonal exchange. The lack of opportunity manifests in not having one's moral demands fully recognized, not having the opportunity to respond when reproached, and not having those one addresses take one's perspective or arguments seriously.

In his contribution to the volume, Manuel Vargas investigates the implications of social oppression for his "agency cultivation" model of moral responsibility. His aim, in particular, is to show how this model can provide a response to the more general skeptical worry that the distinction between culpable and non-culpable actions collapses once we acknowledge the extent to which our psychologies and agency are socially constituted and susceptible to circumstantial variation. In developing a response to this worry, Vargas rejects as implausible any appeal to a notion of "transcendent agency" or "the idea that agency is not importantly constrained by or limited to features of circumstance or experience" (Vargas, chapter 4, this volume). Rather, he argues, an adequate response must move beyond atomistic or individualistic conceptions of agency and acknowledge that "responsible agency is partly a matter of how our social, political, and even ideological circumstances are arranged" (chapter 4, this volume). Vargas's response to the skeptical worry involves three main claims. First, the "responsibility system"—responsibility attitudes and practices, including practices of praise and blame—is justified to the extent that it cultivates agents' ability to recognize and suitably respond to moral considerations. Second, culpability is a scalar matter: degree of culpability is determined by the degree to which an agent has the ability to recognize and respond to the relevant moral considerations, where "for a given moral consideration, the relevant degree of sensitivity is determined by whatever conception of capacity that an ideal observer would pick as best for helping imperfect creatures like us to do the right thing, over time, and in the actual world" (chapter 4, this volume). Third, whether or not an agent's social and circumstantial context is exculpatory depends on the extent to which that context undermines her ability to be sensitive to the relevant moral considerations. Oppressive contexts that drastically limit the morally adequate action possibilities available to an agent, or impair an agent's epistemic and deliberative capacities, may mitigate culpability. Usually, however, these kinds of limitations and impairments are context specific and partial; thus exculpation is likely to be piecemeal rather than global. In addition to these claims, Vargas's response to the skeptical worry highlights the importance of "moral ecology" (or the interpersonal, social, and political environment) for our agential capacities, raising the question of what kinds of social and political intervention might be justifiable to enhance the moral ecology and scaffold the development of responsible agency. In the final section, Vargas sketches out some preliminary answers to this question.

Like Vargas, Jules Holroyd thinks that social practices can help individuals develop the capacities for morally responsible agency. In her chapter for this volume, she compares two different accounts of moral responsibility that share this commitment—Vargas's circumstantialist (or agency cultivation) approach (Vargas 2013, 2015) and Victoria McGeer's scaffolded-responsiveness view

(McGeer 2012; McGeer and Pettit 2015). Her analysis is original in adopting a methodological approach that is "ameliorative." Rather than attempting to achieve a balance between intuitions about difficult cases and current use, Holroyd's ameliorative approach involves asking what purpose the concept of moral responsibility (and thus our moral responsibility practices) *ought to* serve. Holroyd thinks that our moral responsibility practices should cultivate agency and should tend to increase individuals' sensitivity to moral reasons. To evaluate the merits of Vargas's and McGeer's approaches, she explores how they handle the difficult cases of implicit bias and sexist use of gendered pronouns. Vargas's approach, Holroyd argues, has limited resources for expanding the responsibility of agents to cases of this sort. Under his approach, moral responsibility is determined by the agent's current reasons responsiveness and by features of the environment (or "moral ecology") in which she finds herself. In cases of implicit bias, the agent is currently unaware of her bias and so does not consider relevant reasons. Furthermore, the agent is often sheltered from her own biases by aspects of the moral ecology. Agents are thus not responsible for implicit biases on Vargas's approach. In contrast, Holroyd argues that McGeer's scaffolded-responsiveness approach can explain when and how it might be appropriate to hold agents responsible for their implicit biases and sexist use of gendered pronouns. This is because McGeer's approach explains how agents can be sensitized to reasons by a prospective idealized audience ("those whose [anticipated] judgments about our conduct matter to us" [Holroyd, chapter 5, this volume]). Such an audience can prompt us as agents to respond to reasons or points of view that we might not otherwise consider. In addition, Holroyd also reflects on the relationship between moral responsibility and blame. She argues that we should identify responses "beyond blame," such as reproach and moral disappointment, for engaging with morally responsible individuals whose agency we are seeking to expand or scaffold.

Elinor Mason also takes up the complex question of moral responsibility for implicit biases. In her chapter, she considers this alongside responsibility in two other types of cases—explicit biases that the agent lacks resources for identifying as wrong, and so-called glitches in which an agent forgets or is inattentive. She understands all these as cases of wrongdoing without ill will. Despite the lack of ill will, she argues, the agents involved are both morally responsible and blameworthy. Mason engages extensively with the arguments of Cheshire Calhoun (1989), who offered a somewhat different analysis of moral responsibility in contexts where the wrongfulness of a biased action is masked from the agent by social conditions. One such example is the use of harmfully sexist language (such as 'lady' or 'girl' to refer to a woman) in contexts where this is regarded as polite or flattering rather than patronizing. Calhoun argues that agents in such cases are not *blameworthy* for the action, but that responding with blame, or reproach, can nevertheless be justified on forward-looking grounds. In contrast, Mason argues that it is not only appropriate to reproach agents in these cases, but that they are *blameworthy*. Mason's approach is underpinned by a view of moral responsibility as something we *take on* as part of a commitment to maintaining respectful relationships with others. At least part of what is required for an agent to be morally responsible for an action is that she takes responsibility. Thus Mason thinks our propensity to feel guilt once we become aware of our wrongdoing in these cases reveals something important about what it means to be morally responsible and blameworthy. Mason's approach can be distinguished from other views that support a blame-like moral response to actions that stem from implicit bias, including Calhoun (1989) and Fricker (2016), neither of whom accepts that the agent is blameworthy. It can also be distinguished from Holroyd's approach: Holroyd agrees that agents in some of these cases should be held morally responsible, due to the potential of doing so to expand their agency. However, she questions whether blame is an appropriate response in such cases. One challenge for Mason's approach, which she discusses in the final section, is that some people are expected to take on more responsibility and others less. This can sometimes track social identity—as when girls are the focus of education initiatives to prevent unwanted pregnancies, sexual assault, or rape.

Neil Levy's chapter is also concerned with moral responsibility for wrong-doings in contexts where the agent lacks resources for identifying the wrong. However, his analysis of the problem as well as his proposal for addressing it differ considerably from Mason's. Levy's central aim is to challenge the widely accepted view that individual agents are the loci of agency. The view that moral responsibility ascriptions pertain to *individuals* is shared even by most theorists who propose social accounts of moral responsibility, who focus on how social factors influence individual agents' capacities, and how this should be taken into account in ascribing responsibility. But to Levy these social approaches nevertheless exemplify what he describes as an "almost obsessive focus on the individual as the only locus not only of agency but also of responsibility" (Levy, chapter 7, this volume). As an alternative, he proposes that we look first for *agency* rather than *agents*. Sometimes, he argues, this will reveal that systems, or what he calls "supra-agential aggregates," are the loci of agency. Sometimes the supra-agential aggregate is an entity with a structure and clear boundaries that could be held morally responsible and/or liable for its role in the wrongdoing (such cases would often also be captured by theories of collective responsibility). On other occasions, however, the loci of agency may not be something that can be blamed or held responsible. Levy then turns his attention to the epistemic conditions of moral responsibility. Knowledge and its production, he argues, are also distributed among individuals. He offers several examples to illustrate this, including scientific research practices and cultural practices. These practices mean that individuals are "embedded in complex social networks that distribute knowledge" (chapter 7, this volume) and that in making use of these we often also acquire widely shared false beliefs. Unlike Holroyd and Mason, Levy does not think individuals should be held responsible or blamed for holding such false beliefs (which would include implicit biases), or for wrongdoings that arise from them. However, his account gives him resources to deal with these problems differently. He argues that once we recognize that the loci of agency may be supra-agential aggregates rather than individuals, we can explore the possibility of responding to the aggregates or systems involved in widely shared false beliefs. Responses will not always involve ascribing moral responsibility and reacting with blame or punishment—they could include reforming institutions and collectives.

Like the authors of some earlier chapters (McKenna, Mackenzie, Oshana, and Holroyd, for example), Katrina Hutchison's focus is on bringing an existing account of moral responsibility into engagement with apparently oppressive moral responsibility practices. Focusing on P. F. Strawson's distinction between the objective and participant stances, in the first half of the chapter Hutchison picks up on Strawson's suggestion that this distinction is not hard and fast, and that in many cases we take a stance toward others that is neither wholly participant nor wholly objective. She argues that it is reasonable to think of a spectrum between the two, with many real cases falling toward the middle. Some Strawsonians (e.g., Victoria McGeer [2012]) have noted that taking the participant stance toward someone is respectful of that person's agency, whereas the objective stance may be disrespectful. Hutchison explores the relationship between the two stances and respect in some detail, drawing particularly on Stephen Darwall's (2004) distinction between recognition and appraisal respect. She argues that the objective stance involves recognition respect for the individual as a person, despite involving a negative assessment of their agential capacities. In contrast, the participant stance involves appraisal respect for the person's agential capacities. Since appraisal respect can come in degrees, cases that fall toward the middle of the spectrum should involve a corresponding degree of appraisal respect. Hutchison draws on this analysis of the participant and objective stances to better understand several cases in which Indigenous Australian women died in custody due to apparent neglect of urgent medical needs by police, health professionals, and others involved in their supervision. The treatment of the women in these cases appears to reflect systematic biases in the moral community at the time, and as such Hutchison takes them as examples of a corrupt moral responsibility practice, rather than isolated tragic cases. She argues that these cases involved failures of respect—particularly recognition respect. These failures are, however, obscured by the fact that the women were alcohol or drug users and fell somewhere toward the middle of the participant/ objective stance spectrum.

Natalie Stoljar's chapter makes a distinctive contribution to the volume, by examining the relationship between social accounts of responsibility and of autonomy. Stoljar's overarching aim is to defend externalist, constitutively relational conceptions of autonomy against the criticism that such accounts too readily deny autonomy to oppressed or exploited persons. This denial invites the "agency dilemma": while conditions of subservience and oppression undermine autonomy, "claiming that people are non-autonomous just in virtue of oppression erases their agency and disrespects their evaluative commitments" (Stoljar, chapter 9, this volume). Stoljar's subsidiary aim is to take issue with the agency dilemma by offering a critical exploration of "dialogical answerability accounts of autonomy." Independently defended by Paul Benson (2005) and Andrea Westlund (2009), such accounts premise autonomy on a disposition for "responsible self-ownership," where that amounts to a subjective preparedness to hold oneself answerable for one's choices and actions in the face of justificatory challenges. Such accounts are allegedly invulnerable to the agency dilemma in claiming that all choices, even those that signal internalized norms of oppression, are in theory consistent with autonomous agency provided the actor can engage and is willing to engage in reflective dialogue that demonstrates authentic commitment. In doing so, the actor takes responsible ownership of her actions. Stoljar's argument against dialogical answerability is sweeping. Two theses are key to her argument. One is that the agency dilemma can be laid to rest if more nuanced attention is paid to the differences between authentic agency, autonomy, and moral responsibility and to the distinct conditions for each. The second is that we should follow Angela Smith (2005, 2012a) and look to an account of answerability-responsibility that tracks actions that are rationally related to the agent's evaluative commitments. Adopting Smith's approach, Stolar argues, permits us to preserve the moral agency of actors and allows for evaluative appraisal of the actor's authentic choices and actions even in circumstances where the actor's capacity for autonomous choice and action is truncated by systemic social oppression and aberrant socialization. Using the examples of "resisters" (e.g., social reformers such as Martin Luther King Jr.) and "endorsers" (e.g., Jehovah's Witnesses in Nazi concentration camps), she claims that it strains credulity to regard them as autonomous, given the conditions they were forced to navigate. Nonetheless, we can admire their fortitude and psychic integrity, and hold them up as moral exemplars who are responsible and answerable for their choices and actions insofar as these proceed from their evaluative judgments. We can acknowledge that "endorsers" or "resisters" retain valued and valuable aspects of agency at the same time we deny that persons subject to exploitative or oppressive circumstances are autonomous.

In her contribution, Andrea Westlund focuses on the debate among philosophers and popular psychologists about the roles blame and blaming should play within our responsibility practices. Many regard blame as a destructive, essentially hostile practice that does little to serve our moral practices and may even conceal morally suspect attempts to deflect attention away from one's own malfeasance. Westlund agrees that, where blaming takes the form of humiliating speech and hostile affective attitudes, it serves as a destructive rather than constructive response. But she believes these worries can be assuaged by differentiating blame as a potentially hostile reactive attitude in response to perceived ill will and wrongdoing from blaming as an expressive speech act, and by disentangling the variety of forms blaming may take. Following J. L. Austin (1962), Westlund examines the multiple functions blaming can serve: as a "behabitive," a performative utterance that exhibits attitudes and emotional states; as a "verdictive," in which verdicts (including judgments of responsibility) are delivered upon the wrongdoer; and as an "exercitive," a declarative act that "involve[s] the exercise of . . . normative or moral powers to make claims, give reasons, impose obligations, or otherwise alter the normative landscape" (Westlund, chapter 10, this volume). Failing to disentangle these yields a variety of blame that Westlund labels "strongly verdictive" in which the blamer wields power over the blamed party, renders judgment on the blamed party, and exhibits emotions of a punitive variety. Strongly verdictive blaming arrests, rather than furthers, moral dialogue. Yet moral dialogue is precisely what is called for in engaging with others in the community of moral agents. In contrast, Westlund recommends that our responsibility practices take the form of "holding answerable without judgmental blame" (chapter 10, this volume). Holding answerable includes aspects of each form of blame, but with the goals of inviting the blamed party to adopt an alternative viewpoint on her action, and giving the blaming party the opportunity to reconsider the circumstances that led her to assess the actor as she did and to respond as she did. Properly deployed, blame does not humiliate the wrongdoer, foreclosing moral conversation, but prompts the wrongdoer to answer for her conduct—to take responsibility for it. Westlund's account challenges the Strawsonian idea that the reactive attitudes and practices are reserved for persons toward whom we take a participant stance as opposed to the detached and objective, nonconversational stance that we assume in therapeutic and pedagogical contexts. By making thoughtful use of a range of different cases "in which the ability to exercise important normative powers is relationally compromised" (chapter 10, this volume), Westlund establishes how it is possible to express fault with behavior at the same time we demonstrate our regard for the actor as a morally responsible agent and a morally engaged dialogical partner. By adopting the nonjudgmental model of blame into our repertoire of responsibility practices, we offer the (rightly) blameworthy party the opportunity to take responsibility and to choose to act in more rewarding ways.

Bennett Helm offers a Strawsonian reactive attitude analysis of blame that expands the range of those attitudes to include what he calls "communities of respect." Helm's aim is to preserve the reactive attitudes as mechanisms of blame from criticism leveled by T. M. Scanlon (2008, 2012), while clarifying elements of Scanlon's account. Scanlon charges that reactive attitudes analyses fail to explain the fact that blame tracks particular interpersonal relationships and ignores the fact that reactive practices of blaming will vary given the significance the action of wrongdoing has for the wronged individual. Helm answers that this focus on the individual is unduly egocentric and overlooks the crucially communal dimension of attitudes of blame, judgments of blameworthiness, and blaming practices. Neither the content of blame nor the propriety of blaming hang on the personal relationship one bears to the wrongdoer; rather, they hang on the impairment done by the wrongdoer to the moral community of which she is a member. The array of reactive attitudes is founded in relationships that signify membership in communities of respect. Helm notes that Scanlon's account is vague insofar as it fails to provide a principled explanation for our decision to demarcate specific relationships, defined by specific attitudes, as open to blame. Helm locates this explanation in the fact that such violations fail to accord the community recognition respect, thus inviting legitimate blame. What is at issue is not merely injury done to a particular person on a particular occasion, but the significance of the injury for the norms of the moral community of which the person is a part. This explains why persons who are not direct victims of a moral injury because they lack first-person engagement with the wrongdoer—due to remoteness of time or physical distance—nonetheless may possess the standing to adjust their reactive attitudes toward the wrongdoer as the situation allows. The assault on these norms also explains why we do not regard acquiescence to abuse and domination as absolution for responsibility, for "acquiescence does not involve the mutual recognition of each as having the standing and authority to hold the other responsible to the norms of a community of respect" (Helm, chapter 11, this volume). Our respect for shared norms also explains the employment of other attitudes implicated in our responsibility practices, such as forgiveness.

In the final chapter of the volume, Maureen Sie focuses on the role of what she calls "tokens of appraisal" in our moral responsibility practices. In the philosophical literature on moral responsibility, much emphasis has been placed upon identifying the necessary and sufficient conditions for ascribing moral responsibility to individuals, and identifying whether or not they are blameworthy. The appropriateness of moral appraisal is usually taken to depend upon the agent's responsibility status: whether she is morally responsible for the behavior in question. However, Sie argues that this focus on conditions of responsible agency obscures the important social role that our responses to one another play in communicating and coordinating moral expectations. In some respects, Sie's analysis of the role of tokens of appraisal picks up on the same considerations as the scaffolding approaches to moral responsibility developed by Vargas (2013), McGeer (2012, 2013), McGeer and Pettit (2015), and Holroyd (chapter 5, this volume). The similarity is particularly clear in her argument that appraisals play an important role in the development of agential capacities. Just as Holroyd and McGeer think that the response of an audience (real or imagined) can prompt an agent to adjust the moral reasons she takes into account and her evaluation of her own behavior, Sie argues that other people's moral appraisals can challenge our self-understanding, reveal inconsistencies between our values and actions, or help us to identify reasons we ought to be sensitive to in deciding how to behave. In addition, Sie argues that appraisals play an important role in establishing and refining our shared moral standards. Toward the end of the chapter, she uses a case involving implicit bias to illustrate this: those who are subject to implicit bias are often not regarded as equal participants in moral responsibility practices, and may struggle to have their appraisals of others heard. Nevertheless, Sie contends that it is through voicing such challenges—whether or not they are "deserved" by those whose actions reveal biases of which they are unaware— that change occurs. Where Sie departs from other scaffolding approaches is in not attempting to reconcile her account of the social role of tokens of appraisal with an account of the conditions for moral responsibility. It is hard to determine how deep this difference is, particularly between Holroyd and Sie. Holroyd's ameliorative methodology means that she, like Sie, foregrounds the social role of moral responsibility practices. For Holroyd, this process informs the selection of a concept of moral responsibility (and thus the conditions for being held responsible), whereas Sie argues that we should focus on the social function of responsibility practices, rather than the conditions for being responsible, and does not seek to connect the two questions.

Notes

1. Strawson's approach is not the first of this kind. In fact, in "Freedom and Resentment," he engages explicitly with consequentialist approaches to moral responsibility, which were popular with compatibilists at the time and also took social factors to underpin moral responsibility. According to these approaches, our practice of holding one another morally responsible is justified by the social consequences of so doing, particularly the deterring influence of being regarded as apt for punishment. Twentieth-century proponents of this sort of view include Moore (1912); Schlick (1939); Ayer ([1946] 1954); and Nowell-Smith (1948, 1954). Where these approaches apparently fail is in being purely forward-looking. Most of us, even compatibilists, have the intuition that moral responsibility ascriptions must be "deserved" by the agent. Strawson's approach apparently accounts for this backward-looking aspect of moral responsibility—our sense that moral responsibility ascriptions serve more than consequentialist ends.

2. Strawson has another paper on moral philosophy, "Social Morality and Individual Ideal" (1961), and he makes some further comments on free will and moral responsibility in *Scepticism and Naturalism: Some Varieties* (1985). Some philosophers have drawn on these other sources in developing Strawsonian accounts of moral responsibility, perhaps most notably Paul Russell (1992), who draws heavily on the latter in his naturalistic reading of Strawson's argument. But most contemporary Strawsonians do not draw on these papers.

3. In some relationships, we expect a lot more than this. A recent account of the relationship-dependence of the moral demands we make of one another can be found in T. M. Scanlon's *Moral Dimensions: Permissibility, Meaning, Blame* (2008).

4. For other important recent contributions to the literature on blame, see Hieronymi 2004; Scanlon 2012; Smith 2008a; and the essays in Coates and Tognazzini 2012.

5. In fact, Strawson does not talk about paradigm or idealized cases, but it is obvious he is thinking of idealized cases. At various points in the paper, he qualifies what he says about these cases; specifically, he qualifies the implicit claim that such exchanges always unfold in the way he describes, or that our resentments always track others' regard for us in the relevant way, or that third parties generally do or should mirror offended parties in their assessment of the situation. For example, he says, "[P]sychological studies have made us rightly mistrustful of many particular manifestations of the attitudes I have spoken of. They are a prime realm of self-deception" (1962, 210).

6. Similar sorts of considerations are at play in discussions about the difference between education and indoctrination of children (see, for example, Cuypers and Haji 2007) and the extent to which agents are responsible for moral ignorance that results from their upbringing (Levy 2009). See also our discussion below (section 3, note 10) of work in feminist and relational autonomy on adaptive preferences.

7. Of course, this assumption is not made in the *free will* debate, where incompatibilists, for example, are concerned that our ordinary ascriptions of moral agency fail to be sensitive to whether or not physical determinism holds. Thus we might systematically ascribe moral responsibility to one another because we are oblivious to the possibility of universal determinism. But if universal determinism does hold, then none of us would have (what incompatibilists regard as) key capacities required for moral agency. In the free will debate, however, the different parties are not concerned that social hierarchies might lead to the ascription of moral agency to some, but not others, in ways that fail to track underlying capacities. In the free will debate, the question is always about the *possibility* of human moral agency, rather than differences between different agents. If universal determinism rules out free will, it rules it out for everyone, so it would be superfluous to discuss the impact of social hierarchies.

8. Parts of the discussion in this section are adapted from Mackenzie 2017.

9. For an overview of Real Self Theories of moral responsibility, see Kane 2005, chapter 9. Susan Wolf's "Reason" or "Sane Deep Self" view (1987, 1990) is a critical emendation of the standard Real Self view.

10. For a more detailed overview of these criticisms of hierarchical theories, see Mackenzie and Stoljar 2000. For recent discussions on autonomy and adaptive preferences, see Cudd 2015; Mackenzie 2015; Stoljar 2014.

11. Christman's focus on the importance of personal history for autonomy is influenced by the work of Al Mele, specifically his trademark manipulation examples in his contributions to debates about "Frankfurt-type examples" in the literature on the Principle of Alternate Possibilities (see, e.g., Mele 1995). For an overview of the manipulation problem as it applies to Real Self Theories of moral responsibility, see Mele 2002.

12. Again, note the overlap with Real Self Theories of moral responsibility, which hold that agents may be exculpated for actions that do not express their "true selves" or from which they are alienated.

13. Compare Susan Wolf's "Reason View" (1987, 1990), which proposes a normative competence account of moral responsibility.

14. In contrast to Shoemaker, other theorists such as Angela Smith (2012a) think that answerability on its own is adequate to understand moral responsibility.

15. In addition, there have been some studies investigating the role of stereotype threat in "psychological disengagement" (decreased psychological investment in one's success in a specific

domain) and "domain avoidance" (avoiding or distancing oneself from a specific domain). For discussion and references to the empirical literature, see Goguen 2016.

16. In line with this broader understanding, Stacey Goguen defines stereotype threat as occurring "when an individual becomes aware, consciously or unconsciously, that their behaviour in a specific social arena or 'domain' could render salient a negative stereotype about them or their social group" (2016, 217). She also argues that philosophers and psychologists should pay more attention to the epistemic effects of stereotype threat on agents' sense of self-identity, including self-distrust and self-doubt about one's rational capacities. For a detailed critique of Claude Steele's work on stereotype threat as overly narrow, see Blum 2016. Blum argues that Steele's studies focus primarily on the effects of stereotype threat on the academic performance of high-achieving African American students. This focus overlooks broader educational, moral, and political issues about stereotypes. These include the importance of equipping students in stereotype-vulnerable groups "with the intellectual tools to recognize, examine, and criticize stereotypes in general and stereotypes of their group in particular" (Blum 2016, 151) and to distinguish stereotypes from valid generalizations; and the importance of understanding how stereotypes and stereotype threat are embedded in, and interact with, structures that perpetuate social injustice, and are internalized by members of stereotype-vulnerable social groups.

17. Note that Fricker does not think that credibility excesses confer unfair epistemic privilege or advantage on those who enjoy them. In contrast, José Medina (2013) argues that a central feature of epistemic injustice is that those in positions of social advantage and privilege enjoy an undue and unwarranted excess of credibility.

18. See especially the essays in Brownstein and Saul (2016b, volumes 1 and 2).

19. The IAT indirectly measures people's attitudes, for example, toward racial groups, through a task that involves pairing images of black or white faces with positive or negative words associated stereotypically with a specific social group. In some pictures, the correct pairing is compatible with the stereotype; in others, the correct pairing is incompatible. The speed and accuracy with which participants undertake the task is taken as a measure of implicit preferences for black or white faces. For more detailed discussion of implicit bias, including various tasks used to measure it, references to the relevant empirical literature, and theories about the nature of implicit attitudes, see Brownstein and Saul 2016a.

20. The example of whether or not an agent should be held responsible for a sudden outburst of anger is from Adams's (1985) influential version of the nonvoluntarist challenge. The other examples are from Smith (2005).

References

Adams, Robert M. 1985. "Involuntary Sins." *The Philosophical Review* 94 (1): 3–31.

Anderson, Elizabeth. 2010. *The Imperative of Integration*. Princeton, NJ: Princeton University Press.

Arpaly, Nomy. 2004. *Unprincipled Virtue*. New York: Oxford University Press.

Austin, John L. 1962. How to Do Things with Words. 2nd ed. Edited by J. O. Urmson and Marina Sbisa. Cambridge, MA: Harvard University Press.

Ayer, A. J. (1946) 1954. "Freedom and Necessity." Reprinted in Ayer, A. J. *Philosophical Essays*, 271–284. London: Macmillan and Co. Ltd.

Benson, Paul. 1991. "Autonomy and Oppressive Socialization." *Social Theory and Practice* 17 (3): 385–408.

Benson, Paul. 2005. "Taking Ownership: Authority and Voice in Autonomous Agency." In *Autonomy and the Challenges to Liberalism*, edited by John Christman and Joel Anderson, 101–126. Cambridge: Cambridge University Press.

Benson, Paul. 2014. "Feminist Commitments and Relational Autonomy." In *Autonomy, Oppression, and Gender*, edited by Andrea Veltman and Mark Piper, 87–113. New York: Oxford University Press.

Blum, Lawrence. 2016. "The Too Minimal Political, Moral, and Civic Dimension of Claude Steele's 'Stereotype Threat' Paradigm." In *Implicit Bias and Philosophy, Vol. 2, Moral Responsibility, Structural Injustice, and Ethics*, edited by Michael Brownstein and Jennifer Saul, 147–172. Oxford: Oxford University Press.

Brownstein, Michael, and Jennifer Saul. 2016a. Introduction to *Implicit Bias and Philosophy, Vol. 1, Metaphysics and Epistemology*, edited by Michael Brownstein and Jennifer Saul, 1–19. Oxford: Oxford University Press.

Brownstein, Michael, and Jennifer Saul, eds. 2016b. *Implicit Bias and Philosophy, Vol. 1, Metaphysics and Epistemology & Vol. 2, Moral Responsibility, Structural Injustice, and Ethics*. Oxford: Oxford University Press.

Calhoun, Cheshire. 1989. "Responsibility and Reproach." *Ethics* 99 (2): 389–406.

Christman, John. 1991. "Autonomy and Personal History." *Canadian Journal of Philosophy* 21 (1): 1–24.

Christman, John. 2004. "Relational Autonomy, Liberal Individualism and the Social Constitution of Selves." *Philosophical Studies* 117 (1–2): 143–164.

Christman, John. 2009. *The Politics of Persons: Individual Autonomy and Socio-Historical Selves*. Cambridge: Cambridge University Press.

Coates, Justin, and Neil Tognazzini, eds. 2012. *Blame: Its Nature and Norms*. New York: Oxford University Press.

Cudd, Ann. 2006. *Analyzing Oppression*. New York: Oxford University Press.

Cudd, Ann. 2015. "Adaptations to Oppression: Preference, Autonomy and Resistance." In *Personal Autonomy and Social Oppression: Philosophical Perspectives*, edited by Marina Oshana, 142–160. New York: Routledge.

Cuypers, Stefaan E., and Ishtiyaque Haji. 2007. "Authentic Education and Moral Responsibility." *Journal of Applied Philosophy* 24 (1): 78–94.

Darwall, Stephen. 2004. "Respect and the Second-Person Standpoint." In *Proceedings and Addresses of the American Philosophical Association* 78 (2): 43–59.

Darwall, Stephen. 2006. *The Second-Person Standpoint: Morality, Respect, and Accountability*. Cambridge, MA: Harvard University Press.

Dworkin, Gerald. 1976. "Autonomy and Behavior Control." *Hastings Center Report* 6: 23–28.

Dworkin, Gerald. 1988. *The Theory and Practice of Autonomy*. New York: Cambridge University Press.

Frankfurt, Harry. 1971. "Freedom of the Will and the Concept of a Person." *The Journal of Philosophy* 68 (1): 5–20.

Fricker, Miranda. 2007. *Epistemic Injustice: Power and the Ethics of Knowing*. Oxford: Oxford University Press.

Fricker, Miranda. 2016. "Fault and No-Fault Responsibility for Implicit Prejudice—A Space for Epistemic Agent-Regret." In *The Epistemic Life of Groups: Essays in the Epistemology of Collectives*, edited by Michael Brady and Miranda Fricker, 33–50. Oxford: Oxford University Press.

Friedman, Marilyn. 1986. "Autonomy and the Split-Level Self." *Southern Journal of Philosophy* 24 (1): 19–35.

Friedman, Marilyn. 2003. *Autonomy, Gender, Politics*. New York: Oxford University Press.

Glasgow, Joshua. 2016. "Alienation and Responsibility." In *Implicit Bias and Philosophy, Vol. 2, Moral Responsibility, Structural Injustice, and Ethics*, edited by Michael Brownstein and Jennifer Saul, 37–61. Oxford: Oxford University Press.

Goguen, Stacey. 2016. "Stereotype Threat, Epistemic Injustice, and Rationality." In *Implicit Bias and Philosophy, Vol. 1, Metaphysics and Epistemology*, edited by Michael Brownstein and Jennifer Saul, 216–237. Oxford: Oxford University Press.

Hieronymi, Pamela. 2004. "The Force and Fairness of Blame." *Philosophical Perspectives* 18 (1): 115–148.

Kane, Robert. 2005. *A Contemporary Introduction to Free Will*. New York: Oxford University Press.

Khader, Serene. 2011. *Adaptive Preferences and Women's Empowerment*. New York: Oxford University Press.

Levy, Neil. 2009. "Culpable Ignorance and Moral Responsibility: A Reply to FitzPatrick." *Ethics* 119 (4): 729–741.

Levy, Neil. 2013. "The Importance of Awareness." *Australasian Journal of Philosophy* 91 (2): 211–229.

Levy, Neil. 2014. "Consciousness, Implicit Attitudes and Moral Responsibility." *Noûs* 48 (1): 21–40.

Mackenzie, Catriona. 2014. "Three Dimensions of Autonomy: A Relational Analysis." In *Autonomy, Oppression, and Gender*, edited by Andrea Veltman and Mark Piper, 15–41. New York: Oxford University Press.

Mackenzie, Catriona. 2015. "Responding to the Agency Dilemma: Autonomy, Adaptive Preferences and Internalized Oppression." In *Personal Autonomy and Social Oppression: Philosophical Perspectives*, edited by Marina Oshana, 40–60. New York: Routledge.

Mackenzie, Catriona. 2017. "Feminist Conceptions of Autonomy." In *The Routledge Companion to Feminist Philosophy*, edited by Ann Garry, Serene J. Khader, and Alison Stone, 515–527. New York: Routledge.

Mackenzie, Catriona, and Natalie Stoljar. 2000. "Introduction: Autonomy Refigured." In *Relational Autonomy: Feminist Perspectives on Autonomy, Agency, and the Social Self*, edited by Catriona Mackenzie and Natalie Stoljar, 3–31. New York: Oxford University Press.

McGeer, Victoria. 2012. "Co-Reactive Attitudes and the Making of Moral Community." In *Emotions, Imagination and Moral Reasoning*, edited by Robyn Langdon and Catriona Mackenzie, 299–326. New York: Psychology Press.

McGeer, Victoria. 2013. "Civilizing Blame." In *Blame: Its Nature and Norms*, edited by Justin Coates and Neil Tognazzini, 162–188. Oxford: Oxford University Press.

McGeer, Victoria, and Philip Pettit. 2015. "The Hard Problem of Responsibility." In *Oxford Studies in Agency and Responsibility, Vol. 3*, edited by D. Shoemaker, 160–188. Oxford: Oxford University Press.

McKenna, Michael. 2012. *Conversation and Responsibility*. New York: Oxford University Press.

Medina, José. 2013. *The Epistemology of Resistance: Gender and Racial Oppression, Epistemic Justice, and the Social Imagination*. New York: Oxford University Press.

Mele, Alfred. 1995. *Autonomous Agents*. New York: Oxford University Press.

Mele, Alfred. 2002. "Autonomy, Self-Control, and Weakness of Will." In *The Oxford Handbook of Free Will*, edited by Robert Kane, 529–548. Oxford: Oxford University Press.

Meyers, Diana. 1989. *Self, Society and Personal Choice*. New York: Columbia University Press.

Moore, G. E. 1912. *Ethics*. London: Thornton Butterworth Ltd.

Narayan, Uma. 2002. "Minds of Their Own: Choices, Autonomy, Cultural Practices, and Other Women." In *A Mind of One's Own: Feminist Essays on Reason and Objectivity*, 2nd ed., edited by Louise Antony and Charlotte Witt, 418–432. Boulder, CO: Westview Press.

Neely, Wright. 1974. "Freedom and Desire." *Philosophical Review* 83 (1): 32–54.

Nowell-Smith, P. H. 1948. "Freewill and Moral Responsibility." *Mind* 57 (225): 45–61.

Nowell-Smith, P. H. 1954. *Ethics*. London: Penguin Books.

Oshana, Marina. 1997. "Ascriptions of Responsibility." *American Philosophical Quarterly* 34 (1): 71–83.

Oshana, Marina. 1998. "Personal Autonomy and Society." *Journal of Social Philosophy* 29 (1): 81–102.

Oshana, Marina. 2002. "The Misguided Marriage of Autonomy and Responsibility." *Journal of Ethics* 6 (3): 261–280.

Oshana, Marina. 2004. "Moral Accountability." *Philosophical Topics* 32 (1–2): 255–274.

Oshana, Marina. 2006. *Personal Autonomy in Society*. Aldershot, UK: Ashgate.

Oshana, Marina. 2015. "Is Socio-Relational Autonomy a Plausible Ideal?" In *Personal Autonomy and Social Oppression: Philosophical Perspectives*, edited by Marina Oshana, 3–24. New York: Routledge.

Pickard, Hannah. 2013. "Responsibility without Blame: Philosophical Reflections on Clinical Practice." In *Oxford Handbook of Philosophy and Psychiatry*, edited by K. W. M. Fulford,

Martin Davies, Richard Gipps, George Graham, John Sadler, Giovanni Stanghellini, and Tim Thornton, 1134–1152. Oxford: Oxford University Press.

Russell, Paul. 1992. "Strawson's Way of Naturalizing Responsibility." *Ethics* 102 (2): 287–302.

Scanlon, Thomas M. 2008. *Moral Dimensions: Permissibility, Meaning, Blame*. Cambridge, MA: Belknap Press of Harvard University Press.

Scanlon, Thomas M. 2012. "Interpreting Blame." In *Blame: Its Nature and Norms*, edited by Justin Coates and Neil Tognazzini, 84–102. New York: Oxford University Press.

Schlick, Moritz. 1939. "When Is a Man Responsible?" In *Problems of Ethics*, translated by David Rynin, 143–158. New York: Prentice-Hall Inc.

Sher, George. 2005. *In Praise of Blame*. New York: Oxford University Press.

Shoemaker, David. 2011. "Attributability, Answerability, and Accountability: Toward a Wider Theory of Responsibility." *Ethics* 121 (3): 602–632.

Shoemaker, David. 2015. *Responsibility from the Margins*. New York: Oxford University Press.

Smith, Angela M. 2005. "Responsibility for Attitudes: Activity and Passivity in Mental Life." *Ethics* 121 (3): 331–352.

Smith, Angela M. 2007. "On Being Responsible and Holding Responsible." *Journal of Ethics* 11 (4): 465–484.

Smith, Angela M. 2008a. "Character, Blameworthiness, and Blame: Comments on George Sher's *In Praise of Blame*." *Philosophical Studies* 137 (1): 31–39.

Smith, Angela M. 2008b. "Control, Responsibility, and Moral Assessment." *Philosophical Studies* 138: 367–392.

Smith, Angela M. 2012a. "Attributability, Answerability, and Accountability: In Defense of a Unified Account." *Ethics* 122 (3): 575–589.

Smith, Angela M. 2012b. "Moral Blame and Moral Protest." In *Blame: Its Nature and Norms*, edited by Justin Coates and Neil Tognazzini, 27–48. New York: Oxford University Press.

Smith, Angela M. 2015. "Responsibility as Answerability." *Inquiry* 58 (2): 99–126.

Sperry, Elizabeth. 2013. "Dupes of Patriarchy: Feminist Strong Substantive Autonomy's Epistemological Weakness." *Hypatia* 28 (4): 887–904.

Steele, Claude. 1997. "A Threat in the Air: How Stereotypes Shape Intellectual Identity and Performance." *American Psychologist* 52 (6): 613–629.

Steele, Claude. 2010. *Whistling Vivaldi and Other Clues to How Stereotypes Affect Us*. New York, NY: W. W. Norton and Company.

Stoljar, Natalie. 2000. "Autonomy and the Feminist Intuition." In *Relational Autonomy: Feminist Perspectives on Autonomy, Agency, and the Social Self*, edited by Catriona Mackenzie and Natalie Stoljar, 94–111. New York: Oxford University Press.

Stoljar, Natalie. 2014. "Autonomy and Adaptive Preference Formation." In *Autonomy, Oppression, and Gender*, edited by Andrea Veltman and Mark Piper, 227–252. New York: Oxford University Press.

Strawson, P. F. 1961. "Social Morality and Individual Ideal." *Philosophy* 36 (136): 1–17.

Strawson, P. F. 1962. "Freedom and Resentment." *Proceedings of the British Academy* 48: 187–211.

Strawson, P. F. 1985. *Scepticism and Naturalism: Some Varieties*. London: Methuen and Co. Ltd.

Taylor, Charles, 1976. "Responsibility for Self." In *The Identities of Persons*, edited by Amelie O. Rorty, 281–299. Berkeley: University of California Press.

Vargas, Manuel. 2013. *Building Better Beings: A Theory of Moral Responsibility*. New York: Oxford University Press.

Vargas, Manuel. 2015. "Précis of Building Better Beings: A Theory of Moral Responsibility." *Philosophical Studies* 172 (10): 2621–2623.

Wallace, R. Jay. 1994. *Responsibility and the Moral Sentiments*. Cambridge, MA: Harvard University Press.

Wallace, R. Jay. 2011. "Dispassionate Opprobrium: On Blame and the Reactive Sentiments." In *Reasons and Recognition: Essays on the Philosophy of T. M. Scanlon*, edited by R. Jay Wallace, Rahul Kumar, and Samuel Freeman, 348–372. New York: Oxford University Press.

Washington, Natalie, and Daniel Kelly. 2016. "Who's Responsible for This? Moral Responsibility, Externalism, and Knowledge about Implicit Bias." In *Implicit Bias and Philosophy, Vol. 2, Moral Responsibility, Structural Injustice, and Ethics*, edited by Michael Brownstein and Jennifer Saul, 11–36. Oxford: Oxford University Press.

Watson, Gary. 1975. "Free Agency." *Journal of Philosophy* 72 (8): 205–220.

Watson, Gary. 1987. "Responsibility and the Limits of Evil: Variations on a Strawsonian Theme." In *Responsibility, Character, and the Emotions*, edited by F. Schoeman, 256–286. New York: Cambridge University Press.

Watson, Gary. 1996. "Two Faces of Responsibility." *Philosophical Topics* 24 (2): 227–248.

Watson, Gary. 2014. "Peter Strawson on Responsibility and Sociality." In *Oxford Studies in Agency and Responsibility, Vol. 2, "Freedom and Resentment" at 50*, edited by David Shoemaker and Neil Tognazzini, 15–32. Oxford: Oxford University Press.

Westlund, Andrea. 2009. "Rethinking Relational Autonomy." *Hypatia* 24 (4): 26–49.

Wolf, Susan. 1987. "Sanity and the Metaphysics of Responsibility." In *Responsibility, Character, and the Emotions: New Essays in Moral Psychology*, edited by Ferdinand David Schoeman, 46–62. New York: Cambridge University Press.

Wolf, Susan. 1990. *Freedom within Reason*. Oxford: Oxford University Press.

Zheng, Robin. 2016. "Attributability, Accountability, and Implicit Bias." In *Implicit Bias and Philosophy, Vol. 2, Moral Responsibility, Structural Injustice, and Ethics*, edited by Michael Brownstein and Jennifer Saul, 62–89. Oxford: Oxford University Press.

1

Power, Social Inequities, and the Conversational Theory of Moral Responsibility

MICHAEL MCKENNA

> We should think of the many different kinds of relationships which we can have with other people—as sharers of a common interest; as members of the same family; as colleagues; as friends; as lovers; as chance parties to an enormous range of transactions and encounters. Then we should think, in each of these connections in turn, and in others, of the kind of importance we attach to the attitudes and intentions towards us of those who stand in these relationships to us, and of the kinds of *reactive* attitudes and feelings to which we ourselves are prone. In general, we demand some degree of goodwill or regard on the part of those who stand in these relationships to us, though the forms we require it to take vary widely in different connections. The range and intensity of our *reactive* attitudes towards goodwill, its absence or its opposite vary no less widely.
>
> —P. F. Strawson, "Freedom and Resentment"

1 Strawsonian Theories of Responsibility and the (Dubious?) Demand for Good Will

How should we understand the social and relational dimensions of moral responsibility?[1] Understood in one way, this question has an obvious answer: sociality is essential to moral responsibility's nature. So it is for P. F. Strawson (1962) and numerous others embracing a broadly Strawsonian approach to theorizing about moral responsibility.[2] On this approach, moral responsibility is essentially interpersonal because being responsible is conceptually connected to holding responsible, which in turn is understood in terms of social practices. Hence, responsibility turns out to be a deeply social phenomenon. This is intimated in the well-known passage from Strawson's seminal paper "Freedom and Resentment" quoted above.

On Strawson's own proposal, *being* morally responsible in the sense of being either praiseworthy or blameworthy is most fundamentally about the quality of will with which an agent acts—whether it is from good or ill will. How is this thesis conceptually linked with considerations of sociality? Here is how: standards for a competent agent's acting from a reasonable quality of will are understood by reference to the expectations of the moral community positioned to hold responsible. As indicated in the preceding quotation, the community makes the moral demand that agents show a sufficient degree of good will. Deviations from these demands then render fitting reactive responses such as praise or blame in the form of outwardly manifested emotions like gratitude or resentment. In this way, the fittingness of praising and blaming in social practice signals the scope of praiseworthiness and blameworthiness. One involves surpassing the standards set down by the basic demand for good will; the other involves falling below them.

In this essay, I will be concerned with the requirements of sociality in light of the Strawsonian enterprise.[3] More precisely, like other contributors to this volume, I will focus upon a strikingly neglected topic within the literature on free will and moral responsibility: the social and relational dimensions of moral responsibility in light of both social inequities and asymmetrical relations of power. How do, and, perhaps more importantly, how *should* these factors influence our moral responsibility practices and judgments? By drawing upon my Strawson-inspired conversational theory of moral responsibility, I intend to expose a rather unseemly dimension of our moral responsibility practices. To foreshadow what will come, I call attention to Strawson's remark, included in the opening quotation above, that in general we demand some degree of good will or regard on the part of those with whom we are variously related. This widely shared assumption is often heralded as one of the deepest and most celebrated insights in Strawson's paper (e.g., Watson 2014). Of course, in a certain respect it is undoubtedly true, given that it is qualified with 'in general.' Nevertheless, it masks much that is a source of worry, and so perhaps should not be celebrated without caution. After all, not all *do* demand a reasonable degree of good will from pertinent others. For some, there is little point in doing so because there is little reason to expect that their demands will even register at all among those whose authority is liable to have great sway over them. For many others, the forms good will can be expected to take will be settled by standards they have no part in shaping.

In what follows, I will focus primarily upon disparities regarding the forms that good and ill will can be expected to take. By drawing upon my proposed

Strawson-inspired conversational theory of moral responsibility, I will argue that many agents who are morally responsible for their conduct, even when they do act from a reasonable degree of good will, operate in contexts that are morally unfair to them as agents. Or, at any rate, there is something morally suspect about the social conditions facilitating exercises of their agency when they act in ways that are morally praiseworthy (and also morally blameworthy). This is because, as the conversational theory reveals, quality of will is to be identified and explained by a community of interpreters who take some kinds of actions as indicative of good will and other kinds as indicative of lack of good will. Since some in this community are socially empowered, in contrast with others who are socially disempowered, the conditions for what signals good and ill will are liable to arise from potentially unjust social circumstances.

2 The Conditions for Moral Responsibility

I turn to the conditions for moral responsibility. Considering these will help assess the influences on moral responsibility of asymmetric relations of power and various forms of social inequities. I will assume in what follows that we can safely set aside worries about free will and moral responsibility skepticism. Perhaps, contrary to my own position, skeptics like Derk Pereboom (2014) and Galen Strawson (1986) are correct that because no one has free will, no one is morally responsible (in an important sense). I leave that as an open question. But the issue before us is about potential effects on responsibility due to *special* conditions of our sociality. Hence, it will be most useful to assume free will and moral responsibility realism and then proceed by raising questions about unique social and relational conditions in which these can be attenuated, compromised, or extinguished.[4]

Some Strawsonians hope to exhaust the conditions for moral responsibility by focusing upon quality of will alone, or instead quality of will and a general capacity for engaging in adult interpersonal relationships.[5] My own view is that this attempts to do too much with too few resources. I prefer a mixed theory. Moral responsibility as I understand it requires at least two conditions that are neutral between Strawsonian interpersonal theories and other competitor proposals: a *control condition* and an *epistemic condition*.[6] These conditions apply both to the conditions for being a morally responsible agent—which concerns the *status* of some but not all persons—and also to the conditions in which a person who *is* a morally responsible agent is morally responsible *for* something, such as an action, an omission, or the consequences of one of these things.

Attending to the control and the epistemic conditions gives rise to several interesting philosophical issues regarding the influence of significant social inequalities and asymmetric relations of power. The control condition (which can plausibly be understood as a free will condition) invites worries about coercion and duress, especially in contexts of interactions between members from disparate groups whose social status and power are asymmetrically distributed. A further and more subtle possibility here concerns domination in the sense Pettit (2001) intends it. In such cases, a person's options might be constrained in light of the mere prospects that others are easily able to exercise domination over that person with no repercussions. Hence the person self-regulates in ways that are liable to diminish her freedom.[7] These factors can sometimes serve as grounds for mitigating or instead excusing otherwise blameworthy behavior on the part of those who are disadvantaged by the pertinent disparities. Naturally, they can also give rise to *greater* degrees of freedom for those advantaged by these conditions, and so to a potentially greater range of conduct for which one ought to be regarded as accountable.

In the case of the epistemic condition, the social and relational variables at issue raise worries about disproportionate access to education, complex sources of information, or for that matter the opportunity to attend to matters of moral and political concern with sufficient care—people working three jobs to make ends meet, for instance, can perhaps be excused for failing to stay abreast of efforts to properly regulate the banking industry. Hence, some appeals to ignorance or limited understanding as grounds for mitigation or excuse are far more compelling than others.[8] Those massively disenfranchised and without the power to guide the aim of various inquiries will be far more likely to *merit* some form of mitigation or excuse in certain contexts, although it should be noted that, ironically, they are often the same group of people far less likely actually to *be* excused.[9] Likewise, of course, those with *greater* access to epistemic resources are liable to bear a greater degree of moral responsibility for their conduct since the charge "You should have known better" will apply more liberally.

The considerations mentioned in the two preceding paragraphs provide ample resources for exploring the social and relational dimensions of moral responsibility in light of extreme disparities in relations of power and significant social inequities. What insights might we be able to draw specifically from my conversational theory of moral responsibility? Again, my goal will be to attend to the Strawsonian demand for a reasonable degree of good will.

Some Strawsonians apparently think that a quality of will condition on moral responsibility is encompassed by the control and the epistemic condition already identified.[10] When, for instance, an agent knowingly and freely does morally wrong, this alone, some might contend, is sufficient for her having a morally objectionable quality of will and so being morally blameworthy. My own view (McKenna 2012), which I grant is controversial, is that quality of will is a *further* condition over and above the control and epistemic conditions. In the case of blameworthiness, what is involved is either an ill will or an insufficiently good will.[11] Nothing much turns on settling this issue here. Either way, on a Strawsonian theory, when an agent is morally responsible for some action, she *does* satisfy a quality of will condition—either because the control and epistemic conditions already ensure it, or because on a view such as mine a distinct quality of will condition is also satisfied. Moreover, for Strawsonians, it is quality of will that is most salient in settling questions of an agent's responsibility. And quality of will, as explained above, is linked to the moral community since it is the community who, by making demands, sets the bar for what will count as sufficient or insufficient quality of will.

Quality of will, as I understand it (McKenna 2012), is a matter of the value of an agent's regard for others.[12] When we hold morally responsible, what we are reacting to, or what we are prepared to react to, is an agent's quality of will as manifested in her conduct. Eventually, I will further develop the quality of will condition in terms of my conversational theory of moral responsibility. However, before doing so, I turn in the next section to an especially illuminating application of the epistemic condition in evaluating cases of putative blameworthiness. Are those ignorant of largely unrecognized moral wrongs due to conditions of oppression blameworthy for participating in and benefitting from those conditions? Is their ignorance exculpating? This will help shed a light on the particular issue I wish to consider.

3 Excusing Morally Ignorant Oppressors?

In her superbly argued "Responsibility and Reproach," Cheshire Calhoun (1989) confronts a challenge for feminists faced with questions about how to respond to social oppression when carried out or at least perpetuated by seemingly innocent participants to the oppressive practices. Is reproach warranted in such cases? If so, it seems that these apparently innocent participants are not innocent after all but instead blameworthy. If not, it seems that feminists are not entitled to "use moral reproach as a tool for effecting social change" (1989, 389). Each horn comes at quite a cost.

Consider the first horn—that the seemingly innocent are blameworthy after all. As Calhoun rightly notes, many individuals who are, as she puts it, "morally unflawed" (1989, 389) unknowingly commit wrongdoing through participating in oppressive social practices that strongly disfavor women.[13] Yet they do so by means that appear to arise from nonculpable ignorance. How so? In contexts in which some moral knowledge is not widely shared, which Calhoun calls "abnormal moral contexts" (396), it is not just the unsavory, like pimps and other misogynists, who are prone to harm women by means of various oppressive practices, but many well-meaning men (and women too, of course). Calhoun mentions parenthetically "male bias in psychological and other theories, the design of female fashion, the use of 'he' neutrally, [and] heterosexual marriage" (397). Even if one wished to dispute any of these as significant moral wrongs, it is beyond question that various shared social practices regarded widely by many as morally neutral do after all contribute to morally wrong forms of oppression that undermine women's autonomy. To think that reproach *is* warranted even for those Calhoun refers to as "morally unflawed" is, it seems, to think that these moral agents are after all culpable for engaging in what they take to be perfectly innocent behavior. But how could that be? We cannot expect even the most virtuous among us to have access to all the best information about morality. Presumably, we are all vulnerable to moral blind spots at the limits of our current social and cultural settings.

Now consider the other horn—that in these contexts the seemingly innocent are indeed as they seem to be, innocent. If so, it appears that feminists are not entitled to reproach—by which I take it Calhoun means moralized blame. The cost of thinking that reproach is *not* warranted because these parties are not blameworthy means that feminists must let too much pass. The oppression identified is, after all, deeply harmful and far-reaching. Failing to reproach, Calhoun argues, comes dangerously close to endorsement and so to participating in the modes of oppression feminists correctly see as deep forms of moral wrongdoing.

Calhoun offers an elegant solution to this dilemma. She distinguishes between reasons to blame in light of blameworthiness, and reasons to blame as a means of effecting social change. A person could be entitled to blame those who are not blameworthy, say in the context of excused wrongdoing, given *other* powerful moral considerations. A significant need to achieve social reform is such a reason, according to Calhoun, and, moreover, failing to reproach is highly likely to signal endorsement or sanctioning of the moral order (1989, 400–405). (Of course, it should be clear that the reasoning at issue here applies to other cases as well, like that at issue in claims of white privilege or class privilege.)

Some might be inclined to downplay Calhoun's proposal as perhaps correct but no more than a pedestrian application of a simple point: blameworthiness merely provides a pro tanto reason to blame. All blameworthiness ever establishes is that a wrongdoer is deserving of something, blame—and all desert ever provides is a pro tanto reason for some sort of response. But there can be reasons other than desert for treating a person a certain way, and these reasons can override the pro tanto reasons. Or these other reasons can instead do duty to justify a treatment like blame when the desert-based reasons are altogether absent. For instance, young children who are not yet morally responsible agents are not yet blameworthy for their conduct. Hence, they do not deserve blame—granting the near truism that only the blameworthy deserve blame. But we might have good moral reason to blame them as a means of training them up into becoming morally responsible agents who will eventually deserve blame (and praise). So, too, it can be argued, we can have reasons to blame those who are not blameworthy for participating in oppressive practices because it is in the service of an overriding social good. While this might be true, there is nothing especially philosophically illuminating going on here.

To downplay Calhoun's proposal in this way would be to misunderstand the striking philosophical point she brings into relief. Her argument, as I understand it, is not *simply* about overriding reasons to ignore considerations about what a nonculpable wrongdoer does not deserve (blame). It is, rather, about the *special social setting* giving rise to those overriding reasons and how that social setting shapes not only the moral landscape but our moral responsibility practices as modes of responding to that moral landscape. (It is this point in particular that I wish to draw upon in my own proposal as I develop it below.) As Calhoun puts it, the sort of moral wrongdoing at issue in these kinds of cases occurs at the social rather than at the individual level (1989, 394). This gives rise to a special class of moral reasons that can then be "turned back on" our responsibility practices in the hope of refashioning them.[14]

Think about it this way. The architecture of our responsibility practices is, so to speak, built up out of a stock of accessible bits of moral knowledge. Good moral reasoners, being fallible creatures and so lacking moral omniscience, rely upon this stock as a resource for engaging with others in ways that can give rise to blameworthy as well as praiseworthy behavior. But if moral knowledge, like all knowledge, depends upon background social conditions rendering pertinent truths accessible or instead inaccessible, then some forms of moral knowledge will sometimes be, so to speak, outside the reasonable scope of even a well-meaning person's epistemic radar.[15] Of course, perhaps a few elites at the fringes of moral knowledge might be better positioned, but their understanding cannot be expected to be accessible to most others.[16] As such, the moral landscape will be affected insofar as even morally virtuous agents will be liable to participate unwittingly in wrongdoing.[17] And, moreover, because of this, our practices of holding morally responsible will be likewise affected insofar as this sort of epistemic limitation will do two things. First, it will provide legitimate grounds to claim nonculpable ignorance as a basis for excusing conduct that contributes to oppression. Second, it will limit the moral community's resources and so impede the moral community from deploying the very machinery of our blaming practices that could be used to correct these sorts of wrongs.

These special features of our social setting and the pressure they place on our own practices of holding morally responsible provide reasons for justifying blame even when directed at those whose wrongdoing, due to epistemic considerations, is excusable—that is, even at those who do not deserve blame. Doing so allows for the possibility of moral reform. This, I take it, is precisely an application of what Manuel Vargas (2013) has in mind in writing of "building better beings." We modulate our responsibility practices with the aim of encouraging people to be more alive to moral reasons. By blaming those wrongdoers who are not blameworthy in these contexts, we thereby allow for the possibility of making accessible this sort of moral knowledge. *We bring it to light.* This in turn can help refashion our responsibility practices in such a way that those failing to act properly in light of this moral knowledge would no longer be able to claim nonculpable ignorance. Then they could after all be regarded as blameworthy and so not excused. There is, in this sense, a kind "feedback" loop that helps us bootstrap our moral responsibility practices to be better positioned to hold accountable those who unwittingly do engage in wrongdoing that contributes to oppression.

4 The Role of the Conversational Theory and the Demand for Good Will

In the next section, I draw upon Calhoun's proposal to help cast a critical light of a different sort on our moral responsibility practices. In this section, I first set out only briefly my conversational theory as a natural way of extending a Strawsonian account of moral responsibility. As explained above (section 1), on my view, quality of will as manifested in an agent's conduct is a matter of the value of the regard or concern an agent displays for others. The quality of this regard is in turn evaluated in terms of a moral community's implicit demand that co-members display a sufficient degree of good will toward others. Perceived departures are then taken to be grounds for a fitting response in the form of a reactive attitude of some sort. In the case of blameworthiness, this is a matter of responding with resentment or indignation. Overt manifestations of these reactive emotions, when directed at a blamed party, have, as Gary Watson (1987) has noted, not only an expressive but a communicative role; they serve to communicate our moral demands and expectations.

According to my conversational theory, and drawing upon Watson's proposal, I have argued (McKenna 2012) that moral responsibility is not only essentially interpersonal and communicative, but that it also has a *conversational* dimension. This is crucial. On the conversational theory, an agent's actions—those that are candidates for blameworthiness or praiseworthiness—are potential bearers of meaning, where meaning is a function of the quality of an agent's will. This meaning is analogous to the meaning a competent speaker conveys when she engages in conversation. I call this *agent meaning*. Like speaker meaning, agent meaning can be affected by the interpretive framework whereby others interpret the agent. In the case of agent meaning, a moral community assigns saliences to types of actions, and they do so in light of expectations about the cooperative constraints of something analogous to a conversational transaction. Hence, the interpretive community expects that the agents whose actions they interpret will have uptake with respect to the interpretations the community employs. They therefore expect that agents will be able to modulate their behavior in light of those interpretations. For instance, a type of action liable to be interpreted as manifesting poor quality of will gives reason for competent moral agents to avoid signaling such quality of will by acting in this type of way. By emerging conventions, types of conduct come to indicate appropriate or instead inappropriate quality of will. A competent moral agent thus acts in a social context wherein these interpretive pressures are liable to affect her judgments about what does and does not signal good or ill will and so what might or might not be communicated to others who stand prepared to hold her to account by way of praising and blaming practices.

The same applies to the practices associated with various modes of blaming and praising. Consider overt manifestations of reactive emotions like resentment or indignation directed at a blamed party. These modes of expressing emotions involve modulating one's behavior against the backdrop of otherwise expected social interactions, interactions unfolding under the assumption that the basic demand for good will has been met. A blamed person is, for instance, excluded from an otherwise routine lunch outing, or is greeted more coolly in simple exchanges, or directly corrected for some misdeed with angry rather than kind treatment. All of these are modes of interacting by way of altering what would otherwise be regarded as treatment of one who *does* show reasonable good will. In short, just as the actions for which we are accountable have meaning, so too the means of blaming or praising through outward manifestations of reactive emotions have meaning. And in each case, this sort of meaning is shaped in part by a background set of loose interpretive conventions against which instances are evaluated.

One more point about the preceding sketch of the conversational theory. Grice (1957) distinguished speaker from sentence meaning. When we interpret a speaker in actual conversation, our interpretive goal is to understand what the speaker meant by what she said, not just what the sentences mean that the speaker used to convey what she meant. Often these go together, but they can come apart. We can, for instance, use the sentence 'That was a good meal' to mean the meal was terrible by making use of sarcastic cues and the like and relying upon our audience to cooperatively receive our expression as we intended it. So, while conventions regarding sentence-types help shape what we mean to say, they do so in ways consistent with variation that allows for particularizing our own intended meanings and departing from the conventional meanings assigned to sentence-types. An analogous point applies to interpreting the actions of morally responsible agents, and it *also* applies to interpreting the praising and blaming responses of those holding responsible when they react to those blamed (or praised). A shove, for instance, might characteristically show ill will, but in some contexts could be taken to express solidarity or playful aggression (say on a basketball court). Why is this important for what is to come? Because our ability to function in an interpretive space where others are equipped to see us as acting with good will, and our ability to communicate to them our reactive assessment of them when they do not, rely upon an expectation that we share enough interpretive resources to facilitate successful communication. And one kind of resource is just social authority—being positioned to have one's interpretive scheme do the work in settling meaning.[18] This resource, as it happens, is usually not evenly distributed.

Given this very simplified description of the Strawsonian project and my proposed conversational theory as an extension of it, return now to the passage from Strawson with which I started. I repeat it here for ease of reference:

> We should think of the many different kinds of relationships which we can have with other people—as sharers of a common interest; as members of the same family; as colleagues; as friends; as lovers; as chance parties to an enormous range of transactions and encounters. Then we should think, in each of these connections in turn, and in others, of the kind of importance we attach to the attitudes and intentions towards us of those who stand in these relationships to us, and of the kinds of *reactive* attitudes and feelings to which we ourselves are prone. In general, we demand some degree of goodwill or regard on the part of those who stand in these relationships to us, though the forms we require it to take vary widely in different connections. The range and intensity of our *reactive* attitudes towards goodwill, its absence or its opposite vary no less widely. P. F. Strawson "Freedom and Resentment"

Note Strawson's observation about the variability and particularity of our relationships. He focuses on how much we care about how others regard us in their interactions with us (their quality of will) and our demand for good will on their behalf. This extends to our reactions to those who fail to meet the demand when we hold them responsible via a reactive attitude. Note also his observation that the forms we require the demand for good will to take vary widely (compare with the preceding point about the particularity of speaker meaning in relation to generic sentence meaning). Now let us inject into this picture a fact about nonideal human communities. Those who make the demands for a reasonable degree of good will and those prepared to react to departures from those demands are not all equally empowered. If we add familiar facts about significant social inequalities and asymmetric relations of power, we bring to light a set of considerations that are not necessarily so flattering to a Strawsonian understanding of our responsibility practices.

5 Something Insidious Rooted in Our Responsibility Practices?

So now, looking through a critical lens, focus yet again on Strawson's remark that in general we demand some degree of good will or regard on the part of those who stand in varying relationships with us. As it happens, it is a contingent albeit inescapable fact that some who express a demand for good will are taken to have an authority that others lack. As I noted above (section 1), there are some who take their own social status to be so limited that they do not demand that they are shown a reasonable degree of good will—at least in relation to members of comparatively advantaged groups. In some cases, they do not see any point in even making the demand. Others do, but they have no part in settling the interpretive standards regarding what plausibly counts as expressions of good will.[19] In this way they are, in a certain sense, outsiders to those positioned to exercise a greater degree of moral authority.

Consider, for instance, etiquette or manners. While standards of etiquette or manners are usually not directly regarded as relevant to morality (however, see Buss 1999), drawing upon these conventions in how one comports oneself can often be a *vehicle* for showing or instead failing to show deference or respect for others, which is a matter of morality. In this way, especially as understood through the lens of the conversational theory, superficial conventions of etiquette can function as a way of manifesting morally significant behavior. However, the social conventions giving rise to what counts as polite behavior— such as pausing to hold a door open for someone, refraining from interrupting another who is speaking in certain social contexts, how one behaves while dining in certain settings rather than others, the cutlery one uses, when one begins to eat, and so on—are all established by social contexts wherein those empowered set the expectations. Departures from expected behavior can be taken to show a lack of respect or concern for the feelings of others—such as one's hosts. The upshot is that those who act in such contexts have available to them resources for displaying good or ill will, but those resources are themselves structured and constrained by certain groups empowered to set expectations and "police" departures from expected behavior. Of course, if this were limited just to matters of etiquette, there would be little interest here. But my contention is that these interpretive pressures on the (conversational) context of action are ubiquitous.

They pervade nearly every aspect of our social lives. Those marginalized by existing power-structures—cultural, social, and economic—live out their lives shouldering the burdens of acting in a context in which much of the interpretive framework signaling what counts as constituting good or ill will is settled by others whose social lives are in some way alien, inaccessible, or unwelcoming to them.

Return to Calhoun's insight. Special social contexts can provide reasons to blame some who are not in fact blameworthy in order to achieve social change. Her focus was on social structures involving massive disparities in social advantage that supported forms of wrongdoing: contributing to oppressive social conditions through forms of moral ignorance that were exculpating. These social structures helped support the *perpetuation* of the oppressive conditions by deploying the very responsibility practices that, were they exercised by better-informed moral agents, would have instead functioned as a tonic in correcting those oppressive conditions. Calhoun's proposal shows us how to alter our resolution and look upon our responsibility practices critically so as to determine whether their design is in certain respects deleterious. This is what I intend to do in this section.

There is, however, a significant difference between the cases I wish to focus upon and the ones Calhoun was interested in. Calhoun focused on cases of moral *wrongdoing*. She argued that in these special sorts of contexts moral ignorance really was excusing. (She then argued that reproach could be warranted anyway—a conclusion I agree with.) My interest is different. I am interested primarily, albeit not exclusively, in cases where well-intentioned moral agents, those Calhoun would describe as morally unflawed (I would prefer a different term), do *not* engage in moral wrongdoing at all. Instead, they act well. They do right. In doing so, moreover, they act in ways that *do* show adequate moral regard for others. These agents *do* meet reasonable demands for good will. Indeed, they might even be regarded as praiseworthy. My claim is that in many of these cases, those who act well often do so in contexts in which the resources for interpreting their quality of will are framed by the interests of others—sometimes, even often, quite innocently so. (An example is forthcoming in the next paragraph.) Yet these framings have power insofar as a comparatively socially disadvantaged yet fully competent moral agent, in acting from good will, will be responsive to that interpretive framework. The standards the empowered set for signaling compliance with the demand for good will are shaped by those whose status is in some manner or other dominating. And this can happen, as in the sorts of cases Calhoun has in mind, even when the parties in positions of domination are all well-meaning and innocent of any wrongdoing. In such cases, the parties involved need not be individually culpable for any particular conditions resulting in these asymmetric social conditions.

To return for just a moment to a superficial case of etiquette, imagine a young provincial boy from an impoverished family off to college at some very elite school. Through his talent and good fortune, he comes to find himself at "high table" dining with a sophisticated class of people, all well-meaning and welcoming to him. He tries his best to display grace and gratitude, somehow managing to comport himself well in dining and conversing with these elite, even managing to be able to talk a bit about high art, like a recent opera production he was lucky enough to attend. Suppose, all going smoothly, his hosts later think well of him, and he too about himself. Here is the thing. He showed good will (not necessarily *morally* good will, but good will), and were he in various ways to have departed from these forms of etiquette, he could have been *accurately* regarded as an ass—as having shown disrespect for his hosts or other company. Nevertheless, the conventions deployed to discern his good intent, the cues he was aware of as potential signals of disapproval (even if only possible and never actually on display), all arise from a world where the persons setting those interpretive conditions are the ones empowered to do so, while he comes from a world as an outsider. Were he later to feel some pride for being a bit of a success, he might also, not unreasonably, feel degraded and in some way burdened by his disadvantaged place. It is not that there is a type of oppression of which he is a victim, although maybe there is that too. It is rather that his own exercises of responsible agency are shaped by conditions that still are liable to leave him feeling alienated.[20]

My contention is that *this is everywhere*. Our lives are rife with circumstances like this. Academics reading this will naturally think of the familiar dynamics of what counts as appropriate behavior in conferences or colloquia settings, how to maneuver in a graduate seminar, or for that matter, when and how to show deference in responding to a referee. In philosophy settings, there are modes of argumentation, styles of asking questions, or knowing when to shut up, which are simply settled by those empowered. Even when one is at one's best and is regarded as showing the best quality of will in his or her dealings with others, the means of showing that are by conventions shaped by an elite few.[21]

What more is there to say about this observation? Think about the social conditions informing Calhoun's proposal. Special social circumstances—what Calhoun called "abnormal moral contexts"—set a baseline for forms of conduct regarded as acceptable in a way that shields us from accurate moral knowledge. In the cases Calhoun had in mind, certain sorts of moral wrongs, such as those involving gender disparities, were not recognized by most in the moral community, and so objectionable moral behavior was not seen as such. Here, something similar is going on: a baseline for deploying an interpretive scheme regarding what counts as signaling good and ill will is set in place by a set of background cultural practices. Participants to the practices, both those who are comparatively advantaged and those who are not, cannot be expected to have antecedently fashioned these by reference to some morally ideal standard. They come to be taken as given background conditions of the cultural milieu in which agents get trained up into the moral community and learn to function. But as it happens, these interpretive schemes, and the conventional meanings they assign to patterns of action, have baked-in forms of bias that serve as the basis for even well-intentioned people to engage with each other. Moreover, since on the conversational theory the interpretive enterprise involves efforts to understand the particularized meaning of an agent's actions, moral agents rely upon the interpretive community being inclined to interpret them well. Those disadvantaged due to significant asymmetries in relations of power then risk alienation by defying or departing from these conventions, both in attempting to act with good will and in reacting to others when holding them accountable. Hence, our moral responsibility practices—our actual practices as they normally function—are in a sense morally tainted, or at least they are morally dubious. At the very least, they need to be assessed from a critical distance. Perhaps an example will help.

Consider a more serious matter than one simply about etiquette, one that does after all have moral import. In a comical exchange in the opening pages of E. M. Forster's *Howards End* ([1910] 1986, chapter 2), Meg discloses to Aunt Juley her sister Helen's secret—that Helen and young Paul Wilcox are in love. This is taken by Aunt Juley and Meg for apparently different reasons to be a crisis of the first order. Why? The reader is left to infer that two young people being in love is nearly tantamount to an engagement. It seems someone who has Helen's interests at heart is needed to go size up the situation by visiting Helen at the Wilcoxes' estate, where she is staying. Meg and Aunt Juley debate who is suited for this task and how to proceed, with Meg delighted for the news and Aunt Juley wary. The relative social positions of the two families are a central factor in these considerations. (We are led to believe that young Paul Wilcox comes from a wealthy family.) In explaining herself with youthful exuberance, Meg remarks that if Helen had fallen in love with a shop assistant or penniless clerk, it would not matter. Nothing other than Helen's being in love counts—although perhaps a very long engagement might be needed. To this, pleading to be the diplomat, Aunt Juley then remarks to Meg,

> Now, just imagine if you say anything of that sort to the Wilcoxes. I understand it, but most good people would think you mad. Imagine how disconcerting for Helen! What is wanted is a person who will go slowly, slowly in this business, and see how things are and where they are likely to lead. (Forster [1910] 1986, 10)

Of course, as the reader soon learns (only pages later), Helen's relationship with Paul Wilcox quickly falls apart. Nevertheless, this lighthearted opening exchange is very revealing. While Meg and Aunt Juley both have something morally important at stake—the well-being of Helen—they are alive to what would and should count as proper decorum in assessing the situation. Why is this relevant to the current topic? As the reader learns, Meg and Aunt Juley's situation is influenced by asymmetric relations of power shaped by wealth, gender, and social status.[22] They are simply not suitably positioned to exercise much power over the Wilcoxes, given their place in the social life of that time. Revealingly, it never occurs to either that one might just go as relative moral and social equals and speak plainly with the Wilcoxes about the prospects for this young couple. Instead, to show good will and act well (alive to "what most good people would think"), what is needed, as Aunt Juley remarks, is the discretion of one who can signal to these people what is expected of proper folks. Hence Aunt Juley promises just to visit and discretely look about, making no mention of engagements or anything of the sort.

This might seem a curious example for me to pick from *Howards End*, given the famous scene, featured prominently in Angela Smith's (2008) work on moral responsibility, when Meg confronts her husband Henry (Mr. Wilcox, Sr.) for blindness to his own moral hypocrisy in being so unforgiving of Helen for her adultery:

> "Not any more of this!" she cried. "You shall see the connection if it kills you, Henry! You have had a mistress—I forgave you. My sister has a lover—you drive her from the house. Do you see the connection? Stupid, hypocritical, cruel—oh, contemptible!—a man who insults his wife when she's alive and cants with her memory when she's dead. A man who ruins a woman for his pleasure, and casts her off to ruin other men. And gives bad financial advice, and then says he is not responsible. These, man, are you. You can't recognize them because you cannot connect." (Forster [1910] 1986, 243–244)

A critic at this point might object that I have gotten it wrong: Meg's performance in this famous scene places on full display that, disproportionately disempowered or not, Meg has equal moral footing in the moral responsibility game for holding to account those she blames—in this case, her ass of a husband. But as I see it, this deepens my point rather than cuts against it. Why are we to regard Meg as the heroine in *Howards End*? I say it is in part because she is able to act well as a moral agent—as a morally responsible agent—holding to account others who would tarnish her sister or judge her cruelly. But her acting so well is to be regarded by us as heroic partly because she takes her role as a moral agent by operating within a social context in which she and her family are socially disadvantaged. That is, her moral agency is "against the odds," and yet she is able to hold others to account despite her marginalized social position. The earlier lighthearted story gives us a window into the world into which Meg, Helen, and Aunt Juley enter, and we see them socially disadvantaged in the circumstances in which they are initially to engage the Wilcoxes. Apparently, as they see their own circumstances, they are expected to operate within the conventions taken to bear on what counts as showing good will, and so on.[23]

6 Conclusion

In works like *Beyond Good and Evil* ([1886] 1966) and *Genealogy of Morals* ([1887] 1967), Nietzsche famously argued that our moral responsibility practices were benighted. They concealed ugly facts about our nature and our true motivations. Although I have come at it by very different means, I too have attempted in this essay to cast a critical eye on these practices. I have no interest in drawing the sorts of conclusions Nietzsche wished to draw. But I have been at pains to scrutinize an element of Strawson's project that, to the best of my knowledge, no one has ever even considered looking upon critically—the demand for good will that according to Strawsonians serves as the foundation for our moral responsibility practices. Drawing upon my conversational theory of moral responsibility, and attending especially to the interpretive dimension to our perceptions of what counts as good and ill will, I have argued that our moral responsibility practices are tarnished or in some way benighted.[24] They have baked into them problematic moral assumptions placing pressure on those who are comparatively disadvantaged given significant asymmetries of power in the social relations between disparate groups.

When I first encountered this dimension of the Strawsonian enterprise, and when it occurred to me that my conversational theory took on wholesale these problematic elements of our responsibility practices, I took it to be a damning criticism of the Strawsonian enterprise and of my conversational theory. But upon reflection, I do not think it is. Indeed, I now take it to be an advantage of the conversational theory that it helps to bring these facts about our responsibility practices into clear focus. Bear in mind that the point of a Strawsonian theory is to explain our moral responsibility practices and not necessarily to endorse them. So, as a descriptive resource, I think it just helps in getting something correct. As a diagnostic resource, I also think it is useful; we are pointed in the direction of what needs correcting. But what about as a prescriptive resource? Here, I must say, the Strawsonian program and my conversational theory are completely silent.

In the opening section of this essay, I asked how both social inequities and asymmetrical relations of power affect our responsibility practices and

judgments. Drawing upon my conversational theory, I hope I have been successful in the preceding discussion in helping to answer that question. But I also
asked, noting this to be the more important question, how *should* social inequities and asymmetrical relations of power affect our responsibility practices and
judgments? So far as I can tell, to this normative question, Strawsonians have
little to offer, nor do I from the resources of my conversational theory. Perhaps
we might learn from Calhoun's proposal for how we ought to respond to those
in abnormal moral contexts acting from some forms of nonculpable moral ignorance. With an eye to reform, she argues that we ought to treat these parties as if
they are culpable. Maybe something similar is called for here in thinking about
revising our responsibility practices in ways that more equitably reorient the
standards for what counts as signaling good and ill will.[25]

Notes

For helpful advice and comments on this chapter, I would like to thank Keith Lehrer, Kate
Manne, Elinor Mason, David Shoemaker, Jason Turner, and Manuel Vargas. I would also like
to thank Katrina Hutchison, Catriona Mackenzie, and Marina Oshana, for kindly inviting me
to contribute to this volume, *Social Dimensions of Moral Responsibility*, and also for a set of
detailed critical comments.

1. In this essay, I will focus only upon what many now call the *accountability* sense of moral
responsibility wherein one who is responsible is liable to be held to account for her blameworthy behavior. Gary Watson (1996) and then David Shoemaker (2011, 2015b) have carefully identified other senses of responsibility other than the accountability sense. I make no
claims about those other senses in this essay.

2. Gary Watson (2014, 17) offers the clearest expression of the thesis that sociality is at the heart
of Strawson's theory. For those adopting a Strawsonian approach, see, for example, Bennett
1980; Darwall 2006; McKenna 2012; Oshana 1997, 2004; Russell 1992, 2004; Scanlon 2008;
Shoemaker 2015b; Vargas 2013; Wallace 1994; and Watson 1987. Some, such as Oshana and
Scanlon, might reject the Strawsonian project for other reasons (such as emphasizing the
importance of the reactive attitudes), but not, I assume, the tight connection with an interpersonal constraint.

3. Strawsonian interpersonal approaches can be contrasted with intrapersonal approaches
whereby the conditions for being morally responsible are accounted for just by attending
to facts about the agent who is responsible and so without essential reference to considerations of holding responsible (e.g., see Glover 1970; Haji 1998; Zimmerman 1988). The
most familiar version of this alternative strategy is a ledger theory. On a ledger theory, an
agent's moral responsibility, including her praiseworthy and blameworthy conduct, can be
understood on analogy with entries in a ledger of the moral record of an agent's conduct. The
ledger will include, for instance, entries registering culpable violations of one's moral obligations, compliance with one's obligations, supererogatory conduct, and so on. What responses
of holding responsible by praising or blaming are rendered apt, and from whom, are settled
on different grounds. Thus, the social and relational dimensions of the practices of holding
morally responsible are not essential to *being* morally responsible. The two are only contin-
gently related. This is consistent with those contingent relations being deeply embedded in
our practices and informed by important norms regarding social relations between those who
are responsible and those who hold responsible.

4. For similar reasons, we can also remain neutral between those free will and moral responsibility realists who are compatibilists and those who are libertarians. The metaphysics of free

agency is not what is directly at issue here. For a survey of realist views of a compatibilist variety, see McKenna and Coates (2015), and of a libertarian variety, see Clarke and Capes (2017). Another option is to be a free will and moral responsibility realist but also an agnostic about the compatibilist/libertarian divide (e.g., see Mele 1995, 2006).

5. See Bennett (1980), Russell (1992, 2004), and more recently Shoemaker (2015b).

6. This is a widely shared thesis. For example, see Fischer and Ravizza 1998; Haji 1998; McKenna 2013; Nelkin 2011; Sartorio 2016; and Wolf 1990.

7. I am grateful to Dave Shoemaker for pointing this out. Also, as Katrina Hutchison has pointed out in her comments on this essay, there has been a considerable amount of work on this topic on connection with the topic of relational autonomy. See, for example, Baier 1985; Christman 2004; Friedman 1997; Meyers 1989; and Oshana 2006.

8. The following is a comment on this chapter written by Catriona Mackenzie, for which I am grateful: Another set of issues relevant to the epistemic condition and to problematic practices of holding responsible relates to what Miranda Fricker calls "epistemic injustice." To suffer epistemic injustice is to be subject to prejudicial exclusion from knowledge practices on the basis of one's social group membership. Epistemic injustice encompasses testimonial injustices, such as discounting the credibility of a person's testimony due to identity prejudice, and hermeneutical injustice, which is "the injustice of having some significant area of one's social experience obscured from collective understanding owing to hermeneutical marginalization" (Fricker 2007, 158). For another who has also developed the notion of epistemic injustice, see Charles Mills (2007). Thanks to Elinor Mason for the latter reference. For discussion of the relevance of Fricker's work on epistemic injustice for moral responsibility ascriptions, see the chapters in this volume by Catriona Mackenzie and Elinor Mason.

9. Thanks again here as well to Catriona Mackenzie for the insightful observation.

10. The textual evidence is not decisive, but there is some reason to think that Strawson himself (1962) endorses this view, since when he gives his list of pleas that would defeat judgments of responsibility (and acting from objectionable quality of will), they naturally parse into control and epistemic categories. Also, Fischer and Ravizza (1998) endorse a Strawsonian account of responsibility, and seem only to identify a control and an epistemic condition on responsibility.

11. Marina Oshana helpfully advises me to clarify this point. It just comes to the following. In my view, a person might do morally wrong, might do so knowingly and freely, and yet not be blameworthy because she does not act from a morally objectionable quality of will. Suppose, for instance, she acts in the context of a moral dilemma and so cannot avoid wrongdoing. In that case, if she harbors no poor regard for anyone, and if she shows sufficient regard for all involved, then she might do wrong, but she is not blameworthy. Cases like this, I maintain, show that quality of will is a further condition on blameworthiness for wrongdoing beyond a control and an epistemic condition. Again, little turns on it in the present context.

12. This is slightly truncated. My full view also includes not just regard or concern for others but also for, as I have elsewhere put it, salient moral considerations. I include this to capture cases like harm to the environment or to nonhuman animals. David Shoemaker (2015a) has convinced me that there are problems with this formulation, however, but there is no need to work them out here for the purposes of this chapter.

13. I worry that the expression 'morally unflawed' is misleading, since it suggests that what is at issue is a background characterological consideration and that what blameworthiness tracks is that. But Calhoun's point is clear enough regardless. She has in mind, I take it, the idea that those whose quality of will is morally acceptable and even laudable might still engage in certain sorts of wrongdoing by participating in oppressive practices ignorant of the wrong that they are doing.

14. Calhoun never explicitly states this last point, but as I read her, it is clearly an intended implication.

15. See note 8. Also, see the essays in this volume by Jules Holroyd, Neil Levy and Elinor Mason.

16. This is how Calhoun understood the feminist community at the time she penned her essay (1989, 397–398).

17. This is how I think of many of the issues regarding the moral status of nonhuman animals.

18. In her chapter in this volume, Catriona Mackenzie drawing on Fricker (2007), notes a finer distinction that bears on this issue. Testimonial injustice concerns prejudicial failures of

uptake on the part of hearers to have uptake due to a speaker's perceived lack of authority and credibility. Hermeneutical injustice concerns a prejudicial failure of collective interpretive resources to interpret a speaker's experiences. As will become clear, while I am interested in both, it is the latter that is more directly relevant to my thesis.

19. See Andrea Westlund's contribution to this volume, as she discusses this problem.

20. As Marina Oshana has thoughtfully noted, there are two issues at play here. One is about the liability to feel alienated. Another is about a deeper threat: the evaluations of morally responsible agency in the light of which one exercises one's own agency are often shaped outside the reach of one's own influence.

21. Here is another example, suggested to me by Elinor Mason, who permitted me to quote her from our personal correspondence. Mason writes,

> [A]s we welcome our new students this week . . . I am deluged with inadvertently rude emails. It is a constantly frustrating aspect of my job that, as a woman, it is very hard to give critical feedback to students about anything other than their work. So, for example, the terrible emails they write, (which are, of course examples of them getting the etiquette rules wrong: sometimes through social disadvantage, but sometimes the opposite—some of our students are so over-privileged that they think everyone else must be the servant class). I feel like it is part of my job to tell my personal tutees how to write to their professor. But I am always met with instant hostility. So I can't do my job as well as I should be able to do, because my good will in correcting them is perceived as bitchiness or something. If a man did it, it would be perceived as avuncular good advice. So in Fricker's terminology, I am suffering a sort of epistemic injustice. But (and I take it this is part of your point), the particular way in which I am not taken seriously affects my *responsibility*, because I cannot undertake certain things trusting that my will is going to be read correctly. I cannot do my job as well as a man.

The special irony of this case is that when I received her comment, I was having the very same dealings with one of my students, and my experience is pretty much exactly as Mason predicted it would be. Indeed, in all of my years of teaching (over twenty-five now), I have *never once* had my similar corrections be treated in an unwelcome manner.

22. As it happens, we learn that the Wilcoxes apparently have considerable wealth. Moreover, we learn in a prior letter from Helen to Meg, that Mr. Wilcox (Sr.) had found occasion to say "the most horrid things about women's suffrage," but "so nicely" (Forster [1910] 1986, 506), leaving Helen to feel terribly ashamed for saying she believed in equality.

23. Thanks to Katrina Hutchison for suggesting this way of expressing my point.

24. To be clear, I take it as a problem of *any* Strawsonian approach if the demand for good will is uncritically accepted as a foundation for our moral responsibility practices. Focusing on the conversational theory as a way of bringing this to light is helpful, albeit not required to make the point. Why helpful? The theory explicitly attends to a community's interpretive resources as a strategy for discerning the "conversational" significance of an agent's actions (as a way of identifying the quality of her will). This makes it easy to reflect upon how those interpretive resources can be asymmetrically shaped.

25. This project comes down squarely within the boundaries of the approach Manuel Vargas (2013) advocates. He argues that we should evaluate our existing moral responsibility practices with an eye to improving the way agents best respond to moral reasons.

References

Baier, Annette. 1985. *Postures of the Mind. Essays on Mind and Morals.* Minneapolis: University of Minnesota Press.

Bennett, Jonathan. 1980. "Accountability." In *Philosophical Subjects: Essays Presented to P.F. Strawson,* edited by Zak van Straaten, 14–47. Oxford: Clarendon Press.

Buss, Sarah. 1999. "Appearing Respectful: The Moral Significance of Manners." *Ethics* 109 (4): 795–826.

Calhoun, Cheshire. 1989. "Responsibility and Reproach." *Ethics* 99 (2): 389–406.

Christman, John. 2004. "Relational Autonomy, Liberal Individualism, and the Social Constitution of Selves." *Philosophical Studies* 117 (1): 143–164.

Clarke, Randolph, and Capes, Justin. "Incompatibilist (Nondeterministic) Theories of Free Will." *The Stanford Encyclopedia of Philosophy* (Spring 2017 Edition), Edward N. Zalta (ed.), forthcoming URL = <https://plato.stanford.edu/archives/spr2017/entries/incompatibilism-theories/>.

Darwall, Stephen. 2006. *The Second-Person Standpoint: Morality, Respect, Accountability.* Cambridge, MA: Harvard University Press.

Fischer, John Martin, and Mark Ravizza. 1998. *Responsibility and Control: An Essay on Moral Responsibility.* Cambridge: Cambridge University Press.

Forster, Edward M. (1910) 1986. *Howards End.* New York: Penguin Books, Inc.

Fricker, Miranda. 2007. *Epistemic Injustice: Power and the Ethics of Knowing.* Oxford: Oxford University Press.

Friedman, Marilyn. 1997. "Autonomy and Social Relationships: Rethinking the Feminist Critique." In *Feminists Rethink the Self,* edited by D. T. Meyers, 40–61. Boulder, CO: Westview.

Glover, Jonathan. 1970. *Responsibility.* New York: Humanities Press.

Grice, Paul H. 1957. "Meaning." *Philosophical Review* 66 (3): 377–388.

Haji, Ishtiyaque. 1998. *Moral Appraisability.* New York: Oxford University Press.

McKenna, Michael. 2012. *Conversation and Responsibility.* New York: Oxford University Press.

McKenna, Michael. 2013. "Reasons-Responsiveness, Agents, and Mechanisms." In *Oxford Studies in Agency and Responsibility, Vol. 1,* edited by David Shoemaker, 151–184. New York: Oxford University Press.

McKenna, Michael, and Coates, D. Justin. "Compatibilism." *The Stanford Encyclopedia of Philosophy* (Winter 2016 Edition), Edward N. Zalta (ed.), URL = <https://plato.stanford.edu/archives/win2016/entries/compatibilism/.

Mele, Alfred. 1995. *Autonomous Agents.* New York: Oxford University Press.

Mele, Alfred. 2006. *Free Will and Luck.* New York: Oxford University Press.

Meyers, Diana Teitjens. 1989. *Self, Society and Personal Choice.* New York: Columbia University Press.

Mills, Charles. 2007. "White Ignorance." In *Race and Epistemologies of Ignorance,* edited by Sharon Sullivan and Nancy Tuana, 11–38. New York: State University of New York Press.

Nelkin, Dana. 2011. *Making Sense of Freedom and Responsibility.* Oxford: Oxford University Press.

Nietzsche, Friedrich. (1886) 1966. *Beyond Good and Evil.* Translated by Walter Kaufmann. New York: Random House.

Nietzsche, Friedrich. (1887) 1967. *On the Genealogy of Morals.* Translated by Walter Kaufman. New York: Random House.

Oshana, Marina. 1997. "Ascriptions of Responsibility." *American Philosophical Quarterly* 34 (1): 71–83.

Oshana, Marina. 2004. "Moral Accountability." *Philosophical Topics* 32 (1–2): 255–274.

Oshana, Marina. 2006. *Personal Autonomy in Society.* Aldershot: Ashgate Publishing.

Pereboom, Derk. 2014. *Free Will, Agency, and Meaning in Life.* New York: Oxford University Press.

Pettit, Philip. 2001. *A Theory of Freedom: From the Psychology to the Politics of Agency.* New York: Oxford University Press.

Russell, Paul. 1992. "Strawson's Way of Naturalizing Responsibility." *Ethics* 102 (2): 287–302.

Russell, Paul. 2004. "Responsibility and the Condition of Moral Sense." *Philosophical Topics* 32 (1–2): 287–305.

Sartorio, Carolina. 2016. *Causation and Free Will.* New York: Oxford University Press.

Scanlon, Thomas M. 2008. *Moral Dimensions: Permissibility, Meaning, Blame.* Cambridge, MA: Belknap Harvard Press.

Shoemaker, David. 2011 "Attributability, Answerability, and Accountability: Toward a Wider Theory of Moral Responsibility." *Ethics* 121 (3): 602–632.

Shoemaker, David. 2015a. "McKenna's Quality of Will." *Criminal Law and Philosophy* 9 (4): 695–708.

Shoemaker, David. 2015b. *Responsibility from the Margins.* Oxford: Oxford University Press.

Smith, Angela. 2008. "Control, Responsibility, and Moral Assessment." *Philosophical Studies* 138: 367–392.

Strawson, Galen. 1986. *Freedom and Belief.* Oxford: Clarendon Press.

Strawson, Peter F. 1962. "Freedom and Resentment." *Proceedings of the British Academy* 48: 187–211.

Vargas, Manuel. 2013. *Building Better Beings.* Oxford: Oxford University Press.

Wallace, R. Jay. 1994. *Responsibility and the Moral Sentiments.* Cambridge, MA: Harvard University Press.

Watson, Gary. 1987. "Responsibility and the Limits of Evil: Variations on a Strawsonian Theme." In *Responsibility, Character, and the Emotions: New Essays in Moral Psychology*, edited by Ferdinand Schoeman, 256–286. Cambridge: Cambridge University Press.

Watson, Gary. 1996. "Two Faces of Responsibility." *Philosophical Topics* 24 (2): 227–248.

Watson, Gary. 2014. "Peter Strawson on Responsibility and Sociality." In *Oxford Studies in Agency and Responsibility, Vol. 2, "Freedom and Resentment" at 50*, edited by David Shoemaker and Neal A. Tognazzini, 15–32. Oxford: Oxford University Press.

Wolf, Susan. 1990. *Freedom within Reason.* Oxford: Oxford University Press.

Zimmerman, Michael. 1988. *An Essay on Moral Responsibility.* Totowa, NJ: Rowman and Littlefield.

2

Moral Responsibility and the Social Dynamics of Power and Oppression

CATRIONA MACKENZIE

1 Introduction

In "Freedom and Resentment," P. F. Strawson ([1962] 1974) famously characterized moral responsibility as an inescapably social practice. Yet despite the ongoing influence of Strawson's work, much of the philosophical literature on the topic remains recalcitrantly individualistic. Recently, however, a number of philosophers inspired by a Strawsonian approach have begun to challenge the individualistic assumptions prevalent in the literature and to explicate the social and interpersonal dimensions of moral responsibility and of our moral responsibility practices. Manuel Vargas (2013), for example, rejects what he characterizes as prevailing atomistic and monistic assumptions about morally responsible agency. Atomistic views understand morally responsible agency as a "non-relational property of agents . . . characterizable in isolation from broader social and physical contexts," while monism is the assumption that morally responsible agency "is a single, unified capacity that relies on or is constituted by a cross-situationally stable mechanism" (Vargas 2013, 204–205). In contrast, Vargas proposes a view according to which both our agential capacities and our moral responsibility practices are shaped by and dependent upon the broader "moral ecology" (243–248). Moral ecology refers to the social and circumstantial contexts, including cultural norms, practices, and expectations, which scaffold our agency and within which our agential capacities are developed and exercised.

In a somewhat different, but related vein, Michael McKenna claims that moral responsibility is "*essentially* interpersonal" and dialogical (2012, 110). According to his "conversational" model, moral responsibility practices are analogous to conversational practices, and moral responsibility exchanges take the form of an unfolding conversation between agent and interlocutor about the meaning of the agent's attitudes and actions and what these express about her quality of will. Moral responsibility is *essentially* interpersonal on this account, because just as one can only be a competent speaker if one is able to understand and participate in the linguistic conventions and practices of a particular linguistic community, so too one can only be a morally responsible agent insofar as one is able to understand and participate in the moral responsibility practices of a moral community.

This recent focus on the social scaffolding of morally responsible agency and on the interpersonal dynamics at the heart of our moral responsibility practices marks a significant shift from the preoccupation with free will and determinism that has dominated so much of the philosophical literature. Despite this shift toward more socio-relational models of moral responsibility, however, philosophers developing these models tend to operate with fairly idealized conceptions of our social relationships, norms, and practices. McKenna's model, for example, implicitly assumes that the conversational partners are equally socially positioned and thus equally able to participate in reciprocal relations of holding to account. Similar assumptions are operative in McGeer and Pettit's (2015) illuminating analysis of reactive attitudes and blaming responses as exercises in mutually scaffolding or capacitating our sensitivity and responsiveness to moral reasons. Vargas's account of moral ecology, in contrast, does explicitly acknowledge that "non-ideality is the customary condition of our agency" (2013, 221). In other words, we are not ideally rational agents; our agency is shaped and influenced by context and circumstance. Yet while Vargas seeks to develop an account of responsible agency that takes seriously findings from empirical social psychology about the circumstantial constraints on our agency, he does not pay specific attention to the implications of social oppression and inequalities of power for moral ecology or for our moral responsibility practices.[1]

The aim of this chapter is to demonstrate that taking seriously the socio-relational scaffolding of morally responsible agency and the interpersonal dynamics at the heart of our moral responsibility practices requires that we attend also to the impacts of social oppression and inequalities of social power on our agency and practices of holding to account. My understanding of social power and oppression is influenced by feminist scholarship on the topic. Miranda Fricker defines social power as "a practical socially situated capacity to control others' actions, where this capacity may be exercised (actively or passively) by particular social agents, or, alternatively, it may operate purely structurally" (2007, 13). The kind of social power that is of specific interest to my concerns in this chapter is what Fricker refers to as 'identity power.' This is a kind of social control by members of dominant social groups over members of other social groups that depends upon shared conceptions or schemas of social identity, or what Moira Gatens (1996) refers to as 'the social imaginary.' These shared schemas structure our social relations, norms, practices, and institutions, and are internalized in our embodied habits and patterns of thinking, acting, and feeling. Identity power is one form or manifestation of social oppression. Ann Cudd understands social oppression as "an institutionally structured, unjust harm perpetrated on groups by other groups through direct and indirect material and psychological forces" (2006, 25). Material forces include systematic violence or the social threat of violence, economic deprivation and exploitation, discrimination, harassment, inequality of opportunity, and political exclusion or powerlessness. Psychological forces include mechanisms such as stereotyping, explicit and implicit bias, objectification, and cultural domination. These material and psychological forces can cause group and individual psychological harms of humiliation, degradation, and shame. I will draw on this feminist scholarship to show why theorists who seek to explicate the social and interpersonal dimensions of moral responsibility must also address the implications of inequalities of social power and oppression for our moral responsibility practices.[2]

Following Gary Watson, many theorists of moral responsibility distinguish between two dimensions or "faces" of responsibility: attributability and accountability (Watson 2004). Recently, David Shoemaker (2011, 2015) has argued for a tripartite distinction between three distinct but noncompeting dimensions of moral responsibility and of our moral responsibility practices: attributability, answerability, and accountability. Although ordinary agents will typically be eligible for all of these kinds of responsibility, Shoemaker's aim in distinguishing them is to make sense of our ambivalent reactive attitudes and responsibility judgments in a range of cases of marginal agency, including psychopathy, autism, dementia, and mild intellectual disability. The explanation for our ambivalence in these cases, he argues, is that agents suffering from these incapacities will, in different ways, be eligible for some moral responsibility ascriptions but not others, by virtue of having capacities for some qualities of will but not others.

Moral responsibility is both a capacity and a status concept. Shoemaker's focus, in distinguishing these three dimensions of moral responsibility, is to tease out how impairments of *capacity* with respect to one or more of these dimensions affect agents' eligibility for moral responsibility ascriptions. My focus, in what follows, is primarily moral responsibility as *status*. I do not intend to provide an independent defense of Shoemaker's tripartite distinction nor to endorse all aspects of his analysis.[3] Rather, my aim is to adopt his tripartite distinction and use it to tease out how moral responsibility ascriptions and practices are entangled with social dynamics of power and oppression, thereby affecting persons' *statuses* as morally responsible agents. In some contexts, deeply entrenched status inequality can also impair some of the capacities required for morally responsible agency, because the social scaffolding required to develop and exercise these capacities has been severely compromised. However, in many other contexts, including in the examples discussed in this chapter, while the agents in question may have highly developed capacities for morally responsible agency, in the moral responsibility exchanges and practices to which they are subject, they are not treated as having the status of morally responsible agents.

In section 2, I outline Shoemaker's analysis of attributability and draw on feminist work on stereotypes and psychological oppression to demonstrate the impact of social oppression and power inequalities on attributability practices. In section 3, I outline Shoemaker's analyses of answerability and accountability, and McKenna's conversational model of accountability. In section 4, I draw on feminist work on discursive and epistemic injustice to argue that, when enmeshed in social dynamics of power and oppression, both answerability and accountability practices tend to be asymmetrical, rather than reciprocal.

2 Attributability, Social Oppression, and Prejudicial Stereotypes

Responsibility as attributability tracks the quality of an agent's character, as expressed in her attitudes and actions. It thus involves aretaic appraisals and emotional responses to what these attitudes and actions reveal about the kind of person the agent is—what she values, and her virtues and vices, or the faults and excellences of her character (Shoemaker 2015, 38; Watson 2004, 266). Shoemaker claims that the aretaic appraisals involved in our attributability responses are organized around characteristic emotional responses—or what he refers to as "sentimental syndromes" (2015, 25–26)—of admiration or disdain toward others' or our own characters. Admiration is connected with a cluster of cognate emotional responses such as esteem, awe, and pride, while disdain is connected with a cluster of cognate emotional responses such as contempt, hatred, revulsion, and shame (35).

Ideally, our attributability responses ought to be sensitive to whether or not the agent's attitudes or actions are indeed expressive of her character and reflective of her practical identity, or evaluative self-conception, or whether certain excusing conditions might mitigate these responses.[4] Attributability responses are deeply enmeshed in the fabric of our social interactions—in our relations with our friends and intimates, our colleagues, our neighbours, and even in our everyday interactions with strangers. Yet in contexts of social oppression, these responses are often shaped by unjust social stereotypes and social role schemas, for example of race, gender, or class. Stereotypes are "widely held associations between a given social group and one or more attributes" (Fricker 2007, 30), which give rise to empirical generalizations about that social group. Fricker proposes that these empirical generalizations are embodied in images that can condition our judgments without our awareness and may conflict with our endorsed beliefs, explaining their characteristic evidence-resistance. Cudd proposes that the empirical generalizations involved in stereotyping are schemas, or cognitive structures that guide perception, memory, and inferential reasoning. Schemas structure our perceptions in terms of relevant networks of ideas, associations, and emotional responses. Stereotypes work by cognitive processes that refer back and forth between an individual and the generalizations, encoded in schemas, about the social group with which that individual is identified: "We infer from the individual to the group and then project back to the individual. The data we take in is about the individual. The group information stored in schemas is then added to that data, and we project that back onto the individual" (Cudd 2006, 78). In the case of unjust or what Fricker calls "negative identity-prejudicial" stereotypes (Fricker 2007, 35), the attributes and empirical generalizations associated with the group and embodied in images or encoded in schemas are negative, disparaging, and unreliable.

To illustrate the implications of stereotypes for attributability practices, I want to discuss two examples. The first is the example of Tom Robinson in Harper Lee's *To Kill a Mockingbird* (1960), also discussed by Fricker. Robinson is falsely accused of raping a poor white girl, Mayella Ewell, and is on trial for her rape and assault. Because he is a young black man in Alabama in 1935, the jurors' attributability responses to his character are so distorted by identity prejudicial stereotypes of the lying, immoral "Negro," that they literally cannot see his virtuous character traits—of honesty, kindness, and sympathy—for what they are. Instead of eliciting admiration, his character, as perceived via distorting stereotypes, elicits disdain, and no amount of evidence can shift the jurors' prejudicial attributability responses. In cases such as this, the prejudicial stereotype thus not only distorts the interlocutors' initial attributability responses to the agent's character; it also blocks their subsequent appraisal of relevant evidence and their willingness to consider alternative explanations of the agent's actions. Further, interlocutors in the grip of identity prejudicial stereotypes are less likely to be generous in applying any relevant excusing conditions.[5] The kind of social oppression to which Tom Robinson was subject was extreme. Yet similar patterns of prejudicial attributability responses are evident in many contexts involving inequalities of social power.

The second example, the notorious "children overboard" case, is from the recent Australian political context and occurred in November 2001, in the immediate aftermath of 9/11 and just before a federal election, which the conservative government of the time was predicted to lose. Amid public anxiety about terrorism and Islamic extremism, the then conservative government sought to whip up public support by invoking and entrenching identity prejudicial stereotypes about refugees from predominantly Muslim countries, such as Afghanistan and

Iraq. The case involved a vessel carrying 223 asylum seekers and suspected to be operated by Indonesian people smugglers. It was intercepted by an Australian Navy vessel 190 kilometers off Christmas Island and subsequently sunk. A number of government ministers claimed that, before the vessel sank, the asylum seekers had threatened to throw their children overboard if they were not granted asylum in Australia, and that these actions demonstrated their manipulative and callous character. These claims were allegedly supported by photographs published in the *Australian* of children and adults in the sea wearing life jackets.[6] The chief of the navy publicly rejected these claims and said that the photos showed asylum seekers in the water immediately after the vessel had sunk, before they were rescued by navy personnel. A Senate inquiry subsequently supported the navy's version of the events and revealed that the then prime minister, John Howard, knew the claims to be false even while he was publicly repeating them. Yet, despite the evidence of this gross deception, the government was re-elected, and these same identity prejudicial stereotypes continued to shape public perceptions of refugees from predominantly Muslim countries.

Prejudicial stereotypes are insidious not only because they distort attributability appraisals of individual members of the target social group, but also because they are typically internalized, resulting in psychological oppression and its attendant harms. As Fricker explains, "[T]he subject of the injustice is *constituted* just as the stereotype depicts her (that's what she counts as socially), and/or she may actually be *caused* to resemble the prejudicial stereotype working against her (that's what she comes in some measure to be)" (2007, 55). Psychological oppression can take varied forms in an individual's psyche, depending on the nature of the material, economic, and psychological forces to which the agent is subjected. In the feminist literature on psychological oppression and on relational autonomy, analysis has focused on the phenomena of adaptive preference formation, false consciousness, and distorted self-affective attitudes.

Adaptive preference formation arising from social oppression or deprivation is a phenomenon whereby an individual's preferences are harmfully adapted or habituated to the constraints of her situation—harmfully adapted because these preferences may conflict with the agent's needs or with valuable goods, and absent those constraints she is unlikely to have formed these preferences.[7] Agents whose preferences are adaptive in this sense seem to be complicit in perpetuating their oppression. This complicity often arises from false consciousness. False consciousness refers to false beliefs formed under conditions of oppression that support the maintenance of oppressive social relations of dominance and subordination (Cudd 2006, 178–180; Meyerson 1991). Privileged groups often have false beliefs about themselves and about other social groups that rationalize and justify their dominance in the social hierarchy. These beliefs are typically encoded in unjust stereotypes that work to justify the perpetuation of the current social arrangements. However, it is not only privileged groups that are susceptible to and motivated to accept unjust stereotypes and the false beliefs encoded in them. False consciousness also refers to the phenomenon whereby members of subordinate groups accept these false beliefs—sometimes explicitly endorsing them, sometimes by implicitly acquiescing to them, sometimes failing to recognize the role played by these beliefs in their actions and choices. Several examples of adaptive preference formation and false consciousness working in tandem have been discussed extensively in the literature on relational autonomy. These include Thomas Hill's example of the Deferential Wife, who is so devoted to serving her husband's needs and shaping her life around his that "she tends not to form her own interests, values and ideals: when she does, she counts them as less important than her husband's" (Hill 1991, 5); Paul Benson's example of the college student who, despite excelling at her studies, being liked by her friends and acquaintances, and leading an active, challenging life, feels bad about herself because she has internalized the false belief that a woman's worth is determined by her appearance (Benson 1991, 389); and Marina Oshana's example of the Taliban woman who, despite her earlier education as a medical doctor, has come to accept on religious grounds the false belief that women are inferior and should be subordinated to men (Oshana 2003, 104–107). These examples are illustrative of how socially oppressive stereotypes can shape practical identity formation, that is, how agents subject to oppression can be *constituted* by that oppression.[8]

The phenomenon of stereotype threat explains how a person may be *caused* to resemble the prejudicial stereotype. As Claude Steele's (1997) and subsequent empirical studies have shown, when individuals in a situation (e.g., a job interview) or doing a task (e.g., an IQ or math test) are exposed to negative stereotypes about the typical performance of members of their social groups (e.g., women, African Americans) in situations or tasks of that kind, they perform significantly less well than those individuals do when not exposed to the stereotype. The subjects' fear that they will conform to the stereotype, especially if they have an investment in performing well, actually causes them to perform less well. Repeated experiences of stereotype threat over time tends to result in disaffection and continued underperformance, which serves to reinforce the stereotype, thus perpetuating a vicious cycle.[9]

The constitutive and causal dimensions of practical identity formation in contexts of social oppression can result in distorted self-affective attitudes that undermine an agent's sense of her own worthiness. Demeaning stereotypes, oppressive social norms, economic and social inequality, and a myriad of oppressive practices directed toward members of subordinated social groups, including hate speech, violence, harassment, objectification, and social distancing, all convey messages of social inferiority, incompetence, inadequacy, irrationality, untrustworthiness, and unworthiness. These can be internalized in feelings of shame and humiliation, and in affective attitudes of diminished self-respect, self-trust, and self-esteem.[10] Persistent messages of social inferiority and unworthiness, and prejudicial stereotypes about the character traits of subordinated social groups can erode the development of these self-affective attitudes to varying degrees, depending on the severity of the oppressive social forces to which an agent is subject. In his "Letter from Birmingham Jail," Martin Luther King Jr. writes eloquently of this phenomenon, worrying about "the ominous clouds of inferiority beginning to form in her [his daughter's] mental sky," and the "unconscious bitterness toward white people" beginning to "distort her personality." He also writes of "being harried by day and haunted by night by the fact that you are Negro, living constantly at tiptoe stance . . . plagued with inner fears and outer resentments . . . fighting a degenerating sense of 'nobodiness' " (King 1964; quoted in Cudd 2006, 177).

In his discussion of clinical depression and attributability, Shoemaker notes an asymmetry between first- and third-person aretaic responses to people who are clinically depressed (2015, 129–136). From a first-person perspective, the depressed person may feel shame and self-disdain about her sense of apathy and her lack of motivation, regarding this as a character failing, for example as laziness. From an informed third-person perspective, however, others are likely to see her current state as not indicative of who she really is, but as a deviation from her character, attributable to the illness.[11] To the extent that there is such an asymmetry, I suggest that it contrasts with what often happens in contexts of social oppression and stereotype threat. In these contexts, third-person attributability responses are typically internalized by the agent, resulting in first-person attributability responses that often match the stereotypes embedded in the third-person responses. For example, gendered stereotypes of women as less competent and rational, or more emotional and needy than men, and attributability responses by others (such as her husband) that reinforce these stereotypes, can destabilize or erode a woman's trust in her capacities, judgment, and independence, leading her to regard and to present herself as less credible, competent, and worthy than is in fact the case.[12]

In the following two sections, I argue that social oppression and asymmetries of power can similarly distort moral responsibility practices related to answerability and accountability.

3 Answerability and Accountability: Shoemaker and McKenna

Among theorists of moral responsibility who distinguish between attributability and answerability, some hold that attributability is relevant to moral responsibility only insofar as an agent is answerable to others for her attitudes and conduct.[13] Thus they think that the primary focus of our responsibility practices is answerability. Others, for example, McKenna (2012), accept the distinction between attributability and accountability, but do not distinguish answerability from accountability. It is beyond the scope of my discussion in this chapter to engage in this debate or to rehearse the details of Shoemaker's arguments in favor of the tripartite distinction. For the sake of my argument in this section, I assume that answerability and accountability are distinct faces of responsibility. I begin by explaining the distinction, as Shoemaker understands it, and then discuss McKenna's conversational model of accountability. Whether or not one accepts that they are distinct faces of responsibility, the aim of the discussion in this section is to show that answerability and accountability are essentially interpersonal, social processes of reason-giving and holding to account. Drawing on the feminist literature on discursive and epistemic injustice, in the following section I argue that in contexts of social oppression, rather than being equal and reciprocal, these processes are often distorted by asymmetrical relations of power.

Shoemaker argues that whereas moral responsibility in the *attributability* sense is directed toward the quality of an agent's character, responsibility in the *answerability* sense is directed toward the quality of her judgments, as expressed in her attitudes and actions. A person is morally responsible in the *answerability* sense insofar as she is answerable to others' demands that she provide justificatory, evaluative reasons for her actions and attitudes. Such demands often take the form of questions such as "Why did you do (or react like) that?" where the kind of reason that the interlocutor is seeking is not just an explanation of the agent's action, but rather a justification as to why the agent considered the reasons on which she acted, rather than a range of alternative relevant reasons, to be worth acting on. For example, if I am told by her teacher that my child has been punished for hitting another child, I am likely to ask her, "But why did you hit him?" If she replies, "Because he was teasing me," I might prompt her to reflect on the worth of the judgment on which she acted (that hitting the other child is the appropriate response to his teasing), rather than an alternative judgment on which she might have acted (that walking away would be a better response).[14]

Shoemaker (2015) proposes that our answerability practices are organized around the sentimental syndromes of regret and pride when directed toward the quality of our own judgments, and disapproval and approval when directed toward the quality of others' judgments. Disapproval and regret are connected with a cluster of cognate emotional responses, such as disappointment, irritation, frustration, and shame, while approval and pride are connected with a cluster of cognate emotional responses, such as appreciation and approbation (2015, 35). As Shoemaker points out, answerability practices are enmeshed "in a wide variety of practical domains, including the athletic, the aesthetic, the epistemic and the prudential" (78). I can question your aesthetic judgment when you proudly show me your new painting, your epistemic judgment when you confide with me about your latest conspiracy theory, or your prudential judgment when you tell me you are going to marry a person you have known for only two months. And I may respond in these situations with feelings of disappointment, frustration, or disapproval. I may also regret my own judgments in the same domains, for example my imprudent financial decision to invest all my savings in a new car.

Shoemaker and other moral responsibility theorists present answerability practices as symmetrically and reciprocally structured, such that each party has the standing to hold the other answerable for the quality of their judgment. This idealization, however, overlooks the extent to which, in all these domains, including the moral, answerability practices are also deeply enmeshed in social hierarchies of authority and power that determine who has the standing to hold answerable. These authority relations are not symmetrical and reciprocal, even if they may be justifiable. A judge has the standing to hold the defendant answerable, a teacher has the standing to hold students answerable, parents have the standing to hold their children answerable, police have the standing to hold suspects answerable, and so on. In nonideal social contexts, however, these and other kinds of social relations of authority are typically inflected by identity power.[15] In patriarchal societies, for example, only the husband has the social standing to hold his wife answerable; she has no equivalent standing. Similar asymmetries of social standing apply also to accountability practices, including praise and blame, as I discuss in the following section. Before turning to this issue, however, I outline Shoemaker's analysis of accountability and McKenna's conversational model of accountability.

On Shoemaker's analysis, accountability is specifically connected with holding to account, and with practices of praise and blame. Whereas the target of *answerability* is the quality of the agent's judgment, the target of *accountability* is the quality of the agent's regard. A person is morally responsible in the accountability sense insofar as she can appropriately be held to account with respect to the basic moral demands of due respect and regard for others in interpersonal relationships. The demand for regard is the demand that others take one's normative perspective seriously. Shoemaker distinguishes between two kinds of regard: evaluational and emotional. Evaluational regard involves perceiving relevant facts about another's normative perspective as putative reasons that should be taken into account in one's normative deliberations (2015, 98). Emotional regard involves caring about another's normative perspective and being disposed to respond emotionally to the other's cares and concerns. Shoemaker proposes that our accountablility practices are organized around

the sentimental syndromes, on the one hand, of anger and associated negative emotional responses of resentment, indignation, hurt feelings, guilt, and
shame, and on the other hand, of gratitude and associated positive emotional
responses of gratification and warm feelings (35). Agential anger, on this analysis, is a response to perceived failures of regard on the part of another agent, such
as inconsiderateness or insensitivity. Anger aims to communicate to the other,
to make him aware of, the agent's sense that her normative perspective has not
been taken seriously and that she has been slighted.

It is a background assumption of Shoemaker's analysis that our accountability practices are fundamentally social. However, Shoemaker does not explicitly seek to explicate the social dimensions of these practices. In contrast, this
is a central focus of McKenna's (2012) conversational view. Like Shoemaker,
McKenna places both qualities of will and Strawsonian reactive attitudes at the
heart of our accountability practices, including practices of praise and blame.
And like Shoemaker, he regards the reactive attitudes as expressive and communicative. According to his conversational model, just as the utterances of a competent speaker of a natural language are taken to express a distinctive meaning to
which the speaker's interlocutor then responds, so too the actions of a morally
responsible agent bear a distinctive meaning, which is taken by her interlocutor
to express the quality of that agent's will: "By acting as she does, the morally
responsible agent *opens up the possibility of a conversation* about the moral value
of her action, most notably about the quality of her will" (McKenna 2012, 88–
89). In the unfolding stages of the conversation, the interlocutor holds the agent
responsible for the meaning of her action by responding with reactive attitudes to
what he or she interprets to be the quality of will expressed in the agent's action,
thereby inviting her to give a moral account of her conduct. McKenna refers
to the stages of this conversational exchange as those of "Moral Contribution,"
"Moral Address," and "Moral Account" (89). He understands these stages as
a dynamic process of reason-giving, interpretation, and emotional response
between the responsible agent and the one holding her to account—a process
that Victoria McGeer refers to as "co-reactive exchange" (2012). Through apologies, excuses, or defensive reactions, the agent either acknowledges or seeks to
shift the other's interpretation of the quality of will expressed in her action.

What makes our moral responsibility practices of reactive exchange essentially
interpersonal or social, according to McKenna, is that *being* and *holding* responsible are thoroughly intertwined—neither is metaphysically more basic—and
both depend upon inherently social capacities and skills for *participation* in the
practices. A competent morally responsible participant in this process must be
able to grasp and make use of social conventions for understanding the meaning
assigned to actions. Thus, she must be able to grasp the moral significance of her
own actions and to interpret the meaning of others' actions (McKenna 2012,

213). She must be able to understand the meaning of others' reactive attitudes and to express these attitudes herself. She must be able to comprehend and respond to the normative expectations and demands of the moral community, which requires mastery of the relevant social rules and cues (100). She must be able to grasp and apply excuses, justifications, and exemptions. She must be able to participate in dynamic, unfolding responsibility exchanges. In the context of such exchanges, she must be susceptible to feeling and responding to the harms of blame—social exclusion and disapproval—and the benefits of praise.[16]

McKenna's analysis of the complex social competences embedded in our accountability practices is subtle and persuasive, and I cannot do justice to it here. As already noted, however, McKenna's analysis *explicitly* assumes that responsibility exchanges take place between equally capacitated adults, and *implicitly* assumes that these exchanges occur in social and political contexts in which the participants are roughly equally positioned. Both assumptions are questionable.[17] In particular, the assumption that the participants in responsibility exchanges are equally positioned is an idealization that overlooks the way these exchanges, and the social conventions governing them, are frequently distorted and corrupted by oppressive schemas and asymmetries of social power. These schemas and asymmetries can affect the very nature of the act that an agent is taken to have performed in the Moral Contribution stage, the meaning attributed to the agent's quality of will in the Moral Address stage, and the uptake and credibility afforded to her in the Moral Account stage. In the following section, I develop and substantiate this claim using several illustrative examples.

4 Answerability and Accountability: The Effects of Discursive and Epistemic Injustice

In a recent article on the social authoring of agency, Alisa Bierria discusses the example of two photographs published by two different news agencies in the aftermath of Hurricane Katrina in 2005 (2014, 129–130). One photograph depicted two white people carrying food through floodwaters, with the caption "Two residents wade through chest-deep water after finding bread and soda from a local grocery store." The other photograph was almost identical but the subject in the photo was a young black man, and the caption read "A young man walks through chest deep flood water after looting a grocery store in New Orleans." As Bierria points out, the captions frame the actions of their subjects as "finding" or "looting," with reference to two very different social schemas, and in doing so further entrench those schemas. The caption for the photograph of the white people functions to elicit sympathy by socially enfranchising them as "residents" of the city who have suffered loss in the wake of a natural disaster. The caption for the photograph of the black man functions to elicit distrust and reactive attitudes of disapproval by framing his actions in terms of social schemas that equate being young and black with criminality, thereby socially disenfranchising him. The captions thus interpret the nature of the agents' actions in diametrically opposed ways at the Moral Contribution stage of the exchange.

In an ideal responsibility exchange, the Moral Address and Moral Account stages might provide an occasion for the blamed agent to correct any distortions at work in the way her actions have been framed and in the quality of regard these actions are taken to express. However, feminist work on discursive and epistemic injustice shows that inequalities of social power can also distort the dynamics of these stages of responsibility exchanges. Discursive injustice, as characterized by Rebecca Kukla, occurs when, by virtue of her membership in a socially disadvantaged group, it is difficult or impossible for a speaker "to deploy discursive conventions in the normal way, with the result that the performative force of her utterance is distorted in ways that enhance disadvantage" (2014, 441). In Kukla's view, for an utterance or speech act to have performative force, it must secure audience uptake within the context of a complex network of enacted social rituals and conventions that determine the meaning and kind of speech act it is. Uptake is not just a matter of whether the audience correctly understands the speaker's intention. It is determined rather by the kind of impact it has in social space (444). In situations of discursive injustice, a speaker intending and entitled to perform a particular type of speech act whose utterance does not secure uptake as a speech act of this type can end up performing a speech act of a different type, by virtue of the alternative uptake her utterance receives (445). The speaker therefore loses control of her words. Kukla gives the example of a female floor manager in a predominantly male factory whose orders are routinely ignored because they are not taken to be orders but as requests, to which the workers think they are at liberty to accede or decline.

To suffer epistemic injustice, according to Fricker (2007), is to be subject to prejudicial exclusion from knowledge practices on the basis of one's social group membership. Fricker distinguishes two broad kinds of epistemic injustice: testimonial injustice and hermeneutical injustice. In the central case of testimonial injustice, an agent's credibility is mistrusted or impugned—that is, she suffers a credibility deficit—as a result of systematic identity prejudice, and her testimony is discounted or ignored. This is a form of *injustice* because the credibility deficit is entirely due to her social position in an unjust social hierarchy, and it is an *epistemic* injustice because she is wronged specifically in her capacity as a knower.

Returning to the Tom Robinson example, we saw in section 2 how the identity prejudicial stereotypes that frame the jurors' perceptions of Tom distort their attributability responses to his character. A further effect of these prejudicial stereotypes is that they impugn his credibility and the reliability of his testimony and make it impossible for him "to deploy discursive conventions in the normal way" (Kukla 2014, 441). As Fricker explains, Tom knows that he cannot tell the truth that Mayella Ewell attempted to kiss him, because the idea that a white girl would be sexually attracted to a black man would be treated with even more incredulity than is his testimony that he helped her with her chores because he felt sorry for her. Tom also knows that if he does not tell the truth he is equally likely to be found guilty of raping and assaulting her. Thus, just as Tom knew that whether he accepted or rejected Mayella's advances he would be in trouble, he also knows that whatever speech act he tries to perform in the courtroom, he will end up performing a speech act of a different type.

The unjust credibility deficit from which Tom suffers distorts the answerability and accountability practices of the courtroom in exactly the same way as they are distorted in the wider society. Given the prejudicial racist and sexist stereotypes that frame the jurors' perceptions, which mean Tom knows he cannot tell the truth that Mayella attempted to kiss him, it is impossible for him to provide a justification of his judgment that the only course of action available to him was to run away. When asked why he ran away, his response that he was scared is construed as evidence of a guilty conscience.[18] The power dynamics of the accountability exchange in the courtroom, which mirror those in the wider society, are also framed by assumptions about what 'quality of regard' means in contexts of racist oppression. In this context, the only normative perspectives that count are the perspectives of whites. For a "Negro" to exhibit regard can only mean to exhibit due deference to whites, to acknowledge their superiority and authority. The expectations of due regard are therefore structured asymmetrically. There is no reciprocal requirement on the white jurors or on Mayella to exhibit evaluational regard for Tom's normative perspective, or emotional regard for his situation. As a result of these asymmetries, there is no space within the conversational exchange for Tom to properly account for his conduct, as he is not considered an equal with the social standing, authority, or credibility to do so. In other words, although the court proceedings might be thought to exemplify McKenna's stage of Moral Account, this stage in the responsibility exchange is not actually available to Tom due to the discursive and epistemic injustice he suffers. Nor is there space within the responsibility exchange for him to call Mayella to account for falsely accusing him of raping her, for as a "Negro" he has neither the social standing nor the credibility to do so. Thus, McKenna's stage of Moral Address is not available to him.

In contrast to Tom's credibility deficit, Mayella, the white jurors, and the white prosecutor receive an unjust credibility excess, due solely to their privileged positions as white within the social hierarchy.[19] As a result of this credibility excess, Mayella is entitled to initiate the stage of Moral Address without warrant, while being shielded from any reciprocal entitlement by Tom to initiate this stage in an accountability exchange. The excess of credibility attributed to the jurors and prosecutors gives them license to impugn Tom's character with racist slurs and discount the weight of the evidence that he is not guilty. Furthermore, they are able to do so without being held answerable for their judgments or being liable to be called to account by Tom, by the defending attorney, Atticus Finch, or by the wider society in which this drama is played out.

I now want to turn to the second kind of epistemic injustice identified by Fricker (2007), hermeneutical injustice, and use a different example to explain its relevance for practices of answerability and accountability. Hermeneutical injustice is a form of structural discrimination, arising from inequalities of social power and participation. One effect of these inequalities is that the collective hermeneutical resources are skewed toward those with more social power, who have the power to determine social meanings, while those with less social power may be "hermeneutically marginalized." Hermeneutical marginalization is a form of cognitive and epistemic disablement, which makes it difficult to understand and render intelligible certain aspects of one's social experience. One example discussed by Fricker is the experience of sexual harassment, an experience that women employees, despite finding it unwelcome and unpleasant, struggled to articulate and render intelligible until a term was coined in the 1970s to name the experience and, in doing so, define the nature of the wrong. Fricker defines the central case of hermeneutical injustice as "the injustice of having some significant area of one's social experience obscured from collective understanding owing to a structural identity prejudice in the collective hermeneutical resource" (2007, 155). In many cases, hermeneutical injustice is compounded by testimonial injustice, manifesting in "the speaker struggling to make herself intelligible in the testimonial exchange" (159).[20]

A notorious example of the effects of hermeneutical injustice on answerability and accountability practices is the case of DPP vs. Morgan (1976).[21] In August 1973, after an evening of drinking, William Morgan invited three of his friends home to have sex with his wife. Morgan allegedly advised his friends that although his wife might feign resistance, she was "kinky" and actually enjoyed rough sex. When all four arrived at Morgan's home, Daphne Morgan was asleep in her own separate single bed, in the room of their eleven-year-old son. She was awoken, forcibly dragged into another room with a double bed, and raped in turn by the three friends in the presence of the others and then afterwards by Morgan himself, after the others had left the room. She consented to none of the acts of intercourse, and tried to scream out to her older son to call the police, but the assailants covered her face and nose until she could no longer breathe and held her down for the duration of the assault. After the assault had ended, she drove herself to the nearest hospital and told the staff that she had been raped, a claim that was borne out by evidence from the hospital staff about the physical injuries she had sustained.

The specific hermeneutical injustice at the heart of this case was the fact that the crime of marital rape was not recognized as either rape or a crime in British (and Australian) law until the mid-1990s. Hence, although Morgan's friends were each tried for rape as principal offenders, and for aiding and abetting each other as principal offenders, Morgan himself, by virtue of being Daphne's husband, was exempt from prosecution for rape. As Ngaire Naffine explains, "With the husband's immunity from prosecution from rape, the apparatus of the trial could not be engaged when there were allegations of marital rape because there was no crime—no alleged wrong—to engage them. Without a crime there were no prohibited actions to be alleged and none to be explained nor justified. Indeed the raped wife had nothing to complain of and the husband had no need to explain and defend himself" (2016, 2).[22]

In this case, the hermeneutical injustice suffered by Daphne Morgan—her inability to name what her husband had done to her as rape—was caused by and further entrenched state-sanctioned norms of male dominance and female subordination within marriage. In doing so, it also entrenched asymmetrical relations of answerability and accountability. Moral responsibility theorists might respond by invoking a distinction between moral and legal answerability and accountability. In one sense, this is correct—at a personal level, Daphne Morgan could hold William Morgan morally answerable and accountable for his conduct. However, this response skates over two important considerations. First, morality and the law are intertwined. Legal norms and practices embody and lend legitimacy to a community's moral norms and practices. Second, in nonideal social contexts, a person's normative standing to hold others answerable and accountable is deeply intertwined with her social and legal standing. Daphne Morgan's lack of social standing to hold William Morgan legally answerable and accountable effectively eroded her status as an equal and reciprocal participant in moral responsibility practices. If there is no crime of marital rape, then it is more difficult for the wife to identify the husband's Moral Contribution. If, according to the law, a husband is entitled to force his wife to have sex with him, then her entitlement to Moral Address is undermined, and he is not required to give her a Moral Account of his conduct. Nor can the moral community demand this of him either, since according to the law no wrong has been committed.

The asymmetries within moral responsibility practices that are enabled by discursive and epistemic injustice expose victims of wrongs to a further wrong—what Margaret Walker refers to as "moral vulnerability" (2014). Moral vulnerability is an insult and injury to a victim's moral status that arises when the victim's claims are not recognized as such, are discounted or disqualified, either because these claims are denied moral validation or because the person is not recognized as having the moral standing to make a claim for answerability and accountability, or both (2014, 112). Tom Robinson and Daphne Morgan are both morally vulnerable in this sense by virtue of their asymmetrical positions within moral responsibility exchanges.

5 Conclusion

My aim in this chapter has been to diagnose a problem for Strawsonian approaches to moral responsibility. This diagnosis raises the following questions: If moral responsibility is essentially interpersonal and social and yet so many moral responsibility exchanges in our nonideal world are asymmetrical and nonreciprocal, what bearing should this have on our theorizing about moral responsibility? And what are the implications for Strawsonian justifications of our practices? In conclusion, I want to suggest a preliminary response to these questions.

First, several theorists, especially McGeer and Pettit (2015) and Vargas (2013) have recently drawn attention to the capacitating role of moral responsibility practices, in scaffolding our agency and cultivating our sensitivity to moral considerations. In doing so, these theorists have made important moves away from standard conceptions of responsible agency "as a set of properties that describe an agent in a vacuum, free of a context or environment" (Vargas 2013, 226). However, while I agree that moral responsibility is a socially scaffolded capacity and that our moral responsibility practices, when functioning well, can enable this kind of mutual capacitation of our agency, moral responsibility theorists must also start taking seriously the non-ideal social conditions in which many agents develop and exercise their agency. Vargas's attention to the broader "moral ecology" of agency is an important step in this direction. However, moral responsibility theorists need to pay more sustained attention to understanding and explicating the ways in which the social context, and especially social dynamics of power and oppression, can distort moral responsibility exchanges and practices. In this respect, moral responsibility theorists have much to learn from feminist and critical race theorists. My argument in this chapter has focused on the effects of these dynamics on a person's status as a morally responsible agent. More specifically, I have sought to show how an agent's social standing can affect all three dimensions of morally responsible agency distinguished by Shoemaker (2015), distorting not only attributability ascriptions but also practices of answerability and accountability. Although my argument has focused on moral responsibility as a status rather than a capacity, an implication of this argument is that the capacities for morally responsible agency are relational, and hence that deeply entrenched status inequality and distorted moral responsibility exchanges and practices can be de-capacitating. Important tasks for further theorizing are therefore to elaborate the sense in which the capacities for morally responsible agency are relational, to articulate the relationship between the status and capacity dimensions of morally responsible agency, and to explicate how asymmetries of status in moral responsibility exchanges and practices can be de-capacitating.

Second, for Strawsonian theorists such as McGeer and Pettit (2015), McKenna (2012), Vargas (2103), and Shoemaker (2015), an important justification for our moral responsibility practices is their capacitating role. McGeer and Pettit claim, for example, that "the practice of holding one another responsible is of immense importance in human life, providing for a sort of mutual scaffolding or capacitation and enabling us to lift our performance to a level we might not otherwise have attained" (2015, 186). In explaining this mutual capacitation, they propose a two-factor model of reasons responsiveness, as involving both a standing disposition to appreciate and be moved by relevant reasons, and a situationally sensitive higher-order disposition to be "sensitive to audience: the expectations that others hold of you" (2015, 171), which reinforces the disposition to be reasons responsive. However, if in contexts of deeply entrenched inequalities of social power our practices are liable to systematic distortions and are potentially mutually de-capacitating, does this undermine Strawsonian justifications of our practices?

In response to this question, the analysis developed in this chapter might lead in two radically divergent directions. In one direction, it might be taken to lend strong support to a deep skepticism and critique of Strawsonian theories and justifications. If our moral responsibility practices and reactive attitudes are indeed so entwined with dynamics of power and oppression, then how can these practices and attitudes provide any kind of justification for moral responsibility ascriptions? Perhaps what the analysis shows is that these practices and attitudes, despite being deeply embedded in our psychologies and social lives, are fundamentally unjustified.

In the other direction, it might be argued that although the analysis shows why Strawsonian theories need to start from less optimistic and idealized assumptions about our practices, it actually lends support to Strawsonian justifications. What Strawsonian theories show, so the argument goes, is that our agential capacities are inherently social: we only become agents in the first place by being socialized into moral responsibility practices, and our capacities for agency can only be sustained and exercised if they are appropriately socially scaffolded. Our agential capacities are therefore inescapably vulnerable, for better or worse, to the dynamics of social interaction.[23] This is why moral responsibility practices are capacitating in some contexts or for some agents, namely when they sensitize us to relevant moral considerations and expectations. However, when distorted by inequalities of power and oppression that undermine the agential status of some agents, or impair the scaffolding required to develop, sustain, and exercise our capacities, these practices can be mutually de-capacitating, deforming or blunting our reactive attitudes and responsiveness to moral considerations. Because our agential capacities are inherently social, we cannot simply do without these practices. We can and must, however, be vigilant in subjecting them to ongoing scrutiny, critique, and reform.

My sympathies lie in the second of these directions. To develop this argument in more detail would require providing an account of how our moral responsibility practices can be critically evaluated and reformed from within (and without) while still remaining justifiable. This, however, is a project for another paper.[24]

Notes

1. See, however, his contribution to this volume, where Vargas discusses the implications of social oppression for his theory of responsibility.
2. Over the last two decades, feminist relational autonomy theorists have sought to explicate how the material forces and psychological mechanisms characteristic of social oppression can impair the personal autonomy of agents who are subject to them, while recent feminist work on epistemic injustice has sought to explicate their specifically epistemic effects on agents' presumed credibility and trustworthiness. Yet, surprisingly, neither relational autonomy theory nor work on epistemic injustice has received much uptake to date in the philosophical literature on moral responsibility. On relational autonomy theory, see Mackenzie and Stoljar 2000. For more recent contributions to the literature on relational autonomy, see Veltman and Piper 2014; Oshana 2015. On epistemic injustice, see Fricker 2007; Medina 2013.
3. Shoemaker's aim in his (2015) book is to develop a "pure" quality of will theory of moral responsibility that does not appeal to standard conditions such as control or epistemic conditions. Other quality of will theorists, such as McKenna (2012) and Vargas (2013), do not attempt to provide a pure quality of will theory. I do not intend to engage here with the issue of whether a pure quality of will theory is feasible. Angela Smith (2012) criticizes Shoemaker's earlier (2011) version of his tripartite theory. Again, I make no attempt in this chapter to adjudicate the dispute between Smith and Shoemaker.
4. Although theorists of moral responsibility often refer to an agent's "deep self" in relation to authenticity and attributability, I think this term misleadingly suggests that the "deep self" is a metaphysical essence. For this reason, I prefer the notion of practical identity.
5. I return to the Tom Robinson example in section 4, to show how the jurors' prejudicial attributability practices also infiltrate their expectations for answerability and accountability.
6. The *Australian* is a right-wing national newspaper published by Rupert Murdoch.
7. For the original discussion of adaptive preferences, see Elster 1983. For recent feminist discussions of adaptive preferences in connection with autonomy, see Cudd 2006; Khader 2011; Mackenzie 2015; Stoljar 2014; Superson 2005.
8. In the relational autonomy literature, these examples have been used by several theorists to question the plausibility of procedural theories of autonomy, and specifically whether authenticity is a sufficient condition for autonomy. Intuitively, none of the agents in these examples seem autonomous, yet procedural accounts that equate autonomy with authenticity have difficulty explaining why, since these agents authentically embrace the false beliefs and preferences arising from them.
9. See also the discussions of stereotype threat and the self-fulfilling nature of stereotypes in Fricker (2007, 56–57) and Cudd (2006, 79–80).

10. Joel Anderson and Axel Honneth (2005) provide a useful explication of these self-affective attitudes. To regard oneself with self-respect is to think of oneself as the moral equal of others, as having equal standing to have one's views and claims taken seriously. Self-trust is the capacity to trust one's own convictions, emotional responses, and judgments. Self-esteem or self-worth is a fundamentally evaluative attitude. It involves thinking of one's life, one's cares, commitments, and undertakings as meaningful, worthwhile, and valuable.

11. The longer the depression continues, however, the more difficult it is to distinguish between who the person "really is" and who she has become due to the illness. Also, whether or not others are likely to see the person's current state as not indicative of who she really is, but as a deviation from her character, attributable to the illness, depends on how informed those others are about depression and mental illness. Sometimes others, even intimates, can respond to depression with frustration about why the depressed person cannot just "pull herself together."

12. The 1944 thriller *Gaslight*, discussed by Paul Benson (1994), provides a compelling depiction of this phenomenon, as does Mary Wollstonecraft's posthumously published, unfinished novel *The Wrongs of Woman* ([1798] 1980).

13. For example, Watson 2004; Scanlon 2000; Smith 2012. For discussion, see Shoemaker 2015, 70–73.

14. One reason why Shoemaker wants to distinguish answerability from accountability is to explain the ambivalent responsibility responses of caregivers to adults with mild intellectual disability (MID). He argues, rightly in my view, that adults with MID should typically be exempted (or mitigated) from answerability responsibility, in virtue of their impaired capacities for the kind of abstract thought and evaluative judgment involved in considering and being answerable to others' demands for justificatory reasons. However, to the extent that their cares and commitments disclose qualities of character, adults with MID are eligible for attributability responsibility. Further, at least with respect to their family, friends, and caregivers, they are eligible for accountability responsibility. Nevertheless, among ordinary agents, most cases of (moral) answerability will *also* be cases of accountability (2015, 115). Perhaps for this reason, in much of the literature on moral responsibility, accountability practices are understood to involve the kind of demands for justificatory reasons that Shoemaker characterizes as answerability.

15. Marina Oshana also makes this point in her contribution to this volume.

16. Vargas makes a similar point. See Vargas 2013, 262–265. It might be objected that sociopaths and psychopaths can participate in some aspects of reactive exchange, for example grasping and applying excuses, without being susceptible to feeling and responding to the harms of blame. In response to this objection, both McKenna and Shoemaker would argue that because of their incapacities to feel and respond to the harms of blame, and to participate in other aspects of reactive exchange, such as understanding the meaning of others' reactive attitudes, psychopaths are not responsible in the accountability sense, even if they are responsible in the attributability sense.

17. In his contribution to this volume, McKenna acknowledges that the assumption that these exchanges occur in social and political contexts in which the participants are roughly equally positioned is highly problematic.

18. Note the parallels with the recent Trayvon Martin case. Martin, a seventeen-year-old unarmed African American student, was confronted and gunned down by a white vigilante, George Zimmerman, while walking home from a grocery store. Zimmerman assumed that Martin, who was young, black, and wearing a hooded sweatshirt, must be a "gangsta" and therefore dangerous. Zimmerman was not convicted of Martin's murder on the grounds of self-defense. Media commentators repeatedly raised the question of why Martin did not simply run away from the armed Zimmerman when confronted by him. See the discussion of this case in Marina Oshana's chapter in this volume.

19. While Fricker (2007) argues that credibility excesses do not confer epistemic privilege or advantage, Medina (2013) disputes this. I agree with Medina on this point.

20. In the case of Tom Robinson, we see this compounding effect, as the prevailing social norms could not render intelligible the possibility that a white woman could be attracted to a black man and that this attraction might not reciprocated. For a parallel, see Chimamanda Ngozi

Adichie's novel *Americanah* (2013). The novel's central character, Ifemelu, a Nigerian immigrant to the United States, whose boyfriend in one part of the novel is a handsome, wealthy, white man, describes the incredulous stares she receives from white women who cannot fathom that this man could really be her boyfriend.

21. DPP vs. Morgan. 1976. AC 182 House of Lords. My discussion of this case is indebted to Naffine (2016).

22. As Naffine argues, another extraordinary thing about the case is that subsequent legal debate in the following forty years has focused almost exclusively on the principle of the importance of the proof of subjective mens rea, no matter how unreasonable the defendants' beliefs (in this case, the belief that Daphne Morgan consented on the basis of what her husband had told them), rather than on the issue of the husband's immunity from prosecution.

23. Thanks to Tori McGeer for helping me to clarify this point.

24. For extremely helpful comments on earlier versions of this chapter, I am grateful to my coeditors, Katrina Hutchison and Marina Oshana. Earlier versions of this chapter were presented at the University of Amsterdam, Freie Universität Berlin, a workshop on "Extended Responsibility" at the University of New South Wales, and the Australasian Moral Philosophy Workshop. For helpful comments, thanks to the audiences at these events, especially Robin Celikates, John Christman, Stefan Gosepath, Serene Khader, Tori McGeer, Mari Mikkola, and Beate Roessler.

References

Anderson, Joel, and Axel Honneth. 2005. "Autonomy, Vulnerability, Recognition and Justice." In *Autonomy and the Challenges to Liberalism*, edited by John Christman and Joel Anderson, 127–149. Cambridge: Cambridge University Press.

Benson, Paul. 1991. "Autonomy and Oppressive Socialization." *Social Theory and Practice* 17 (3): 385–408.

Benson, Paul. 1994. "Free Agency and Self-Worth." *Journal of Philosophy* 91 (12): 650–668.

Bierria, Alisa. 2014. "Missing in Action: Violence, Power, and Discerning Agency." *Hypatia* 29 (1): 129–145.

Cudd, Ann. 2006. *Analyzing Oppression*. New York: Oxford University Press.

Elster, Jon. 1983. *Sour Grapes*. New York: Cambridge University Press.

Fricker, Miranda. 2007. *Epistemic Injustice: Power and the Ethics of Knowing*. Oxford: Oxford University Press.

Gatens, Moira. 1996. *Imaginary Bodies: Ethics, Power, and Corporeality*. London: Routledge.

Hill, Thomas E., Jr., 1991. *Autonomy and Self-Respect*. New York: Cambridge University Press.

Khader, Serene. 2011. *Adaptive Preferences and Women's Empowerment*. New York: Oxford University Press.

King, Martin Luther, Jr. 1964. *Why We Can't Wait*. New York: Harper & Row.

Kukla, Rebecca. 2014. "Performative Force, Convention, and Discursive Injustice." *Hypatia* 29 (1): 440–457.

Lee, Harper. 1960. *To Kill a Mockingbird*. London: William Heinemann.

Mackenzie, Catriona. 2015. "Responding to the Agency Dilemma: Autonomy, Adaptive Preferences and Internalized Oppression." In *Personal Autonomy and Social Oppression*, edited by Marina Oshana, 48–67. New York: Routledge.

Mackenzie, Catriona, and Natalie Stoljar. 2000. "Introduction: Autonomy Refigured." In *Relational Autonomy: Feminist Perspectives on Autonomy, Agency and the Social Self*, edited by Catriona Mackenzie and Natalie Stoljar, 3–31. New York: Oxford University Press.

McGeer, Victoria. 2012. "Co-Reactive Attitudes and the Making of Moral Community." In *Emotions, Imagination and Moral Reasoning*, edited by Robyn Langdon and Catriona Mackenzie, 299–326. New York: Psychology Press.

McGeer, Victoria, and Philip Pettit. 2015. "The Hard Problem of Responsibility." In *Oxford Studies in Agency and Responsibility, Vol. 3*, edited by David Shoemaker, 160–188. New York: Oxford University Press.

McKenna, Michael. 2012. *Conversation and Responsibility*. New York: Oxford University Press.

Medina, José. 2013. *The Epistemology of Resistance: Gender and Racial Oppression, Epistemic Justice, and the Social Imagination*. New York: Oxford University Press.

Meyerson, Denise. 1991. *False Consciousness*. Oxford: Oxford University Press.

Naffine, Ngaire. 2016. "Definition and Justice in Criminal Jurisprudence: *DPP vs Morgan* Revisited." Unpublished manuscript, cited with author's permission.

Ngozi Adichie, Chimamanda. 2013. *Americanah*. London: 4th Estate, Harper Collins Publishers.

Oshana, Marina. 2003. "How Much Should We Value Autonomy?" *Social Philosophy and Policy* 20 (2): 99–126.

Oshana, Marina, ed. 2015. *Personal Autonomy and Social Oppression*. New York: Routledge.

Scanlon, Thomas. 2000. *What We Owe to Each Other*. Cambridge, MA: Harvard University Press.

Shoemaker, David. 2011. "Attributability, Answerability, and Accountability: Toward a Wider Theory of Responsibility." *Ethics* 121 (3): 602–632.

Shoemaker, David. 2015. *Responsibility from the Margins*. New York: Oxford University Press.

Smith, Angela. 2012. "Attributability, Answerability and Accountability: In Defense of a Unified Account." *Ethics* 122 (3): 575–589.

Strawson, Peter F. (1962) 1974. "Freedom and Resentment." In *Freedom and Resentment and Other Essays*, edited by Peter F. Strawson, 1–25. London: Methuen.

Steele, Claude. 1997. "A Threat in the Air: How Stereotypes Shape Intellectual Identity and Performance." *American Psychologist* 52 (6): 613–629.

Stoljar, Natalie. 2014. "Autonomy and Adaptive Preference Formation." In *Autonomy, Oppression and Gender*, edited by Andrea Veltman and Mark Piper, 227–252. New York: Oxford University Press.

Superson, Anita. 2005. "Deformed Desires and Informed Desire Tests." *Hypatia* 20 (4): 109–126.

Vargas, Manuel. 2013. *Building Better Beings: A Theory of Moral Responsibility*. New York: Oxford University Press.

Veltman, Andrea and Mark Piper, eds. 2014. *Autonomy, Oppression and Gender*. New York: Oxford University Press.

Walker, Margaret. 2014. "Moral Vulnerability and the Task of Reparations." In *Vulnerability: New Essays in Ethics and Feminist Philosophy*, edited by Catriona Mackenzie, Wendy Rogers, and Susan Dodds, 111–133. New York: Oxford University Press.

Watson, Gary. 2004. "Two Faces of Responsibility." In *Agency and Answerability*, edited by Gary Watson, 260–288. New York: Oxford University Press.

Wollstonecraft, Mary. (1798) 1980. "The Wrongs of Woman; or Maria, a Fragment." In *Mary and "The Wrongs of Woman,"* edited by J. Kinsley and G. Kelly. Oxford: Oxford University Press.

3

Ascriptions of Responsibility Given Commonplace Relations of Power

MARINA OSHANA

1 Introduction

The task of this chapter is to address an underappreciated problem exposed by asymmetries in social manifestations of responsibility. The asymmetries operate on two dimensions: there are *asymmetries of power* in the relations between parties to responsibility practices, and there are *asymmetries within responsibility practices*. The former asymmetries are, more generally than not, typical of the dynamics between the presumed responsible party and those who judge her responsible. Indeed, an asymmetry of power is an accepted and acceptable feature of many types of relationship. Parents and children, teachers and students, employers and employees, physician and patient form relationships that are marked by asymmetries of authority and of credibility that define the relationship and that are vital to the integrity of the relationship. Abuses of power do, of course, occur in tokens of these types of relationship; the fact that a position of authority is socially accepted does not insulate individuals within the relationship from such abuses.[1] Too often, the fact that the asymmetry of power *is* socially accepted makes challenges to the abuse less likely to occur. The point I want to make is that there exist relationships defined in part by asymmetries of power that are relationships of a type we value.

Where the asymmetry of power is legitimate, we assume that the practices that constitute moral responsibility will be legitimate as well. That is, we assume that the practice of holding one another accountable will not give way to inappropriate inequities or problematic asymmetries of responsibility practice. This is a grave mistake, but one that nearly every theorist of responsibility, myself included, has committed. Asymmetries of power and asymmetries of responsibility practice have received little attention even within nonmetaphysical accounts of responsibility that highlight the expressivist or interlocutive tenor of responsibility practices and in explicitly social analyses of responsibility of the sort I have defended (Oshana 1997, 2004). They have gone unnoticed, I think, because those of us who write about responsibility have focused almost exclusively on the status of the presumed responsible agent. Like the majority of contemporary analyses of responsibility, attention is directed almost entirely on criteria that the presumed responsible agent must satisfy. And, typically, these criteria are of an epistemic and a metaphysical stripe: Did the agent understand what moral and nonmoral requirements obtained? Was she competent to assess the circumstances and consequences of her actions? Were her actions her own, ones she endorsed? Was the putatively responsible party able to account for her actions, and were the actions rightly credited to her? Having determined that specific conditions requisite to being held accountable had been met by this agent, it seemed a short and entirely straightforward journey to the verdict that the agent met, or fell short of, conditions for responsibility.

This focus has left a lacuna in the literature on two fronts. First, little if any attention has been paid to asymmetries within practices of responsibility. Scant attention is given to the status of the party positioned to hold another responsible relative to that of the party from whom an account is expected. The issue of which persons among a community of interlocutors have the standing to hold others responsible has been largely unexplored. For instance, there is little said on the question of who decides upon standards of evidence for credibility: Who in the interlocutive community determines the worthiness of others to stake claims for accountability and to lay charges of responsibility? Who determines whether a claim has merit? Who determines whether the terms of the practice—such as in providing an account of one's actions that is meant to excuse or justify or explain—have been satisfactorily met? The second, and more general, point is that little if any attention has been paid to the social, economic, and political power dynamics—often asymmetric—that structure the context within which evaluations of responsibility occur.[2]

But to be inattentive to the fact of asymmetries, as happens when attention is thrust, lopsidedly, upon the qualifications of one party for responsible agency, is to run the risk of ignoring pernicious asymmetries of power. I shall argue that such oversight risks the integrity of agents and can place fundamental principles of justice at stake.[3] In addition, depending on the practices associated with holding a person responsible, a person may be sanctioned in a variety of ways, many of which are quite harsh and liberty limiting. Thus the oversight may be a grave one. As Margaret Urban Walker reminds us, "We can make judgments assigning responsibility and we can also raise moral questions about the way we make them" (2007, 68). It behooves those of us who are serious about understanding the social dimensions of responsibility to raise these questions and to integrate them among the philosophical analyses of responsibility we offer.

Not all philosophical discourse about responsibility has ignored the asymmetries entirely. A notable exception to the oversight is found in feminist discourse. This is not surprising. Feminist moral philosophy, feminist philosophy of law, and feminist epistemology have long been the vanguard in highlighting the systematic devaluation of women's standing as credible interlocutive partners. Feminist philosophy attends to the consequences that inequities of power have on moral, legal, epistemic, and social standing, and on decisions about which parties are deemed full agents, positioned to hold responsible and to be held responsible.[4] In what follows, I draw most notably on some lessons acquired from feminist work in moral epistemology.

In the course of my argument, I explore the idea that who we are and how we have been represented to the world shapes expectations about our agential competence and capabilities as responsible partners. Such expectations inevitably infiltrate our professional lives and our public lives as citizens. In the interest of full disclosure, let me state that a number of the examples I employ are drawn from personal experience and from testimonial and anecdotal reports of friends, colleagues, acquaintances, and the news. The findings are not scientific, but they are not meant to be, nor need they be. We can gain philosophical insight into the concept of responsibility and the practices that give shape to that concept from empirical evidence of experiences of a direct, first-personal, and yet shared sort. Indeed, philosophical theorizing about the concept and practices of responsibility is of greater significance when experiential and testimonial resources are brought to bear.

Section 2 begins with some general remarks about responsibility as I understand the phenomenon. To be clear, the account I describe is not an account of the various responsibilities or duties we have to ourselves and to others. It is an account of responsibility practices—an account of what it means to be responsible, to be held responsible, and to hold responsible. While I do not plan on revising my view that ascriptions of responsibility are essentially expectations that an account be forthcoming from the actor, I do believe this is too myopic a picture. It is one that blithely assumes that the power dynamic involved in ascriptions of responsibility is, if not symmetrical, then nonpernicious, or nonexploitative and just. What I want to offer is a limited but, I hope, fruitful examination of the effect of asymmetries of power and of practice upon ascriptions of responsibility. In sections 3 and 4, I use the phenomena of stereotype threat and implicit bias as indicators of these asymmetries. I examine two scenarios in which the power had by interlocutors and those held accountable is relativized to their gendered, economic, and ethnic social status, and in which responsibility practices are regularly rendered perniciously asymmetric because of gender, class, and ethnicity.

The scenarios occur in the context of academic life and the context of interacting with law enforcement officials. I characterize the perniciousness as malignant in that it increases in scope and strength the longer it persists.

The discussion is restricted by the very narrow range of cases I examine. I do not have the luxury of space or time to develop the exhaustive examination of situations where malignancies of asymmetry often appear.[5] The concluding section of the chapter gestures—but does no more than gesture—toward our prospects for rendering social relations more symmetric. I am pessimistic that a wholesale reordering of the social structures that underpin such asymmetries is feasible, and I leave an exploration of that promise to others less pessimistic than myself.

2 What Is Responsibility?

Often, when we judge a person responsible—whether morally, legally, professionally, socially, or causally—we are holding the person accountable (Oshana 1997, 2004, 2010).[6] We are affirming that the person should clarify her beliefs and, if fathomed, her intentions about her behavior. (Sometimes, these may be beliefs about what the person had a duty to do.) We are affirming that the person should do so, usually, to an audience of others who are (or can be) affected by her actions. If the audience addressed is incapable of appreciating the significance of the account, as is true of small children, severely incapacitated humans, or animals, an account is nonetheless appropriate and should be expected. The responsible party should recognize herself as bearing the charge and as having acted in a way that makes an explanation fitting even if not deliverable, or even if uptake is impossible.

Accountability is a proficiency of the responsible agent; to be responsible, a person must be capable of a type of interlocution. An account ought to be forthcoming because expectations about the interlocutionary and normative proficiencies of the agent are assumed. Absent evidence to the contrary, we assume that the agent is alert to (or can be alert to) reasons that support or challenge the activity for which responsibility is purported. These reasons are interpersonally salient, and it is apparent that the agent recognizes them as such. The agent is capable of making contact with the normative aspects of the action. Ideally, these are reasons that the party held accountable and others in the relevant moral, legal, or social community are prepared to accept as directives for action.[7]

Among the questions we need to answer in navigating our responsibility practices are questions about epistemology: If a person is to be held accountable, what must the person know or be capable of knowing? What is it that a person should be aware of if the person is to have moral, legal, practical, and cultural knowledge of the sort that responsibility assumes? There is, in addition, a question to be asked about knowledge acquisition: What are the right, or best, ways of acquiring knowledge of a sort requisite to being responsible and to holding responsible? Finally, there is a question to be asked about the epistemic environment: What must conditions on the ground be like in order to develop the faculties for being responsible?

The concept of responsibility and the practices that give shape to the concept reflect the character of the social realm in an essential way, just as they reflect in an essential way the capabilities of the individual actors. The practice of ascribing responsibility engages co-awareness, in which persons appraise one another as suitable participants in the interpersonal relationships definitive of responsibility. It is usually a dialogical practice, involving the request for, the giving of, and the receiving of reasons. It is almost always judgmental, involving the assessment of the reasons given as rising to or falling short of expected standards of justification. It is judgmental, as well, in evaluating the personality of the actor. The practice partners one or more actors who, by way of allegedly free and intentional, or free and reasonably foreseen action, have behaved in such a way that others may have some claim upon them: a claim of justice, of duty, or of simple explanation. Most critically, our responsibility practices are inextricably bound with our status as robust agents: "In making each other accountable to certain people for certain states of affairs, we define the scope and limits of our agency, affirm who in particular we are, show what we care about, and reveal who has standing to judge and blame us. In the ways we assign, accept, or deflect responsibilities, we express our understandings of our own and others' identities, relationships, and values" (Walker 2007, 16).

This account of responsibility is meant to be general. It is meant to describe what responsibility means in a variety of realms: the moral, the legal, and the social. The general idea of responsibility practice is that of having the standing to hold and to be held to account. The normative standards against which assessments of accountability are made and the content of a responsible agent's epistemic repertoire will vary depending on whether the matter at hand is one of moral responsibility, legal responsibility, practical responsibility, or responsibility within the contours of a profession. The account is holistic in its treatment of the responsible subject and the circumstances that prompt responsibility practices. The account is holistic because it pursues questions about responsibility from a vantage point that broadens the foci beyond concerns about the free will of the actor or concerns about the psychological control conditions for responsible agency, as is customarily the case. The account is attentive to the socio-relational circumstances that shape the aretaic profile—the character and the values—of responsible agents and that help structure the positions they occupy in the interpersonal exchange. The account of responsibility aspires to be democratic rather than autocratic, and to encourage participatory engagement as opposed to docility and compliance. Ideally, we should understand responsibility as essentially relational in its treatment of the conditions for accountability and answerability.

Representing oneself as a responsible agent and being recognized by others as a responsible agent is a function of the quality of one's interactions with others (Oshana 2010). More precisely, representation and recognition hinge on the positive or negative corroboration one's representation provokes. *Successful* representation and recognition necessitate awareness on the part of the agent and those who hold her responsible of the roles both play. Successfully representing ourselves as responsible agents dictates that we remain alert to the impressions others have of us, especially in contexts that are fertile ground for bias. Successful representation and recognition mean that careful attention must be given to the dynamics of power that shape these interactions, for it is within dynamics of social power that the normative expectations we have of ourselves and of each other originate. It is within dynamics of power that persons take part in the formation of the moral, legal, professional, and cultural traditions through which responsibility practices are filtered. It is within dynamics of power that persons come to be regarded (or disregarded) as dependable moral, legal, and practical agents and as credible members of moral, legal, professional, and cultural communities. In sum, successful practices of responsibility mandate effortful co-awareness of the roles we inhabit and of the configurations of power within which we operate.

3 Malignant Asymmetries I

3.1 Stereotype Threat and Implicit Bias

The claims I have made about the social character of responsible agency and about asymmetries of power can be substantiated by considering the effects of stereotype threat and implicit bias upon the responsibility credentials of certain groups of persons in society. As members of particular groups—socioeconomic, professional, ethnic, gendered, and even geographic—we are regarded by our peers and by outsiders as more or less qualified—more or less "credentialed"— responsible agents. We are treated as more or less entitled to hold others accountable and to be held to certain standards of accountability. Stereotype threat and explicit as well as implicit bias erode proper regard. To be clear, I am not suggesting that the asymmetries involved in the web of responsibility practices are due to stereotype threat or implicit bias. The bases for the inequities of power that undergird assessments of responsibility and responsible agency, and that typify responsibility practices, are far more complex and systemic. They cannot be traced to one phenomenon (just as implicit bias and stereotype threat themselves are not straightforwardly traced to one source). My point is that stereotype threat and implicit bias offer fertile and fairly ubiquitous manifestations of pernicious and malignant asymmetries that compromise relationships of responsibility. The scenarios I explore below find evidence of both stereotype threat and implicit bias and thus offer a launching point for discussion.

Stereotype threat is "the risk of confirming, as self-characteristic, a negative stereotype about one's group" (Steele and Aronson 1995, 797). It "manifests itself when members of a group that is negatively stigmatised at some task are made aware of their group membership in a high stakes situation where they care about doing well" (Saul 2015). The upshot threatens the performance of the stereotyped members because they are apprehensive, even if unconsciously so, of corroborating the salient group stereotype. Implicit biases are unconscious preconceptions that emotionally influence the manner in which we approach one another, assess one another, and cooperate with one another. Implicit biases are reflected in the traits we confer upon one another. While bias may benefit members of the targeted group ("boys are good at logical reasoning"), just as often biases hinder and work to the detriment of the group ("boys are not good at nurturing"). Too often, bias has a basis in social practice. For example, men are associated more readily than women with competence in political leadership and accepted as naturally suited for political leadership because of a paucity of women in positions of political leadership.

Both stereotype threat and implicit bias are pernicious. They infect responsibility practices when members of the salient groups are adversely stigmatized and deemed less credible partners in the enterprise of holding accountable; when they are regarded as less trustworthy, reliable, and deserving of authority because of their perceived membership in a less socially powerful group. The following scenarios illustrate, to varying degrees, the role of stereotype threat and implicit bias in delivering such asymmetries of power.

3.2 Women and Minorities in the University Classroom

The first case I discuss is one in which a (usually) proper asymmetry of power is challenged by an inappropriate asymmetry of responsibility practices given social bias and inequity. The university classroom is a context in which power asymmetries are obvious. Both teachers and students enter the classroom recognizing that asymmetries of power are in place. These are asymmetries of design and convention, and they are accepted for a host of reasons. The teacher is assumed to be better acquainted with the subject matter than is the student. The student is there to learn something she does not know from someone who possesses that knowledge and is there to share it. As a measure of this exchange, the teacher possesses authority her students lack and experiences power (including punitive power) over her students.

Most notably, the teacher has the power, and the student does not, to set criteria for student success and set the terms for assessment. This type of authority engages professional as well as moral responsibilities. Other varieties of power within the classroom signal asymmetries of a conventional sort. For example, the student may not, unless invited, address the teacher with the same level of familiarity that the teacher may address the student. And so forth. The asymmetries correspondingly allow students to hold their instructors accountable, notably for the execution of certain job-related duties. As instructors, we can be held accountable by our students for our failure to be clear, or to utilize effective pedagogy. As instructors, we are duty-bound to acknowledge the possibility of error on our part, and to be fair in our interactions with the students. We are rightly accountable to our students when we fall short in these tasks. The asymmetry of power is accepted because the nature of the student-instructor relationship requires it (general expectations of the profession), and because it is generally benign and just (moral expectations).

The classroom is unmistakably a realm in which the credibility and authority of the instructor are matters of professional concern. As a professor in a classroom, your role is to instruct and to engage your students with the subject matter. To do this successfully, you must not simply lecture, offering up the wealth of scholarly expertise in your possession. You must also initiate and sustain a discussion and, in disciplines such as philosophy, a critical dialogue in which the merits of a theory or position are explored. You must be forceful but not uncivil; you must summon respect without appearing imperious.

Now consider the position of women professors in the classroom. Jennifer Saul, a philosopher at the University of Sheffield, states the obvious: "Women's experiences as teachers are ... likely to be different from men's" (2013, 45). Saul cites a 2010 study that concluded that women "are more likely to encounter incivility in the classroom, ranging from sleeping or checking e-mail to aggressive and bullying interruptions" (46).[8] I can attest that all of these, and more, have been regular occurrences in my classes, from my first days as a novice (when a young white male student interrupted a lecture with the assertion that "you're wrong!" about Plato's tripartite theory of the soul) to the days of my (visibly) seasoned presence in classes well within my area of expertise. My female colleagues, junior and senior, corroborate this. Repeated assurances and demonstrations of our qualifications often do little to blunt these behaviors; it matters not that we hold advanced degrees, that we are respected by our peers, that we have proven track records of academic and professional success. To an extent and with an intensity not experienced by our male colleagues, our right to establish the terms of dialogue and debate in the classroom is tested. Our credibility as members of what is ordinarily regarded as a respected professional cohort, entrusted to circumnavigate our pedagogical responsibilities, is defied, sometimes in subtle, at other times flagrant, ways. Some challenges are polite, as when we are repeatedly addressed as "Mrs." rather than "Professor." Other encounters are blatantly insubordinate and disrespectful. Years ago, a young black male student invited me to dinner at a (relatively) "romantic" restaurant to discuss his abysmal grade. Another felt no inhibition in commenting on my attire and placing his hand on my knee. Recently, a male student complained to the chair of my department that I could not be trusted to give him a fair grade because I was a feminist. In isolation, these occurrences are locally disruptive of the professor-student dynamic. Systemically, they accumulate into what one of my colleagues likens to "death by a thousand paper cuts"; individually minor irritants but cumulatively debilitating injury to one's identity as a professional.

The challenges I have highlighted reflect assumptions about gender and race—about what persons must look like and act like in order to claim legitimate instructional authority. These assumptions often emanate from socially cultivated implicit bias, and they frequently generate stereotype threat. The stereotype threats are cultivated in the early junctures of academic life. A study conducted on the reasons undergraduate women disproportionately choose not to pursue philosophy concluded that "[w]hen women are preoccupied (either consciously or unconsciously) with worries about confirming stereotypes about women in a given area, they feel more stressed in those settings, are less motivated, and are less able to devote their full attention and effort to the tasks of responding in class discussions, writing papers, and preparing presentations. This consequence is unfair to women students. It is also evidence of a pedagogical problem, since instructors should aim to connect with and help all of their students" (Thompson et al. 2016, 3).

Among the biases—not necessarily ones that invite stereotype threat, but nonetheless serve to weaken the professional credibility of women in the academy—are the notions that women naturally are, and therefore should be, deferential, accommodating, and "nice."[9] This seems to be the case in an anecdote Saul shares from Louise Antony, a senior philosopher at the University of Massachusetts:

> [When] I taught a course to engineers that was usually taught by a male colleague, he advised me to brook absolutely no excuses for late papers, and to announce (as he always did) that students would simply be docked 5 points for every day late. When I found that I had over 40 late papers (in a class of 300+), and that many of them were so late they would have a failing grade before I even read them, I asked him what he did: did he disregard the announced policy, or did he let the chips

fall where they may (leading to failing grades for quite a few students). His answer: that's never happened to me. Thus, he never had to face the dilemma of either undermining his own authority by not following his announced policy, or evoking the ire of 40 students in a class that didn't like you to begin with. (Saul 2013, 46)[10]

Incivility and microaggression on the part of one's students amount to pernicious asymmetries within responsibility practices, especially when such behavior is ignored or casually written off as unintentional or as immature. Challenges to proper pedagogical dynamics of power within responsibility practices are heightened for women faculty in predominantly male fields of study such as philosophy. This type of pedagogical dynamic is experienced to an even greater degree for women of color; I would assume the situation also intensifies for professors who are members of identifiable religious minorities, sexual minorities, and professors with visible disabilities. There are far fewer women of color in the academy than there are women of European ancestry, and even fewer identifiable religious minorities and professors with visible disabilities. It is no secret that descriptive stereotypes of gender, race, religious affiliation, and ability carry heightened perceptions of incompetence.[11] If one is a member of a racial, religious, or sexual minority, or less-abled body class, or if one's socioeconomic upbringing renders one an outlier, one's perceived competence deficit is compounded: minority faculty "face problematic student attitudes and behaviors, including students inappropriately questioning both their authority and credibility in the classroom" (Tuitt et al. 2009, 66). In my case, students have been prone to question whether, as a female, or as a faculty of color, I will be fair. Can I, they wonder, set aside my race and/or gender when assessing their work? While few openly question my competence to assess their work, some have worried that, although I am competent to teach the material, the fact of my race and gender will invariably color my judgement of their performance. Their worries often surface in the tenor of the responsibility practices that occur between us. They are far more inclined to question my right to hold them accountable: why should *they* be accountable to *me*?

This is especially the case when, having navigated life as white, male, and perhaps economically privileged, they find themselves in a context where they have less power than me, and where I am an unknown quantity. (Interestingly, female students of color, especially African-American and Latina students, are less inclined to challenge the accepted asymmetry of power.) Some of my students have been unabashedly upfront about this and interpret their skepticism as a sign of sensitivity to racial and gender difference: they know I differ in superficial respects from other professors and so assume that my presentation of the material and approach to their work will be affected, and negatively so, by my difference. They have not interacted in a classroom with a professor who looks like me; I am one of a handful of African-American/mixed race professors they have encountered (if they have encountered any). Almost certainly, I am the only African-American/mixed race woman philosopher they have seen, and may ever see.[12] The young white male who rudely declared that I was wrong may simply find the experience of a woman of color teaching him to think logically, no less holding him accountable to do so, so rare as to be unfathomable. He may believe that men have an advantage in skills of argument and logical assessment that women of all stripes lack, and these beliefs become apparent in his incivility. Jacqueline Scott, an African-American philosopher at Loyola University in Chicago, offers one anecdote:

> It is amazing how in many ways people literally don't see me. I remember my first job out of graduate school was at the University of Memphis. It was in my second semester and I was teaching a class of 180 students. It was in two classrooms and it wasn't even tiered or anything. So, it was just these long rows. And I sat in a chair just to the side waiting for the students to come in. And they were talking and they were like "Oh, yeah, I've heard she's really hard but she tells funny jokes." And they were just talking on and on and on. And then I waited until class started and I stood in the front and they still didn't get quiet. And so I said, "OK, we're ready to begin. We're ready to begin." And they kind of looked and said, "Well, when's the professor coming?" They thought I was one of the graduate students. And I said, "I am the professor." And there was a sort of silence. And there were heads turned to the side like, "A black woman philosophy professor? What is that?" Also, the students often called me Mrs. Scott, and every time I would find myself looking for my mother saying, "Where's my mom? She's here?" Even though I always referred to myself as Professor Scott, this is what happened. And they were so kind, but they were always saying, "So, when are you going to get that Ph.D.? It is so great that you are teaching. You are really funny." And I would say, "Well, I already have it." And again it was the pause and the head turned to the side like "What is that?" I still get that sometimes. They call me Mrs. You know, it's a nice title; it's perfectly fine. I don't insist on being called professor, but I wonder about my male colleagues, particularly my white male colleagues, and whether it is ever assumed that when they get in front of the classroom they don't have a Ph.D. (Scott, in Allen et al. 2008, 177–178)[13]

I have described at length circumstances where responsibility-competence is wrongly discredited owing to stereotype, bias, and marginalization. Having done so, we are in a position to investigate how the shared experiences of minority faculty offer evidence of underscrutinized asymmetries of power latent in communities of responsible interlocutors. To repeat, it is within dynamics of power that persons come to be considered reliable agents, credible interlocutors, and deserving members of the moral and broader community. It is within dynamics of social power that the normative expectations we have of ourselves and of each other originate. It is within dynamics of social power that persons judge one another as apt participants in the interpersonal relationships that characterize responsible agency. The classroom and, more broadly, the university experiences of women and minority faculty cast a pall on what I suggested at the outset of this section are benign, expected, and useful asymmetries of professional power. Almost invariably, the agential expectations we have of ourselves qua professional academicians are disturbed. Our credibility as interlocutors is undercut, and our entitlement to authority is tested. My experiences, and Antony's, and Scott's, and of too many women and minorities in the academy highlight myriad hindrances we must negotiate in representing ourselves as professional agents and in being acknowledged by others as such. Our students and some of our colleagues may (consciously or unconsciously) feel entitled to challenge our rightful authority and to disregard the proper conventions of accountability practice—for example, by demanding of us proof of our credentials to teach them—because of the enhanced social power they have come to expect given their privileged racial, socioeconomic, or gendered status. The incivility, microaggression, and skepticism encountered by underrepresented faculty can be traced to these social inequities.

Notably, though these challenges occur in the context of the university, the encumbrance is not confined there. Because the challenges touch at a staple of our identities, the effect is a diminution of the regard we might otherwise claim as responsible agents among our privileged, shielded peers. The more essential and frequent the context of the interaction, the more pervasive and consequential the effects. Academic faculty spend a good percentage of their adult lives interacting with students and with their colleagues. Recall that representation, and recognition or acknowledgment, hinge on confirmation of one's contribution as a credible player in the community. Members of other, more powerful ethnic, gendered, economic, and religious groups within the interlocutive community that is academe have monopolized the popular imagination as the prototype of that community. By virtue of their visibility and owing to the recognition they have been afforded, they have been authorized to decide the standards by which other members of the academy are acknowledged as credible practitioners of the discipline, and are deemed capable of setting the terms of academic and pedagogical practice. Persons such as Antony, Scott, and myself, who have not been reflected in the initial prototype, are thus vulnerable to lopsided expectations that we account for our academic practices to others, and that we justify, defend, and explain our professional agential standing. Others have presumed the right to expect accounts of our actions in the classroom, verification of our competence to execute properly our responsibilities, and to sometimes voice incredulity that we are epistemically sophisticated enough to understand what would constitute holding our students responsible in ways appropriate to the nature of our relationship with them.

While the bulk of these asymmetries are systemic, borne of the history of higher education, they may be compounded by stereotype threat. As women and as minorities, we may have brought to the dynamics of the classroom and to our professional relations the anxiety and insecure footing that implicit bias provokes. As women and as minorities, we are acting out the professorial role in a context fraught with pervasive biases about the group(s) with which we have some visible or emotional kinship. These biases are ones we are likely to have absorbed, though we may fight their influence. Consider a soundtrack about stereotyped intellectual capability, which both students and teachers have absorbed: this is the unrelenting dialogue (inescapable in philosophy departments and professional conferences) about "who is smart." Saul decries this feature of the profession of philosophy as a "vice" and one that is in all probability a byproduct of implicit bias.[14] Saul cites Eric Schwitzgebel, who notes,

> I have been collecting anecdotal data on seeming smart. One thing I've noticed is what sort of person tends spontaneously to be described, in my presence, as 'seeming smart.' A very striking pattern emerges: In every case I have noted the smart-seeming person has been a young white male. . . . Seeming smart is probably to a large extent about activating people's associations with intelligence. . . . And what do people associate with intelligence? Some things that are good: poise, confidence (but not defensiveness), giving a moderate amount of detail but not too much, providing some frame and jargon, etc. But also, unfortunately, I suspect: whiteness, maleness, a certain physical bearing, a certain dialect (one American type, one British type), certain patterns of prosody—all of which favor, I suspect, upper- to upper-middle class white men. (Saul 2015)

As minorities in the academy, the impression we may have of ourselves, and the impression our students and colleagues may have of us, can be that we just are not smart enough or smart in the "right" way. We may come to believe that we will do, and are expected to do, an inferior (or, at best, "different") job of educating our pupils. (A common refrain I hear is the worry that we will be unmasked as the frauds we fear we are.) As members of groups that are marginalized, or at least underrepresented in the context wherein agential responsibility is at stake, we must confront socially entrenched preconceptions about how we will perform—and the onus will be on us to prove that we can outstrip these presumptions.

This perversion of agential competence need not be owing to bigotry and animus, though implicit bias almost certainly contributes. This perversion of agential competence may be traced to the "exclusively or nearly exclusively male reading lists, overwhelmingly male lecturers, department seminar speakers" (Saul 2015), who are exhibited as the face of the discipline. Students in areas of study that, like philosophy, heavily emphasize logic, competence in which is stereotyped as the province of white males, rarely encounter and are unlikely to seek out as mentors women or people of color among the faculty. Scholarship by women and people of color are standardly absent from their course syllabi, though many teachers have come to appreciate the problem and have made concerted efforts to remedy the omission. Misguided views of agential competence may be due to well-entrenched ideas about femininity and proper behavior from people whose membership group is denigrated and divested of social power.

But that the perversion is innocent in origin and addressable in theory does not alter the injurious effect it has upon those party to it. I have no doubt that, as curricula in philosophy become more representative of the work of women, of ethnic, religious, and sexual minorities, and of persons with disabilities, attitudes in the profession will change for the better. However, we need vigilantly to draw attention to the default stance of discredit that underrepresented faculty confront as reliable interlocutors within the classroom. As participants in the exchanges that characterize ascriptions of responsibility, underrepresented professors should be presumed by their students (and colleagues) to be competent, credible, reliable, and trustworthy. If they are regarded as suspect in their ability to judge or to question the words, the behavior, and the performance of their students, whether or not this regard is tracked to nonculpable ignorance or implicit bias, their professional proficiency and operative authority are compromised. At best, they are forced to negotiate for a status that others are granted as a matter of course.

Let me close this section by stating just how mentally and emotionally arduous a task this can be. If, due to innocent but pervasive implicit bias, a person's standing to hold accountable and to be held accountable is diminished, and the onus is on the person to resurrect herself as a competent interlocutor, the person has effectively been relegated to inferior status qua robust agent. She must assume an additional task—that of proving herself entitled to the status she claims—where others in her professional situation carry no such burden. The burden is contoured to the expectations we have of persons of that type, and intensified by these:

> Women . . . remain in a bind. Engaging in agentic behaviors allows them to overcome descriptive stereotypes of lesser competence (Rudman 1998), but dominative agentic traits, such as being forceful, directive, and competitive, are incompatible with a prescribed communal orientation [of being nice, adaptive, accommodating, and so forth]. (Rudman and Glick 2001, 745)

4 Malignant Asymmetries II: Administering the Law in a Democratic Society

The second type of case I want to explore features an asymmetry of coercive power wielded by officers of the law coupled with asymmetrical responsibility practices on the part of law enforcement. Both asymmetries are suspect, as both exploit systemic social biases and inequities of power. Each type of asymmetry is anathema to democratic political engagement in large part because of the effect each has upon the responsible agency of participants in democratic processes. We should attend to the effects of bias and inequities of power upon persons in their capacity as responsible partners in the enterprise of democratic public life, if for no reason other than a concern for and fidelity to the principles of democracy. The US Department of State offers an official declaration of the ideals of democracy in action:

> Although nuances apply to the world's various democracies, certain principles and practices distinguish democratic government from other forms of government. . . . Democracies understand that one of their prime functions is to protect such basic human rights as freedom of speech and religion; the right to equal protection under law; and the opportunity to organize and participate fully in the political, economic, and cultural life of society. Democracy subjects governments to the rule of law and ensures that all citizens receive equal protection under the law and that their rights are protected by the legal system. (US Department of State 2016)

One essential component of democratic citizenship is the ability to converse with others about matters of law and public policy that affect their lives. This ability can be traced to the possession of civil rights. In societies such as the United States, many of these rights are constitutionally enshrined and include the rights to freedom of movement, peaceful assembly and protest, and the right to bodily security. The execution of these rights depends on the presumption that those who enjoy them are competent to make proper use of the rights and are deserving of them. The conditions for competence are liberal; one need not be capable of complex reasoning to claim a right to bodily security or to freedom of association. However, as with most rights, one is at liberty to partake of these in a wider range of circumstances as one matures and as one's interaction in the world increases.

A second essential element of democratic life is protection under the rule of law rather than the rule of persons. While the American Bar Association (ABA) acknowledges that there is no precise definition of a system in which laws rather than persons rule, the World Justice Project of the ABA has proposed a working definition consisting of the following four principles in conjunction:

1. A system of self-government in which all persons, including the government, are accountable under the law;
2. A system based on fair, publicized, broadly understood and stable laws;
3. A fair, robust, and accessible legal process in which rights and responsibilities based in law are evenly enforced;
4. Diverse, competent, and independent lawyers and judges.
   (American Bar Association, Division for Public Education. Accessed May 16, 2016, 5)

The ABA notes that "our understanding of the rule of law in the United States did indeed develop around the belief that a primary purpose of the rule of law is the protection of certain basic rights" (4). A gloss might be that to assert the rule of law is to assert that laws and legal procedures pertain to all citizens equitably, equally, and with due process:

> The rule of law protects the rights of citizens, maintains order, and lim-its the power of government. All citizens are equal under the law. No one may be discriminated against on the basis of their race, religion, ethnic group, or gender. . . . No one is above the law, not even a king or an elected president. The law is fairly, impartially, and consistently enforced, by courts that are independent of the other branches of gov-ernment. If you are detained, you have the right to know the charges against you, and to be presumed innocent until proven guilty according to the law. (Diamond 2004)[15]

Together, these fundamentals of democratic life showcase the need for prac-tices of responsibility that are genuinely dialogical, just, and respectful. This is the third marker of democratic life. To take seriously civil rights and the rule of law is to take seriously the necessity of responsibility practices that are attentive to the asymmetrical dynamics that inform the activity of ascribing responsibility. It is to be sensitive to asymmetries that are present in being called upon to give an account of one's behavior. Respecting the rule of law calls upon those subject to it, and most importantly those who wield powers of enforcement, to question divergences in the confidence parties to the exchange have in the law and legal process. Responsibility practices that fall within the ambit of law enforcement in a democratic society should ensure all parties to the practice a standing that empowers them to be heard, to raise questions, and to persuade one another, and those party to the practices should be mindful that each party has this standing. Indeed, such practices should cultivate this empowerment. What I am calling the "democratic" elements of responsibility practice operate even where legitimate asymmetries of authority and credibility obtain, as where doctor and patient are accountable to one another for different things and with greater or lesser moral and legal consequence, or when trained and certified law enforcement professionals are granted coercive power over the public. The practices must be authorized or "owned" by all those who are affiliates to it. Interactional practices of responsibility that are merely permitted out of courtesy or whim, or are granted as an act of largesse, are not owned equally by the participants. Instead, they are practices that reflect the supremacy of selected, influential parties.[16] They are practices that signal the presence of questionable asymmetries of power and asymmetries within responsibility practice that jeopardize the democratic rule of law.

The past few years in the United States have spawned a flood of documented incidents of violence involving the abrogation of civil rights where this abrogation is correlated with race, sexual orientation, gender, religion, national origin, and disability. In the aftermath, stereotypes of the victims are circulated in the social media, conveying the message that the victim's conduct and mannerisms—manner of dress, manner of speech, and posture—signaled a threat. On many of these occasions, treatment of the victim has been captured in recordings and on video. These recordings indicate a refusal on the part of the assailant to regard the victim as a person in possession of civil rights, and as able and entitled to question the treatment meted out. Each incident bears witness to a flouting of accepted practices of respectful interlocutionary exchange and evaluative assessment. These practices, which constitute holding and being held accountable, are founded on a good-faith reliance that they will occur within the boundaries of the rules of law and with respect for the basic civil rights of the participants. These are incidents in which pernicious asymmetries of power, built upon social inequity, destabilize and render problematically asymmetric practices of moral and of legal responsibility.

The victims I have chosen to name are familiar. The stories of Oscar Grant III,[17] Trayvon Martin,[18] Eric Garner,[19] Michael Brown,[20] Tamir Rice,[21] Walter

Scott,[22] Freddie Gray,[23] Sandra Bland,[24] and Samuel DuBose[25] have, in little over six years, become synonymous with a defining lack of recognition of and respect for the agential standing accorded to people of color, and black males in particular.

Trayvon Martin's death—the first in the age of social media to capture the attention of the national news media—again forced the topic of disparities in assessments of moral responsibility and enforcement of law into the forefront of a national conversation.[26] At the time of his death, Martin was returning to his father's home from a nearby convenience store. He carried on his person a bottle of iced tea and a bag of Skittles candy. Martin was clad in a hooded sweat-shirt, something his killer, George Zimmerman (and others) likened to "gangsta" wear.[27] Despite being warned by an emergency police dispatcher not to pursue the matter on his own, Zimmerman followed Martin, claiming that Martin's behavior was "suspicious." This much is clear from Zimmerman's remarks to the dispatcher.

Zimmerman also felt justified in confronting Martin. We have only Zimmerman's word that Martin behaved in a way that marked him as some-one against whom lethal force was defensible under law, just as we have only Zimmerman's testimony that Martin *provoked* him to employ lethal force. Whatever the facts of their exchange, there was scant legal reason under Florida law for Zimmerman to withdraw from a confrontation. The lack of legal rea-son to refrain from violence—indeed, the existence of legal reason to mount a violent response—effectively shrouded from scrutiny the uncomfortable fact that Zimmerman failed to treat Martin as a person to whom respect and agen-tial standing were due. The law lent a patina of acceptability to what many have argued was Zimmerman's racist behavior.

Consider the provisions made for aggressors by Florida's self-defense ["Stand your ground"] law[28] under which Zimmerman mounted his defense. Consider their implication for practices of moral as well as legal responsibility. The rele-vant portions of the statute follow, with my italics to indicate those that figured prominently in Zimmerman's plea:

776.012   Use or Threatened Use of Force in Defense of Person

— (2)   *A person is justified in using or threatening to use deadly force if he or she reasonably believes that using or threatening to use such force is necessary to prevent imminent death or great bodily harm to himself or her-self or another or to prevent the imminent commission of a forcible felony. A person who uses or threatens to use deadly force in accordance with this subsection does not have a duty to retreat and has the right to stand his or her ground if the person using or threatening to use the deadly force is not engaged in a criminal activity and is in a place where he or she has a right to be.*[29]

776.041 Use or Threatened Use of Force by Aggressor

The justification described in the preceding sections of this chapter is not available to a person who:

(2)   *Initially provokes the use or threatened use of force against himself or herself, unless:*

(a) *Such force or threat of force is so great that the person reasonably believes that he or she is in imminent danger of death or great bodily harm and that he or she has exhausted every reasonable means to escape such danger other than the use or threatened use of force which is likely to cause death or great bodily harm to the assailant; or*

(b) In good faith, the person withdraws from physical contact with the assailant and indicates clearly to the assailant that he or she desires to withdraw and terminate the use or threatened use of force, but the assailant continues or resumes the use or threatened use of force.[30]

Judge Debra Nelson, presiding over *State of Florida v. George Zimmerman*,[31] did not refer to the "aggressor" clause of the law in her instructions to the jury.[32] Rather, she stated the standard to which George Zimmerman should be judged as follows:

In deciding whether George Zimmerman was justified in the use of deadly force, you must judge him by the circumstances by which he was surrounded at the time the force was used. *The danger facing George Zimmerman need not have been actual; however, to justify the use of deadly force, the appearance of danger must have been so real that a reasonably cautious and prudent person under the same circumstances would have believed that the danger could be avoided only through the use of that force. Based upon appearances, George Zimmerman must have actually believed that the danger was real. . . .* George Zimmerman . . . had no duty to retreat and had the right to stand his ground and meet force with force, including deadly force, if he reasonably believed that it was necessary to do so to prevent death or great bodily harm to himself.[33]

The prosecutor in *State of Florida v. George Zimmerman* did not succeed in persuading the jury that Zimmerman's belief that Martin presented "imminent danger of death or great bodily harm" was baseless.[34] Richard Thompson Ford, of the Stanford School of Law, notes that Zimmerman's acquittal was not surprising:

There were no witnesses to the events that led to the shooting, so no one to directly refute Zimmerman's version. Police mishandled crucial evidence, giving the defense an opening to discredit it. A very polished and credible forensics expert backed up Zimmerman's account, while the prosecution's expert seemed befuddled and uncertain. And, perhaps most important of all, Florida law is extremely lenient with respect to the use of deadly force in self-defense. In many states, deadly force is justified only if the shooter could not retreat and avoid the confrontation, but in Florida, there is no duty to retreat. All of this multiplied the possible scenarios that would justify shooting a teenager armed with a bag a candy and a can of iced tea. (2013)

Ta-Nehisi Coates (2013) similarly notes that the law as it applied to Zimmerman's defense in fact required very little of Zimmerman:

> Effectively, I can bait you into a fight and if I start losing I can legally kill you, provided I "believe" myself to be subject to "great bodily harm." It is then the state's job to prove—beyond a reasonable doubt—that I either did not actually fear for my life, or that my fear was unreasonable. In the case of George Zimmerman, even if the state proved that he baited an encounter (and I am not sure they did) they still must prove that he had no reasonable justification to fear for his life.

One might ponder the compatibility of Statute 776 with our professed fidelity to civil liberty and to the rule of law. I will set that question aside; I could not fairly tackle it in the space of this chapter. For that matter, it is not obvious how clarification on this would shed light on the problem at hand. The problem at hand is how persons, particularly persons of color in interactions with institutions of law enforcement, might find their standing as responsible agents reduced. My suggestion is that this reduction will be due, in large part, to a malignant asymmetry of power.

To appreciate this, let us begin by asking what might have put Zimmerman in imminent fear for his life. What was distinctive of the situation with Trayvon Martin that resulted in an escalation with lethal consequences? What did Zimmerman assume of Martin? The prosecution alleged, as did a good portion of the public, that nothing about the situation should have alarmed Zimmerman, unless one regards Martin's ethnicity, gender, age, and attire as cause for concern. Clearly Zimmerman did regard these as cause for concern that rose to the level of immediate danger. A ready explanation for why Zimmerman reacted this way is summed up by Robert Weisberg, a professor of law at Stanford University. Weisberg (2013) says,

> Suffice to say that in the United States today, perceptions of possible deadly threats are all-too-often race-inflected. Race-blindness in

resolving a case like this is impossible. Subtracting race from the case was a daunting challenge for the jurors. Race would have been implicit in the legal arguments and was sure to be unmentioned in the jury instruction. But the facts were these: Zimmerman knew Martin was African-American. Martin may have made assumptions about Zimmerman because Zimmerman was a non-black confronting a black. And trying to surmise how Zimmerman and Martin perceived each other was crucial to this case.

This explanation is not universally accepted. Given the muscle accorded to those who use deadly force by Statute 776, it is plausible that the legally correct, indeed unavoidable, verdict in the case was one of "not guilty." It is even arguable—although not, I would say, plausible—that *State of Florida v. George Zimmerman* should never have become a public forum about civil rights, "rather than a simple homicide case."[35]

But the philosophical issue with which I am concerned is not whether the proper verdict was reached under the law. Nor, as I have said, is the congruity of Statute 776 with preservation of the civil rights the central philosophical issue. The philosophical issue is whether the interactions between Zimmerman and Martin reflected a pernicious asymmetry of credibility, of recognition, and of regard for civil rights. The case urges us to ask these questions whether or not we believe justice was served. We need to ask why Martin was not afforded the opportunity to offer an account—even if Zimmerman was not entitled to demand one—of his presence in the neighborhood. We need to take seriously the likelihood that, whether due to entrenched stereotypes about race or fear of young adult males, the asymmetry is institutionalized in law. A person who is susceptible, because of race, sexual orientation, gender, religion, national origin, or disability, to treatment that stereotypes and degrades is a person whose life is one in which all three markers of democratic life are in short supply. A person who is susceptible, because of race, sexual orientation, gender, religion, national origin, or disability, to treatment that stereotypes and degrades is shortchanged in the possession of civil rights, in protection under the rule of law, and in access to practices of responsibility that are sincerely dialogical, just, and civil. In all, she is regarded as a less than fully capable participant in public life.

Acknowledging one another as equal participants in the interpersonal relationships definitive of a participatory democracy is essential to sustaining faith in the ideals of democracy. Being taken seriously as a competent interlocutive partner is a prerequisite to satisfying public interaction. This is true in everyday discursive exchanges as well as in more momentous circumstances, such as communicating one's expectations regarding medical care, negotiating one's wages, or interaction with institutions of the state. But this takes on critical urgency where confrontations involving the legally sanctioned and unprovoked use of lethal force are commonplace. Incidents of the sort I have described make a mockery of these ideals, just as they make a mockery of the lives of the people who are expected to uphold them.

5 Conclusion

The scenarios I have described, in which one suffers a loss of credibility as a responsible agent, constitute forms of social injustice. As Gerald Marsh reminds us,

> Credibility is, among other things, a kind of social power. Credible per-
> sons have an ability to control how things go in their social world vis à
> vis their power to control knowledge production. When we take the
> word of a credible informant, the informant thereby exercises social
> power: she influences what we believe. . . . Credibility is also often a
> kind of identity-power. Some persons are accorded credibility merely
> in virtue of who they are: male, white, upper-class, whereas some per-
> sons are not given credibility merely in virtue of who they are: working-
> class, black, female. (2011, 281)

When someone is denied the opportunity to offer an account, to require an account, or to have the account asked of them receive fair uptake, it is often owing to malignant asymmetries of authority that short-circuit respectful representation and recognition. Success in the social practices of being represented as a responsible party and being recognized as such turns on conscientious attention to the dynamics of power that shape the normative expectations we have of one another. Some persons, such as Oscar Grant III, Trayvon Martin, and Tamir Rice, were afforded no opportunity to offer an account. Others tried to assert themselves—consider Eric Garner's now catchphrase "I can't breathe," Freddie Gray's pleas for assistance as he was transported to a police station, or Sandra Bland's challenge to the officer who cited her for a traffic violation. But all suffered from perniciously asymmetric responsibility practices in which they were regarded with suspicion and derision because of their membership in a minority group. All were preemptively assessed and discredited as unworthy or "flawed" responsible agents. The assumption of an upright character, a benign quality of will and of action, plausibility of testimony, and the opportunity to speak that might be credited to members of more powerful social groups were wholly lacking in these exchanges. Thus it is arguable that those who held dominance in the responsibility exchanges—officers of the law or self-appointed neighborhood watchmen—felt at liberty to treat membership in the minority group as grounds for silencing, sanction, containment, and peremptory use of force. It is arguable that those who held dominance in the asymmetry of coercive power exploited this asymmetry, merging it with asymmetrical responsibility practices premised on systemic social biases. The result: responsibility practices that treated membership in the minority group as legitimate reason to suspend the hallmarks of democracy. They are de facto abrogations of civil liberty and of the rule of law. They are de facto abrogations of equitable responsibility practice. They are examples, of the most urgent and heart wrenching sort, of the need to take seriously the fact that in circumstances of asymmetrical power, those in positions of dominance may spurn (and are sometimes legally authorized to spurn) the standards and practices of shared accountability that are essential to a satisfactory interpretation of moral responsibility.[36]

Notes

1. I thank Catriona Mackenzie for raising this point.
2. Catriona Mackenzie explores these issues as well in her contribution to this volume.
3. 'Integrity' as in "the state of being sound and undamaged." *Encarta Dictionary* (North America).
4. I understand agency as a fairly robust state. An agent is a being who deliberates, reflects, decides, intends, and brings about states of affairs. Ideally, an agent sets standards of behavior for herself and is in control of herself, unlike a patient, or a being that is acted upon, managed, or caused to assume various states. See Oshana 2015, 96.
5. A few such situations are the negotiation of parenting and housekeeping duties; the negotiation of advancement in salary and position in the workforce; the negotiations involved in securing housing and in acquiring a mortgage; and the negotiation of unbiased representation in social media.
6. We are not always doing this. Judging responsible may go no further than crediting causal involvement, or may go as far as implicating one for what is blameworthy or praiseworthy. For helpful discussion of the spectrum, see Watson (1996) 2004; Smith 2012; and Shoemaker 2007, 2011.
7. See Oshana 2016.
8. See also Superson 1999; and Hanrahan and Antony 2005.
9. "Traditional gender relations clearly fit this mode. Women, who are societally subordinate to men, are stereotyped as being nicer (Eagly & Mladinic, 1989) and are more likely to enact subordinate roles that require communal traits (Eagly, 1987)" (Rudman and Glick 2001, 744).
10. The expectation that female faculty should conform to stereotyped gender roles is reflected in the evaluations they receive from their students. A not-infrequent complaint on my teaching evaluations is that I am not nice enough (sometimes, though, I receive a higher numeric evaluation when a student judges that I am nice). Speaking of the disparities in student evaluations for male and female professors of philosophy, Superson (1999, 7) notes that "[t]o reward a professor for being a good professor is to acknowledge that she or he does and should have institutional power. In contrast, to reward a female professor for conforming to gender stereotypes is to reward her for exhibiting traits that are typically inconsistent with having power and being able to use it in a meaningful way, including being subservient, nurturing, easy—in short, non-threatening."
11. See Rudman and Glick 2001, 744.
12. Donna-Dale Marcano reports that "[to] be a black woman in philosophy is an anomaly. We must remember that woman is herself an anomaly in the canon but to be black and a woman

is to be the extreme opposite of philosophy's canonical figures. The black woman's intellectual capacity and philosophical engagement is believed to be nothing less than a void. . . . My white male students may never articulate their aspirations to be a Socrates or Plato, and yet it is not unusual for many of them to envision themselves as purveyors of the tradition" (2008, 165). At the time I received my PhD, I was (by my best estimate) the fourteenth black woman in the United States to do so.

13. The struggle for power in the classroom obtains even in disciplines in which women and minorities are well-represented proportional to their numbers in the general population. Sociology is one such discipline. Tuitt et al. (2009) report that, at one large university in the Midwestern United States, a group of junior faculty of color in the fields of sociology and psychology compiled a narrative of their common experience as members of predominantly white institutions of higher education. The narrative describes what they characterize as "being in the line of fire," and "dealing with the micro-aggressions and macro-oppressions that are endemic to [their workplace]" (69). At the invitation of the Faculty Senate president, the narrative was presented to the faculty at large. The objective was to showcase and "challenge the ways that race and racism play a role in . . . pedagogical interactions," with the hope that in doing so their (predominantly white) colleagues would "better understand how race impacts our lives as faculty members on a daily basis" (71). The authors labeled their particular narrative "fictional" because it represented a distillation of the common experiences of the five junior faculty members. As a group, they reported the impact their racial identities had upon their experiences within the classroom and within the broader culture of their academic institutions. Here is a representative passage from the narrative:

> I have come to understand that I do not have the privilege of walking into a classroom and having students assume that I am a capable and credible teacher. Nor do I have the privilege of walking into a classroom and having people assume that I have earned my position through hard work and determination. I have to be deliberate in the subject matter that I teach so that others do not see me as an exception to their assumptions about who is qualified, about who has a right to be here. I also do not have the privilege of having people know that I am a well-educated person with three degrees, who teaches at a university, and who is an expert in my discipline. And throughout my journey in the academy, I have had plenty of experiences that remind me of the privileges that I do not have. I will continue to be suspect to my students, my peers, and to the world around me, regardless of my qualifications or academic accomplishments. (69)

14. "After all, they're judgments about what someone's capable of rather than their actual output: For example, 'He's really smart, but it just doesn't come through in his work' is a perfectly normal sort of thing to say. The same is true of the negative judgments: For example, 'She writes good papers, but that's just because she works so hard. I don't think she's really smart' " (Saul 2013, 54).

15. See also Diamond 2016.

16. Elsewhere I have argued that this would signal an absence of autonomy on the part of some of the discussants (Oshana 2006, 132–133).

17. "Oscar Grant III (1986–2009) was a young African-American man who was fatally shot in the early morning hours of New Year's Day 2009 by BART Police officer Johannes Mehserle in Oakland, California, United States. Responding to reports of a fight on a crowded Bay Area Rapid Transit train returning from San Francisco, BART Police officers detained Grant and several other passengers on the platform at the Fruitvale BART Station. Officer Johannes Mehserle and another officer had restrained Grant, forcing him to lie face down. Mehserle was unable to remove Grant's right arm from under his body in order to handcuff him. Mehserle drew his pistol and shot Grant once in the back. He later claimed that he had intended to use a Taser on him. Grant was unarmed. He was pronounced dead the next morning at Highland Hospital in Oakland. The events were captured on multiple official and private digital video and privately owned cell phone cameras. . . . On July 8, 2010, Mehserle was found guilty of involuntary manslaughter and not guilty of second-degree murder and voluntary manslaughter. . . . On November 5, 2010, Mehserle was sentenced to two years, minus time served. . . .

Mehserle was released under parole after serving 11 months. Oakland civil rights attorney John Burris filed a $25 million wrongful death claim against BART on behalf of Grant's family. BART settled with Grant's daughter and mother for a total of $2.8 million in 2011" (*Wikipedia* 2017).

18. On the evening of February 26, 2012, Martin—an unarmed seventeen-year-old African American student—was followed, confronted, shot, and killed near his home by George Zimmerman, a neighborhood watch captain in Sanford, Florida.

19. On "the afternoon of July 17, 2014, when two officers approached Mr. Garner as he stood unarmed on a sidewalk, and accused him of selling untaxed cigarettes. One of the officers used a chokehold—prohibited by the Police Department—to subdue him, and that was cited by the medical examiner as a cause of Mr. Garner's death" (Goodman 2015).

20. Brown, an unarmed black teenager, was shot and killed on August 9, 2014, by Darren Wilson, a white police officer, in Ferguson, Missouri, a suburb of St. Louis (Buchanan et al. 2015).

21. Tamir Rice, a twelve-year-old boy, was shot and killed by police on November 22, 2014, in Cleveland, Ohio. Two police officers responded after receiving a police dispatch call of a male black sitting on a swing and pointing a gun at people in a city park.

Because of multiple layers in Cleveland's 911 system, crucial information from the initial call about "a guy in here with a pistol" was never relayed to the responding police officers, including the caller's caveats that the gun was "probably fake" and that the wielder was "probably a juvenile." What the officers, (46-year-old) Frank Garmback and his (26-year-old) rookie partner, Tim Loehmann, did hear from a dispatcher was, "We have a Code 1," the department's highest level of urgency. When the officers raced into action, they took a shortcut that pointed their squad car straight into the park, pulling up so close to Tamir that it made it difficult to take cover, or to use verbal persuasion or other tactics suggested by the department's use-of-force policy. Within two seconds of the car's arrival, Officer Loehmann shot Tamir in the abdomen from point-blank range, raising doubts that he could have warned the boy three times to raise his hands, as the police later claimed. And when Tamir's 14-year-old sister came running up minutes later, the officers, who are white, tackled her to the ground and put her in handcuffs, intensifying later public outrage about the boy's death. When his distraught mother arrived, the officers also threatened to arrest her unless she calmed down, the mother, Samaria Rice, said. Officers Garmback and Loehmann did not check Tamir's vital signs or perform first aid in the minutes after he was shot. But Officer Garmback frantically requested an emergency medical team at least seven times, urging the dispatcher to "step it up" and to send medical workers from a fire station a block away. It would be eight minutes before they arrived. (Dewan and Oppel Jr. 2015)

22. Scott was shot and killed on April 4, 2015, in North Charleston, South Carolina, following a routine daytime traffic stop for a nonfunctioning brake light by Michael Slager, a white North Charleston police officer. "The case initially failed to engage national media attention, with Slager maintaining that he had killed Scott because he feared for his own safety after Scott had attempted to take his Taser. But . . . eyewitness video emerged, filmed on a cellphone and telling an entirely different tale. The footage showed Scott running away from Slager, who fired eight times, striking the unarmed Scott four times in the back" (Laughland 2015).

23. Twenty-five-year old Gray died April 19, 2015, a week after he was chased and restrained by police officers. Gray suffered a fatal spinal injury while being transported in their custody (Stolberg and Nixon 2015).

24. Sandra Bland was a 28-year-old black woman who was found hanged in a jail cell in Waller County, Texas, on July 13, 2015. Her death was classified as a suicide by the county coroner and was followed by protests against her arrest disputing the cause of death and alleging racial violence against her. Bland had been pulled over for a minor traffic violation [failure to signal a lane change] on July 10 by state trooper Brian Encinia. He arrested her following an escalating conflict during which he alleged that she had assaulted him and which was recorded by his dashcam and by a bystander's cell phone. After authorities reviewed the

dashcam footage, Encinia was placed on administrative leave for failing to follow proper traffic stop procedures. (*Wikipedia* 2016)

Following a grand jury investigation, Encinia was indicted for perjury (Montgomery 2016).

25. Samuel DuBose was killed by a white officer during a routine traffic stop in what a prosecutor called a "senseless, asinine shooting." . . . Mr. DuBose, 43, was shot and killed on July 19 [2015] by Officer Ray Tensing, who pulled him over in a Cincinnati neighborhood adjacent to the campus because his car lacked a front license plate. The shooting was captured on a body camera, and Officer Tensing, who was fired from the department, faces trial on a charge of murder. (Stolberg 2016)

The publically funded University of Cincinnati agreed to a settlement of nearly $5 million (USD) with DuBose's family after two days of mediation.

26. I say 'again' because the conversation is one that the nation regularly confronts. No sooner has the name of one victim of law enforcement's mistreatment of minorities faded from memory (to wit, a prostate Rodney King, viciously beaten by members of the Los Angeles police force in 1991; Abner Louima, violently sodomized with a broomstick by officers of the New York City Police Department at a Brooklyn precinct station house in 1997 [see Chan 2007]) than another arises.

27. Coates (2013) decries "the criminalization of Martin across the country," citing "the Trayvon Martin imagery used for target practice (by law enforcement, no less)," "the theory . . . floated by Zimmerman's family that Martin was a gun-runner and drug-dealer in training." "Or the theory floated that the mere donning of a hoodie marks you a thug, leaving one wondering why [Trayvon Martin wearing a hoodie] is a criminal and [Brad Pitt wearing a hoodie] is not." Of Martin's death, Geraldo Rivera of *Fox News* commented, "You dress like a thug, people are going to treat you like a thug. That's true. I stand by that." https://www.mediamatters.org/video/2013/07/14/foxs-geraldo-rivera-you-dress-like-a-thug-peopl/194866. Accessed June 11, 2016.

28. 2011 Florida Statutes Title XLVI, Chapter 776, Section 041, https://www.flsenate.gov/Laws/Statutes/2011/776.041. The current law can be found at 2016 Florida Statutes, Title XLVI, Crimes, Chapter 776, "Justifiable Use of Force," http://www.leg.state.fl.us/statutes/index.cfm?App_mode=Display_Statute&URL=0700-0799/0776/0776.html.

29. 2011 Florida Statutes Title XLVI Chapter 776 Section 041. https://www.flsenate.gov/Laws/Statutes/2011/776.041. Accessed January 7, 2016.

30. 2011 Florida Statutes Title XLVI Chapter 776 Section 041. https://www.flsenate.gov/Laws/Statutes/2011/776.041. Accessed January 7, 2016.

31. *State of Florida v. George Zimmerman*, Case Number 592012-CF001083-A, 18th Judicial Circuit in and for Seminole County, Florida. Decided July 13, 2013, Judge Debra Nelson presiding.

32. In fact, instruction on this law

was discussed by the prosecution and defense at the hearing on the jury instructions. . . . The prosecution wanted the judge to instruct the jury on that law, allowing the jury to conclude that Zimmerman was the "aggressor." The prosecution claimed that "profiling" and "following" Martin made Zimmerman an "aggressor" under that law. The defense, relying on *Gibbs v. State of Florida*, 789 So. 2d 443—Fla: Dist. Court of Appeals, 4th Dist. 2001, http://scholar.google.com/scholar_case?case=15783778784317286558 argued that the law was clear that, in order to be the "aggressor," or in order to provoke the use of force against you, you have to be the first one to use or threaten actual force. "Profiling" and "following" are not using or threatening actual force, and therefore doing those things does not make Zimmerman the "aggressor" under that law. The defense said the judge should not give the "aggressor" instruction because the prosecution had not presented the court with evidence that Zimmerman was an "aggressor" under that law. The judge ruled that the Court would not give the instruction (essentially ruling for the defense). (Hartmann 2013)

33. My italics. Judge Debra Nelson, July 12, 2013. http://www.cnn.com/TRANSCRIPTS/1307/12/cnr.11.html. CNN NEWSROOM, Zimmerman Trial Deliberations to Begin Shortly. Aired July 12, 2013 - 14:00 ET. Accessed November 3, 2017.

34. The six jurors—all of them women—deliberated for 16½ hours. Five of the women are white; one is a minority. The jury had three choices: to find Zimmerman guilty of second-degree murder; to find him guilty of a lesser charge of manslaughter; or to find him not guilty. For second-degree murder, the jurors would have had to believe that Martin's unlawful killing was "done from ill will, hatred, spite or an evil intent" and would be "of such a nature that the act itself indicates an indifference to human life." (Botelho and Yan 2013)
35. Sridutt Nimmagadda of the *Independent Political Report*, a starkly conservative-leaning website, presses this view at Nimmagadda, 2013, ". . . AND JUSTICE FOR ALL: An Analysis of the State of Florida vs. George Zimmerman Case," http://independentpoliticalreport.com/2013/07/sridutt-nimmagadda-an-analysis-of-the-state-of-florida-vs-george-zimmerman-case/.
36. A version of this chapter was presented at the XIX Philosophy Colloquium on Action, Agency, and Responsibility at Unisinos in Sao Leopoldo, Brazil in October 2016. I am grateful to the audience, and especially to Marco Azevedo, Adriano Naves de Brito, David Copp, Isabel Limongi, and Sofia Stein for their comments. Thanks, too, to Catriona Mackenzie and Katrina Hutchison for helpful comments on prior drafts of the chapter, and to Wendy Carlton for her careful editorial assistance.

References

Allen, Anita, Anika Maaza Mann, Donna-Dale L. Marcano, Michele Moody-Adams, and Jacqueline Scott. 2008. "Situated Voices: Black Women in/on the Profession of Philosophy." *Hypatia* 23 (2): 160–189.

American Bar Association, Division for Public Education. "Part I: What Is the Rule of Law?" Accessed May 16, 2016.

Botelho, Greg, and Holly Yan. 2013. "George Zimmerman Found Not Guilty of Murder in Trayvon Martin's Death." CNN.com Sun July 14, 2013. http://www.cnn.com/2013/07/13/justice/zimmerman-trial/index.html.

Buchanan, Larry, Ford Fessenden, K. K. Rebecca Lai, Haeyoun Park, Alicia Parlapiano, Archie Tse, Tim Wallace, Derek Watkins, and Karen Yourish. 2015. "Q&A: What Happened in Ferguson?" *New York Times*, last updated August 10. http://www.nytimes.com/interactive/2014/08/13/us/ferguson-missouri-town-under-siege-after-police-shooting.html.

Chan, Sewell. 2007. "The Abner Louima Case, 10 Years Later." *New York Times*, August 9. https://cityroom.blogs.nytimes.com/2007/08/09/the-abner-louima-case-10-years-later/comment-page-1/?_r=0.

Coates, Ta-Nehisi. 2013. "Trayvon Martin and the Irony of American Justice." *Atlantic*, July 15. http://www.theatlantic.com/national/archive/2013/07/trayvon-martin-and-the-irony-of-american-justice/277782/.

Dewan, Shaila, and Richard A. Oppel, Jr. 2015. "In Tamir Rice Case, Many Errors by Cleveland Police, Then a Fatal One." *New York Times*, January 22. http://www.nytimes.com/2015/01/23/us/in-tamir-rice-shooting-in-cleveland-many-errors-by-police-then-a-fatal-one.html.

Diamond, Larry. 2004. "What Is Democracy?" Lecture at Hilla University College for Humanistic Studies, Babylon, Iraq, January 21. https://web.stanford.edu/~ldiamond/iraq/WhaIsDemocracy012004.htm.

Diamond, Larry. 2016. "Democracy Education for Iraq—Nine Brief Themes." Accessed May 16. https://web.stanford.edu/~ldiamond/iraq/DemocracyEducation0204.htm.

Ford, Richard Thompson. 2013. "The Law That Acquitted Zimmerman Isn't Racist. But That Doesn't Mean the Outcome Wasn't." *New Republic*, July 16. https://newrepublic.com/article/113873/zimmerman-trial-racist-laws.

Goodman, J. David. 2015. "Eric Garner Case Is Settled by New York City for $5.9 Million." *New York Times*, July 13. https://www.nytimes.com/2015/07/14/nyregion/eric-garner-case-is-settled-by-new-york-city-for-5-9-million.html.

Hanrahan, R., and Louise Antony. 2005. "Because I Said So: Toward a Feminist Theory of Authority." *Hypatia* 20 (4): 59–79.

Hartmann, Thom. 2013. "Why Were Trayvon Martin and George Zimmerman Held to Two Different Standards of Justice?" Truthout. July 17. http://www.truth-out.org/opinion/item/17637-why-were-trayvon-martin-and-george-zimmerman-held-to-two-different-standards-of-justice.

Laughland, Oliver. 2015. "Walter Scott: Hundreds Gather in Church and in Rain to Mourn Man Shot by Officer." *Guardian*, April 11.

Marcano, Donna-Dale. 2008. "Situated Voices: Black Women in/on the Profession of Philosophy." *Hypatia* 23 (2): 160–189.

Marsh, Gerald. 2011. "Trust, Testimony, and Prejudice in the Credibility Economy." *Hypatia* 26 (2): 280–293.

Montgomery, David. 2016. "Texas Trooper Who Arrested Sandra Bland Is Charged with Perjury." *New York Times*, January 6. http://www.nytimes.com/2016/01/07/us/texas-grand-jury-sandra-bland.html.

Nimmagadda, Sridutt. 2013. ". . . AND JUSTICE FOR ALL: An Analysis of the State of Florida vs. George Zimmerman Case." http://independentpoliticalreport.com/2013/07/sridutt-nimmagadda-an-analysis-of-the-state-of-florida-vs-george-zimmerman-case/.

Oshana, Marina. 1997. "Ascriptions of Responsibility." *American Philosophical Quarterly* 34 (1): 71–83.

Oshana, Marina. 2004. "Moral Accountability." *Philosophical Topics* 32 (1–2): 255–274.

Oshana, Marina. 2006. *Personal Autonomy in Society*. Aldershot: Ashgate.

Oshana, Marina. 2010. *The Importance of How We See Ourselves: Self-Identity and Responsible Agency*. Rowman and Littlefield: Lexington Books.

Oshana, Marina. 2015. "Memory, Self-Understanding, and Agency." In *The Philosophy of Autobiography*, edited by Christopher Cowley, 96–121. Chicago: The University of Chicago Press.

Oshana, Marina. 2016. "A Feminist Approach to Moral Responsibility." In *The Routledge Companion to Free Will*, edited by Meghan Griffiths, Neil Levy, and Kevin Timpe, 623–632. New York: Routledge.

Rivera, Geraldo. 2013. "You dress like a thug, people are going to treat you like a thug. That's true. I stand by that." https://www.mediamatters.org/video/2013/07/14/foxs-geraldo-rivera-you-dress-like-a-thug-peopl/194866.

Rudman, Laurie A., and Peter Glick. 2001. "Prescriptive Gender Stereotypes and Backlash Toward Agentic Women." *Journal of Social Issues* 57 (4): 743–762.

Saul, Jennifer. 2013. "Implicit Bias, Stereotype Threat, and Women in Philosophy." In *Women in Philosophy: What Needs to Change?*, edited by Fiona Jenkins and Katrina Hutchison, 39–60. Oxford: Oxford University Press.

Saul, Jennifer. 2015. "Women in Philosophy." *TPM: The Philosophers Magazine*, January 23. https://www.philosophersmag.com/opinion/9-women-in-philosophy.

Scott, Jacqueline. 2008. "Situated Voices: Black Women in/on the Profession of Philosophy." *Hypatia* 23 (2): 160–189.

Shoemaker, David. 2007. "Moral Address, Moral Responsibility, and the Boundaries of the Moral Community." *Ethics* 118 (1): 70–108.

Shoemaker, David. 2011. "Attributability, Answerability, and Accountability: Toward a Wider Theory of Moral Responsibility." *Ethics* 121 (3): 602–632.

Smith, Angela. 2012. "Attributability, Answerability, and Accountability: In Defense of a Unified Account." *Ethics* 122 (3): 575–589.

Steele, Claude M., and Joshua Aronson. 1995. "Stereotype Threat and Intellectual Performance of African Americans." *Journal of Personality and Social Psychology* 69 (5): 797–811.

Stolberg, Sheryl Gay, and Ron Nixon. 2015. "Freddie Gray in Baltimore: Another City, Another Death in the Public Eye." *New York Times*, April 21. https://www.nytimes.com/2015/04/22/us/another-mans-death-another-round-of-questions-for-the-police-in-baltimore.html.

Stolberg, Sheryl Gay. 2016. "University of Cincinnati to Pay $4.85 Million to Family of Man Killed by Officer." *New York Times*, January 18. https://www.nytimes.com/2016/01/19/us/university-of-cincinnati-to-pay-4-85-million-to-family-of-man-killed-by-officer.html.

Superson, Anita 1999. "Sexism in the Classroom: The Role of Gender Stereotypes in the Evaluation of Female Faculty." *American Philosophical Association Newsletter on Feminism and Philosophy* 99 (1): 46–51. Citations refer to a pre-publication copy provided by the author.

Thompson, Morgan, Toni Adleberg, Sam Sims, and Eddy Nahmias. 2016. "Why Do Women Leave Philosophy? Surveying Students at the Introductory Level." *Philosopher's Imprint* 16 (6): 1–36.

Tuitt, Frank, Michele Hanna, Lisa M. Martinez, María del Carmen Salazar, and Rachel Griffin. 2009. "Teaching in the Line of Fire: Faculty of Color in the Academy." *NEA Higher Education Journal* (Thought & Action) 25: 65–74.

US Department of State. 2016. "Principles of Democracy." US Department of State's Bureau of International Information Programs. Accessed May 16. https://www.state.gov/j/drl/democ/.

Walker, Margaret Urban. 2007. *Moral Understandings*. 2nd ed. New York: Oxford University Press.

Watson, Gary. (1996) 2004. "Two Faces of Responsibility." Reprinted in *Agency and Answerability*, 219–259. Oxford: Clarendon Press.

Weisberg, Robert. 2013. "Some Thoughts on State v. Zimmerman." SLS Blogs. July 18. https://law.stanford.edu/2013/07/18/some-thoughts-on-state-v-zimmerman/.

Wikipedia. 2016. "The Death of Sandra Bland." Accessed June 22. https://en.wikipedia.org/w/index.php?title=Death_of_Sandra_Bland&oldid=726215993.

Wikipedia. 2017. "The Shooting of Oscar Grant." Accessed March 19. https://en.wikipedia.org/w/index.php?title=Shooting_of_Oscar_Grant&oldid=770795805.

4

The Social Constitution of Agency and Responsibility

Oppression, Politics, and Moral Ecology

MANUEL R. VARGAS

1 Introduction

When people are subject to oppression, does that fact undermine their culpability for wrongdoing?[1] No uncomplicated answer is appealing. On the one hand, it seems callous to insist that someone's being subject to oppression is never relevant to her culpability. On the other hand, it seems implausible and disrespectful to insist that no one is ever responsible for wrongdoing under oppression.

One skeptical view is that this puzzle about oppression is the product of a deeper problem. The conviction that people can be responsible under oppression is a recalcitrant conviction grounded in the naïve belief that people are free in a way that allows them to transcend their circumstances. Similarly, the exculpatory impulse that emerges when we think about oppression is a species of the more general thought that *all* actions are conditioned in the same sort of way, as products of prior causal forces. On this view, the puzzle about culpability under oppression is just the conflict between our naïveté and our recognition that we are products of circumstance.

If this skeptical worry is familiar, so is the reply. Optimists insist that there is a way to ground the difference between culpable and nonculpable action. They typically appeal to some privileged bit of psychological functioning: the possibility of acting from values, commitments, or rationality; the reasonability of asking people to justify themselves; or the putatively theory-neutral commitments of affective responses to wrongdoing. In the context of thinking about culpability under oppression, however, there is something prima facie dissatisfying about the optimist's strategy. To point to psychological features as the basis of responsibility misses the force of the worry that oppression undermines culpability. The skeptical worry *just is* that our psychologies are shaped by social context in a way that makes us not culpable.

There are two ways forward. One is to insist on the philosophically fraught possibility of our being able to transcend our circumstances in some robust way. A second, perhaps less intuitively appealing approach is to show how to acknowledge that our agency is socially constituted without surrendering the distinction between culpable and nonculpable actions. This chapter pursues the second path.

An idea that animates some of what follows is that we tend to think about culpability in the wrong way, as almost exclusively settled by intrinsic features of the agent and her actions. Culpability is a function not just of agents, but of the agent's relationship to circumstances and the governing normative practices. The foundations of culpability are as much political and normative as metaphysical. Oppression is particularly interesting because it has varied effects on culpability: sometimes it eliminates it, sometimes it makes it harder to do the right thing, and other times, it enables responsible agency. The upshot is that the nature of culpability under oppression—and what we can do about it—is complex.

Section 2 outlines the basic puzzle and reasons for rejecting the idea that we possess a transcendent form of agency that obviates the need to explain how social forces might affect culpability. Section 3 provides an account of the basis of moral culpability that accommodates the fact of the social constitution of our agency while specifying the normative function of responsibility practices. On this picture, responsible agency is socially constituted in two ways. First, the acquisition of our values and dispositions, and how they are maintained are fundamentally social matters, continuously shaped by social feedback. Second, facts about what social practices are effective at fostering moral considerations—facts outside the head of the agent—fix what capacities matter for culpability and determine whether a given agent's psychology can be rightly said to be able to respond to moral considerations. Section 4 applies this account to culpability under oppression, arguing that oppression can affect our ability to respond to moral considerations as well as the standards that determine what it is for us to be able to respond to moral considerations. The final section explores the implications of this picture for larger questions about the social and political ecology of culpable agency. Once we see culpability as partly a function of the social constitution of agency, we have reasons to reflect on the limits of social and political interventions that structure that agency. In sum, agents can be culpable under oppression, and this is something we have some control over, but the particulars matter.

2 Agency in Circumstances

I began by noting that it can seem both disrespectful and too forgiving of oppressed people to maintain that they are not culpable for wrongdoing under oppression. The skeptic will object that, respectful or not, it is false that people can be responsible under oppression. I reject the skeptical view, but it is instructive to begin by considering an idea that animates it, namely, the evident tension between two families of truisms about the agency required for culpability.

One set of truisms about individual agency includes the following: people are ordinarily agents; sometimes they act intentionally, and other times they don't; some actions are freely undertaken, and others are not; some actions deserve moral praise and blame, and others do not. A second set of truisms concern the relationship of context and agency. This set includes thoughts of this sort: what people do is a matter of their circumstances; circumstances matter both for what we care about and what we can do; what seems valuable or appealing to an agent is a product of upbringing and socialization; what powers a person has in a given situation are products of history and forces outside of the control of the agent.

It is unclear how both sets of ideas could be simultaneously true. Our common-sense ideas of culpable agency—that agents are at fault, that they deserve blame and condemnation for wrongdoing—seem to require some independence from circumstances. When the effects of circumstances are particularly salient, as when one is stressed or subject to some unusual pressure, we tend to excuse the effects of those circumstances. That exculpatory impulse can seem like the thin edge of a wedge. Once we recognize the fact that who we are and what we do is a product of either antecedent forces or circumstances over which we have no control (as we do when we forgive someone for being stressed or exhausted), it is unclear how this is different in kind from any circumstantial source of our dispositions and behavior. Accountability threatens to dissipate in the face of appeals to circumstance.

The challenge here is not always one of clear contradiction. Rather, it seems to be a matter of one explanation trumping or undermining another (cf. Björnsson and Persson 2013). In our interpersonal lives, we tend to act as though our ideas about individual agency are fundamental and secure. When we shift our attention to context, though, the fact that agency seems to be a product of social (and other) kinds of circumstances somehow makes the truisms about individual agency seem less evident. In the social sciences, this tension is often characterized in terms of the structure-agency problem. Especially (but not exclusively) in sociology, a persistent challenge is how to square explanations that emphasize the explanatory or causal role of social structures with the idea that individual agents make free choices. In philosophy, variants of the problem tend to emerge in debates about moral luck, free will, moral responsibility, and autonomy.

Determinism, mechanism, socialization, and the social structuring of an agent's option set are taken to threaten the possibility of various ideals of agency, including morally responsible agency (e.g., Pereboom 2001; Greene and Cohen 2004).

Some caution is in order. We sometimes talk of agency, full stop, as though it were a single thing, the contours of which we all agree upon. This way of talking can mislead, both about the variety of forms of agency and about the particular challenges that threaten distinct forms of agency. There are convictions about agency that are unaffected by attention to circumstances. Creatures resolve practical challenges with different kinds of deliberation: the squirrel decides whether to go for the acorn, the writer decides whether to keep typing, and the reader decides whether to take notes. These sorts of facts—facts about some pedestrian forms of agency—are not undermined by our acknowledging that these agents are part of a larger social or environmental context. The agency of the squirrel-as-acorn-pursuer, person-as-typist, and reader-as-note-taker is entirely compatible with thinking each is structured by, and a part of, external forces. Contrary to one reading of Nagel, agency does not always shrink "to an extensionless point" when we consider context and antecedents (1979, 35).

Redirecting our attention to wider social or environmental forces can diminish the salience of particular psychological facts about given agents. Diminished salience is only that, however. It is not the more radical and unwarranted claim that there is no genuine agency—that agents do not believe, desire, decide, intend, and attempt. What is more plausibly threatened by attention to circumstances are those forms of agency that make a claim about normative standing. Whether someone is free in a politically or morally relevant sense, whether we should take seriously someone's preferences in formulating our plans, whether we can appropriately praise and blame, whether someone acts autonomously— we can become uncertain about such questions when we highlight the role of context. Where values, sensibility, and the perception of reasons are structured or constituted by culture, norms, and values, and where the range of available acts is constrained by institutions, resources, and wider social meanings, it is harder to be confident about our normative assessments of agents.

Even if we were convinced that, in general, agency can be suitably distinguished from the wider causal fabric in a way that might support responsibility attributions, the internal structure of our practices shows some concern for the social origins of our motivations, values, and judgments. At first pass, we tend to suppose that an adult of ordinary knowledge and capabilities is culpable for knowingly putting a child at risk of unnecessary injury. So, if a soccer parent harms a child by insisting on unreasonable athletic performance—e.g., insisting on the child playing through a significant injury—we are inclined to hold the parent responsible. (We are also often prepared to find fault for modestly indirect effects of parenting choices on the maturing child.) However, that initial presumption of culpability is vulnerable to exculpatory pressures *internal to the practice*. Suppose we learn that our soccer-crazed adult grew up in a sports-obsessed environment, one that downplayed the seriousness of the risk to the child while glorifying the risk-taking of playing while injured. For many of us, this additional bit of information makes the initial certainty that the parent is fully culpable at least somewhat less certain. To the extent that one acquires normative standards by cultural osmosis, and one is in a cultural milieu that discourages and even attempts to disable critical reflection on those standards, it is less obvious that the offending adult is as culpable as our initial reactions tend to suggest. The fact of the always-lurking exculpatory element of context invites further explanation.

There is a more general phenomenon at work here. When our values, knowledge, or moral convictions are at some remove from those we are considering condemning, there is some tendency—for at least us, here and now—to be unsure how to proceed in our assessments of blame. We might still find their behavior repugnant, ill-considered, or reprehensible. The strength of these reactions and what follows presumably reflects, among other things, our sense of the degree to which the offender is a member of our in-groups, the nature of the perceived offense, and so on. However, our confidence that some action is morally reprehensible can rest (perhaps with some discomfort) alongside our uncertainty about the culpability of those performing it (Watson 1987). Wrongfulness and culpability come apart.

A good deal of our moral sensibility is socially constituted. However, it is not merely that social influences sometimes bypass our rational, valuing agency, but that these influences *just are* the things that generate and sustain our motivations, cares, values, and habits of regard in the first place. That's why the typical approach of optimists about responsibility—rooting distinctions of culpability in privileged bits of psychology, whether in desires, values, rational capacities, commitments, or judgments—seems unresponsive to the thread of thinking that seems to animate one part of our attitudes about oppression. Once we attend to it, the usual way we acquire values and commitments seems to undermine culpability.[2]

Here some will interject with the claim that it is the possession of free will that allows us to disregard questions of social context.[3] If an appeal to free will is supposed to help explain why agents can be influenced by context but still culpable, then free will must be the sort of thing that licenses our praising and blaming of one another—even in the face of the evident fact that our choices, values, and aspirations have been subject to social and other influences.[4] Transcendent agency is roughly the idea that agency is not importantly constrained by or limited to features of circumstance or experience. The idea that we have a kind of "contra-causal" freedom, perhaps coupled with something like substance dualism, is one way of giving expression to this elusive thought.

The appeal of this picture of agency is clear. If we do have such freedom, then the social dimensions of the structure and exercise of our agency is mostly irrelevant, precisely because it can be transcended or overcome. Moreover, the view seems to have deep roots in aspects of ordinary convictions about agency (Vargas 2013a; Nichols 2015).

Alas, the idea of transcendent agency is more aspirationally alluring than philosophically satisfying. First, it is not clear what basis there is—or could be—for transcending anything. On standard philosophical and scientific models of agency, anything we do is a product of circumstance, biology, physical structure, or the interaction of these things. To the extent to which these forces are not in our control, it is not clear how anything we do could count as transcending these influences, absent some special story that is at odds with most current scientific and philosophical views. Second, it is not clear what the basis for decision-making would be, even if we could transcend the particulars of our context, biology, or underlying physical structure. It is not obvious why decision-making entirely disconnected from the discernible features of the context of decision would be an appealing picture for the basis of culpability. Transcendent agency would also be opaque to us—inasmuch as it would be radically disconnected from our understanding of the physical, causal world, it is not clear how we could understand its basis, when it occurs, or whether someone is systematically incapable of such transcendence for some or another reason.[5]

It is not irrelevant that the various brain, cognitive, and behavioral sciences suggest that our everyday notion of agency is systematically mistaken in a number of different ways, and that may include our sense of our being transcendent agents. Conscious, reflective agency seems to play a considerably lesser role in what we do than ordinary conceptions of agency presume (Nahmias 2010; Levy 2014; Doris 2015). We are prone to invisible biases whose operations are not always readily discernible, and seemingly irrelevant features of situations and contexts propel and sometimes disable agency in ways agents fail to recognize and would tend to disavow if informed (Doris 2002; Nelkin 2005; Nahmias 2007; Vargas 2013b; Doris 2015; McKenna and Warmke, forthcoming). This is not to make the radical point that conscious control is illusory, that we never understand our motives, or that self-aware agency is impossible to attain. There are various reasons to think that the most radical versions of these views are implausible (Mele 2009). It nevertheless remains true that we oftentimes have an uneasy grip on why we do what we do.

What I take to be the general lesson of contemporary cognitive science is this: we underestimate the degree to which our actions are structured by situational pressures and automatic processing that operates below the level of conscious awareness. In turn, this suggests a kind of challenge to views that insist on our transcendence—even if we really did sometimes transcend our circumstances, biology, and physical relations, it is clear that automatic processing, regular, discernible patterns of bias, situational effects, and so on are the order of the day. Given that most exercises of agency do not suggest a radical independence from the causal and social order, we are back to the basic challenge: to the extent that we are a part of—embedded in, we might say—a social order, and given the forms of agency that are compatible with a causal, naturalistic conception of humans, can we show that people are culpable?

The issues here are complex. Does social deprivation (in the form of poverty or social stigma, for example) impair responsible agency? Is otherwise culpable action subject to mitigation when performed under conditions of oppression (as when a battered spouse kills the batterer)? Does unjust or repeated exposure to risks or harms change the moral significance of some otherwise culpable acts?[6] The philosophical literature on freedom and responsibility has been mostly silent on these questions, but if we accept that culpability has a relationship to the social constitution of our agency, these questions are not peripheral.

It would be a mistake to suppose that political and legal considerations exhaust the way in which our agency is socially structured. There is a web of more broadly social categories and roles that structure which actions seem appealing and how we think about ourselves (Hacking 1995; Haslanger 2012), which values are easier to live out, and the control one has over the perception of one's intentions (Bierria 2014). The wrong sorts of socialization seem to undermine one's suitability as a target of the reactive attitudes (Wolf 1987; Watson 1987). If one goes on to think that, in general, our agency is socially scaffolded (Vargas 2013a; McGeer 2015; Doris 2015; Huebner 2016), or dependent on interaction and feedback from other agents, then both the presence but also *the absence* of certain kinds of social feedback will affect whether someone is a responsible agent. The issue here is not just whether one is responsible or not. Sometimes the stakes are subtler. A particularly insidious way for the social world to be structured is where, perhaps invisibly, the context makes it particularly difficult to exercise one's responsible agency.

One promising idea is that it is better to think of sociality as an enabling condition of our agency, rather than a constraint. Vindicating this idea is no easy task. Beyond accommodating the idea that who we are and what we value are frequently given by, or at least structured by, social context, an adequate account will also need to accommodate the idea that what *opportunities* we have are often socially structured. Collectively, these thoughts suggest that we do poorly to approach responsible agency in atomistic or individualist terms. If the nature of our agency and the social structure of our opportunities are products of, among other things, political institutions and practices, then responsible agency is partly a matter of how our social, political, and even ideological circumstances are arranged. Call this *the challenge of social circumstances for moral responsibility.*

Let's turn to how we might answer that challenge.

3 Agency Cultivation

Here, I propose a way of balancing our commitments to the idea of responsible agency with facts about the social structuring, scaffolding, and constitution of that agency. There are two desiderata governing what follows. First, the ambition is to offer a metaphysically modest account of moral responsibility that allows for *the social constitution of agency.* Second, the account must provide an *adequate normative basis* for culpability judgments. I begin with the first desideratum, concerning the social constitution of agency.

Nonderivative culpability for wrongdoing is a function of at least three things: *rational capacities, psychology,* and *environment.* Culpable agency involves a suitable ability to recognize and respond to what moral considerations there are.[7] However, our psychology involves bundles of relatively circumscribed cognitive and affective processes (some more abstract and deliberative, some more concrete and automatic). So, following standard views in the cognitive sciences, I maintain that our psychological dispositions are less cross-situationally stable, general, or content neutral than common-sense views tend to suppose. Instead, they are clusters of dispositions that function best in relatively circumscribed contexts. As a result, the boundedness of our rationality means that our rational capacities are better- and worse-suited to specific and circumscribed environments. In short, our rational agency—and thus, our culpability—is a product of the fit between our psychologies and our environments.

These three foundations of culpability (our rational agency, its psychological underpinnings, and the environment) have a dynamic relationship to one another. We can "train up" cognition for particular environments. Environments can foster particular patterns of cares and commitments that shape what agents perceive as reasons. We can also restructure our environments to better exploit our cognitive and affective dispositions, and to better express and realize our cares and commitments. As Hurley has noted, both higher-level cognition—e.g., explicit metarepresentation—and lower-level, more automatic processes have a "public ecology" that fosters and sustains situated rationality (2013, 206). The socially scaffolded nature of our agency is thus not an incidental but a central feature of the kinds of creatures we are.[8]

Here, though, the animating challenge of social circumstances becomes central. If the social constitution of our agency is what makes oppression look exculpating, then how does a socially situated picture of rational moral agency solve the problem? To answer this question, we must turn to the second aspiration for the present account. That is, we need to show how the proposal is *normatively adequate*, or capable of doing the normative work we need for a theory of responsibility. The account succeeds if it can show how socially constituted, circumstantially variable features of agency can license, justify, or make normatively apt our culpability judgments and their characteristic attitudes.

In what follows, I offer an account with three important elements: (1) a justification for responsibility attitudes and practices (the "responsibility system"); (2) an account of the form of agency required for culpability; and (3) an explanation of how this is compatible with an ecological, nontranscendent picture of agency. Together, these elements provide the resources for showing that culpability is compatible with the social constitution of agency. I say more about each element in order, but an initial sketch of the overall picture may be useful.

On this proposal, the underlying function of our responsibility attitudes and practices is the cultivation of a certain form of agency, one that recognizes and responds to moral considerations. Call this justification of our general system of responsibility practices the *agency cultivation model*. However, the norm-structured practices of moralized praise and blame only rightly apply to agents who are suitably capable of responding to moral considerations. Importantly, the involved capacities of responsiveness are *circumstantialist*, or sensitive to a distinctive set of social and normative considerations that vary across circumstances. This conception of capacity is tied to the justifying aim of the practice: the relevant notion of capacity is the one that, were it adopted and internalized by the relevant agents, would be at least co-optimal for improvements in the agency of those governed by the practice. Together, these ideas can provide a unified story about whether and when agents are culpable for wrongful action under conditions of oppression.

Let's begin with the justification of the responsibility attitudes and practices. Social practices that admit of a distinction between the justification of the practice and the content of the particular rules of the practice provide a helpful model for thinking about the relationship of culpability to the justification of responsibility practices. For example, consider a system of foul calls in a typical sport. A standard justification for having foul calls in a sport is that it helps protect the players, and, perhaps not unrelatedly, the enjoyment of the fans. Internal to a game, though, fouls are assessed on the basis of the foul rules. Whether a player deserves a foul is not determined by the referee in light of whether it is appealing to the fans, or whether the calling of the foul will in fact protect a given player. Rather, the basis of the foul is the rules that govern the game and the players in it. When one violates those rules in particular ways, one deserves a foul. To be sure, a given referee's decision about whether to call the foul can be subject to a range of epistemic and pragmatic considerations. Sometimes it is unclear whether a foul was committed. A minor but genuine foul in the waning moments of a game that is already decided may not seem worth the call. Even so, the propriety of the foul, considered as a foul, is settled by the actions of the players and the applicable rules. Importantly, it is *not* a matter of whether making the call in a particular instance contributes to the teleology of a system of foul calls.

Culpability—or blameworthiness—functions in a way analogous to a system of foul calls. That is, an agent is blameworthy when she has failed to act with due moral concern and is the right sort of agent for the application of those norms. Like a system of foul calls in a sport, the overall practice of moral blame has a teleology to it. This teleology is not operative at the level of first-order determinations of culpability (or a foul). In both practices, considerations about the justification of the system of norms and practices may be entirely invisible to participants in the practice. However, what makes a system of blame justifiable (when it is) is that it cultivates moral considerations-sensitive agency. Call this the *agency cultivation model* of moral responsibility. To the extent to which a system of moralized praise and blame helps refine and extend our ability to recognize and suitably respond to moral considerations, it has a justification. To the extent to which it fails to support this form of agency—and absent some further justification—it fails to be normatively adequate.[9]

The norms of blameworthiness apply to some agents and not others. Infancy and some varieties of mental impairment are commonly regarded as conditions that preclude membership in culpability practices. On this account, some baseline ability to recognize and suitably respond to moral considerations is a prerequisite for the applicability of the blameworthiness norms. When one has that baseline ability, then one is a responsible agent, that is, a proper subject of the norms of responsibility, and a candidate for culpability. When one fails to have the requisite ability—e.g., because one cannot recognize the relevant moral reasons, or because of some systemic volitional incapacity to that class of considerations—then one is not a responsible agent, and thus, incapable of culpability.[10]

Crossing that threshold of ability is part of what makes someone properly (or if you like, truly) responsible, as opposed to it being merely useful to blame that person. With children, we oftentimes feign blame as a tool for teaching children about what is blameworthy. Ersatz blame is one of the ways we nurture and develop the capacities required for genuine blameworthiness, and thus, help foster genuine blameworthiness over time. However, blame (of the sort that expresses a judgment of culpability) is distinguished from moral education in part by the blamer believing the blamed to be an agent of the right sort. Where the blamed agent is missing the requisite set of recognitional and volitional capacities, the agent is not culpable. So, any blaming (or feigning of blame) requires some other basis.

A consequence of this approach is that culpability is "patchy." One might be a responsible agent with respect to some considerations and not others. The same person might be responsible with respect to those considerations only in some circumstances and not others. Responsible agency is therefore not an always-on or always-off matter, and one's suitability for blame can shift in highly context-sensitive ways. Borderline cases or atypical psychologies raise a range of puzzles for ordinary practices. However, where there is a suitable degree of sensitivity to the relevant moral considerations, one is a responsible agent, thereby potentially culpable for wrongdoing.

On this picture, our rationality is bounded or tied to circumstances, and more generally, agency is structured by contextually or "ecologically situated" dispositions to respond to information in the environment. The difficult issue is how to understand claims that agents *can* respond in the relevant ways in the identified contexts. What sort of threshold of sensitivity to moral considerations would constitute the possession of the capacities required for culpability? Answering this question has been a long-standing difficulty for accounts of free will and responsibility that are intended to be compatible with the thesis of determinism. An important part of the appeal of transcendent pictures of agency is that they seem to provide more principled answers to this question than compatibilist proposals.

We can deliver an account of (nontranscendent) capacities that fits with this ecological conception of agency. Let's assume that culpability presumes agency that is sensitive to moral considerations. So, the issue is how to specify that sensitivity or capacity in a way that can be integrated into the agency cultivation model. Here's the solution: for a given moral consideration, the relevant degree of sensitivity is determined by whatever conception of capacity that an ideal observer would pick as best for helping imperfect creatures like us to do the right thing, over time, and in the actual world. Call that conception of capacity the *responsibility-relevant notion of ability*.[11]

The responsibility-relevant notion of ability can't be so strict as to entail that no one has any possibilities other than the ones she actualizes (as, for example, a conception of ability on which people can only do one thing under determinism). That wouldn't enable a well-functioning system of blame to achieve its effects. Similarly, the notion of capacity can't be so general as to entail that everyone always is blameworthy for everything causally connected to her choices. Such a conception of ability would make it impossible for agents to reasonably manage the risks of culpable choices. So, the relevant notion of capacity has to be a Goldilocks notion of capacity: not too strict and not too lax, or, just right for enabling a well-functioning system of blame.

One can get a sense of how this framework can help us understand the way oppression affects culpability by considering the idea of degrees of culpability.

On this account, the ability to recognize and respond to moral considerations is a scalar matter. However, there are plausibly three distinct parts of that continuum that matter for culpability. First, there are agents who fall below the requisite degree of sensitivity to moral considerations in a circumstance and are therefore not culpable. Second, there are agents who cross the requisite threshold so that they are properly subject to the norms of blame, and thus, are culpable for the relevant bit of wrongdoing in the considered context. Among these agents, there is a further division codified in common sense, between agents whose wrongdoing is mitigated because of morally significant difficulty in exercising the relevant capacity, and those who have no such mitigating element.

The present approach has the tools to capture this idea. The ability of an agent to respond to a relevant moral consideration is a function of how the observer's conception of ability maps the agent's intrinsic properties on to a modal profile. This modal profile determines whether the agent has the ability to recognize and respond to the relevant considerations, and it comes in degrees. Agents whose modal profile just crosses the required threshold for culpability are distinct from those whose profiles cross the requisite threshold by a considerable margin. This difference suggests a useful distinction between the second and a third level of ability to recognize and respond to moral considerations. The latter, third level of responsiveness concerns modal profiles where it can be said that there is no morally salient difficulty in complying with the relevant moral norm. Variation in the quanta of blame directed at agents within this third level is, presumably, primarily a matter of the significance of the operative moral consideration and the quality of the will evinced by the agent in the considered context.[12]

The metaphysics of ability talk is not everyone's cup of tea. Nevertheless, it provides something too many compatibilist accounts lack: a specification of what it means to say someone had the ability to respond to moral considerations in a context. Modeling the metaphysics of culpability-relevant ability in a way tied to a concern for achieving and sustaining moral considerations-sensitive agency blocks the worry that compatibilists are helping themselves to a cheat (i.e., a story about a nonlibertarian conception of ability or capacity). It also provides an explanation of why capacities understood in this way matter for the appropriateness of blame, and this will matter for how we understand the significance of oppression for culpability.

I now turn to how this picture connects with the social constitution of our agency. Let's begin with the idea that we value being regarded as competent at navigating the social world in light of moral considerations. To be seen as incompetent in this way is to lose an important kind of social standing, and considerations like these plausibly underpin our willingness to be called to account (cf. Raz 2011). Given that one of the best ways to be reliably seen as morally competent is to be *actually* competent, practices that foster and extend such competence are important. The present account captures both our interest in being a certain kind of agent, and why culpability would be sensitive to whether, in a given situation, we meet some standard or expectation of competence at recognizing and responding to operative moral considerations. We also have a robust interest in *other* agents being sensitive to moral considerations. Our engagements with other agents become incredibly fraught when we think they are insensitive to moral considerations (or, at least, what we take to be moral considerations). Individually and collectively, we have a pervasive interest in the kind of agency at the heart of the agency cultivation model.

Notice that all of this is compatible with, and even depends on, the socially constituted nature of agents. Blameworthiness does not require a transcendent self, detached from the causal order. Culpability for wrongdoing depends on agents, the narrow circumstances of the action, and the justified norms, which in turn shape the practice-dependent specification of the abilities that matter for culpability. Changes in each of these elements can alter culpability. Holding fixed the circumstances and wider situation, a change in the agent's intentions or the psychological structures of agency can alter culpability. Holding fixed the intrinsic properties of an agent, the agent's culpability can change if the circumstances of action are altered. Coercive circumstances, for example, can alter the culpability of an agent even when the agent's intrinsic features remain the same. Finally, even if we hold fixed the intrinsic properties of the agent and the narrow circumstances (for example, circumstances of moderate coercion), wider social or cultural contexts can ground different norms concerning whether caving in to that coercion is culpable. The ideal observer's judgments about those norms will vary depending on what particular norms (and what specifications of capacity) best achieve the justifying aim of the responsibility system. Thus, the account offers a principled basis for distinguishing between culpability in some circumstances and not others, without denying the possibility of constitutive luck and luck in circumstances.

Culpability is not a function of whether some bit of blaming will in fact produce the justifying good in that context. The underlying normative structure of this account is teleological, but not in the way of widely repudiated consequentialist accounts of yore. That is, it does not presume that individual judgments of responsibility are exclusively forward-looking, or only applicable to the extent to which they modify the downstream attitudes or behavior of a given agent. Akin to a system of foul calls, there is a forward-looking basis for a system of responsibility practices with backward-looking standards of evaluation. Plausibly, those norms of blameworthiness are concerned with quality of will, or failures of to meet expected standards of moral concern. Culpability is thus a function of an agent's action, plus (typically backward-looking, quality of will-focused) norms of blameworthiness. And all of this presumes that agents have the responsibility-relevant sense of ability, specified in a way that enables a practicable and justified system of blame.

As in the case of the relevant notion of capacity, the standards of culpability are somewhat coarse-grained, on pain of making the norms and practice of responsibility too difficult to internalize and deploy. A system with a more direct and fine-grained tie to a particular justifying outcome—for example, the building out of that agent's capacity by blaming in that particular instance (e.g., McGeer 2014, 2015)—imposes considerable cognitive demands on agents. Moreover, it introduces greater unpredictability into our social practices in a way that undermines the prospective control an agent has over whether he or she is blamed (Schmidt 2016). The advantage of a view that distinguishes the justification of responsibility practices from the particular norms that achieve the specified end is that it avoids the omnipresent tyranny of instrumental blaming.

The teleological aspect of this account, even in the form at work here, can still give pause to those who feel the intuitive pressure to think that moral responsibility must be the kind of thing that is grounded in noncontingent features of the world, or even rooted in a radical kind of human freedom that sets humans apart from the rest of the causal order. Despite the pull that transcendent pictures of agency may have on many of us, such accounts are not necessary to justify and make sense of familiar practices of moralized praising and blaming. The present account is a proposal for how we should go forward given what we now know about our agency, and it shows how practices like ours can be in good stead. We need not substitute "moral sadness" for full-throated culpability-imputing blame, as some views would have it (cf. Pereboom 2001). A sufficiently nuanced teleological account has the resources to capture the everyday phenomena of actual, messy, human praising and blaming that sent some philosophers searching for a picture of transcendent agency and left others seeking a diluted or even skeptical picture of responsibility.

4 Responsibility and Situated Agency

Culpability for wrongful acts arises when responsible agents (i.e., agents with the requisite capacities to recognize and respond to moral considerations) fail to exercise moral considerations-responsive capacities in the morally appropriate way. Estimates of blameworthiness for wrongdoing can be also construed as evaluations of an agent's quality of will. Where a responsible agent fails to conduct herself in a way that reflects due concern for morality, there is blameworthiness. For agents with the requisite capacities, the agent's quality of will is partly a function of the quality of the options and the norms or expectations that are properly applicable to those kinds of situations.[13] Where the options in those circumstances provide no morally adequate actional possibility to the agent, and the absence of those options are no fault of the agent, then the agent is not culpable. With the foregoing account in hand, we can now address the relevance of oppression to culpability and the distinctive way the appropriateness of blaming can be asymmetric.

Oppression can render invisible the wrongfulness of an act to both oppressor and oppressed. It can also obscure the moral significance of acts in oppressive situations. Thus, oppression seems relevant to the culpability of the oppressed, but also to the oppressor (Calhoun 1989). Given an account of culpability that requires that agents have the ability to recognize the relevant moral considerations, the invisibility of the wrongfulness of an act, because of oppression, can seem to exculpate both the oppressor and oppressed. This result is worrisome in each case. As noted at the outset, it seems implausible and disrespectful to insist that those who are oppressed are never culpable. Second, the belief that oppression *always* or even frequently exculpates the oppressor (in virtue of the oppressor's moral ignorance) seems to have the consequence that if one is potentially enjoying the benefits of oppressive social arrangements, on pain of acquiring new culpability one has reason to be unreflective about social arrangements.

Here is the core idea in what follows: oppression alters the morally adequate and deliberatively significant possibilities available to agents. Moreover, the way oppression interacts with the norms of blameworthiness (and the underlying requirements on culpability) explains a good deal of what is otherwise puzzling about culpability for wrongdoing under conditions of oppression. Given a context and a set of justified norms for that context, wrongful actions are culpable when the agent fails to exercise her moral considerations-sensitive capacities in ways that constitute a suitable quality of will.

Oppression can affect both what an agent can *do* but also an agent's *deliberations* and *beliefs*. Start with the case of oppression affecting what an agent can do. For an agent to lack due moral concern—to have ill will—the agent has to have available to her morally adequate possibilities of action. However, oppression can eliminate or reduce the morally adequate actional possibilities available to an agent. When the secret police require you to accuse your neighbor of disloyalty to the party, lest they kill or imprison your family, your accusing your neighbor has a different quality of will than when you accuse your neighbor with no corresponding threat. That is, one may act wrongly without a correspondingly poor quality of will.

Importantly, the fact of oppression does not always make agents acting under oppression not blameworthy, because oppression does not always remove all the morally adequate actional possibilities. So long as morally adequate options remain intact, and the agent remains a responsible agent (i.e., capable of discerning and suitably responding to the relevant moral considerations in that context), the agent can fail to have an adequate quality of will, even when subject to oppression.[14]

Oppression can also alter epistemic agency by changing which possibilities are deliberatively accessible to the agent. If one has internalized oppressive norms or cultural scripts, these things shape one's deliberations about what actional possibilities are relevant in a given circumstance. In shaping an agent's deliberations, an agent may lose the relevant degree of access to deliberatively significant and morally adequate action possibilities, in comparison to circumstances devoid of that oppression. One effective way of perpetuating oppressive social conditions is for the costs of oppressive arrangements to be made obscure from those who benefit from those policies, whether by patterns of residence, schooling, media choice, or the formulation of policy. For members of advantaged groups, conditions of oppression might reduce the salience of, for example, complaints about aggressive policing in a racially marginalized community. Or, it might obscure the effects of particular economic policies on low-income wage earners. In general, privilege tends to obscure the costs it imposes on nonprivileged populations. If the loss of access to deliberatively significant and morally adequate action possibilities is sufficiently robust—that is, if in a large enough proportion of deliberatively similar circumstances the agent fails to recognize and respond to the relevant moral consideration(s)—then the agent will not be a responsible agent, and thus not culpable, at least with respect to those considerations in that context.

Not all weakenings of a capacity constitute an incapacitation. The loss of deliberatively relevant possibilities (read: the diminution of the proportion of relevant worlds in which the agent recognizes and suitably responds to the consideration) brought on by oppression may be only mitigating. An agent can satisfy the minimum standards for responsible agency, but the fact of oppression may also impair that capacity, blocking full culpability for wrongdoing. The wrongdoing by an agent impaired in that way does not express the same poor quality of will were the wrongdoing to have been performed by an unimpaired agent.

Oppression can also affect the capacities for responsible agency without any material significance for culpability. Some instances of oppression can reduce the proportion of worlds in which the considered agent suitably recognizes and responds to the relevant moral considerations in the relevant circumstances, but where this reduction is insufficient to pull the agent's capacity underneath what is required for full culpability. Such changes of the agent's modal profile do not mitigate culpability. Moreover, sometimes oppression is entirely tangential to an agent's ability to recognize and suitably respond to moral considerations. In those cases, the fact of oppression does not affect culpability or blameworthiness. In these cases, the badness of oppression is not a function of its effects on the culpability of agents. Finally, oppression may *enable* agents to have a greater sensitivity to a relevant class of moral considerations, for example, in making certain kinds of injustice more visible to those who suffer from it. Oppression may thus enable responsible agency.[15]

The narrowness of the scope of exemptions, or the idea that someone isn't a responsible agent, is a distinctive feature of this account. If we think of responsible agency as requiring circumstantial sensitivity to considerations, typical losses of responsible agency are frequently patchy or variable across contexts. That is, we ordinarily lose responsible agency with respect to a *kind* of consideration in a *kind* of circumstance. Except in the most dramatic circumstances, one does not lose responsible agency with respect to all moral considerations across all possible circumstances. So it goes for losses of culpability due to oppression. The loss of responsible agency is typically neither total with respect to a class of considerations, nor global with respect to contexts. Nor are losses of responsible agency necessarily losses of other forms of agency—potentially, one may have diminished or absent capacities relevant to responsibility without necessarily having diminished agency with respect to other normatively or psychologically important conceptions of agency.

This approach also allows us to acknowledge some of the moral significance of oppression. Oppression can, and frequently does, entail a kind of loss of agency. To the extent to which there are second- or third-personal reasons to want other agents to be competent at navigating moral demands, a loss of this form of agency is plausibly a loss of something we value. To the extent to which we have first-personal reasons to want to be competent at navigating moral demands, there is a loss there, too. In either case, we might think such agency is inherently valuable, quite apart from an agent's actual regard for the possession of that form of agency.

Especially under conditions of unjust social inequality, the appropriateness of blame can have an asymmetric structure. For example, those who are socially disadvantaged may seem to have standing to blame those with social advantage, even when the reverse is not true, if those with social advantage are complicit in the creation or perpetuation of the social disadvantage. Oppressors can enjoy an especially nefarious social arrangement, blaming and punishing parties whose culpability is partly a byproduct of the choices of those with social advantage. Those complicit in the creation or persistence of oppressive social schemes plausibly lose their standing to blame the oppressed in those contexts (cf. Tadros 2009).

The extent to which oppressors are complicit in oppression that produces wrongdoing is often unclear. Disentangling real-world causal and normative relations is seldom easy, and it is made even harder by the subtle ways oppression alters the epistemic agency and actional possibilities of agents. So, assessing culpability for wrongdoing under real-world conditions of oppression is oftentimes an extraordinarily difficult task. The present approach permits us to make a few general observations, however.

First, even if concerns about complicity can affect the standing of the oppressors to blame the oppressed, blame will frequently be entirely appropriate from oppressed to oppressor. The former slave owner may lack suitable standing to condemn the wrongdoing of the former slave, but this in no way precludes the slave from condemning the wrongdoing of the slave owner. Indeed, by the lights of the oppressed, those who are socially advantaged and permit the ongoing persistence of oppression will often seem negligent or even exceptionally ill-willed. Yet the facts about culpability are not a matter of perceived negligence. As noted above, oppressors can be insufficiently able to discern the relevant considerations, and thus, not culpable for their wrongdoing. So, many of the real-world difficulties in discerning culpability can be explained, but they are not readily eliminated.

There is a further dimension worth noting here. The responsibility system earns its keep in virtue of the role that moralized praise and blame play, over time, for creatures with psychologies like ours. Many of the psychological benefits are not at all direct, and it is an error to search for those benefits in every individual instance of holding one another responsible. However, one underappreciated role of blameworthiness and its intimate connection to angry emotions of reaction is the work they do in animating subordinate groups to fight against conditions of oppression. Moral anger helps call attention to the wrong, but it can also bind people together in shared commitments to change social practices and institutions. The protestive dimension of moral blame can be a powerful tool in motivating and sustaining the kinds of coalitions that reshape social norms and the attendant moral practices (Smith 2013). Given that the primary normative function fulfilled by a system of blame just is the enhancement of moral considerations-sensitive agency, there is good reason to think that the norms of blame will typically support angry blaming by subordinate groups against superordinate groups.[16]

Let's take stock. Culpability under oppression is a function of some familiar features of our agency and the context-specific norms of responsibility as well as the way in which oppression interacts with those norms and the morally adequate options available to oppressed agents. One's status as a responsible agent or not, and whether one is blameworthy or not, are not facts prior to, or independent of the normative concerns and particulars of circumstance that structure our agency. Social context, in the form of individual or structural oppression, can impair or even undermine responsible agency. Other times, it leaves it wholly intact. The overriding lesson, though, is the relatively piecemeal nature of these interactions. Culpability is local, but it is variegated in how it arises from the matrix of agency and socio-normative forces.

5 Moral Ecology

I have argued that agency is at least partly socially constituted, a product of an ecology that variously scaffolds and hinders morally appealing forms of agency. We rely on others to attune and calibrate our tracking of moral considerations (cf. Bennett 2002; McKenna 2012, 68; McGeer 2012; Vargas 2013a, 261–265; Hurley 2013). Social feedback and contextual cues do considerable work in norm inculcation, and failing that, in directing our attention to what reasons there are in a given context. When the operative norms are not justified, practices of praising and blaming can reify oppression and other forms of moral error. If we accept that culpability turns on whether we have particular capacities that are both products of and occurrently structured by social context, circumstances should not be an afterthought for a theory of moral responsibility. Rather, they are a central constituent of what it means for us to be responsible agents. So, the *moral ecology* of our agency matters precisely because it is one of the constituents of our responsible agency.

According to the agency cultivation model, the primary engine for the fostering of our moral considerations-sensitive agency is the internalization of moral norms and their consequent effects, especially in connection with culpability assessments. When moral norms are internalized, they structure how agents perceive actional possibilities, and they also provide an impetus for agents to attend to the relevant moral considerations. Our interest in being regarded as competent at navigating moral demands and avoiding blame shapes our prospective behavior. Similarly, we respond to others on the defeasible presumption that those agents are normatively competent and capable of deserving blame in light of how they exercise their agency.

In order to be effective, culpability norms must have sufficient currency in the relevant group, and this ordinarily involves common knowledge about the content of the norms.[17] However, social norms do not always require internalization to succeed in shaping the sensibility and conduct of agents. Awareness of a norm, especially combined with incentives (e.g., avoiding loss of status, avoiding unpleasant experiences of being blamed) can prospectively shape one's behavior, in ways often compliant but sometimes not compliant with the norm. Repeated norm compliance sometimes suffices to produce internalization of the norm. Sometimes it doesn't. With sufficient acceptance, however, prevalent norms can structure deliberation and conduct, orienting agents to the relevant moral considerations even when intrinsic motivation is absent.

Given a picture of agency that allows for its social constitution, we should expect that the content of laws, the shape of economic opportunities, and the various social scripts with currency will each structure our agency in diverse and oftentimes subtle ways. In addition to adopting and promulgating social norms with particular content, we might also hope to shape the moral ecology by attending to the way in which some of these other elements shape our agency. I conclude with some brief remarks about how a concern for culpability and fighting oppression might go if we take seriously the idea that we might alter our agency by altering the moral ecology of that agency.

From the outset, it seems clear that some interventions into our moral ecology—and thus, how we scaffold our agency—will be more and less palatable. Adjustments to our moral ecology that operate on our agency in ways that allow for a kind of rational mediation are preferable to interventions that bypass or subvert our sensitivity to moral considerations. It is now a familiar point that some changes to institutional "choice architecture" need not bypass considerations-sensitive agency (cf. Thaler and Sunstein 2009). Some so-called nudges can be interventions in a moral ecology that work through rational mediation. Others operate by exploiting fundamentally irrational processes or otherwise bypassing an agent's sensitivity to the relevant moral considerations.[18]

Some structuring of choices and environment seems compatible with rational mediation by the agent, and this is clear in nonmoral cases. Putting salad rather than strawberry shortcake at the front of the lunch buffet—an intervention suggested by Thaler and Sunstein (2009, 11)—does not have to bypass someone's rational agency. If the way this nudge functions is to permit the reasons to eat salad to be more salient, or more difficult to ignore, or less likely to be forgotten, there is little reason to think it subverts an agent's rationality. So, if some interventions on moral ecology function in this way—by making moral considerations salient—there is less reason for qualms about those interventions.

Interventions that attempt to restructure local dispositions in ways that are not plausibly mediated by rational sensitivities are, on the face of it, less ethically palatable. Even so, once we accept a socially structured conception of agency, it is not always clear how we should think about mediation by rational agency. Conscious, reflective agency is relatively rare, and anyway, there is good reason to think it too is structured by situational and social pressures (Doris 2015). For accounts that emphasize that sensitivity to moral considerations can operate de re—i.e., without agents consciously thinking of them as such (e.g., Arpaly 2003)—it may be tenable to maintain that some interventions into our moral ecology will work in ways that are consonant with accurate informed reflection, but which may not require it in a given instance. Some mental processes are sensitive to considerations without active, conscious, deliberative assessment— e.g., reflexively pulling one's hand away from a hot stove is rational in a range of contexts. So long as those processes are ones that reason can respect, as it were, the absence of conscious, deliberative moral assessment is less problematic (cf. Doris 2015, 52).

Private and individual adjustments to our ecology of agency are all well and good. However, by omission or commission, oppression is frequently a product of the social and political organization of states. Even if we assume states will regularly tolerate some oppression, intentional attempts to shape circumstances to support responsible agency, and thus, culpability, might seem to require state intervention. However, given an antecedent commitment to some or another form of political liberalism, the possibility of direct state intervention into our moral ecology is not unproblematic. If states are prepared to exercise their power to back particular kinds of interventions, there is a traditional family of worries that states would be taking a de facto stance on substantive moral doctrines about which there is reasonable dispute. In doing so, some have worries that this is a move toward totalitarianism (Berlin 1958), or less dramatically, toward a kind of domination at odds with a serious commitment to individual liberty (Pettit 2015).

Four potential lines of reply are worth noting. First, liberal states *can* have grounds for building ecologies that favor agents being sensitive to some moral considerations and not others. For example, substantive moral considerations that are part of an overlapping consensus of what morality favors can be per-missible under some forms of liberalism (e.g., considerations against genocide and slavery, and considerations grounded in widely accepted human rights). More generally, in the absence of a substantive theory of morality and politics, reasonable constraints on such interventions may be readily identifiable. Such elements may include requirements of publicity (i.e., that the interventions be known); respect for the moral, rational, and political agency of those affected by the interventions; an assessment of the net costs and benefits for various other moral and political ideals (e.g., autonomy, nondomination, dignity); and ongo-ing support and concern for ordinary forms of rational persuasion (cf. Hausman and Welch 2010; Hurley 2013).

Second, shaping the moral ecology, even to overcome oppression, need not require state intervention.[19] Individuals, institutions, and communities can make changes in the currency of social norms and substantially alter the scaffolding of our agency. Antibigotry interventions, from Stetson Kennedy's 1940s "Frown Power" campaign (which involved openly frowning at expressions of racism) to modern practices of "calling out" biased behavior, have reshaped local practices. Community protests of businesses, norms of crossing picket lines, and boycotts are old and familiar tools in the fight against perceived injustice. Decisions about curricula in schools, the promulgation of new workplace norms, and framing choices to serve the public good may also contribute to combating oppres-sion's culpability-undermining effects. Even if we accept the restriction on state neutrality about comprehensive moral issues, we still have important tools at our disposal to reshape the moral ecology. As Mackenzie argues in a different context, "[R]uling out coercive political means ... does not entail ruling out other political means for encouraging citizens to pursue valuable goals—for example, incentive and reward schemes" (2008, 529). Incentives and reward schemes are not tools limited to government actors, so we are not bereft of non-governmental resources for shaping our moral ecology.[20]

It remains an open question whether or not incentives, rewards, and limiting the reshaping of our moral ecology to methods and commitments palatable under political liberalism will provide for much in the way of ecology-shaping. In a posthumously published paper, Susan Hurley (2013) explores an interesting further option. She argues that traditional forms of political liberalism rely on a picture of agency that is at odds with our situated rationality. What is called for, she claims, is a revisionist and ecologically rational liberal conception of government. As she puts it, "Traditional liberalism tends to view government as the primary source of interference with responsible action by private individuals. [Her alternative, revisionist conception of] liberalism should instead view government as having a counter-manipulative and positive role in the public ecology of responsibility" (209). On her account, a revised liberal form of government would be distinguished by a commitment to two principles that reflect a more naturalistically plausible conception of our agency. The first is a broadly negative principle, according to which government should regulate and counter manipulative influences on citizens' beliefs and behavior. The second is a broadly positive principle, in which government is tasked with designing and creating a better public ecology for our rational agency. This latter project coheres in various ways with the project of nudges espoused by Thaler and Sunstein (2009), with a special emphasis on avoiding manipulative uses of government influences. So, re-envisioning the permissible scope of liberal state interventions in a way that allows some nontrivial reshaping of the moral ecology is a third possibility.

A final possibility is to simply reject the ideal of liberal neutrality, and to defend some or another alternative account for the basis of state (or other interventions) in the moral ecology.

Here, I do not take a stand on which of these approaches, or what combination of them, is the most promising in fostering responsible agency under oppression. In supporting responsible agency and mitigating the effects of oppression, we may do well to fashion all the tools we can.[21]

Notes

1. *Oppression* is an elastic term in the wider philosophical literature, admitting of wide differences in its characterization (Haslanger, Tuana, and O'Connor 2015). Let *oppression* be the property of unjust or immoral treatment, social relations, or distributions of opportunities, when it is produced by immoral or unjust social and political arrangements (cf. Cudd 2006,

20). The basic idea can be refined in distinct ways, with varied emphases on the role of institutions (Cudd 2006, 50), subordinate group membership (Haslanger 2012), or oppression's characteristic psychological, social, or material conditions (Young 2004). What follows is compatible with standard refinements of the idea of oppression.

2. This account is neutral on whether positively valenced notions—moral credit and praise—can be modeled on assessments of (negative) culpability.

3. Let *free will* pick out a power or capacity distinctive of creatures properly subject to evaluation in terms of praiseworthiness and blameworthiness. Nothing in this way of framing matters precludes the possibility of alternative understandings of the term. Ongoing disagreements about what free will *is*, what it *means*, and what it *refers to* are partly artifacts of the wide range of philosophical concerns that have been pursued under the guise of theories of free will. Accounts of distinct aspects of agency—deliberation, the phenomenology of freedom, causal origination, authorship, the ability to do otherwise, and so on—each plausibly fix on some property that might reasonably be characterized as free will. It is not obvious that they all come to the same thing (cf. Vargas 2011).

4. These issues are plausibly related to both *the socialization problem* in the autonomy literature, especially as it is concerned with relational notions of autonomy (cf. Mackenzie and Stoljar 2000; Westlund 2009; Oshana 2014, 2015) and to worries about adaptive preferences (Stoljar 2014). For present purposes, I am neutral on the relationship of moral culpability to various notions of autonomy.

5. One motivation for some forms of libertarianism about free will is presumably the desire to capture the idea of transcendence. It is unclear the extent to which all or any philosophically credible libertarian view adequately captures a potentially more basic and radical appeal to transcendence. Libertarianism remains a controversial view, and I have argued against it elsewhere (e.g., Vargas 2004, 2013a, 2016).

6. Questions about degree of blame and the moral valence of individual acts might seem separable from questions about whether someone is a responsible agent, i.e., an apt target of moral responsibility. Although questions of responsible agency and degree of culpability (and indeed, the relevant moral valence of the act) are conceptually independent, I argue that the way social facts can undercut responsible agency turns out to matter for these other questions, too.

7. For present purposes, I am neutral on how reasons are related to our cares and commitments.

8. There are more and less radical ways to accommodate the idea of the circumstance-specific powers of our agency. As will become clear, I favor an approach according to which the normatively significant powers of agency alter by context even if the material substrate, as it were, is stable. However, the basic theoretical demand is more modest than that. What is required is that a theory of responsible agency has *some* way of capturing the way circumstances seem to impinge on agency.

9. For more detailed statements of this approach, see Vargas 2008, 2013a. Related accounts include Arneson 2003; and McGeer 2014, 2015.

10. Here, and throughout, I am bracketing cases of derivative culpability, i.e., cases where one's present responsibility is not grounded in occurrent features of the agent but instead derives from a prior instance of responsibility.

11. More precisely: the responsibility-relevant capacity is the one that, were we to internalize that conception of ability, it would generate practices of moralized praising and blaming in the actual world that are at least co-optimal for agents recognizing and suitably responding to moral considerations in the likely circumstances of action, given our psychologies and the existing socio-historical circumstances. This capacity allows us to specify a modal profile for agents, which we can construe in terms of possible worlds. Roughly, the observer-specified notion of capacity tells us what kinds of worlds count as relevant. We look to those worlds, and if in a suitable proportion of those worlds the agent responds in the relevant way to the relevant considerations, we say the agent has the relevant capacity. For details, see Vargas 2013, 213–228.

12. Moral considerations may not all be on a par with respect to the modal profile they have. In the case of especially important moral considerations, the effects of blame may be particularly important in orienting our attention and shaping our moral concerns. So, the threshold of

sensitivity for being a responsible agent may be lower for such considerations. In contrast, for less important moral considerations, the threshold may be higher simply as a matter of managing reasonable demands on our agency.

13. Recall: the applicable norms will be those relatively general norms that tend to cultivate the right kind of agency, holding fixed various psychological and social features of the community to whom the norms apply. The question of how to individuate options is complex, although the relevant conception of options allows for the possibility that two acts may be behaviorally similar but deliberatively distinct options, which in turn affects evaluations of the agent's quality of will. This approach is functionally similar to the "fair opportunity" approach developed by Brink and Nelkin (2013).

14. In virtue of removing actional possibilities, oppression can count as a form of domination, as understood by Pettit (2015). Action under domination can be culpable if one retains responsible agency and has available morally adequate possibilities. This picture is compatible with a range of views about the relevance of the number of discernible morally adequate options for evaluation of an agent's quality of will. Presumably, an agent's failure of due concern is worse when there are a variety of readily discernible morally adequate options, as opposed to a case in which there is only one option that is difficult to discern. Moreover, as Christopher Lewis (2016) has emphasized in a different context, *how* options are incentivized is plausibly relevant, quite apart from concerns about domination and injustice. Adaptive preferences and morally suspect socialization may work by foreclosing and incentivizing certain options, so that even if agents retain freedom in some or another sense, they can suffer from impairments to the sort of freedom required for moral responsibility. For a pertinent discussion, see Stoljar 2014.

15. There is a closely related idea in standpoint epistemology about the way in which social position, including oppressed social positions, enables particular forms of knowledge. For an instructive discussion, see the introduction and first two chapters of Medina 2012.

16. There is a complexity here having to do with the disposition of dominant groups to regard anger by those in oppressive circumstances as misplaced or unreasonable. I trust that concrete examples in contemporary political life are not hard to find. This significance of this phenomenon for the shape of a normatively ideal system of angry blame depends, in part, on whether there are noninstrumental justifications for moral anger.

17. Allowing for important variations between these accounts, one can find strands of these ideas in Copp (1995), Bichierri (2006), McTernan (2013), and others.

18. There is some debate about how to characterize nudges. Some ways of regimenting Thaler and Sunstein's construal of nudges makes their nonrational nature a matter of definition (e.g., Hausman and Welch 2010). On such construals of nudging, the present point is that there are many nonnudging adjustments to choice architecture that need not entail a bypassing of rational capacities.

19. There is an interesting question about when deployment of state power is counterproductive. My suspicion is that alienation from the state or conditions of low social trust can undermine the effectiveness and credibility of state interventions.

20. A caveat: with sufficient comprehensiveness in scope and distribution, as well as sufficient motivational force attached to incentives, a system of incentives can become a de facto system of coercion. If an enormous range of options are incentivized such that only a few options do not receive the benefit, those options will be perceived as costly. Such a system of incentives is coercive in all but name. This suggests that there is a conceptual problem for one way of thinking about domination and the constraints on republican government. However, for present purposes we only need the relatively innocuous thought that there are ways to encourage norms and adjustments to choice architecture that don't amount to coercion.

21. My thanks to the Gunnar Björnsson, Bryce Huebner, Sofia Jeppsson, Per-Erik Milam, Ben Matheson, Sam Murray, David Pizarro, Grant Rozeboom, Tamler Sommers, Andras Szigeti, the members of seminars at UC Berkeley, University of Gothenburg, and Georgetown, as well as the terrific students and faculty at California State University Bakersfield, for discussions of ideas in this chapter. I'm particularly grateful to Michael McKenna, Emily McTernan, and the editors of this volume for extensive written feedback on earlier versions of this chapter.

References

Arneson, Richard J. 2003. "The Smart Theory of Moral Responsibility and Desert." In *Desert and Justice*, edited by Serena Olsaretti, 233–258. Oxford: Oxford University Press.

Arpaly, Nomy. 2003. *Unprincipled Virtue*. New York: Oxford University Press.

Bennett, Christopher. 2002. "The Varieties of Retributive Experience." *The Philosophical Quarterly* 52 (207): 145–163.

Berlin, Isaiah. 1958. *Two Concepts of Liberty*. Oxford: Clarendon Press.

Bichierri, Christina. 2006. *The Grammar of Society: The Nature and Dynamics of Social Norms*. New York: Cambridge University Press.

Bierria, Alisa. 2014. "Missing in Action: Violence, Power, and Discerning Agency." *Hypatia* 29 (1): 129–145.

Björnsson, Gunnar, and Karl Persson. 2013. "A Unified Empirical Account of Responsibility Judgments." *Philosophy and Phenomenological Research* 87 (3): 611–639.

Brink, David O., and Dana Nelkin. 2013. "Fairness and the Architecture of Responsibility." In *Oxford Studies in Agency and Responsibility, Vol. 1*, 284–314. New York: Oxford University Press.

Calhoun, Cheshire. 1989. "Responsibility and Reproach." *Ethics* 99 (2): 389–406.

Copp, David. 1995. *Morality, Normativity, and Society*. New York: Oxford University Press.

Cudd, Ann E. 2006. *Analyzing Oppression*. New York: Oxford University Press.

Doris, John. 2002. *Lack of Character*. New York: Cambridge University Press.

Doris, John. 2015. *Talking to Ourselves: Reflection, Skepticism, and Agency*. New York: Oxford University Press.

Greene, Joshua, and Jonathan Cohen. 2004. "For the Law, Neuroscience Changes Everything and Nothing." *Philosophical Transactions of the Royal Society B*. 359: 1775–1785.

Hacking, Ian. 1995. "The Looping Effects of Human Kinds." In *Causal Cognition: A Multi-Disciplinary Debate*, edited by Dan Sperber, David Premack, and Ann James Premack, 351–383. New York: Oxford University Press.

Haslanger, Sally. 2012. "Oppressions: Racial and Other." In *Resisting Reality: Social Construction and Social Critique*, 311–338. New York: Oxford University Press.

Haslanger, Sally, Nancy Tuana, and Peg O'Connor. 2012. "Topics in Feminism." *The Stanford Encyclopedia of Philosophy* (Fall 2015 Edition), Edward N. Zalta (ed.), URL = <http://plato.stanford.edu/archives/fall2015/entries/feminism-topics/>.

Hausman, Daniel M., and Brynn Welch. 2010. "Debate: To Nudge or Not to Nudge." *The Journal of Political Philosophy* 18 (1): 123–136.

Huebner, Bryce. 2016. "Implicit Bias, Reinforcement Learning, and Scaffolded Moral Cognition." In *Implicit Bias and Philosophy, Vol. 1, Metaphysics and Epistemology*, edited by Michael Brownstein and Jennifer Saul, 47–79. Oxford: Oxford University Press.

Hurley, Susan. 2013. "The Public Ecology of Responsibility." In *Responsibility and Distributive Justice*, edited by Carl Knight, and Zofia Stemplowska, 188–215. Oxford: Oxford University Press.

Levy, Neil. 2014. *Consciousness and Moral Responsibility*. New York: Oxford University Press.

Lewis, Christopher. 2016. "Inequality, Incentives, Criminality, and Blame." *Legal Theory* 22 (2): 153–180.

Mackenzie, Catriona. 2008. "Relational Autonomy, Normative Authority and Perfectionism." *Journal of Social Philosophy* 39 (4): 512–533.

Mackenzie, Catriona, and Natalie Stoljar. 2000. "Introduction: Refiguring Autonomy." In *Relational Autonomy: Feminist Perspectives on Autonomy, Agency, and the Social Self*, edited by Catriona Mackenzie and Natalie Stoljar, 3–34. New York: Oxford University Press.

McGeer, Victoria. 2012. "Co-Reactive Attitudes and the Making of Moral Community." In *Emotions, Imagination, and Moral Reasoning*, edited by R. Langdon and C. Mackenzie, 299–326. New York: Psychology Press.

McGeer, Victoria. 2014. "P. F. Strawson's Consequentialism." In *Oxford Studies in Agency and Responsibility, Vol. 2*, edited by David Shoemaker, and Neal A. Tognazzini, 64–92. New York: Oxford University Press.

McGeer, Victoria. 2015. "Building a Better Theory of Responsibility." *Philosophical Studies* 172 (10): 2635–2649.

McKenna, Michael. 2012. *Conversation and Responsibility*. New York: Oxford University Press.

McKenna, Michael, and Brandon Warmke. Forthcoming. "Does Situationism Threaten Free Will and Moral Responsibility?" *Journal of Moral Philosophy*.

McTernan, Emily. 2013. "How to Make Citizens Behave: Social Psychology, Liberal Virtues, and Social Norms." *The Journal of Political Philosophy* 22 (1): 84–104.

Medina, José. 2012. *The Epistemology of Resistance: Gender and Racial Oppression, Epistemic Injustice, and Resistant Imaginations*. Oxford: Oxford University Press.

Mele, Alfred. 2009. *Effective Intentions: The Power of the Conscious Will*. New York: Oxford University Press.

Nagel, Thomas. 1979. "Moral Luck." In *Mortal Questions*, 24–38. Cambridge: Cambridge University Press.

Nahmias, Eddy. 2007. "Autonomous Agency and Social Psychology." In *Cartographies of the Mind: Philosophy and Psychology in Intersection*, edited by Massimo Marraffa, Mario De Caro, and Francesco Ferretti, 169–185. Berlin: Springer.

Nahmias, Eddy. 2010. "Scientific Challenges to Free Will." In *A Companion to the Philosophy of Action*, edited by Timothy O'Connor and Constantine Sandis, 345–356. Malden, MA: Wiley-Blackwell.

Nelkin, Dana. 2005. "Freedom, Responsibility, and the Challenge of Situationism." *Midwest Studies in Philosophy* 29 (1): 181–206.

Nichols, Shaun. 2015. *Bound: Essays on Free Will and Responsibility*. New York: Oxford University Press.

Oshana, Marina. 2014. "A Commitment to Autonomy Is a Commitment to Feminism." In *Autonomy, Oppression, and Gender*, edited by Andrea Veltman and Mark Piper, 141–162. New York: Oxford University Press.

Oshana, Marina. 2015. "Is Social-Relational Autonomy a Plausible Ideal?" In *Personal Autonomy and Social Oppression: Philosophical Perspectives*, edited by Marina Oshana, 3–24. New York: Taylor and Francis.

Pereboom, Derk. 2001. *Living without Free Will*. Cambridge: Cambridge University Press.

Pettit, Philip. 2015. "Freedom: Psychological, Ethical, and Political." *Critical Review of International Social and Political Philosophy* 18 (4): 375–389.

Raz, Joseph. 2011. *From Normativity to Responsibility*. Oxford: Oxford University Press.

Schmidt, Andreas. June 10, 2016. "Consequentialism and the Ethics of Blame." Unpublished manuscript. Microsoft Word file.

Smith, Angela. 2013. "Moral Blame and Moral Protest." In *Blame: Its Nature and Norms*, edited by D. Justin Coates and Neal A. Tognazzini, 27–48. New York: Oxford University Press.

Stoljar, Natalie. 2014. "Autonomy and Adaptive Preference Formation." In *Autonomy, Oppression, and Gender*, edited by Andrea Veltman and Mark Piper, 227–254. New York: Oxford University Press.

Tadros, Victor. 2009. "Poverty and Criminal Responsibility." *Journal of Value Inquiry* 43 (3): 391–413.

Thaler, Richard H., and Cass R. Sunstein. 2009. *Nudge: Improving Decisions about Health, Wealth, and Happiness*. New York: Penguin.

Vargas, Manuel. 2004. "Libertarianism and Skepticism about Free Will: Some Arguments against Both." *Philosophical Topics* 32 (1–2): 403–426.

Vargas, Manuel. 2008. "Moral Influence, Moral Responsibility." In *Essays on Free Will and Moral Responsibility*, edited by Nick Trakakis and Daniel Cohen, 90–122. Newcastle, UK: Cambridge Scholars Press.

Vargas, Manuel. 2011. "The Revisionist Turn: Reflection on the Recent History of Work on Free Will." In *New Waves in the Philosophy of Action*, edited by Jesus Aguilar, Andrei Buckareff, and Keith Frankish, 143–172. New York: Palgrave Macmillan.

Vargas, Manuel. 2013a. *Building Better Beings: A Theory of Moral Responsibility*. Oxford: Oxford University Press.

Vargas, Manuel. 2013b. "Situationism and Moral Responsibility: Free Will in Fragments." In *Decomposing the Will*, edited by Till Vierkant, Julian Kiverstein, and Andy Clark, 325–349. New York: Oxford University Press.

Vargas, Manuel. 2016. "The Runeberg Problem: Theism, Libertarianism, and Motivated Reasoning." In *Free Will and Theism: Connections, Contingencies, and Concerns*, edited by Kevin Timpe and Daniel Speak, 27–47. New York: Oxford University Press.

Watson, Gary. 1987. "Responsibility and the Limits of Evil." In *Responsibility, Character, and the Emotions*, edited by Ferdinand David Schoeman, 256–286. New York: Cambridge University Press.

Westlund, Andrea C. 2009. "Rethinking Relational Autonomy." *Hypatia* 24 (4): 26–49.

Wolf, Susan. 1987. "Sanity and the Metaphysics of Responsibility." In *Responsibility, Character, and the Emotions*, edited by Ferdinand David Schoeman, 46–62. New York: Cambridge University Press.

Young, Iris Marion. 2004. "Five Faces of Oppression." In *Oppression, Privilege, and Resistance*, edited by Lisa Heldke, and Peg O'Connor, 37–63. Boston, MA: McGraw Hill.

5

Two Ways of Socializing Moral Responsibility

Circumstantialism versus Scaffolded-Responsiveness

JULES HOLROYD

1 Introduction

This chapter is concerned with the implications of two important developments in the recent literature on moral responsibility: first, there has been a sustained defense of the view that moral responsibility is constituted by our social practices, rather than any metaphysically deep notion antecedent to our social relations (the *social thesis*). Second, it has been asked whether and why we might want such practices (the *justification thesis*). The answers to these questions then guide the articulation and justification of the standards for responsible agency and the norms internal to the practice that govern when individuals are liable to the moral responses of praise or blame.

My main aim here is to evaluate two competing views of morally responsible agency, each of which has been developed to sit within a view of responsibility that endorses the *social thesis* and the *justification thesis*. These two views are Vargas's *circumstantialism* (2013, 2015)—the view that responsible agency is a function of the agent and her circumstances, and so highly context sensitive—and McGeer's *scaffolded-responsiveness* view (2015; McGeer and Pettit 2015), according to which our responsible agency is constituted by our capacity for responsiveness both to reasons themselves, and to the expectations of our audience (whose sensitivity may be more developed than our own). I develop and defend a version of the *scaffolded-responsiveness* view. I then make some suggestive remarks about how such a view might be located within a broader conception of our practices of responsibility: that such a view coheres with a picture of our practices in which moral responsibility is implicated in a range of moral responses beyond blame or praise. Finally, I suggest that these conclusions about moral responsibility and the range of moral response may be further bolstered by approaching these issues via what has been called an "ameliorative" (cf. Haslanger 2000) rather than revisionist analysis. Revisionist analyses seek to revise our existing concept of responsibility, and so remain anchored in our extant concept. Instead, an ameliorative analysis starts by asking what we want the concept of responsibility for and what concept will serve those purposes, with no assumption that the answers we give will yield an analysis that closely tracks our existing understanding of moral responsibility.

2 The Social Thesis

If we want to know what moral responsibility is and when we are warranted in deploying the concept, how should we conduct our inquiry? One approach would be to analyze our intuitions about the concept, revealing what conditions have to be in place in order to be warranted in deploying the concept in our interactions with others. What does the world have to be like (what metaphysical conditions must obtain) and what do we have to be like as agents, in order to stand in certain relations to our actions such that we are morally responsible for them?

Revisionists argue that the concept of moral responsibility must be revised if it is to deliver a coherent set of conditions for responsibility. This idea is supported by pointing to seemingly inconsistent intuitions about responsibility (for example, that ultimate control is, and is not, necessary for responsibility; that determinism is, and is not, necessary for responsibility). Some of these intuitions, then, must be forsaken, and a revised concept adopted. How might one go about this revisionary project? A revisionist approach considers (1) what work the concept of moral responsibility does for us in our social practices, (2) whether these practices are justifiable, and (3) whether a defensible notion of responsibility is embedded within those practices, or can be developed from our understanding of them. Revisionism about responsibility has been most fully developed and defended in the recent work of Manuel Vargas (2013, 2015). In Vargas's revisionism, we end up with a revised concept that rejects incompatibilist intuitions, according to which responsibility is dependent upon some metaphysically deep feature of agents and their actions (say, the need or possibility of ultimate control). Rather, when we look at our social practices, we find a concept that (1) has a role in keeping track of deserved praise and blame. Vargas claims that (2) these practices can be justified if the practices as a whole serve to cultivate a certain valuable kind of agency, namely, agency that is sensitive to moral considerations. And the notion of responsibility that is embedded within these practices is (3) a circumstantialist view of responsible agency—more details of which to follow. Whilst the core of the social thesis is that morally responsible agency is a matter of standing in certain social relations (rather than certain metaphysical conditions obtaining), there are various revisionist alternatives consistent with this position. Some such alternatives may hold little appeal: consider, for example, the options of nihilism—the view that moral responsibility is impossible for us—or eliminativism—the prescription that the notion of moral responsibility should be eliminated from our normative discourse. Each of these latter options rejects some of our intuitions about moral responsibility. But there would be costs to endorsing either view—in particular, giving up the important benefits that can be gained from our practices of holding each other responsible (cf. Vargas 2013, 107). If an adequate justification of the social practices of holding certain agents responsible can be delivered, and if the conception of responsibility derived from this is a defensible one, then we have little reason to pursue either of these bleaker alternatives.[1] However, even if we seek to reject these two bleak options, there may be other—still revisionist— alternatives to Vargas's circumstantialism about moral responsibility, such as the scaffolded-responsiveness view defended here.

3 The Justification Thesis

The *social thesis* has been defended before, both by consequentialists, and famously by P. F. Strawson (1962). Both views see responsibility as constituted by a set of social practices: but each give different accounts of what justifies those practices, and thereby of what responsibility is. On a 'Strawsonian psychologism,' we hold that we cannot but engage in these practices—our psychology is simply geared up to feeling the reactive attitudes (resentment or gratitude) in response to the (poor or good) quality of will we find manifested in others' actions. To be responsible is to be liable to be held responsible, on this view. But this justification takes a strong view on our psychological limits, and supposes implausibly that these patterns of affective response are unchangeable: a fixed point in human relations. Moreover, even if we accept such constraints, this would explain, rather than justify, our practices (cf. Vargas 2013, 160).[2]

However, the Strawsonian option has seemed all the more appealing when set alongside the competing claim, from consequentialist thinking, that what justifies the practice is the good outcome of praise and blame. On this view, praise and blame have a certain moral influence, encouraging people to do good and discouraging or deterring them from bad action. You simply are morally responsible if you are susceptible to be influenced in this way. You are blameworthy if blaming you effects good outcomes (see, e.g., Smart 1973). This sort of view seems coldly manipulative, and it circumvents the agential capacities that we might hope to be engaged in moral communications (see Vargas [2013, 166] for detailed discussion of each of these views).

Both of these views endorse the *social thesis*, and see responsibility as essentially a social rather than metaphysical fact: an agent is responsible and liable to blame given the constraints of our psychological dispositions to view her in that way, or given the efficacy of viewing her thus. But neither of these views provides adequate justification to shore up these social practices.

An alternative option has recently been developed by Vargas (2013) and "heartily endorsed" by McGeer (2015, 2637). Vargas's important revisionary move is to develop a revised moral influence view, which points to the good effects of the responsibility system for fostering a certain sort of agency, namely, agency that is sensitive to moral considerations. This is the 'agency cultivation model.' On this view,

> when we hold one another responsible, we participate in a system of practices, attitudes and judgments that support a special kind of self-governance, one whereby we recognize and suitably respond to moral considerations. So, roughly, moralized praise and blame are justified by their effects, that is, how they develop and sustain a valuable form of agency. (Vargas 2013, 2; cf. McGeer 2015, 2637)

The practice as a whole—the norms regulating judgments about and expressions of deserved praise or blame—can be justified if it promotes this valuable sort of agency.[3] Insofar as the practice has this function—supporting a certain kind of self-governance, cultivating and sustaining agency that is sensitive to moral considerations—it looks like we have good reason to regard these practices as justified.

4 Morally Responsible Agency

If responsibility is constituted by a social practice, and that social practice can be justified, we still lack an answer to our question of what responsible agency is: when is an individual a responsible agent? In other words, *who* is a participant in those practices? We should hope the account of responsible agency has independent plausibility—that it coheres with our intuitions, or the contours of the practices with which we are familiar, and that it resonates with why we care about responsibility. We have additional resources we can draw on in evaluating an account of responsible agency, as provided by the *social thesis* and *justification thesis*. The account of responsible agency should be one that can function in the social practice of holding each other responsible. Further, the notion of responsible agency should be such that, when deployed, it coheres with and even promotes the overall aims of the practice, namely, the cultivation of morally sensitive agency (cf. Vargas 2013, 220). We already have a head start in this task, since Vargas and McGeer both endorse this revisionist approach, and have each developed accounts of morally responsible agency, located within this framework. However, they each arrive at radically different conceptions of morally responsible agency. Next I articulate the competing accounts; then I go on to evaluate them.

4.1 Circumstantialism

Circumstantialism about moral responsibility builds in a familiar claim about the relevance of the agent's reasons-responsiveness to her responsibility. This form of morally responsible agency is understood in terms of a (context-specific) capacity to recognize moral considerations, and to govern ourselves in light of our recognition of these. As with standard reasons-responsive accounts, the capacity involves responsiveness in sufficiently many (counterfactually specified) occasions, in a sufficiently systematic way. But unlike the more familiar versions of reasons-responsiveness views (e.g., Fischer and Ravizza 2000), Vargas rejects atomism and monism about responsibility. That is, he rejects the claim that the relevant capacity is a nonrelational property of agents (Vargas 2013, 204); and he rejects the claim that there is one psychological structure or mental capacity that is important for or constitutive of being suitably responsive to reasons.

Instead, we get a picture whereby the relevant capacities are relational: "a function of whether the agent (with the relevant features in the considered context of action) stands in a particular relationship to the normative practice" (Vargas 2015, 2622); and whereby the capacities are plural: there are "multiple agential structures of combinations of powers that constitute the control or freedom required for moral responsibility" (Vargas 2013, 205). There are good reasons for adopting this sort of relational and plural view of the relevant capacities: literature from empirical psychology has demonstrated that an individual's ability to respond to reasons can be highly dependent on the particular circumstances, and influenced by, for example, the primes provided by the environmental context. One example that Vargas uses to illustrate "the startlingly localized and context-specific potential for degrading our rational capacities" (2013, 207) is that of stereotype threat: the phenomena whereby the activation of a stereotype provokes a stress response that can hinder an individual's performance—desensitize them to reasons, we might say. In a context in which stereotype threat is in operation, an agent's capacities are degraded by those circumstances and the stereotypes activated in them, which impair an individual's ability to respond to the reasons she otherwise would.[4] Even from the armchair, Vargas suggests, it would appear that various different capacities are involved in different aspects of moral agency (2013, 208). For example, the capacities involved in seeing that someone is upset, or in arguing that one has a particular duty, or in recognizing a right, may each differ significantly. Perceptual, emotional, and cognitive reasoning capacities may each be demanded, and different situations may demand more or less from one or other of these capacities. Moreover, situational features may impair each capacity in variegated and unexpected ways.

What we end up with is a view whereby highly context-sensitive sets of capacities are the constituents of an agent's reasons-responsiveness. But the crucial question for this kind of view is what degree of reasons-responsiveness an agent must be capable of in order to be a responsible agent. We already know that for the circumstantialist this will not be an all-or-nothing judgment: for Vargas, an agent might be a responsible agent in one context, and not in another. What does it take in any one context, though? For any context, there is no antecedently given answer to how sensitive to reasons an agent must be. Rather, that standard is given by the forward-looking aims of the practice, to cultivate the agent's moral sensitivity. Accordingly, it depends on "whether the relevant specification of the capacity would best support agents in the actual world in the recognition and suitable response to moral considerations" (Vargas 2015, 2622). The relevant standard—the degree and kind of responsiveness—constitutive of responsible agency in a context is set by a standard, which is "actually co-optimal or better for fostering agency that recognizes and suitably responds to moral considerations in the actual world, in ordinary contexts of action" (Vargas 2013, 219).[5] Vargas notes that a secondary aim in setting this standard is that it should serve to expand the contexts in which agents demonstrate such sensitivity (Vargas 2013, 220). So, a particular contextual feature (such as stereotype threat) may impair an agent's sensitivity to reasons; but whether it does so in a way that undermines an individual's responsibility is not something that can be answered without recourse to the forward-looking aims of the practice. Would a system of norms that supports holding the agent responsible in such contexts, given such sensitivities, better serve the aims of cultivating sensitive agency?[6] This delivers the answer to whether an agent, in a context, is responsible. We will consider an example of how responsibility is determined in more detail shortly.

There are two crucial points to emphasize about this circumstantialist view: first, the circumstantialist claim is one about morally responsible agency, rather than liability to blame. This means that our responsible agency is more "patchy" on this view than on others. For example, if an environment blocks our sensitivity in some way, it is not simply that we are responsible agents who are excused: rather, our responsible agency itself is absent. One implication of this is that much attention is needed to the "moral ecology" in which we function as moral agents (Vargas 2013, 243–249; see also 2017) and the environmental and social relations that might best cultivate such sensitivity. Secondly, it is important to note that Vargas is keen to avoid specifications of the relevant standards for sensitivity in a way that would render almost no one responsible. For example, we shouldn't require sensitivity across *almost all* possible similar contexts, articulated in fine-grained terms, as almost no one would meet that standard, and "we would be required to forgo the real benefits of responsibility" (Vargas 2013, 219). This wish to avoid general skepticism is motivated in part by Vargas's principle of conservation (that we should not too radically revise our conception) and by the idea that we should seek to preserve the benefits attendant on the practices of responsibility.

4.2 Scaffolded-Responsiveness

Let us now contrast this circumstantialist view with what I am calling the *scaffolded-responsiveness view* of morally responsible agency, developed by McGeer (2015), and McGeer and Pettit (2015) across a series of papers. As mentioned above, both McGeer and Vargas articulate their respective accounts of responsible agency within a view that sees responsibility as constituted by social practices, and that maintains that these practices are justified by a forward-looking aim of fostering morally sensitive agency. However, the conceptions of responsibility yielded are in many respects radically divergent. Like Vargas, McGeer (2015) endorses a broadly reasons-responsive view of responsible agency, whereby an agent must have the capacity to register and respond to certain reasons to qualify as a responsible agent. However, whilst both Vargas and McGeer reject atomism, they do so in different ways. As set out above, Vargas construes the capacities as standing in relation to a normative practice in a context. Meanwhile, on the *scaffolded-responsiveness* view of reasons-responsiveness, this capacity is not simply a matter of being able directly, here and now, to register and act on certain reasons—McGeer and Pettit (2015) draw attention to another way in which we might be responsive to reasons: namely, indirectly. On this view, one is reasons-responsive also if one is able to adjust or sensitize to the reasons that there may be. Just as an immune system has the capacity both to defend against diseases it is already sensitized to, it can also become reactive to new diseases. Similarly, we may already be sensitive to some reasons, but also we may have the capacity to become sensitized to new reasons (McGeer and Pettit 2015, 163). In particular, this capacity to become sensitized operates via our sensitivity to our "audience"—those whose (anticipated) judgments about our conduct matter to us (168). Accordingly, "as a reason-responsive agent you can be expected, not only to be moved by the reasons you confront in making a choice, but also by the audience, actual or prospective, that you confront" (170).

The audience should provide an environment in which "we are continually exhorted by one another to exercise that capacity; to think about our actions; to justify them to one another; to work on our weaknesses . . . to nurture our strengths" (McGeer 2015, 2647). The expectation of one's audience provides a "situational force"—one that we may care about both in itself and instrumentally. Accordingly, the responsibility-relevant capacities are relational in that their scope is dependent on one's audience, and this may expand the range of reasons to which an individual is sensitized: both those she is able to detect, and those she is sensitized to via her (actual or prospective) audience.[7] In this way, others "scaffold" our responsiveness to reasons, expanding the range of reasons to which we may be properly said to be responsive.

Note that this articulation of audience involves a certain optimism: for some, the audience may not in fact provide this sort of scaffolding. Thus, one under-specified aspect of the account is the interpretation of one's *prospective* audience: does this include only the audience one realistically expects to face? If so, there may be cases in which one's actual audience is uncritical and unsupportive. On this interpretation, an uncritical audience closes off opportunities for enhancing sensitivity. Alternatively, the conception of 'prospective audience' may extend to audiences one can conceive of, and who populate the moral community, but whom in fact one is unlikely to face in one's actual experience.[8] For example, under one idealization, one's audience will include the sorts of subgroups with new moral insights, who problematize unconsidered moral issues and "force attentiveness in agents who are already, for the most part, morally reflective and sensitive" (Isaacs 1997, 681). On this interpretation, even if one's sensitivity is restricted by one's actual audience, it is enhanced if one could be sensitized to the reasons pointed to by this possible prospective audience.

On either way of developing the view, the scaffolded-responsiveness picture rejects atomism and articulates a relational standard for the sensitivity required for responsible agency. Note the contrast with circumstantialism, which indexes the scope of the agent's capacities to include her circumstances. This has the effect of limiting the scope of an agent's responsibility: where circumstances impair or degrade an agent's capacities, she may not be responsible in that context. In contrast, on the *scaffolded* view, making the constituent sensitivity relational to *others'* sensitivity has the function of potentially expanding her capacities and the range of considerations to which an agent might be—directly or indirectly—sensitive. Crucially, even if an agent's capacities are not in fact expanded, the insight that to be a responsible agent is to have the potential to be scaffolded by our (actual or prospective, realistic or idealized) audience captures an important relational dimension of responsible agency.[9] This, it is argued, coheres with the forward-looking aims of the practice, since engaging with individuals as responsible agents—engaging in moral response such as expressions of blame—can serve to bolster or reinforce those capacities, exhorting the agent to exercise it and aim for greater (direct) attentiveness to reasons. As McGeer and Pettit (2015) put it, addressing each other as morally responsible agents can expand the scope of reasons to which we are responsive: we can *capacitate* each other.[10]

We have, then, two considerably different pictures of responsible agency that we may plug into our framework for understanding morally responsible agency as grounded in social practice. Is one or the other of these views more defensible? In the next section, I outline some considerations that speak in favor of the scaffolded-responsiveness view.

5 How Should We Think about Responsible Agency?

How might we decide which account of responsible agency to endorse?[11] First, we can consider which notion might best serve the justificatory aim of the practice. Second, we can consider which notion has independent plausibility. Third, we can look to our existing practices and ask how they might inform our thinking about which notion of responsibility we should endorse. To this end, we can start our evaluation with some examples of cases that have already generated much critical reflection; this helps us to see both how *circumstantialism* and *scaffolded-responsiveness* would deal with these cases, and the extent to which the considerations articulated above are met.

Instructive cases to focus on are the cases that fall under what Vargas describes as "new, unusual and particularly challenging" (2013, 183) contexts of action, since the two accounts (as we shall see) deal radically differently with such cases. Furthermore, we have a wealth of critical reflection on just such cases, since they have been the focus of much philosophical attention. These sorts of cases include those in which a moral issue is not conceived as such, so as to make difficult or inaccessible the moral insight required for sensitivity to the moral reasons at issue. One such case, discussed by Cheshire Calhoun (1989), concerns the use of gendered pronouns in a way that perpetuates sexist assumptions, and the difficulty of recognizing this in a cultural context in which language use of this sort is not widely considered a "moral issue":[12]

> C1: Bert, a male philosopher writing in the second half of the twentieth century, always uses the male pronoun "he" to refer to supposedly universal individuals, whilst writing his philosophical papers. He does so in a cultural context in which this is the norm, and in which the idea that the use of gendered language, in this way, is problematic is extremely marginal—maintained only by a few themselves marginalized feminist

thinkers. It is certainly not a moral viewpoint with which Bert is familiar, and indeed he has not even considered this aspect of his language
use as a "moral issue."

Another sort of case, recently much discussed, can also be thought of as a
special case of moral ignorance: namely, cases of discriminatory behavior that
results from implicit bias. In these cases, we can suppose, our concern is that
agents are largely ignorant of the reasons that they have to avoid implicitly
biased, discriminatory behavior: namely, the fact that they likely harbor implicit
associations, which influence their judgments and behaviors.

> C2: Alfred is evaluating the CVs of predominantly white male and
> female philosophy graduates, with a view to drawing up a shortlist of
> candidates for a job. Alfred harbors implicit biases that influence his
> judgments of the CVs of female graduates, and those graduates who are
> not racialized white: although showing qualities comparable with those
> on the CVs of the white male graduates, he sees the latter as "shining"
> with a quality that the other CVs don't seem to have. He draws up an
> all-white, all-male shortlist for the job. Alfred is not aware of the role of
> implicit bias in his judgment, nor indeed of facts about the risk of bias,
> and is confident that he has picked "the best" candidates.

As with the case of sexist language, for many people—Alfred included—it may
not even register that there is a "moral issue" to which they are being insensitive.
Yet the individual fails to be appropriately responsive to reasons that there are—
to adopt procedures that may insulate decisions from bias, for example—and
thus the question of their responsibility for this failure is activated. The general
question of the blameworthiness of individuals in cases of moral ignorance—
and indeed, in cases of implicit bias—is one that has been widely addressed,
so I do not consider that here.[13] Rather, what I want to ask is what determinations are made on either the circumstantialist or scaffolded-responsiveness view
of responsible agency. This helps us to build a plausibility argument for one or
other of the accounts.

5.1 Circumstantialism about Moral Ignorance

On the circumstantialist approach, whether individuals such as Bert or Alfred
are morally responsible will depend upon whether they stand in the right relation to the normative practice. That is, it depends on whether the agent is sufficiently sensitive; but our determinations of what "sufficient sensitivity" involves
look to the degree of sensitivity requisite according to the forward-looking aims

of the practice. In other words, the degree of sensitivity that an agent must have is specified according to whether holding agents responsible, in such contexts, serves to improve sensitivity to the relevant moral considerations—in these cases, the moral reasons that there are to use nonexclusionary language or to attend to the possibility of bias. Note that this is not a question of whether any particular token of blame or instance of holding responsible will be effective in cultivating sensitivity. Rather, the question concerns whether a system that specifies *this* standard (whatever that turns out to be) of sensitivity required for responsibility in such contexts will have these agency-improving effects.

Of course, this is an empirical question. It is not at all clear to me from the armchair what the answer to this question might be. However, Vargas's application of circumstantialism to "new and unusual" cases indicates the conclusion that agents are *not* responsible agents in such cases, that the requisite sensitivity in that context is not yet present, such that moral response (notably, blame) for failure to conform with reasons would not cultivate greater sensitivity. In relation to these sorts of cases, Vargas indicates that the agent's capacities are not supported by the context—the environment blocks the agent's sensitivity (2013, 183)—such that we reach the conclusion that the individual is not a responsible agent. And, recall that on the circumstantialist account responsible agency is patchy—the agent is not simply excused from blame; rather, they simply lack the status of morally responsible agent; hence they are not a candidate for liability to blame, given the circumstances. This is because on the circumstantialist view it is responsible agency, rather than any excusing condition, that does the work here.[14] (This strikes me as problematic, but I hold off further evaluation until section 5.3.)

We get a clearer statement of this conclusion when Vargas takes circumstantialism in application specifically to the case of implicit bias (see Vargas, 2017). There may be some reasons to think that holding responsible may have good, sensitizing, effects: it may provide helpful moral feedback and promulgate narratives of self-governance that help agents to live up to them (25). However, all things considered, Vargas argues that the present context is not one in which agents are responsible for implicitly biased actions: blaming may provoke hostility and may prevent individuals from "buying in" to norms that prohibit implicit bias (26). Further, too few individuals are equipped with the relevant knowledge about the phenomenon of bias, or the possibility of mitigating it, to suppose that our current context is sufficiently supportive of sensitive agency. As such, Vargas suggests that the forward-looking aims of the practice are not met by holding people responsible: we do not yet have the moral ecology that supports such determinations (but may yet, in the not too distant future) (31).[15] So, in "new, unusual or particularly challenging contexts" (2013, 183) such as the ones I have described, circumstantialism delivers the verdict that the individuals do *not* meet the standards for responsible agency.

5.2 Scaffolded-Responsiveness about Moral Ignorance

Before we evaluate the circumstantialist response, let us consider what the alternative view of responsible agency delivers in relation to this case. The scaffolded-responsiveness view is again concerned with whether the agent has the requisite capacities to register and respond to the reasons to avoid (in this example) gendered language. On this view, the capacity for sensitivity includes not only an individual's capacities here and now to register the moral reasons in play, but also an agent's capacities given the ability to adjust or sensitize to the reasons there are via sensitivity to an "audience." An individual meets these conditions for responsible agency—meets the standard of sensitivity—either if she is presently sufficiently sensitive to the reasons, or if her present capacities are such that she can be further capacitated by the prospective moral address of others—address thus furthers the forward-looking aims of the practice of improving sensitive agency. Recall that much depends on how audience is specified within the scaffolded-responsiveness view. If one is scaffolded by one's actual audience, then in instances in which one's audience is uncritical and provides no new considerations or challenges, one's sensitivity will not be enhanced by its presence. But, as we saw, an interpretation of the view that incorporates some idealization—that one's prospective audience does include those with moral insight or who present moral challenges—will provide greater opportunity for capacitation.

One example of the sort of capacitating interaction at issue may be the sorts of address discussed by feminist philosophers' engagement with such cases. (McGeer and Pettit [2015] do not suggest this; I am hereby elaborating their account in what I take to be defensible ways.) In dealing with cases of moral ignorance, a range of responses have been considered: Miranda Fricker (2010) delineates the notion of moral disappointment to articulate the contours of the appropriate moral response where we might have *hoped* for greater moral insight, even whilst cultural norms make that insight hard to achieve.[16] Michelle Moody-Adams suggests there is scope for a kind of "forgiving moralizing" (1994, 303) in cases of moral ignorance, whereby we continue to maintain that an individual's moral agency has been implicated in a wrong, but also recognize *the great effort needed* to adopt an appropriately critical stance toward heretofore unquestioned aspects of the cultural context. Cheshire Calhoun has argued for the importance of reproach in such cases, in order to convey the obligation to change behavior (e.g., avoid sexist language), to *motivate* individuals to reflect and do better, and to *reinforce* a view of each other as agents capable of registering and reacting to the relevant reasons (i.e., to be "self-legislating," as Calhoun puts it [1989, 404]).

I do not here want to take a stance on which of these responses is the appropriate one in particular: the important point is that all of these authors focus on these kinds of moral responses to individuals as appropriate despite the agent's failure of direct responsiveness to the moral reasons. Thinking about cases of moral ignorance helpfully provides substance, I think, to the claim from McGeer and Pettit (2015) that our sensitivity is a function not just of our present responsiveness to reasons, but also of our sensitivity to audiences and their exhortations to adjust and expand the range of our direct attentiveness to reasons. Let us briefly note—this is a point to which we later return (in section 6 below)—that none of these authors focus on blame or blameworthiness per se as the appropriate reaction to the moral agents involved. The main point to tease out for now is that these forms of moral address are construed as appropriately directed toward the agent's failure of sensitivity. Moreover, the responses are construed as capacitating and enabling the agent to adjust so as to be directly sensitized to the considerations at issue. Thus, the scaffolded-responsiveness view yields the determination that agents in the sorts of moral ignorance cases I have described may yet be responsible agents. What matters is that they have the capacity to be sensitive to reasons indirectly, via a (perhaps idealized) prospective or actual audience (as well as the capacity to be directly sensitive to certain reasons themselves).

5.3 Which View?

The two views under consideration appear to yield substantially different conclusions about how to deal with cases of moral ignorance. Is one approach more defensible? In this section, I use three parameters in order to evaluate the competing views. First, I consider whether either view better serves the aim of the practice (of cultivating moral-considerations-sensitive agency). Second, I ask whether each view has independent plausibility. Third, I consider the extent to which each view coheres with our extant practices of holding each other responsible.

The Aims of the Practice

Each view of responsible agency is positioned within the *social thesis* and the *justification thesis*, whereby responsible agency arises out of our social practices, which have the purpose of cultivating reasons-sensitive agency. Each view positions itself as able to serve that aim. Yet the views, as I understand them in relation to our cases of moral ignorance, deliver radically different pictures of responsible agency and its implications in these cases. Do we have reason to believe that one or other of these views would better serve the aim of cultivating reasons-sensitive agency?

One of the key insights from the feminist literature on moral ignorance is that moral responses to failures of sensitivity are important for moral change.

As Calhoun puts it, "[A]n excusing response to moral ignorance precludes the social growth of moral knowledge" (1989, 406). And whilst Vargas raises worries about holding individuals responsible in such new and unusual cases—that this may provoke hostility or backlash (2017, 25)—some empirical studies suggest otherwise. In the case of implicit bias, moral confrontations have been found to reduce the later expression of bias (Czopp, Monteith, and Mark 2006). And, in a study specifically on the effects of blaming responses, whilst blame did not reduce implicit bias significantly more than neutral social interactions, nor did it increase bias; and, most significantly, blamed individuals more strongly expressed intentions to change future behaviors to avoid bias (Scaife et al., ms.). So, holding each other responsible may well increase sensitivity to moral reasons. Moreover, there is the danger, to which Vargas is alert, of promulgating hopelessness or complacency via narratives of lack of control. Indeed, in one empirical study, when people were told about the pervasive nature of implicit bias, in the absence of a strong moral norm against this pattern also being communicated, more implicit bias was subsequently displayed (Duiguid and Thomas-Hunt 2015). The circumstantialist view exempts individuals from moral responsibility if contexts do not support sensitivity to the relevant reasons. But in fact, this recent evidence supports Calhoun's contention that in cases of culturally supported moral ignorance, morally engaging individuals may better cultivate moral sensitivity, and so foster the aims of the practice.

Independent Plausibility

Even whilst offering a revisionary account of moral responsibility, we should still hope that the account offered remains recognizably a concept of moral responsibility, one that resonates with the notion—or notions—we deploy in our social practice. It is worth noting that much of the philosophical discussion of moral ignorance has focused on *what kind of* moral response toward the morally responsible agent is appropriate, rather than on the question of whether the individual *is* a responsible agent to whom moral responses are appropriate. The defeasible assumption here, then, is that the agents *are* morally responsible, such that some form of moral response is appropriate; the issue is what mode of response is most effective in increasing sensitivity to the norms at issue. The warrant for such moral responses depends upon holding the individual responsible for her failure of sensitivity. These practices provide support for a view that yields the verdict that individuals are responsible for such failures. The scaffolded-responsiveness view generates this verdict.

One might deny that our practices provide support for the scaffolded-responsiveness view, by suggesting that all the observations I have made show is that the agent must be in general sensitive to such considerations, such that there is a point in engaging her in moral response. The cases I have described do not show that the individual was sensitive to the relevant considerations *at the time at which they behaved problematically*—and so do not support the idea that the agent was at that time morally responsible. There are two responses to this worry. First, the moral responses I outlined above are not properly understood as directed at the agent in recognition of her general sensitivity to moral reasons. They are responses of disappointment, forgiveness, or reproach directed toward the agent *for their failure* to behave as they were expected to. They are ways of holding the individual responsible *for that failure*. These responses are quite different from that of merely pointing out reasons in the hope that the individual will notice them in future. But this latter response seems to be the only one available to the circumstantialist, who, as we have seen, is committed to holding that individuals in such cases are not responsible agents.

The second response returns to the adjudication that the circumstantialist *should* make. If it turns out that holding agents morally responsible in such cases does in fact foster morally sensitive agency—as I suggested above—then the circumstantialist *should* seek an account that also delivers the verdict that the agent targeted by these responses is morally responsible. But the circumstantialist view developed by Vargas does not seem to present us with those resources, since emphasis is placed not on the capacitating relational aspects of responsibility, but on the ways circumstances may impair or erode our capacities. These considerations suggest that it is the scaffolded-responsiveness view that has greater independent plausibility.

Coherence with Practice

There is another dimension of our practices that an independently plausible account of moral responsibility should seek to respect. This feature—and indeed, one of the points of grounding an account of moral responsibility within such social practices—is that, for the most part, we do interact with each other on the assumption that we are morally responsible agents. In the Strawsonian phrase, we occupy "the participant standpoint" (Strawson 1962) in our dealings with each other much of the time. Accordingly, an account that is independently plausible would avoid the determination of widespread skepticism about responsible agency—that is, it would avoid the implication that we lack responsible agency much of the time. Indeed, part of the revisionist project is to save the notion of responsibility from the skepticism oft generated by incompatibilism. This is due to the recognition that responsible agency is valuable, and being able to interact with each other as such is an important—and beneficial—part of human life. Hence Vargas's aspiration that we should avoid setting the standards for responsibility such that almost no one is responsible, as we miss out on the benefits of these social practices.

But the circumstantialist view is in fact ill placed to avoid such skepticism and shore up such value. On the one hand, for all we know, we may frequently be in situations of moral ignorance. For much of the time, there may be reasons to which we are not (yet) sensitized. On the other hand, for all we know, there may be many ways in which situational and contextual factors impinge on our agency. If such moral ignorance or situational influences are—as the circumstantialist view prescribes—precisely the sorts of impairments that render us (not excused, but) *not responsible agents*, then for all we know, we lack moral responsibility in relation to some or other moral consideration much of the time. McGeer also presses this challenge when she argues that, for Vargas, "the fact that [an agent] is *pro tanto* blameworthy for failing to respond to [moral] considerations M in [context] C does not mean that she is blameworthy *tout court*" (2015, 2645). This is because there may be a range of other considerations in play in C to which the agent is not sensitive. Accordingly, "circumstantialism actually raises the bar for (*tout court*) blameworthiness" (2015, 2645). But the point holds not just with respect to blameworthiness, but also with respect to responsible agency itself. For the range of considerations in relation to which sensitivity is lacking, the agent may not be a responsible agent if the moral ecology is not yet in place. This is a direct function of having the concept of moral responsibility do the work of exempting agents from responsibility in such circumstances, rather than the notion of excuse, which upholds the agent's status as morally responsible whilst mitigating blame (see Vargas 2013, 183). This means, as Vargas acknowledges, this account of responsibility is "more targeted" than those views that endorse a generalized capacity for responding to reasons (Vargas 2013, 228). As a result, this targeted approach leaves circumstantialism open to skepticism, insofar as it is eminently likely that there are almost always some moral considerations in a context to which we lack sensitivity. Accordingly, it may never by the case that we are responsible agents *tout court*. This is to countenance a form of skepticism about morally responsible agency that does not cohere with the plausible assumption that we can adopt the "participant standpoint" in our daily interactions; that we can engage with each other as responsible agents—albeit imperfect, often defective responsible agents, with much to learn—much of the time. The scaffolded-responsiveness view—which identifies the ways in which our sensitivity may be incomplete but open to adjustment via sensitivity to others' viewpoints—seems better placed to capture this aspect of our responsibility practice.

Of course, a proponent of circumstantialism may respond that she too can capture this feature of our practice: any specification of the standards of responsibility that generated such skepticism about responsible agency would indeed be at odds with the aims of the practice, so the specification should be adjusted so as to permit the judgment that we are responsible agents on more occasions than the skeptical determinations supply. However, once that move is made, it is not clear what remains *circumstantial* about the circumstantialist view. Setting the standard for responsibility in a way that insulates responsibility from pervasive threats from situational context or culturally pervasive ignorance removes the supposed sensitivity to the circumstances of responsibility. I think this is a good move, but it is not one that renders responsible agency *circumstantial*.

The considerations raised in this section suggest that the circumstantialist view does not cohere with valuable aspects of our practice, and they also reveal tensions within the competing aims of the account: to capture the context sensitivity of our capacities, whilst also setting the standard for the relevant capacities guided by the forward-looking aim of the practice. The circumstantialist restricts the scope of responsible agency, and must maintain that there is some discontinuity in the kind of agency implicated in cases of moral ignorance and that displayed in cases where the agent is in fact (according to the circumstantialist) morally responsible. Meanwhile, the scaffolded-responsiveness view is better placed in terms of the independent plausibility of a notion that delivers determinations of responsibility that are consistent with the value of adopting the participant standpoint in our everyday interactions.

Moreover, whilst the scaffolded-responsiveness view is a somewhat revisionary characterization of reasons-responsiveness as understood within the philosophical literature, the view in fact better coheres with the social practices we engage in (cf. McGeer and Pettit 2015, 174). I take it that the examples from the literature on moral ignorance bear out this claim. Insofar as some sort of moral response is engaged (reproach,[17] forgiveness, moral challenge, disappointment), this is because the agent has the capacities, in the scaffolded sense, to be sensitive to these considerations. This consideration, then, provides further support for the scaffolded-responsiveness view, rather than the circumstantialist account of responsible agency.

However, one crucial point on which we should remark is that our attention to these social practices engages a host of moral responses that are not coextensive with blame. How can we maintain that responsible agency is engaged in such cases, if the moral responses involved are not blame? After all, isn't liability to blame simply what it is to be a responsible agent, such that if we are not concerned here with blame, we cannot then be concerned with responsible agency? Both proponents of circumstantialism (Vargas 2013) and scaffolded-responsiveness (McGeer 2015; McGeer and Pettit 2015) seem to endorse what we can refer to as the *liability assumption*: that to be a responsible agent is to be liable to praise or blameworthiness. We see this in the claim that what it is "to blame someone [is] to hold them responsible in a negative sense" (McGeer and Pettit 2015, 161). Similarly, Vargas proceeds on the assumption that being morally responsible is simply a matter of the agent having the relevant capacities and deploying them in an action that is praiseworthy or blameworthy (2013, 213). Later, it is explicitly held that "we should reserve the phrase 'is morally responsible' for cases in which moral praise and blame can arise" (309). If *this* is how we are thinking about moral responsibility—as tightly bound with praise or blameworthiness—then the fact that we find moral responses such as disappointment, moralizing forgiveness, reproach, and moral confrontation in cases of moral ignorance, does nothing to support the claim that there is morally responsible agency present. If this is right, then no support is garnered by the scaffolded-responsiveness view, and the circumstantialist seems better placed to capture this absence of responsible agency. However, in the next section, I point toward strong reasons for rejecting the characterization of moral responsibility as liability to praise or blame.

6 Beyond Blame

The story so far: I have presented some examples of culturally pervasive moral ignorance—about language use, about implicit bias—and considered how circumstantialism and scaffolded-responsiveness views of moral responsibility deal with them. We have arrived at the following possible positions regarding the responsibility of the agents involved:

1. We could maintain that agents in these cases are not responsible (circumstantialism), so not blameworthy (I raised various concerns about this approach);
2. We could maintain that agents in these cases are responsible (scaffolded-responsiveness) and so are blameworthy (given the liability assumption);
3. We could maintain that agents are responsible (scaffolded-responsiveness) but may not be blameworthy (reject the liability assumption).

Given the considerations we have aired so far, I have suggested there are reasons to construe moral responsibility on the model of scaffolded-responsiveness, such that agents in moral ignorance may be morally responsible. I suggest this move is strengthened if we reject the liability assumption. Whilst a full defense of this claim is beyond the scope of this chapter, I suggest that such a move coheres with a view of responsibility grounded in our social practices.

In articulating the regulatory norms of the practice, Vargas focuses on the norms governing praise and blame: indeed, the concept of responsibility itself is set up as serving the purpose of keeping track of deserved praise and blame (2013, 250). Importing a broadly Strawsonian picture within the social practices, the regulatory norms hold that blame is deserved if a suitably sensitive agent demonstrates a deficit of good will; and praise is deserved when good will is manifested (see Vargas 2013, 250). But is this really an adequate characterization of the use to which we put the notion of moral responsibility? Certainly it is part of the use of the concept. This is a particularly important aspect of the concept from the point of view of metaphysical conceptions of moral responsibility: we must be the kind of agents—ultimately in control, free from deterministic forces—who *deserve* either punitive blame or the rewards of praise (cf. Strawson 1994).

But once we endorse the social thesis and focus on our social practices, the exclusive attention on praise and blame is unwarranted. Rather, my proposal is that whilst deserved praise and blameworthiness are among the regulatory norms of this practice, there is also a range of other moral judgments and responses that do important regulatory work—those implicated where moral failures warrant responses other than blame, for example. These are illustrated by our cases of moral ignorance above. Indeed, it is notable that when P. F. Strawson first introduced the reactive attitudes as constitutive of the social practice of holding responsible, his focus was not limited to praise and blame, but extended to a range of attitudes including resentment, gratitude, indignation, pride, and love. At least, then, it looks like a mistake to preclude, via conceptual fiat, the importance of other kinds of moral response to moral failures. Further, there are good reasons to suppose that these kinds of moral response may be at least as well placed as praise or blame to serve the purpose of cultivating sensitive agency. We should hope for a characterization of responsible agency and moral response that respects these broader possibilities.

How should we make room for these other kinds of moral response? One option would be to see moral responses such as disappointment, reproach, indignation, and so on simply as part of, or subsumed within, a model of blame and the regulatory norms governing its attribution and expression. With this move, the various moral responses are already captured by the liability assumption: that an agent is responsible when she is liable to blame (or praise) broadly construed. But this is obfuscatory on two counts. First, characterizations of blame are often importantly distinct from these other moral responses; supposing that all of them are a species of blame obscures important differences between them. For example, blame may aim to make an individual feel guilty; indignation may not. Blame may aim to cause suffering; disappointment may not (cf. Bennett 2002). Second, this move obfuscates the notion of liability, since there may be different conditions of warrant for these different kinds of moral response. For example, the warrant for blame may require that the agent meets epistemic conditions (she should have known the language was exclusionary); the warrant for disappointment may not (cf. Fricker 2010).

Another option, then, is to see these other modes of moral response as distinct from blame, and filling out our conception of the kinds of moral responses with which we engage each other as morally responsible agents. These other modes of moral response sit alongside blame as ways of holding each other to account (on tokened occasions) and improving our sensitivity to moral considerations (via our engagement in the practice). There are independent reasons for making this move: reflection on our practices does indeed reveal a broader range of moral communication than is captured by simply blame and praise. Some philosophical literature has addressed these modes of moral response, analyzing the structure and role of responses such as indignation, anger, contempt, and disappointment (e.g., Srinivasan 2017; Mason 2003; Fricker 2010; Westlund, chapter 10, this volume). Yet these responses and analyses are ignored by a conception of responsibility that treats responsible agency as constituted by liability to blame (or praise), narrowly construed.

Such a broadening of our moral responses is particularly appealing in combination with a scaffolded-responsiveness view of responsible agency. This view permits that agents may be morally responsible for failures of responsiveness in virtue of their capacity to be sensitized. Where sensitivity is indirect (via prospective audience), liability to a wider range of moral responses than blame may be particularly apt. There is clearly much more to be said here in articulating a fuller picture of these modes of moral response and the conditions for their warrant. My main aim in this section has been to motivate a framework that makes room for such work.

7 Beyond Revisionism about Responsibility

I have been engaged with the following set of theses about our practices of holding each other morally responsible:

- The social thesis
- The justification thesis
- Scaffolded-responsiveness about responsible agency
- A rejection of the liability assumption and an expanded repertoire of moral response.

This set of theses together stand in need of further defense. I want to close by offering some suggestive remarks about the methodological approach we might take whilst developing these theses. My proposal is that they can better be defended if we frame the task of doing so as an explicitly ameliorative analysis of responsibility, rather than as merely a revisionary project. What distinguishes these two approaches, and why does it matter which we adopt?

Revisionism, as we have seen, starts with "our" concept of moral responsibility, but acknowledges that we may have to revise some aspects of thinking about the concept and embrace certain new implications. But the method of inquiry is essentially conceptual analysis, with a commitment to rationalizing that concept as far as possible. We proceed by testing intuitions about the limit of our concept of responsibility (when someone is or is not responsible, and why), and try to get an analysis that best matches it whilst being both consistent and capable of doing the justificatory work needed. But such a project is essentially bound by a "principle of conservation," whereby "even though we are entertaining a revisionist proposal, there is still reason to limit the scope of revisions" (Vargas 2013, 103), so as not to depart too far from "our" concept. Such an analysis is therefore beholden to what Kelly McCormick (2013) calls the reference-anchoring problem: the problem of showing that the revised concept of responsibility yielded remains sufficiently close to the folk psychological concept, in order to avoid the charge of changing the subject. Moreover, revisionists face what McCormick calls the normativity-anchoring problem, which challenges the revisionist to explain why we should care about the new concept. Revisionists are skeptical about the force of folk intuitions per se, jettisoning some (incompatibilist ones) in formulating a revisionary account. Then, when we ask the justificatory question of why we should care about the revised concept—in this case, of responsibility-related practices—we find an appeal to the value of a certain form of agency. But the revisionist cannot appeal to intuition in support of this value, for, as we have seen, the revisionist is skeptical about folk intuition. So either revisionists must explain why some intuitions count for more than others, or—absent further argument—we lack adequate justificatory grounds for the revised concept.

I want to propose that an ameliorative analysis of responsibility is preferable and in particular is on a better footing in relation to these problems.[18] Ameliorative analyses do not try to unpack and articulate our concept. Instead, this sort of inquiry is normatively motivated: we start by asking what the legitimate purposes are for which we want and use the concept, and then, having articulated those purposes, we identify which concept we ought to use given those purposes. For example, an ameliorative analysis of moral responsibility could start by asking, do we want the concept to maximize utility? Or to track desert? Or to improve morally sensitive agency? Do we want the concept to be inclusive or elitist? Or do we want the concept at all? These questions are foregrounded in an ameliorative analysis, and the concept that can serve the legitimate purposes is then formulated. As such, there is no need for a principle of conservation, since the aim is not to give an analysis of "our" concept, but to set out an account of what the concept should be and should be used for. For example, we might identify the legitimate purpose to which we put the notion of moral responsibility as that of cultivating a certain kind of agency, via the means of moralized response.[19] We then ask what concept of responsibility we ought to deploy for this purpose. Such an approach avoids the reference-anchoring problem, since the ameliorative approach asks what our concept *ought to be*, and so it maintains no pretense that the analysis will yield a concept close to the extant folk concept. It is not an attempt at conceptual analysis of "our" concept: an ameliorative approach is explicit that it may change the subject. To the extent that the ameliorative analysis has to deal with questions about how far the analysis departs from our intuitive concept, this is a practical question about whether people could and will take up the newly formulated notion of responsibility, and not simply a worry about "changing the subject."

Further, conceiving of the project as an ameliorative analysis can also address the normativity-anchoring problem. Such an analysis need not reject (some, or all) intuitions as useful in theorizing. Indeed, proponents of this analysis can maintain that intuition—for example, about the value of certain aspects of our practice—provides important data for conceptual analysis. But the ameliorative project is simply different in kind: it attempts to ask what concept we ought to use for our legitimate purposes (rather than ask what our concept is). Accordingly, adopting this sort of analysis brings no methodological commitment to general skepticism about intuition, and we can rely on intuition as helpful and method-ologically respectable in guiding our understanding of what we want the concept to do for us, or in explaining the values that underpin the justification of the practice. Moreover, the ameliorative project needs to show that the concept argued for serves legitimate purposes, and it would have to argue for those purposes as legitimate. In this context, say, we would have to argue for the purpose of cultivating moral-considerations-sensitive agency as legitimate.[20] Arguing that this aim is legitimate is in principle consistent with conceptual pluralism; we might have different concepts for different legitimate purposes, subject to feasibility constraints.[21]

These considerations provide some reason for pursuing an ameliorative analysis, rather than a merely revisionary approach. However, there is a further strong reason for adopting this approach: doing so leads us to explicitly reflect on the question of what we want our concept of responsibility for and what work the concept *ought* to be doing for us. If our practices of responsibility are social practices, and thus contingent on the sustaining, critiquing, and reforming of certain social arrangements, it is right that we should carefully scrutinize and ask whether those social practices can be altered or improved. That is, once the social thesis is endorsed, and we move away from a view on which responsibility is simply a matter of certain metaphysical conditions being met, the question of how we want our responsibility practices to be is opened up.

I have suggested that if we want the concept to be doing work for us in practices that aim to cultivate moral-considerations-sensitive agency, then we should endorse the scaffolded-responsiveness account of moral responsibility. This view can serve those purposes by expanding the range of reasons to which we are (directly and indirectly) responsive at any time. This enables us to see morally responsible agency as implicated in a range of cases—such as those of moral ignorance—in which moral responses other than blame are engaged in order to further sensitize agents to the reasons in play. Some of the considerations I raised in defending the scaffolded-responsiveness view indeed drew on features of our practices as we find them. But this view may be best defended, I have suggested, by pursuing an ameliorative analysis. Such an account is better suited to engage both the role of the social practice of holding responsible, and of responsible agency, in contexts in which we often find ourselves, namely those in which our moral understanding is impoverished, but—we hope—improving. And surely this is what we want these social practices for.[22]

Notes

1. Note that revisionists face certain challenges: first, they must show that the account remains an analysis of *moral responsibility*. That is, they must show that the revisions made have not ended up changing the subject (McCormick [2013, 5] calls this the reference-anchoring problem). Second, they must show why the account delivered remains one we should still care about: since it does not capture all of our intuitions, does it still capture other important ones—or are there other things that can shore up the value of the practice we are left with (what McCormick [2013, 13] calls the normativity-anchoring problem)? Addressing these two concerns will be aided by facing a further challenge: namely, articulating what the practical implications are of adopting revisionism. For example, Vargas notes that if revisionism requires us to give up incompatibilist intuitions (intuitions that favor alternative possibilities, or require ultimate control, say), "there may be isolated pockets of our practice that . . . cannot continue as before" (2015, 2623). However, Vargas does not articulate what those parts that we may have to jettison would be. Yet my sense is that it will be difficult to fully meet the first two challenges before we have a good grasp on exactly how our responsibility practices themselves (rather than our concept) may change. I address these methodological issues in the final section.
2. We might worry about the fairness of Vargas's objections to Strawsonian psychologism, critiquing the practice as a whole (our dispositions, as humans, to engage in certain kinds of practice) by using a case that focuses on an individual's psychological dispositions (the example of jealous Dave, who has certain fixed psychological dispositions to feel jealous of his partner's other friendships, but comes to question the justifiability of the expression of these feelings [Vargas 2013, 162]). Just because individuals' dispositions are explanatory rather than justificatory, this does not mean that the set of dispositions as a feature of agents engaged in a practice has no justificatory power. Sommers (2013) has also raised this concern.
3. There are important differences between Vargas's model, which focuses on the effects of the system as a whole (i.e., a system of norms that regulate praise and blame), and McGeer's model, which focuses rather on the cultivation of sensitivity in particular tokens of moral response (such as blame or praise).
4. Vargas wants to resist framing this in terms of the agent's capacities remaining the same, but exercising them becoming more difficult—since this just pushes the issue back a step: our

abilities to exercise those capacities are not cross-situationally stable, even if the capacities themselves are (2013, 208). I actually think that "pushing the issue" back a step matters a great deal, for reasons articulated in section 5—namely, it allows us to maintain the claim that the individual is a responsible agent, albeit an agent who did not exercise her capacity to recognize reasons in that context.

5. Vargas spells out the details of how sensitive agents must be to qualify as responsible in counterfactual terms, which concern the frequency ("a suitable proportion of worlds" [2013, 214]) with which one would respond to moral considerations in relevantly similar contexts. Details are needed about this frequency (what proportion of possible worlds?) and about the description of contexts that are relevantly similar (coarse- or fine-grained descriptions of morally relevant considerations and contexts?). These matters are settled by looking to what proportion of possible worlds, described at what degree of fine- or coarse-grainedness up for discussion, is at least as good as any other in fostering moral-considerations-sensitive agency (2013, 219).

6. Of course, this is a difficult question for us to answer. Vargas relies on an ideal observer to determine this. It is not clear to me how this part of the picture integrates with an account whereby responsibility is constituted by our social practices, but I set this worry aside for another occasion.

7. McGeer and Pettit (2015) develop this model to explain how we should understand blame: as a sanction that enforces a specific or general injunction against inattentiveness to reasons, and that serves as a post hoc exhortation to be attentive. I am not persuaded by this aspect of their account, but it is not entailed by the scaffolded-responsiveness view, so we can regard these parts of the account as separable.

8. A related issue concerns the remarks about one's audience being "authorized" as a source of moral guidance or challenge (McGeer and Pettit 2015, 172), and whether this includes those one in fact views as authorized, or those one *should* authorize qua members of the moral community. The issue here and in the text is ultimately how much idealization is built into the conception of audience in the account.

9. I am grateful to Marina Oshana for helping me to pinpoint this dimension of difference between the two accounts. For an alternative way of formulating the relational aspects of responsibility, see Westlund, chapter 10, this volume.

10. On their view, the sanctioning component of the blame serves to fulfil the promised threat that accompanies the exhortation "attend to reasons or else" (McGeer and Pettit 2015, 183–185). I am not persuaded by this part of their view, but it seems to me inessential to the scaffolded view of responsible agency. I offer an alternative way of thinking about moral response, in section 6. Note also that this feature of McGeer and Pettit's view applies to particular tokens of blame, rather than the practices as a whole, which is a point at which their justification departs from Vargas's.

11. Or indeed, any notion of responsible agency—there may be others that fare better than either of the two available. I consider this the start of our inquiry, which may end up with a different account yet.

12. Other prominent examples in the literature on moral ignorance include Michele Moody-Adams's (1994) discussion of the alleged difficulty of recognizing the wrong of slavery in cultures in which slave ownership was common. Another, from Miranda Fricker's (2010) work, is that of a schoolteacher whose cultural context makes it difficult to grasp the moral insight that corporal punishment is wrong. I focus on Calhoun's case because it is (I assume) more proximal to the cultural context in which readers are located. This is not to say there are not many other analogous cases to which similar thoughts may apply (exploitation of cheap labor, climate pollution, the food industry, and so on and so on).

13. See Isaacs 1997; Calhoun 1989; Moody-Adams 1994; Fricker 2010; Saul 2013; Holroyd 2012; Brownstein 2016; and Washington and Kelly 2016.

14. Vargas writes, "[I]f the threat to a responsibility ascription operates via some threat to the normal capacity to respond to moral considerations (as seems more likely in cases of new, unusual, or particularly challenging contexts of action), then the issue is how these concerns are accommodated internal to some account of the capacities required for being subject

to the responsibility norms. In other words, we look to our theory of responsible agency" (2013, 183).

15. Note that it seems not at all clear that we should say similar things in the more standard case of moral ignorance: that holding responsible for gendered language is inappropriate since it provokes hostility, prevents buy-in to the norms against gendered language, and that the knowledge is not in place to permit sufficient sensitivity. This, for me, provides additional reason for doubting the circumstantialist view.

16. Though note that Fricker is concerned with cases in which we are at a historical distance from the wrongdoers, such that it may no longer be possible to capacitate them.

17. Note, however, Calhoun's detachment of the justification of reproach (responsibility) and its point (moral change).

18. For a statement of ameliorative analyses, see Haslanger 2000. For discussion of the contours of such an inquiry see Burgess and Plunkett, 2013a, 2013b.

19. Compare a consequentialist ameliorative analysis, which might specify the legitimate purpose as maximizing utility and specify a concept of responsibility that serves this purpose: blameworthy if susceptible to moral influence.

20. Compare Haslanger's (2000) ameliorative analysis of gender, which argues that ending gender inequality is the legitimate aim.

21. See Saul 2006; Jenkins 2016.

22. I am grateful for extremely useful feedback from the editors of this volume, and for constructive discussion with Federico Picinali, Yonatan Shemmer, Manuel Vargas, and audiences at Macquarie University and the University of Sheffield.

References

Bennett, C. 2002. "The Varieties of Retributive Experience." *The Philosophical Quarterly* 52 (207): 145–163.

Burgess, A., and D. Plunkett. 2013a. "Conceptual Ethics I." *Philosophy Compass* 8 (12): 1091–1101.

Burgess, A., and D. Plunkett. 2013b. "Conceptual Ethics II." *Philosophy Compass* 8 (12): 1102–1110.

Brownstein, M. 2016. "Attributionism and Moral Responsibility for Implicit Bias." *Review of Philosophy and Psychology* 7 (4): 765–786.

Calhoun, C. 1989. "Responsibility and Reproach." *Ethics* 99 (2): 389–406.

Czopp, A. M., M. J. Monteith, and A. Y. Mark. 2006. "Standing Up for a Change: Reducing Bias through Interpersonal Confrontation." *Journal of Personality and Social Psychology* 90 (5): 784–803.

Duguid, M. M., and M. C. Thomas-Hunt. 2015. "Condoning Stereotyping? How Awareness of Stereotyping Prevalence Impacts Expression of Stereotypes." *Journal of Applied Psychology* 100 (2): 343–359.

Fischer, J. M., and M. Ravizza. 2000. *Responsibility and Control: A Theory of Moral Responsibility.* Cambridge: Cambridge University Press.

Fricker, M. 2010. "I—The Relativism of Blame and Williams's Relativism of Distance." In *Aristotelian Society Supplementary Volume* 84 (1): 151–177.

Jenkins, K. 2016. "Amelioration and Inclusion: Gender Identity and the Concept of Woman." *Ethics* 126 (2): 394–421.

Holroyd, J. 2012. "Responsibility for Implicit Bias." *Journal of Social Philosophy* 43 (3): 274–306.

Haslanger, S. 2000. "Gender and Race: (What) Are They? (What) Do We Want Them to Be?" *Noûs* 34 (1): 31–55.

Isaacs, T. 1997. "Cultural Context and Moral Responsibility." *Ethics* 107 (4): 670–684.

Mason, M. 2003. "Contempt as a Moral Attitude." *Ethics* 113 (2): 234–272.

McCormick, K. 2013. "Anchoring a Revisionist Account of Moral Responsibility." *Journal of Ethics & Social Philosophy* 7 (3): 1–19.

McGeer, V. 2015. "Building a Better Theory of Responsibility." *Philosophical Studies* 172 (10): 2635–2649.

McGeer, V., and P. Pettit 2015. "The Hard Problem of Responsibility." In *Oxford Studies in Agency and Responsibility, Vol. 3*, edited by D. Shoemaker, 160–188. Oxford: Oxford University Press.

Moody-Adams, M. M. 1994. "Culture, Responsibility, and Affected Ignorance." *Ethics* 104 (2): 291–309.

Saul, J. 2006. "Philosophical Analysis and Social Kinds: Gender and Race." In *Aristotelian Society Supplementary Volume* 80 (1): 119–143.

Saul, J. 2013. "Implicit Bias, Stereotype Threat, and Women in Philosophy." In *Women in Philosophy: What Needs to Change?*, edited by K. Hutchison and F. Jenkins, 39–60. New York: Oxford University Press.

Scaife, R., T. Stafford, A. Bunge, and J. Holroyd. "The Effects of Moral Interactions on Implicit Bias." Unpublished manuscript.

Smart, J. J. C. 1973. "An Outline of a Utilitarian System of Ethics." In *Utilitarianism: For and Against*, edited by J. J. C. Smart and B. Williams, 3–76. Cambridge: Cambridge University Press.

Sommers, T. 2013. Review of *Building Better Beings: A Theory of Moral Responsibility*, by Manuel Vargas. *Notre Dame Philosophical Reviews*. https://ndpr.nd.edu/news/42827-building-better-beings-a-theory-of-moral-responsibility/.

Srinivasan, A. 2017. "The Aptness of Anger." *The Journal of Political Philosophy*. doi: 10.1111/jopp.12130.

Strawson, G. 1994. "The Impossibility of Moral Responsibility." *Philosophical Studies* 75 (1): 5–24.

Strawson, P. F. 1962. "Freedom and Resentment." *Proceedings of the British Academy* 48: 1–25.

Vargas, M. 2013. *Building Better Beings: A Theory of Moral Responsibility*. Oxford: Oxford University Press.

Vargas, M. 2015. "Précis of *Building Better Beings: A Theory of Moral Responsibility*." *Philosophical Studies* 172 (10): 2621–2623.

Vargas, M. 2017. "Implicit Bias, Responsibility and Moral Ecology." In *Oxford Studies in Agency and Responsibility, Vol. 4*, edited by David Shoemaker, 219–247. Oxford: Oxford University Press.

Washington, N., and D. Kelly. 2016. "Who Is Responsible for This?" In *Implicit Bias and Philosophy, Vol. 2*. edited by M. Brownstein and J. Saul, 11–36. New York: Oxford University Press.

6

Respecting Each Other and Taking Responsibility for Our Biases

ELINOR MASON

1 Introduction

One puzzling feature of a world like ours, one riven with various sorts of prejudice and oppression, is that oppressive behavior is not always malicious. An individual who has simply absorbed the attitudes of his social world might be entirely well meaning, honestly doing his best. The old-fashioned sexist, who takes his own behavior to be appropriate and chivalrous, has no idea that he is actually patronizing and belittling the women around him. From his point of view, he is acting entirely appropriately, and furthermore, he is justified in that view, given the world in which he has been raised. In that case, there is a puzzle about how and why such a person might be blameworthy.

The standard view about blameworthiness is that, in order to be blameworthy, it is crucial that the agent has bad motives of some sort: what philosophers tend to call a bad will. But once we think about the nature of the agent's environment in cases like the old-fashioned sexist, it is not clear that we can locate the problematic aspects of the agent's behavior in the agent's will—rather, the problem comes from outside, from the nature of the society. It seems that such agents are nonculpably ignorant of the relevant moral truths. Thus the bad act does not reflect a poor quality of will. Yet, when people act in sexist and racist ways, through implicit bias, or more or less explicit bias, we are not inclined to take such agents to be beyond reproach. So the question I attempt to answer in this chapter is, in what way can we blame such agents? What is the basis, if any, for blaming them?

The answer I give is that agents are sometimes blameworthy (where I really mean that they are blame*worthy*, and not just that it is permissible to reproach them), even if they do not have any bad will. I argue that although the paradigmatic account of blameworthiness is based on quality of will, we can and should be willing to allow that there are nonparadigmatic cases. I argue that the zone of responsibility can be extended to include acts that we are not fully in control of, and acts whose moral status we are nonculpably ignorant about at the time of acting. This extension of responsibility happens through a voluntary *taking* of responsibility. In what follows, I argue that there are certain conditions under which we should take responsibility, and that when we do so, we genuinely are responsible.

I start by arguing that it is indeed possible that some racist and sexist agents act without bad will, and so there is a category of problematic behavior that is not covered by traditional approaches to blameworthiness. I argue that Cheshire Calhoun's suggestion (1989), that we should make a distinction between blame and moral reproach, does not go far enough in the cases that I am interested in. Intuitively, in these cases, we need something closer to full-blown blame, despite the admitted lack of bad will. Finally, I present my own suggestion, which is that we should think of a sphere of responsibility that is not based on bad will, but rather, is based on agents' *taking responsibility*. I argue that we can understand the reasons for taking responsibility in terms of our relationships with others, whether those are personal relationships, or the relationships we have in virtue of a shared society.

2 Quality of Will

The central compatibilist idea, an idea we originally see in Hobbes and Hume, that gets refined by more recent philosophers such as Strawson (1962) and Frankfurt (1971), is that the crucial thing for moral responsibility is the *quality of will* behind the act.[1] The phrase 'quality of will' (due to Strawson 1962) is now a term of art in this field, but I will very briefly explain what I mean by it. It would be a mistake to think that 'will' in 'quality of will' picks out something sui generis or mysterious. Rather, the word is being used to refer to an everyday notion: the motivations that lead to an action. So saying that what matters for moral responsibility is quality of will is just saying that what matters is how an agent was motivated.[2]

One major disagreement in the contemporary literature on compatibilism is over whether nonculpable ignorance is always an excuse. Volitionists argue that if an agent does not know what she is doing when she acts, she cannot be held responsible—she does not have the right sort of quality of will. According to volitionists, there is a control condition on responsibility, such that an agent must be in control of what she is doing, where that includes knowing what she is doing under the relevant description. For a hard-line volitionist, nonculpably acquired ignorance is always an excuse. So an agent who does not know that the money she donates to charity is actually going straight into the pockets of oligarchs cannot be held responsible for that, and the agent who does not know that he is insulting someone by calling her 'young lady' cannot be held responsible for that, and so on.[3]

By contrast, attributionists argue that quality of will can be good or bad *without* self-conscious knowledge of what is being done.[4] Attributionists argue that we can be blameworthy or praiseworthy as a result of our unconscious motivations. In Angela Smith's example (2005), the agent forgets her friend's birthday. She didn't forget deliberately, and there is (let's assume) nothing she deliberately did that caused her to forget. But her forgetting is caused by her bad will, by the fact that she does not care enough about her friend. An agent may tell herself that she is acting well, but in fact be driven by bad motivations. Words of "kindness" are sometimes passive aggressive. Omissions and forgettings often indicate carelessness. A slip is sometimes Freudian. Thus, according to attributionists, we can say that the agent is blameworthy, even though she acted in ignorance.

My own view is that these are both ways of having a relevant quality of will, and although they give rise to slightly different sorts of blameworthiness, they are both important ways of being responsible.[5] One way to have a bad will is to act badly knowing exactly what you are doing. Another way to have a bad will is to have bad motivations that one is not aware of. Having bad motivations is a way of having a bad will, even when there is no history of self-aware, culpable acts that led to these bad motivations. Of course, it may not be easy to determine what is going on in a particular case. Even in one's own case it is not always easy to tell how deep motivations are working, and what knowledge one has at a subconscious level. But there is nonetheless a fairly clear foundation for blameworthiness here: blameworthiness depends on bad will, understood in one of these two ways.[6]

3 Bad Actions without Bad Will

In this section, I discuss three categories of bad action that (arguably) do not emanate from a bad will. In all three cases, the standard view is that we are not blameworthy for these actions. But we rightly, I argue, feel some unease with the standard view. Blameworthiness in these cases may be complex, but it is not obvious that there is no blameworthiness.

Some of the ways in which an agent can produce a bad outcome without a bad will are entirely innocent and uncontroversial—cases where the bad outcome is entirely down to obscurity or glitches in the outside world, and has nothing to do with agency per se. For example, an agent whose car breaks down

in a completely unpredictable way is not blameworthy for consequently missing a meeting. An agent is not to blame for wasting a charitable donation when
the money is, through hidden and obscure means, going astray. An agent whose
well-meaning words of kindness hit a raw nerve and offend someone in a way
that could not reasonably have been expected is not blameworthy for the offense.

But there are also cases where although it is plausible that an agent does not
have a bad will, it is not completely clear that the agent is off the hook. These are
the cases that I focus on here.

3.1 Implicit Bias

One such case is the phenomenon of implicit or unconscious bias. I want to
remain neutral on what sort of attitude or attitudes implicit bias is composed of.[7]
All I want to commit to is that implicit biases are revealed in our behavior (our
hiring behavior, for example) and that we are not aware of having these biases.

There is broad agreement, both in the volitionist camp and in the attributionist camp, that we can be *indirectly* responsible for our biases in a fairly straightforward way.[8] If we are aware that we have biases, or are likely to, and if we know that
there are things we can do to avoid having or manifesting biases, then obviously
we should do those things, and if we do not, we are blameworthy. This is just
analogous to indirect responsibility for our car malfunctioning. If we know that
the brakes need to be checked, and we don't check them, we are blameworthy
for the accident that is caused by the brakes failing.

However, there is disagreement over whether we can be *directly* responsible
for our biases, or for the actions caused by our biases, and this is a hard question
even for attributionists. Our biases are usually the result of absorbing problematic ideas from our culture. Thus they are importantly different from character
traits, though they may appear to work in the same way. An innately misanthropic
person is like that by nature, and so although we do not blame him for acquiring
the trait (after all, he did not acquire it deliberately or though carelessness), we
do blame him for the behavior that manifests the trait. We also judge the person
for *being* misanthropic—for having (though not for acquiring) the trait.[9]

An implicit bias is not usually acquired deliberately or through carelessness,
and so the agent is not usually blameworthy for acquiring the bias.[10] However,
the mere fact that a bias is caused by external forces does not mean that it does
not implicate the agent's will. We must be careful not to confuse the origin of a
trait with its nature. A misanthrope may be misanthropic because of a virus con-
tracted in infancy, but that does not make a difference to how misanthropic he
is. His quality of will is not affected by the fact of a certain history (and though
of course different histories tend to produce different qualities of will, they may
not). If we consistently stick to the claim that it is just the quality of will itself

that merits blame, then the *origin* of the trait cannot deliver an excuse.[11] The question, then, is not just where the trait comes from, but to what extent is the agent's will engaged in the exercise of the trait?

There is good reason to think that implicit biases often implicate the agent's will. People who test positive for implicit racist biases also tend to exhibit avoidance behavior, suggesting that there is something visceral going on, something that it would be hard to characterize without referring to the agent's deep motivations.[12] Compare a tendency to underestimate certain sorts of probability—the likelihood that two people in a room have the same birthday, for example. This tendency, which many of us have, is probably innate, but it does not seem to implicate our will in any interesting way. We do not make the error out of any suspect motivation. We just make it because our brains are pretty bad at dealing with probabilities. Implicit bias of the sort I am discussing here, by contrast, is very much involved in the moral texture of the world. It is very plausible that our deep motivations make us susceptible to implicit biases, that we are predisposed to accept hierarchies that favor us or that resonate with other morally suspect motivations.

So the attributionist account gets a foothold here. Our biases are very likely to go hand in hand with problematic motivations such as contempt, disgust, and so on. Thus there is a way to defend the view that implicit bias is, in itself, directly blameworthy: it may be a way of having a bad will. I think it is likely that many cases of implicit bias are like this.

However, there *may* be biases that do not involve bad will. Returning to the point that implicit biases seem to come from outside us, there is another way to understand this so that it makes more sense as a potential excuse. It might be that the operation of biases *bypasses* our will. We might just absorb information about stereotypes and reproduce it in our behavior without any attitude being involved at all. On this picture, we are, as animals, as machines, partly automated. I have no idea if that is correct, but it seems at least passingly plausible.[13] If our biases operate by bypassing our wills, then it cannot be said that we have a bad will in exhibiting bias.

In that case, neither volitionism nor attributionism could make sense of direct responsibility for biases. We would be left with a picture whereby, so long as we have taken all the measures that we reasonably could to avoid bias and its results, we would not be responsible for remaining biased. In the actual world, where we do not have good techniques for avoiding or ameliorating bias, that would leave a lot of bias and manifestation of bias blameless.

Perhaps this conclusion is acceptable, though it strikes me as unsatisfactory. Agency is complex. There isn't a clear dividing line between what we do through our will in the sense relevant for blameworthiness, and what just happens. Even if implicit biases are automated and do not engage my motivations, and so do not reflect bad will, they nonetheless seem to issue from my agency. They do not seem to be in the category of mere events—if I unknowingly discriminate against the women on the shortlist, this is something *I have done*. It seems too quick to say that I am not responsible in any way. So we have a puzzle here—on the one hand, it might be that implicit bias does not involve bad will. On the other hand, there is a strong pull to find it blameworthy.

3.2 Explicit Bias

Explicit bias may not involve awareness of wrongdoing, but it also probably involves bad will most of the time, and so the attributionist sort of blameworthiness is applicable.[14] Both racism and homophobia seem intimately related to obviously problematic attitudes, like disgust and contempt. Racist and homophobic attitudes may be couched in terms of factual claims (about intelligence, or God's will, or whatever), but it does not seem likely that these factual mistakes are mere factual mistakes. It is fairly obvious that these mistakes are motivated by hostile attitudes.

Sexist attitudes, like racist and homophobic ones, also usually seem to depend on false factual beliefs. But it is very often plausible that sexist attitudes are not hostile and that they are not underlaid with contempt or disgust. Consider this example from Cheshire Calhoun:

> Imagine, for example, a man who always refers to women as "girls" or "ladies." He, too, is uncoerced into doing so and is in complete possession of normal adult reasoning faculties. Yet it seems he ought not to be blamed for linguistically infantilizing or patronizing women, for, from his point of view, one cannot reasonably expect him to see anything wrong with his actions. We may suppose that in his childhood, his father and mother referred to women as "girls" or "ladies." He may also have come to understand that the former is flattering because it suggests youth and the latter simply polite. We may suppose that the people to whom he was exposed when he was growing up gave him examples only of this linguistic use and this understanding of its significance. From his point of view, it is natural to conclude that "girl" is flattering rather than infantilizing and that "lady" is polite rather than patronizing. (Calhoun 1989, 398)

In this example, arguably, the man has no bad will at all. He is ignorant, for sure, but he is ignorant in an understandable way—he is not culpably ignorant. Nor is he exhibiting bad will in the attributionist sense. All his motivations toward women are benign. They are patronizing, and he would probably assent to various claims that are patently false, such as that women are less good drivers than men. But from his point of view, his attitudes are apt, just as we believe (I hope correctly) that patting a dog, calling it a "good doggy," and praising it for sitting on command, are apt rather than patronizing. We can make a distinction between sexism and misogyny: not all sexism involves misogyny.[15]

There is an important point worth emphasizing here, and that is that the more historically isolated the case, the more likely we are to think that it is possible for the agent to be sexist without a bad will. Miranda Fricker (2007) considers an example of sexism that involves no bad will (though she does not frame it quite in those terms). In Fricker's example, taken from Patricia Highsmith's novel, *The Talented Mr Ripley*, the character of Herbert Greenleaf repeatedly discounts the views of Marge, the young woman who would have become his daughter-in-law had his son not been murdered. Marge is actually correct about the identity of the murderer, but Greenleaf repeatedly ignores her insights. From his point of view, Marge is not worth taking seriously (Fricker 2007, 14–15).[16]

Fricker's main argument is that one of the ways that a social hierarchy affects us is by affecting the credibility levels we accord to others.[17] As Fricker points out, and as others have argued before her, we do not give as much weight to the testimony of people who are lower down in the social hierarchy.[18] So the question arises, are people blameworthy for committing this testimonial injustice? Fricker argues that the agent is not blameworthy (100–101).[19]

Fricker's background thought is that Greenleaf's ignorance is non-culpable. His attitude toward Marge is not hostile or contemptuous on a personal level. He believes, and is justified in believing, that her perspective is inferior. We can imagine for the sake of argument (especially as he is fictional) that he has made no epistemic slips, there is nothing he missed, nothing going on that he is not in control of. The problem is in the world, not in him. Let's also stipulate that there is no bad will. It seems plausible that agents in solidly sexist eras are in the grip of cultural norms that are so powerful that the agent can accept them without any extra push from suspect motivations.

Things look different when the relevant evidence is readily available. Most of us now have evidence that we are all prone to biases, and that there is systematic discrimination against women and people of color, and so on. When the evidence is "available," it becomes less likely that someone who gets things wrong has no bad will. However, there are various reasons why available evidence might not be availed of. One reason is bad will. But there are other reasons: the agent might be isolated from the evidence by peculiar circumstances or by non-sinister character traits. In what follows, I will be working on the assumption that it is possible that even in our era, people can be in the grip of sexist conceptual frameworks that, though sexist, do not reflect a bad will.

I agree with Fricker that when the evidence is not available, there is some undermining of blameworthiness for false moral views.[20] Of course, the issue of evidence may not be necessary to establish blameworthiness: it may be that the attitude itself involves a bad will, and as I pointed out earlier, the attributionist account is sufficient to establish blameworthiness. But let's assume that it is possible to have sexist (or otherwise problematic) attitudes without having a bad will. My hunch is that in both the historical and present-day cases, we think that the agent is blameworthy in some way for those attitudes, even when the agent does not have a bad will. My aim in this chapter is to vindicate that thought. I also explain why an agent in the historical case is less blameworthy than the agent in the present day, given that (by hypothesis) neither has a bad will.

3.3 Glitches

I want to briefly mention one more area where there are bad acts without bad will. This category of acts is not connected with our prejudices, but with the flawed nature of our agency. Sometimes, we just forget things, or don't notice them, in ways that do not reflect a bad will. Randolph Clarke (2014) imagines a man who has promised his spouse that he will get milk on the way home. Imagine that there is nothing that he has failed to do that he should have done in order to remember. He could have set reminders, but it would have been "borderline compulsive" behavior to do so. He could have stopped himself from thinking about his work on the way home, but he often thinks about his work, and with no bad effects (2014, 165).[21] In other words, we are to imagine a case where an agent forgets something and there is no bad will. Forgetting the milk is not very important, but we sometimes forget things that are much more important, and again, it seems possible that there is no bad will in these cases. From now on I will call these unmotivated forgettings "glitches."

Many philosophers have argued that in this sort of case, if there really is no bad will, then the agent is not responsible.[22] Clarke disagrees; he says that the agent is responsible, and responsible just because he has fallen below a standard (2014, 167). The problem with that response is that it is not clear what 'falling below a standard' means. If it means that the agent did it knowingly, or with unconscious bad will, then we are back to the standard accounts of what renders an agent blameworthy: some sort of bad will. If, on the other hand, the agent fell below a standard without realizing it, without intending it, or without being poorly motivated with respect to that standard, then we have no reason to think the agent is blameworthy. There are many ways of falling below a standard that have no implications at all for blameworthiness—I might simply be too short to go on the rollercoaster.

In all of the cases I have mentioned (some implicit biases, some explicit biases, and glitches), we are pulled in two directions. On the one hand, the absence of a bad will seems to indicate an excuse, as it usually does. In these cases, the will is not engaged in the action in the right way for the standard accounts of responsibility to get a hold. In some (but not all) cases of implicit bias (at least possibly), the will is bypassed by some heuristic the brain has. In some cases of explicit bias (again, the claim is not that all cases are like this, just that it is a possibility), so long as the beliefs are not inherently contemptuous, it is possible to accept them "innocently." In the case of glitches, obviously, there is just a glitch—sometimes we just slip for no reason.

On the other hand, it is not obvious that the agent is off the hook. Think about how we would feel on realizing that we have acted badly in one of these ways. Imagine being presented with evidence that our selection of job candidates was racially biased. Or imagine being presented with video evidence that we did not listen to a suggestion or argument from a female colleague, and yet when the same point was presented by a man we took it seriously. And of course, the experience of realizing that we have forgotten something important is familiar. In all those cases, I think, we are likely to feel something akin to guilt.

Introspection is not a completely reliable test here. First, we sometimes take on more or less guilt than we should—I return to that point in section 6. Second, what we should immediately do when presented with the evidence as in the above cases, and what most of us would immediately do, is examine our own conscience for bad will. Did I in fact forget your birthday because I don't care about you? Do I subconsciously undervalue people of color, or women? We might feel guilty because we assume that we do harbor bad will, even when we cannot find it, and it is probably a good thing that we are inclined to self-examination in these cases, and inclined to find ourselves guilty until proven innocent. But this is not the sort of guilt (or blameworthiness) that I seek to vindicate here.

So let's stipulate that in these cases there is no bad will. Let's imagine, further, that we are presented with the explanation for our behavior. Imagine that the mechanisms of the brain, the way it absorbs and encodes information, the way it glitches, and so on, are all explained to us. Should we now feel that we can safely distance ourselves from our actions, that our actions are not our fault, but rather are things that happen to us, just as if we were blown by the wind? I think not. I think it would be *apt* to feel responsible in these cases, and I will defend that view in the rest of the chapter.

4 Reproach

Let's return to Calhoun's discussion of the well-meaning man, whose basic framework for understanding the world is sexist. Calhoun herself does not put the issue in terms of whether the man has a bad quality of will.[23] She tacitly takes for granted that the man does not have a bad will, and that therefore he is not blameworthy. Calhoun's concern is whether we should nonetheless blame him. Calhoun's answer is that we cannot let him off the hook, because that amounts to condoning his behavior, and it impedes moral progress. Calhoun argues that although this man is not strictly blameworthy, we should *reproach* him.

I am entirely in agreement with Calhoun's argument for reproach in this case, but as Calhoun herself says, that is not the same as saying that he is blameworthy. It is worth stressing this distinction. Our reasons for reproaching, that is to say, the act of reproaching, can differ from what we think of as the paradigm reasons for holding responsible without becoming the wrong sorts of reasons. The paradigm reason for holding someone responsible is that they *are* responsible. On the compatibilist account, that means that they have a relevant quality of will. But there can be other valid reasons for reproaching people.[24] For example, we may reproach children for things we don't actually take them to be responsible for in order to teach them how to *be* responsible. The sense in which Calhoun suggests we should hold the benignly motivated sexist responsible is not quite like that, because the context is very different, as she points out (1989, 401). But the justifying reasons for holding responsible are similar, in that they are forward-looking; they relate to the way we would like things to be, as opposed to being an assessment of what an agent has done in the past.[25]

My focus here is not on holding responsible; it is on *being* responsible, and on blame*worthiness*. In the next section, I argue that there is a way to make sense of blameworthiness proper in cases like the old-fashioned sexist.

5 Taking Responsibility

Before I present my argument for taking responsibility for biases, I need to make clear that I am talking about responsibility in the sense of blameworthiness, and not about *liability*. Liability, legal or conventional, is just the duty to make amends in the event that a bad outcome occurs. Strict liability (as it is called in law) does not imply that the agent who is liable must have a bad will, or even that she herself performs the relevant act: one can be liable for what one's tenant, or children do, and for what the wind does, or what just happens. Liability does not imply blameworthiness.

I am not talking about liability here. It may well be that we should take on liability in some of the cases I am interested in, but I am suggesting something more ambitious. I am suggesting that we should take on *responsibility* for these actions. We should *own* them: we should feel about them as we feel about the actions that we do deliberately, or out of good or bad will that we were not aware of at the time. We should be willing to extend the realm of our own responsibility.

Or, to put it another way, we should be willing to limit the excuses that we take ourselves to be entitled to appeal to. In general, we can appeal to various sorts of luck, accident, inadvertence, and ignorance as an excuse, but the kind of inadvertence that is in play here will not count as an excuse.

I shall motivate my claim that we should sometimes take responsibility by using an example.[26] Imagine a conversation between Angela and her friend, after Angela has forgotten an important birthday. Imagine that Angela searches her own conscience and finds no flaw in her will at all. Let's say, for the sake of argument, that she is accurate in her introspection. It is not the case that she failed to care enough. Rather, her forgetting her friend's birthday was just a glitch. Imagine that she now says to her friend, "Hey, you have nothing to worry about, it's not a big deal, I just forgot." There is something lacking in this response. The friend might justifiably feel that an apology is owed even if there was no bad will: she might feel, and with good reason, it seems, that the lack of bad will is not entirely exonerating.

We can imagine further, that Angela accepts that she should apologize. She accepts liability (though we do not usually talk about liability in contexts where restitution consists only, or mainly, of an apology). Her friend might still feel something is amiss. The friend might ask whether Angela feels bad, and meet this response: "No, I don't feel bad. As I said, it was a glitch. I have nothing to feel bad about. I have apologized. What more do you want?" There is a natural thought that her friend might reasonably reply, "I want you to feel bad about it! I want you to feel guilty—to take responsibility. This is not about you. It's about me. I hoped for a card from you on my birthday, and you just forgot!"

There are, of course, complexities in this story. One possible line of objection points to the fact that in most cases where we fail in a duty, even if it is completely clearly not blameworthy, it would be cold-hearted not to feel *anything* in response to the failure, but the appropriate feelings are not necessarily guilt and remorse; they are more like regret, sympathy, and empathy. The problem with Angela in this story, we might say, is just that she seems so cold-hearted.

It is true that when we fail in a duty, even when it is not through bad will, it is usually fitting to feel sympathy and empathy and so on, and it is true of course that we don't tend to like people who shrug off those feelings as unimportant. But there is more than that going on with Angela. Angela insists that she does not feel bad. She takes a very strict approach to her own responsibility—she knows that she had no bad will, and for her, that is the end of the story. But her friend wants more; their relationship demands more.

You might think that the friend is just wrong about things, and that Angela's clear-sighted assessment of the situation is preferable. But I am not arguing about what the reasons or evidence supports. I am talking about what we want from our loved ones, and the attitudes that we take as evidence that they are committed to us in the right sort of way. The idea here is that it is not always appropriate to insist on the paradigmatic criteria for blameworthiness. As an analogy: the paradigmatic criteria for love might preclude loving our dogs. But the clear truth is that we do love our dogs. So we must adjust our conception of what love is.

In the example above, I focused on a personal relationship and the way in which personal relationships can have internal demands that do not align with philosophical conceptions of blameworthiness. Next, let's turn to failures to do one's duty to other people, where the duty is not a duty arising from a personal relationship, but just a duty we have to our fellow people. Start with implicit bias. Imagine that we discover that we are one of the subjects in the well-known hiring bias experiment, in which CVs associated with female names, or traditionally black names, are judged as less worthy than identical CVs that appear to belong to white men (Steinpreis, Anders, and Ritzke 1999; Bertrand and Mullainthan 2004). Imagine that you are confronted with the evidence that you have done this. In many cases, this may involve bad will, of familiar or more complex kinds.[27] But let's stipulate again, that in the cases I am discussing, there was no bad will. The act is like a glitch, in that it just happens, though of course the causal mechanism is slightly different in a glitch.

Again, there are complexities here. Of course you should accept liability: you should be willing to do your best to rectify the situation. And you should feel emotions like regret and sympathy. But, I argue, as a member of a society in which there are women and people of color, and a history of oppression, you should be willing to take on extended responsibility for this sort of failing. You should feel, not just regret, but something akin to guilt or remorse. Taking on that responsibility is constitutive of respecting your fellow community members in the appropriate way. Taking on responsibility reflects the gravity and nature of the offense. In treating someone as less valuable because of race or sex, we are undermining their personhood. We go some way to restoring it by taking on extended responsibility for our error.

Again, I will try to motivate the claim by using an example. Take an example of explicit bias: imagine that we explain to Calhoun's character (call him Stan) that "young lady" is patronizing, and that he should not think of men and women as having different roles and properties. Let's assume, as before, that Stan had no bad will, and that he approaches the issue with a willingness to believe that he has made a mistake. He tries hard to understand that age is irrelevant, and that gender neutrality is best, but that if there is no gender-neutral way to address someone, "woman" is better than "lady." Imagine two attitudes he might take to his own future errors:

Stan Doing His Best:
This is all very complex. I'm not sure that I am going to get it right.
If I get it wrong, though, it's just an innocent mistake. Don't blame

me. I really am trying. I am doing my best. You can't ask more of me than that.

Stan Responsible:
This is all very complex. I'm not sure that I am going to get it right. I will feel terrible if I get it wrong in future, now that I understand more about all this, and I apologize in advance. But of course I am absolutely going to try my best.

Let me stipulate that each really is willing to try their best, that each *believes* that 'young lady' is patronizing. Nonetheless, Stan Responsible has taken the seriousness of the issue to heart, in a way that Stan Doing His Best has not. The fact that he will feel terrible shows that he is thinking about the women he will encounter in the future, and the way that his attitude to them will affect them. He is thinking of himself as having a relationship with other members of the community, a relationship that requires respect. So even though he knows that he may accidentally get something wrong in the future, and he knows that doing so would not betray a bad will on his part, he *takes* responsibility—he does not allow himself to appeal to inadvertence as an excuse.

By contrast, Stan Doing His Best seems more concerned with himself. He seems to have examined his conscience, found it clear, and takes it that doing his best is enough. What more can he do? He can't do more, of course, and my argument is not that he should do more than his best—he should do his best. But he should also eschew the excuse that further slips would be entirely inadvertent. He should take on responsibility.

Think about the way in which we are all Stan. We are, most of us, in a situation where we know that we are likely to be in the grip of various problematic views and assumptions, ways of framing the world and social relations that we have inherited and have not yet had our consciousness raised about. What should we be more concerned with: our own consciences, or the people to whom we are being unfair in our ignorance? The issue of whether or not we have a bad will is not the important issue. The important issue is that we take seriously that we are wronging someone. Taking it seriously involves taking responsibility for it, feeling bad about it.

And think about how we feel as the injured party. What do we want from our fellow members of society? We want them to do their best to avoid being biased against us, obviously. And I am not denying that that is the main thing we want. But that doesn't mean that we don't also want them to take seriously the wrongs they do us. Imagine a conversation between a woman and her male head of department, where he apologizes for having failed to promote her a few years ago. He explains that he now sees that although he did not have any bad will at all, he was unfortunately biased in various ways, and that he will now rectify the situation.

Again, he may or may not take on responsibility as well as liability. Understanding that he has actually taken responsibility, that he feels remorse, makes a huge difference to this exchange and to how things are in the future. Liability is not enough. Being a decent fellow member of a department, being a decent fellow member of a society, requires taking on responsibility for inadvertent injustices. So, when we inadvertently fail in our duties to others, where those duties are duties of relationships, personal or impersonal, we should take on responsibility.

The 'should' here is normative, but it does not indicate a moral duty. This is usefully illustrated by contrasting my argument with an argument presented by David Enoch. Enoch (2012) argues that we sometimes have a moral duty to take responsibility in areas where agency is 'penumbral'. Enoch's account of the range of actions for which we might take on responsibility is much wider than mine: Enoch talks about responsibility for what one's child does, for an accident that kills a pedestrian, and for what one's country does.[28] Thus our concerns are slightly different. I am concerned with actions that are genuinely an agent's actions. This illustrates an important problem in Enoch's account. The area of "penumbral agency" is not really an area of agency at all. It is an area in which we might reasonably be held *liable*, but it would be stretching things to say that we might be genuinely responsible, or blameworthy in my sense. Enoch conflates taking on responsibility with taking on liability.

The difference between taking on liability and taking on responsibility is a difference in the psychology of the agent—the attitudes and feelings that they are taking on. When we feel responsible for an action, we must feel that it is our action, that we did it, that we own it. Feelings of remorse and so on are apt when the agent herself acts badly, but are not apt in regard to the actions of others. Thus we cannot take on responsibility for the actions of others. We can take on liability. Taking on liability is just willingness to perform acts of recompense in the event of a bad outcome. It does not involve ownership, or the attendant feelings of remorse and so on.

It might be objected that what one should feel when one has inadvertently acted badly is not remorse, but something more like what Bernard Williams calls "agent regret" (1981, 27; 1993, 69). Indeed, Miranda Fricker, in a recent article, makes exactly this claim (2016). Fricker imagines someone who, through no epistemic fault, is in the grip of sexist prejudices. Such a person might be innocent in having acquired such bad views (they have come from the epistemic environment), and also justified in thinking that she is free of such prejudices. Fricker compares that person to Oedipus, as discussed by Williams (1993). Fricker says, "Both do voluntary things the significance of which, through no fault of their own, they do not grasp; and in both cases their failure to grasp it is down to their circumstances or environment. They both suffer a kind of *environmental* bad luck" (2016, 45).

The notion of agent regret is much weaker than the notion of remorse. It is also much broader. Williams (1981, 1993) uses various examples to justify his idea that agent regret is an overlooked moral emotion. One example depends on outcome luck: he compares two lorry drivers who drive with the same level of care: one kills a child, and one does not. The example of Oedipus seems a bit different, as Fricker points out. Oedipus acts deliberately, but he doesn't know what he is doing; he is unaware of some important facts. And what would we say about Helen of Troy—should she feel agent regret? Did she launch a thousand ships? Of course not, but at the same time, we might think it odd if Helen feels absolutely nothing about the fact that the Trojan War started because of her face. To be fair to Helen, her face did nothing—it was perceived in certain ways by certain people, and *they* started the Trojan War, but still, it was Helen's face, and even if her actions were beyond reproach, it would be odd of her to feel nothing at all. So we might be drawn to the view that there are shades of agent regret, varying in both quantity and quality.

This leads to the very natural thought that remorse as well as agent regret comes in various shades. Remorse is paradigmatically appropriate when one has knowingly and deliberately done something bad, when one is blameworthy on the volitionist account, in other words. As I said earlier, attributionists argue that one can be blameworthy without self-awareness. One way to understand the debate between volitionists and attributionists is as a dispute over what a univocal notion of blameworthiness applies to. But as Gary Watson (1996, 2004) influentially pointed out, we could think in terms of different sorts of responsibility.[29] I think that one is blameworthy in a slightly different way when one acts without awareness, but it is still genuine blameworthiness, and the agent should feel a very close relative of remorse. It would be a shame to conflate the distinction between these two ways of being blameworthy, but that does not downgrade either of them.[30]

So, returning to the distinction between taking on liability and taking on responsibility, the above reflections on shades of remorse do not undermine the distinction, even if they make us think that the boundaries might be vague. Taking on responsibility is more personal, more emotional, and more weighty than taking on liability. There is also an important difference in the sorts of reason one might have for taking on liability or responsibility. I have argued that the reason for taking on responsibility in certain cases is that it is constitutive of respectful relationships. There are some contexts in which, when we inadvertently let someone down, we have to own that. We have to take it on, give it the same status as the acts that issue from our will. We do not, however, have a *moral* duty to take on responsibility. We could eschew the whole relationship. The point is rather that if we are committed to the relationship, whether personal or social, we must act in certain ways.

Enoch (2012), by contrast, is interested in diagnosing a moral fault. He argues that the fault in the lorry driver who does not take on anything after (nonnegligently) having killed a pedestrian is that he has violated his moral duty to take responsibility (2012, 110–111). But although the lorry driver has a moral duty to take on liability—at the very least to apologize, and to make amends in other small ways if possible—he has no duty to take on responsibility or blameworthiness. Nothing hangs on him taking on more than liability—it is not required by the relationship in play.

Enoch thinks that taking on responsibility is an act of will, and that justifies his view that it is something we sometimes have a duty to do it. I agree if we understand him as talking about liability: in nonlegal contexts, taking on liability can be an act of will. But taking on responsibility is more like a disposition. Some people are inclined to take on responsibility; they do not actively *do it* so much as discover that they have done it. Ideally, their taking on responsibility is responsive to their relationships in an appropriate way. To respect your partner is (assuming that this is what your partner wants) to automatically feel bad about having let him down, even when you let him down inadvertently. To respect your fellow people is to feel bad when you wrong them.[31] Of course, our dispositions to take on responsibility are not always perfectly responsive to the genuine and legitimate needs of our relationships. They can be distorted in various ways. I return to that point below.

First, I want to briefly return to historical cases. I have argued that we should take responsibility for the ways in which we inadvertently let people down. But that doesn't clearly apply to people who never realize that they have let people down. Fricker's Greenleaf is just a man of his time, and he is trapped in his time. It seems that it does not make sense to say of Greenleaf that he should take responsibility for his mistakes, because he is not even remotely aware of the possibility that he is making that sort of mistake.

I agree that it does not make sense for Greenleaf to take responsibility. Ideally he would come to see things differently, of course, but if we imagine him in the historical context he is in, he does not have enough distance from his own oppressive actions and tendencies to take responsibility for them. Thus, my view makes sense of our ambivalence about historical cases. First, we can understand why it might be that the agent has no bad will—the epistemic circumstances are bad. And second, whereas we expect, both normatively and predictively, our peers to take responsibility for their inadvertent oppressive actions or tendencies, we know that someone who is historically isolated will not have done so, and will have had very limited opportunity to do so. As Fricker remarks, it would take someone really exceptional to see through the orthodoxy of the day (2007, 101). This is not to say that we have no critical resources. We still think, of course, that the agent should not have been so biased, that he has done something wrong in being so biased, and so on, and that the world itself is problematic and needs to be changed.

There is one last point to make, and that is that when an agent takes on responsibility, she *is* responsible. One might think that taking on responsibility is artificial in some way, or, like taking on liability, it does not really involve the deep sense of responsibility. But my argument is that one can change one's standing with regard to an inadvertent action, and if one takes on responsibility for it, one really is responsible. This is not a radical claim: it is just a development of what the compatibilist needs for the compatibilist view to get going. Compatibilism requires a certain amount of good faith. It is always possible to turn around and suddenly see things in the light of determinism. If we do that, we can stop seeing ourselves as responsible at all. So the argument I am making here is just a development of that point; it builds on what compatibilism must already rely on: that we are willing to see ourselves as responsible.

6 Feminist Implications

I shall close with some feminist implications of this proposal.[32] It is a "well-known fact," in the sense that is likely to be taken for granted in popular cultural forms such as magazine articles and sitcoms, that women feel more guilt than men do.[33] We feel guilty about our children, our spouses, our pets, about what we eat, about how we speak, about how we look, about what we say, about how hard we work, about how messy our houses are, and, even more disturbingly, it seems that we feel guilt if we are assaulted or raped or harassed. It is always our fault. Men, by contrast, at least in the popular imagination, breeze through life, feeling guilty only about what they can control.

The alleged problem (it may be a figment of the popular imagination, but I will assume that the impression is accurate for the sake of argument) is not simply that women feel worse about what they have done. It is that women take on responsibility for more of what happens than men do. And that is not simply a matter of taking on more responsibilities (though it seems that women do that too, as the well-documented phenomenon of the "second shift" illustrates[34]). The point is that, as I have argued, we have some leeway over what we take responsibility for, and women seem to take on more.

The social context of this picture is, of course, a patriarchal society. Thus, as I suggested above, the ways in which we are inclined to take on extended responsibility are themselves hostage to the social environment we are immersed in. If women really do feel more guilt then men, it is partly because women are blamed more, are *held* more responsible than men are. For example, efforts to prevent unwanted pregnancies, rape, and sexual harassment often focus on educating girls. Girls are taught to think that it is up to them to learn how to say "no" effectively, how to insist on condom use, how to dress so as to avoid unwanted attention, and so on. So it is not surprising that failure to prevent bad things happening feels like a failure. Part of what is going on here is that women are unfairly being made to take responsibility, to feel guilty, about things that others do.

But my argument suggests another explanation for the (putative) fact that women feel more guilt than men. I have argued that we take on extended responsibility because our relationships require it. As I pointed out earlier, our close personal relationships require what we *think* they require: we make our own relationship conditions. We make them partly on an individual basis, but we also make them culturally. In some cultures, arranged marriages seem fine; in others, they do not. What we can accept and what will make us happy depend very much on what we have been brought up to expect. And what we will accept depends on our bargaining position. The bargaining positions of those in oppressed groups are, of course, weaker than those of the privileged.

So it might seem that my view leaves little room for normative criticism of relationships that are shaped by oppressive social structures. If what people expect from women in a relationship is more responsibility than what they expect from men, that *makes it true* that the relationship requires more from women. And this is indeed the lived experience of many women in heterosexual relationships. In order for the relationship to work, to feel right, the woman has to take on an awful lot of extended responsibility.

The solutions are, of course, not out of reach. I find it interesting that once we understand responsibility as involving an element of taking responsibility, and once we see that that is connected to our social relationships, it is evident that the nature of our social relationships must be examined carefully. We cannot simply take for granted how we respond to others; rather, we should interrogate our responses. We cannot take for granted the shape of our relationships, but should examine them for ideological distortions. My view is not that we should take everything for granted and base responsibility on that. My view is rather that *especially* because responsibility is intertwined with our social world, it is important that we are critical of our social world.

7 Conclusion

I have argued that there is an interesting category of acts that do not betray bad will, but that are nonetheless not clearly ones that we should let people off the hook for. Such acts are *our* acts, in that they come from our agency in a broad sense. Some forms of implicit and explicit bias fall into this category. I have argued that we should *take* responsibility for these actions in the situations where doing so is necessary for the relevant relationship. So if there is no relationship at all, taking responsibility is not required. What we should take responsibility for varies with the relationship. In personal relationships, we should take responsibility for a wide range of glitches as well as our biases. In our broader social relationships, we need to take responsibility for our biases. Taking responsibility is constitutive of respecting in the appropriate way.[35]

Notes

1. I am not claiming that all compatibilists would accept this as a characterization of the view. My point here is that quality of will is the *central* feature of a compatibilist account. In fact, many compatibilist views depart from a quality of will view, bringing in notions such as history and capacity that are not intrinsic qualities of an agent's will, but extrinsic ones. There is also disagreement over what sort of quality of will is relevant, and not just over whether self awareness is necessary, but over what levels of reasons responsiveness are needed and how reasons responsiveness is understood, and over what sort of identification with one's own will is required.
2. See also Michael McKenna's very clear account of what 'quality of will' means (2012, 58–59), though I disagree with McKenna on whether 'quality' only refers to moral worth.
3. See Wallace (1994, 138–139); Zimmerman (1997 and elsewhere); Rosen (2002 and elsewhere); Levy (2011 and elsewhere).
4. See Watson (1996, 2004) where the term 'attributionism' originates. The view is developed (in various different ways) by others, including Nomy Arpaly (2003 and elsewhere); Angela Smith (2005 and elsewhere); T. M. Scanlon (1998 and elsewhere); Matthew Talbert (2008 and elsewhere).
5. See Mason 2015.
6. I focus on blameworthiness and fault rather than praiseworthiness and achievement because in general we are more tolerant of luck in praiseworthiness; we are less reluctant to allow luck to play a role in praiseworthy outcomes because less is at stake for the actor.
7. See Michael Brownstein's *Stanford Encyclopedia* article (2016) for a review of the various views on that.
8. See, e.g., Kelly and Roeder 2008; Holroyd 2012; Vargas 2013, esp. chapter 8.
9. See Adams (1985) for a very clear justification of that outlook, which of course is the basis of the attributionist view.
10. Indirect responsibility for biases depends on the cultural situation—in a situation where there is lots of awareness of bias and good and well-known techniques for countering bias and avoiding acquiring bias, it will be much easier to assign blameworthiness for acquiring and having biases.
11. Gary Watson points out this problem (1987; 2004, 247).
12. Research by Fazio et al. (1995) shows a correlation between implicit racism and sitting further away from people of that race. Bessenof and Sherman (2000) demonstrate a similar correlation between bias against fat people and avoidance behavior. These and other results are discussed in Dasgupta (2004).
13. This view is suggested by the psychologist John Bargh (2005). I owe the reference to Holly Smith's discussion (2011, 135). Smith concedes that if there are indeed fully automatic processes, then we are not blameworthy for them, and her overall view is that we are blameworthy only if a sufficient proportion of our attitudes are involved in our behavior.
14. The volitionist has a harder time making sense of blameworthiness for explicit bias, because the agent who is genuinely in the grip of false views all the way down, who has never engaged in culpable self-deception, cannot be blameworthy on the volitionist view. This is one reason the volitionist view seems implausible when proposed as the sole account of responsibility.

15. And of course it is possible that we could tell a similar story about other biases, including racism and homophobia.

16. Fricker also draws on Anthony Minghella's screenplay, in which the character of Greenleaf says at one point, "Marge, there's female intuition, and then there are facts" (2007, 1).

17. I think that epistemic injustice can manifest as both implicit and explicit bias. It appears as implicit bias when the agent is not at all aware that she is listening less to, and taking less seriously, members of the oppressed group. It appears as explicit bias when people consciously believe things like "women are more intuitive than men and men are more rational then women."

18. See, e.g., Mills (1998), who argues the point in relation to race.

19. Fricker claims that to call the agent blameworthy in this sort of case would be hubris (2007, 105). Instead, she argues for something that we can justifiably do (or feel) in place of blame. She suggests that when someone's circumstances are epistemically limited, although we cannot aptly feel the resentment of blame, we can aptly feel "resentment of disappointment" (104). I return to this below.

20. Arpaly makes this point too: she gives an example of a young boy raised in an entirely sexist and segregated society (2003, 104).

21. Clarke is interested in responsibility for omissions, but for the sake of my argument here, nothing hangs on this being a case of omission. What I call a "glitch" is often called negligence, though that is misleading in various ways. For other examples with this structure, see Vargas 2005; King 2009; Sher 2009; Raz 2011; Tannenbaum 2015. See also Mason 2018, forthcoming.

22. Volitionists, of course, argue that the agent is not responsible in these cases, as the control or knowledge component is missing, and this case is, from the volitionist perspective, even more clearly a case of blamelessness than cases where the control/knowledge condition is missing but the attributionist can point to bad will. Others are more inclined to admit that the case is puzzling.

23. In the passage quoted above, it looks as though Calhoun is assuming a volitionist approach to understanding bad will, but we have no reason to assume that she would rule out an attributionist approach, and the example works well as a case where there is neither the volitionist type of bad will nor the attributionist. Calhoun's main concern is with the nature of the circumstances, what she calls "an abnormal moral context," (1989, 390) in which the behavior is wrong but widely thought to be permissible.

24. There is a different sense in which we hold people "responsible" without really believing that they are responsible: we assign liability. For example, we hold people responsible for what their dogs do. I am not talking about liability, but about responsibility, as will become clear.

25. Vargas (2013) argues that we should allow forward-looking considerations a more substantial role in our responsibility practices than we currently do.

26. See also Andrea Westlund's chapter in this volume for a discussion of the difference between holding responsible and blaming. The idea that we should take responsibility for things that are not under our control is not new. Joseph Raz, in his discussion of negligence (inadvertent fault), argues that we should take responsibility for negligence because our self-respect demands it (2010, 17). I discuss Raz's view in detail, as well as the literature on negligence, in Mason (2018, forthcoming). Robert Adams suggests in passing that we should take responsibility for traits that are not under our control (1985, 15). Susan Wolf suggests that there is a virtue of taking responsibility (2001, 10); David Enoch (2012) argues that we sometimes have a moral duty to take responsibility: I discuss his view below. There may be others that I have missed. Fischer and Ravizza (1998, 207–239) talk about taking responsibility, but it is clear that they intend for it to be apt only when the agent's act is under her control. Bernard Williams thinks that we are responsible for things that go beyond the boundaries of our wills, though he does not talk about *taking* responsibility (1993, 55–56).

27. See, e.g., Shoemaker's account (2015) of the various ways in which we might be impaired, and yet nonetheless have bad will.

28. It seems obvious that we couldn't be responsible in my sense for what others freely do (though we might be liable), but there is another interesting notion in this neighborhood, that I do not go into here, and that is "guilt by association" or "moral taint"—see, e.g., Oshana 2006.

29. See also Shoemaker 2015.
30. I defend this view in more detail in Mason 2015.
31. This is not supposed to be a complete account of respect. Obviously I am using an account such that respect involves affect. There is another sense of respect such that it is just a matter of treating someone appropriately, and in that sense I do think we have a moral duty.
32. For some different but not unrelated thoughts about feminist approaches to responsibility, see Oshana 2016.
33. A recent study (Extebarria et al. 2009) showing that women feel more guilt than men was much discussed on the Internet, and the discussion overwhelmingly has the tone, "tell me something I don't know."
34. First put into words by the sociologist Arlie Hochschild (Hochschild and Machung, 1989). For another relevant sociological study on gender differences in taking responsibility, see Walzer 1996.
35. Thanks to David Enoch, Alex Guerrero, Jen Morton, Monique Wonderly, and the editors of this volume for comments on earlier drafts.

References

Adams, R. M. 1985. "Involuntary Sins." *Philosophical Review* 94 (1): 3–31.
Arpaly, N. 2003. *Unprincipled Virtue: An Inquiry into Moral Agency.* Oxford: Oxford University Press.
Bargh, J. A. 2005. "Bypassing the Will: Toward Demystifying the Nonconscious Control of Social Behavior." In *The New Unconscious*, edited by R. R. Hassin, J. S. Uleman, and J. A. Bargh, 37–60. Oxford: Oxford University Press.
Bertrand, M., and S. Mullainathan. 2004. "Are Emily and Greg More Employable than Lakisha and Jamal? A Field Experiment on Labor Market." NBER Working Papers from National Bureau of Economic Research, Inc., No. 9873.
Bessenoff, G. R., and Sherman, J. W. 2000. "Automatic and Controlled Components of Prejudice toward Fat People: Evaluation Versus Stereotype Activation." *Social Cognition* 18 (4): 329–353.
Brownstein, M. 2016. "Implicit Bias." *The Stanford Encyclopedia of Philosophy.* http://plato.stanford.edu/entries/implicit-bias/.
Calhoun, C. 1989. "Responsibility and Reproach." *Ethics* 99 (2): 389–406.
Clarke, R. 2014. *Omissions: Agency, Metaphysics, and Responsibility.* Oxford: Oxford University Press.
Dasgupta, N. 2004. "Implicit Ingroup Favoritism, Outgroup Favoritism, and Their Behavioral Manifestations." *Social Justice Research* 17 (2): 143–169.
Enoch, D. 2012. "Being Responsible, Taking Responsibility, and Penumbral Agency." In *Luck, Value and Commitment: Themes from the Ethics of Bernard Williams*, edited by U. Heuer and G. Lang, 95–132. Oxford: Oxford University Press.
Etxebarria, I., M. J. Ortiz, S. Conejero, and A. Pascual. 2009. "Intensity of Habitual Guilt in Men and Women: Differences in Interpersonal Sensitivity and the Tendency Towards Anxious-Aggressive Guilt." *Spanish Journal of Psychology* 12 (2): 540–554.
Fazio, R. H., J. R. Jackson, B. C. Dunton, and C. J. Williams. 1995. "Variability in Automatic Activation as an Unobtrusive Measure of Racial Attitudes: A bona fide Pipeline?" *Journal of Personality and Social Psychology* 69 (6): 1013–1027.
Fischer, J. M., and M. Ravizza. 1998. *Responsibility and Control: A Theory of Moral Responsibility.* New York: Cambridge University Press.
Frankfurt, H. G. 1971. "Freedom of the Will and the Concept of a Person." *Journal of Philosophy* 68 (1): 5–20.
Fricker, M. 2007. *Epistemic Injustice: Power and the Ethics of Knowing.* Oxford: Oxford University Press.
Fricker, M. 2016. "Fault and No-Fault Responsibility for Implicit Prejudice—A Space for Epistemic Agent-Regret." In *The Epistemic Life of Groups: Essays in the Epistemology of Collectives*, edited by M. Brady and M. Fricker, 33–50. Oxford: Oxford University Press.

Hochschild, A. R., and A. Machung. 1989. *The Second Shift*. New York: Penguin Books.

Holroyd, J. 2012. "Responsibility for Implicit Bias." *Journal of Social Philosophy* 43 (3): 274–306.

Kelly, D., and E. Roedder. 2008. "Racial Cognition and the Ethics of Implicit Bias." *Philosophy Compass* 3 (3): 522–540.

King, M. 2009. "The Problem with Negligence." *Social Theory and Practice* 35 (4): 577–595.

Levy, N. 2011. *Hard Luck: How Luck Undermines Free Will and Moral Responsibility*. Oxford: Oxford University Press.

Mason, E. 2015. "Moral Ignorance and Blameworthiness." *Philosophical Studies* 172 (11): 3037–3057.

Mason, E. (2018, forthcoming) "Between Strict Liability and Blameworthy Quality of Will: Taking Responsibility." *Oxford Studies in Agency and Responsibility* 5.

McKenna, M. 2012. *Conversation and Responsibility*. Oxford: Oxford University Press.

Mills, C. W. 1998. *Blackness Visible: Essays on Philosophy and Race*. Ithaca, NY: Cornell University Press.

Oshana, M. 2006. "Moral Taint." *Metaphilosophy* 37 (3–4): 353–375.

Oshana, M. 2016. "A Feminist Approach to Moral Responsibility." In *The Routledge Companion to Free Will*, edited by M. Griffiths, N. Levy, and K. Timpe, 623–632. New York: Routledge.

Raz, J. 2011. *From Normativity to Responsibility*. Oxford: Oxford University Press.

Rosen, G. 2002. "Culpability and Ignorance." *Proceedings of the Aristotelian Society* 103 (1): 61–84.

Scanlon, T.M. 1998. *What We Owe to Each Other*. Cambridge, MA: Belknap Press of Harvard University Press.

Sher, G. 2009. *Who Knew?* New York: Oxford University Press.

Shoemaker, D. 2015. *Responsibility from the Margins*. Oxford: Oxford University Press.

Smith, A. 2005. "Responsibility for Attitudes: Activity and Passivity in Mental Life." *Ethics* 115 (2): 236–271.

Smith, H. 2011. "Non-Tracing Cases of Culpable Ignorance." *Criminal Law and Philosophy* 5 (2): 115–146.

Steinpreis, R., K. Anders, and D. Ritzke. 1999. "The Impact of Gender on the Review of the Curricula Vitae of Job Applicants and Tenure Candidates: A National Empirical Study." *Sex Roles* 41 (7–8): 509–528.

Strawson, P. F. 1962. "Freedom and Resentment." *Proceedings of the British Academy* 48: 1–25.

Talbert, M. 2008. "Blame and Responsiveness to Moral Reasons: Are Psychopaths Blameworthy?" *Pacific Philosophical Quarterly* 89 (4): 516–535.

Tannenbaum, J. 2015. "Mere Moral Failure." *Canadian Journal of Philosophy* 45 (1): 58–84.

Vargas, M. 2005. "The Trouble with Tracing." *Midwest Studies in Philosophy* 29 (1): 269–291.

Vargas, M. 2013. *Building Better Beings: A Theory of Moral Responsibility*. Oxford: Oxford University Press.

Wallace, R. J. 1994. *Responsibility and the Moral Sentiments*. Cambridge, MA: Harvard University Press.

Walzer, S. 1996. "Thinking about the Baby: Gender and the Division of Infant Care." *Social Problems* 43 (2): 219–234.

Watson, G. 1987. "Responsibility and the Limits of Evil." In *Responsibility, Character, and the Emotions*, edited by F. Schoeman, 256–286. New York: Cambridge University Press.

Watson, G. 1996. "Two Faces of Responsibility." *Philosophical Topics* 24 (2): 227–248.

Watson, G. 2004. "Responsibility and the Limits of Evil." Reprinted in *Agency and Answerability: Selected Essays*, 219–259. Oxford: Oxford University Press.

Watson, G. 2004. "Two Faces of Responsibility." Reprinted in *Agency and Answerability: Selected Essays*, 260–288. Oxford: Oxford University Press.

Williams, B. 1981. *Moral Luck: Philosophical Papers, 1973–1980*. Cambridge: Cambridge University Press.

Williams, B. 1993. *Shame and Necessity*. Berkeley: University of California Press.

Wolf, S. 2001. "The Moral of Moral Luck." *Philosophic Exchange* 31 (1): 5–19. http://digitalcommons.brockport.edu/phil_ex/vol31/iss1/1.

Zimmerman, M. J. 1997. "Moral Responsibility and Ignorance." *Ethics* 107 (3): 410–426.

7

Socializing Responsibility

NEIL LEVY

1 Introduction

With few exceptions, work on moral responsibility in the Anglophone world is resolutely individualist.[1] The individual is not merely the primary unit of analysis and bearer of value; for the most part, individualism is taken for granted to such an extent that philosophers are no more aware of their individualism than fish are of the water in which they swim. In this chapter, I suggest that concerns about *agency* may pull apart from concerns about *agents*, when "agents" are identified with individuals (i.e., human organisms, with boundaries defined by their skin). Put another way, I suggest that if we identify agents with the loci of agency, we will sometimes find that agents are not identical to individuals: they may be constituted by individuals, or parts of individuals, together with extra-individual objects and entities, including *other* individuals (cf. Rovane 1998). Since it is agents, understood as loci of agency, who are (very plausibly) the bearers of responsibility, both our normative interests in the distribution of obligations and of blame and our explanatory and predictive interests in the causes of changes in the world should lead us to abandon individualist presumptions in favor of a focus on agency, whenever and wherever we find it.[2]

Changing our focus from biological individuals to a more inclusive way of understanding the loci of agency is, I claim, justified on grounds that are conceptual and normative. It is justified on conceptual grounds because we cannot understand individual agency except by situating individuals within broader contexts (especially, though not only, the broader contexts of the other agents who constitute the social groups to which they belong). We cannot, that is, hope to understand responsible agency by developing accounts of individual agency, on the one hand, and collective agency, on the other.[3] Individual agency depends on the social context in which individuals are embedded, both for its genesis and its continued existence. Individuals owe their powers and their limitations to stable collectives as well as to much smaller and perhaps transitory groupings (even groupings as small as a dyad), and only by understanding this context can we understand how their agency is realized, the constraints upon it, and the ways in which agents may reasonably be expected to exercise it.

The change of focus from biological individuals to the broader contexts in which individuals are situated is justified on normative grounds for several reasons, but a principal justification is the corrective role it can play in identifying how (alongside other resources) institutions distribute individual-level blameworthiness. Agents who perform wrongful acts while satisfying standard individual-level criteria for blameworthiness *very* often have fewer resources (psychological and financial) and less (in the way of resources and social standing) to lose from punishment than those who do not, and these facts about them are explained by how resources are socially distributed. They have less self-control, for instance (self-control is correlated with socioeconomic status, and the neural mechanisms for this fact are slowly being elucidated [Hackman, Farah, and Meaney 2010]). They are subjected to a double dose of unfairness: first they are positioned socially and psychologically such that they face greater incentives to crime and have less capacity to resist these incentives; then they are blamed and punished when they fail to resist. Addressing the enormous and growing disparities within developed countries requires the redistribution of resources of many kinds, but a heavy emphasis on "personal responsibility" is a barrier to the policies that would lead to such redistribution. If we come to see that individual responsibility is itself frequently distributed, and refocus our attention on the collectives and institutions that are the agents of the reproduction of inequality, we may be better placed to allocate blame and to enact better policies (both the official policies formulated by political and social organizations and the informal policies that govern our behavior toward one another).

In the first half of the chapter, my focus is on the locus of agency and on questions concerning how it is exercised. Roughly, this half focuses on what is often called the control condition on moral responsibility, and its purpose is to clear the way for refocusing our concern with responsibility from individuals to broader contexts, especially the contexts provided by collectives. I argue on conceptual grounds that the focus on individuals abstracted from their contexts is unjustified, showing that the kinds of capacities that have plausibly been held to be sufficient for moral responsibility may be possessed by supra-agential aggregates (constituted of several agents, of agents embedded in institutional contexts, or of agents and artifacts).[4] In the second half of the chapter, I turn to the other condition on moral responsibility that is often identified: the epistemic condition.[5] If considerations concerning the control condition force us to give up an exclusive focus on agents understood as individuals, there is no principled reason why we ought to retain it when assessing whether the epistemic condition is satisfied, and by whom it is satisfied. Broadening our perspective allows us to broaden the range of individuals and institutions who are obligated to satisfy the epistemic condition and who may be held responsible if it is not satisfied. In the conclusion, I draw the two threads of the chapter together, suggesting that we might best identify the agents responsible for failures to satisfy the epistemic condition by reference to the locus of agency, rather than preconceived ideas about who agents are. We may thereby find that the obligations to bring it about that individuals are better informed are themselves as truly social—falling on social institutions and governments, for example—as are the agents who bring about significant changes in the world.

2 Agency: Individual and Extra-Individual

The past two decades have seen a revival of interest in debates over the control condition on free will and moral responsibility. Incompatibilists—those who maintain that free will and moral responsibility are incompatible with causal determinism—have developed new lines of attack against their compatibilist counterparts, while compatibilists have developed sophisticated accounts of agency to ward off these attacks (for some of the many highlights of the debate in its agency-focused incarnation, see Kane 1996; Fischer and Ravizza 1998; Clarke 2003; Steward 2012; Vihvelin 2013; Pereboom 2014). These debates have been fruitful: they have illuminated essential aspects of human agency and led to a better understanding of how it can be constrained and undermined. But the accounts of agency developed by compatibilists and libertarians alike share a commitment to individualism that dramatically and, I think unjustifiably, limits their scope. They are silent on how agency is supported and even partially realized by a scaffold that extends beyond our skins, and therefore on the extra-agential, deeply social conditions that may make the difference between responsibility and excuse.

Let me illustrate this individualist commitment with a discussion of a recent debate between compatibilists and incompatibilists. Recent controversy has often centered on *manipulation cases* (some philosophers believe that manipulation arguments constitute the central difficulty facing compatibilism; see Mele 2006). In brief, arguments based on manipulation cases proceed as follows: a scenario is presented in which one agent covertly manipulates another in a manner that leaves the manipulated agent satisfying whatever set of conditions a compatibilist might adduce as sufficient for freedom, but which is supposed to be intuitively responsibility-subverting nevertheless. Having generated the intuition that an agent may be unfree despite satisfying plausible compatibilist conditions on free will, the incompatibilist then proceeds to argue that there is no relevant difference between being covertly manipulated to act in this way and being determined to act in the same way. Perhaps the manipulation case that has attracted the most attention is Derk Pereboom's Four-Case Argument (Pereboom 2001, 2014), which has the virtue (among others) of making the parallel between manipulation and determinism very clear.

In Case 1 of the Four-Case Argument, neuroscientists using very advanced technology to produce Plum's moment-to-moment states manipulate him into murdering Ms. White for rationally egotistic reasons. But Plum nevertheless satisfies plausible compatibilist conditions on free will. He does not, for instance, experience an irresistible desire, and his reasoning is consistent with his character (he is frequently manipulated into acting for rationally egoistic reasons, though he also often acts for moral reasons). He endorses his first-order desire to kill Ms. White, and he satisfies conditions on reasons responsiveness and reactivity (his reasoning processes would recognize reasons, including some moral reasons, to do otherwise, were they presented, and there are possible scenarios in which he would actually do otherwise in response to such reasons).[6] Nonetheless, Pereboom claims that it is intuitive that Plum is not responsible in Case 1: the manipulation undermines his freedom.

Pereboom then proceeds to construct three further cases. In the first two, Plum is manipulated into killing Ms. White as before and for the same reasons, but each case is less outlandish and closer to an ordinary case involving wrongdoing in a deterministic world than its predecessor. In Case 2, Plum is not locally manipulated, as in Case 1. Rather, he has been created by neuroscientists who have "programmed" him to weigh reasons egotistically (though not exclusively so), such that in the circumstances in which he finds himself he is causally determined to form a desire to kill Ms. White and to act on it. As before, the desire is not irresistible, Plum endorses it, and the mechanisms upon which he acts are moderately reasons responsive. In Case 3, Plum has been indoctrinated from infancy in such a way that he often (though not exclusively) acts for egotistical reasons, such that he is determined in the situation in which he finds himself to form a desire to kill Ms. White and to act on it. In Case 4, Plum is not manipulated at all: rather, he is an ordinary agent in a deterministic world, who often (though not exclusively) acts for egotistical reasons, such that he is causally determined in the situation in which he finds himself to form a desire to kill Ms. White and to act on it.

Pereboom argues that if one accepts that Plum in Case 1 is not responsible—and one should, he maintains—then one should also accept that Plum is not responsible in Case 2 either. After all, he points out, the difference between the cases consists merely in *when* the manipulation occurs. But if one accepts that Plum is not responsible in Case 2, Pereboom argues, one should also think he is not responsible in Case 3, since it differs from Case 2 only in *how* Plum's mental states were created. Indoctrination need not be less constraining than neural manipulation, after all, so it is hard to see why it ought to undermine moral responsibility any less. But, finally, Pereboom argues that if one accepts that Plum in Case 3 is not morally responsible for killing Ms. White, one should accept that Plum in Case 4—which features an ordinary agent acting in a deterministic world—also fails to be morally responsible. According to Pereboom, if Plum's mental states and values arose by chance or without anyone intending them, he would be no more responsible than he is in a world in which he has been manipulated into having them. Accepting that Plum is not responsible in Case 4, however, is accepting that compatibilism is false: ordinary agents cannot be morally responsible in deterministic worlds.

It is tempting to reply to the manipulation argument by trying to identify a difference between the manipulated agent and ordinary agents in deterministic worlds. Michael McKenna (2008) calls this kind of move a *soft-line* reply to these cases. He argues that soft-line replies will ultimately fail: even if we succeed in demonstrating a responsibility-relevant difference between an agent who features in a manipulation case and the kinds of agents whom compatibilists think are morally responsible for their actions in a deterministic world, the incompatibilist can simply build that condition into their revised manipulation argument. The only condition the compatibilist could cite that the incompatibilist cannot bring on board is the stipulation that the agent not be manipulated, but that stipulation looks ad hoc and question-begging without an account of *why* manipulation undermines moral responsibility but determinism does not.

McKenna therefore advocates a *hard-line* reply to manipulation cases: rather than deny that the agents who feature in such cases are relevantly similar to determined agents, he denies that manipulation necessarily undercuts responsible agency. This bullet-biting maneuver requires us to accept that one agent may manipulate another into performing an action for which that second agent is nevertheless fully responsible (which does not entail, of course, that the manipulator is not *also* responsible for the action; responsibility may be able to be shared without any particular agent's portion diminishing relative to a situation in which responsibility is hers alone). No matter what set of conditions we identify as sufficient for moral responsibility, that is, we must accept that manipulators can bring it about that agents satisfy these conditions (unless we stipulate a question-begging "no manipulation" condition). But that fact should not shake our faith in those conditions. If they are independently plausible as sufficient conditions on moral responsibility, we should accept that agents who satisfy them *are* morally responsible, even if they are manipulated into satisfying them, McKenna maintains.

John Martin Fischer's enormously (and deservedly) influential account of morally responsible agency shares with McKenna's an emphasis on the rich set of internal capacities displayed by most actual adult agents. For Fischer (see Fischer and Ravizza 1998; Fischer 2006), agents are morally responsible when their actions are caused by moderately reasons-responsive mechanisms. Roughly, a mechanism is moderately reasons responsive if it is capable of recognizing a sufficient range of reasons to do otherwise were they presented, and there is at least one possible world in which the mechanism would cause the agent to do otherwise in response to such a reason.[7] This account is genuinely illuminating. We really do discover important things about agents by asking about counterfactuals in precisely the way Fischer suggests. We discover what reasons they are capable of recognizing and responding to, and whether there are distinctive gaps in the patterns of such responsiveness, and so on. But in the hands of McKenna, Fischer, and other philosophers, the answers to these questions are gerrymandered to reflect individualist commitments.

For Fischer and for McKenna, an agent exemplifies a rich enough set of agential capacities and is therefore morally responsible when she herself—understood as the person bounded by her skin—remains capable of appropriate response. When manipulation, for instance, leaves her unable to respond in that way, she is not responsible. But there is another way of dividing up cases. We can ask not about *agents*, in a way that is guided by our intuitions about who or what is an agent, but about *agency*. Rather than asking, with Fischer (for instance), "Is the agent appropriately responsive and reactive to reasons?" we might ask, "Is appropriate responsiveness and reactiveness to reasons exemplified?" Asking that question will yield a different way of picking out agents, and one that might be better justified.

To pave the way for this kind of move, it might be worth comparing Pereboom's Four-Case Argument with a different thought experiment, Searle's Chinese Room experiment (Searle 1980, 1990). That thought experiment features a native English speaker, with no knowledge of Chinese, who is locked in the room with a box of Chinese symbols and an instruction book. Native Chinese speakers write questions in Chinese and post them through a slot in the room. The agent inside the room uses her instruction book to produce (to her, meaningless) symbols on a piece of paper, which she then posts back to the people outside. The instruction book and database of symbols are so cleverly constructed that she is able to intelligently answer any question put to her in Chinese. But she understands neither the questions nor the answers she returns. Searle thinks it is obvious that the agent inside the room does not understand Chinese; he takes the thought experiment to show that rule-governed manipulation of symbols can never be sufficient for genuine thinking; syntax alone can never be sufficient for semantics.

One popular reply (or set of replies—here I abstract from the difference between the Systems Reply and the Virtual Minds Reply) argues that though the agent inside the room does not understand Chinese, there is an agent who does understand it. That agent is identical to or supervenes on the system as a whole: the person inside the room, the input and output devices, and the internal processes together constitute an agent who understands Chinese (see Cole 2014 for discussion). This reply changes our focus from agents to agency: from a (possibly arbitrary) focus on loci of agency held to be bounded by skins to the identification of appropriate response functionally. This same move is available to us in response to manipulation cases, of course. Instead of, or as well as, asking whether Plum is responsible, we can ask whether there is agency that meets the conditions for responsibility. Is the system composed of Plum *and the scientists manipulating him* appropriately responsive and reactive to reasons? Asking that question will help free us from the individualist prejudice, according to which agency is always a property of those entities we intuitively identify as agents, and that, in turn, will allow us to identify the actors who play an indispensable role in shaping the physical and natural world.

What, besides a taken-for-granted presumption in favor of individualism, explains why philosophers have not asked this question? Perhaps they take it to be inappropriate, for reasons centered on pragmatic considerations. A morally significant event has occurred—Ms. White has been murdered, say—and we want to know if someone is to blame, should be punished, or have obligations to make amends. There is no one other than Plum and other individuals (say the neuroscientists who manipulate him) of whom to ask this question. This worry has some force: sometimes there is no agent who can be held to account, for pragmatic reasons or because there is no mechanism for holding them to account. But there are cases in which this is not true. More importantly, understanding the true loci of agency and thereby freeing ourselves from the grip of the individualist prejudice clears the way for better policy: if agency is in fact exercised by supra-agential aggregates, then understanding the world, and having a chance of shaping it as we would like, requires us to focus on such aggregates as well as (and sometimes instead of) individuals.

Suppose that the system composed of Plum and the neuroscientists exemplifies moderate reasons responsiveness but that neither Plum nor any individual neuroscientist meets these conditions. This might occur if, for some reason, no individual was in a position to grasp the nature of the actions they helped to bring about, because they each responded to a narrow slice of information in such a manner that the ensemble of responses manifested moderate reasons responsiveness. We might think that in such a case, we would have moral responsibility without an agent that could be blamed, punished, or under an obligation to make amends. But that is far from obviously the case. If agency is constituted by a set of agents, then there *is* an entity that might be blamed or otherwise held to account. Of course there are practical problems with holding it to account *without* also (unjustifiably) holding the individuals who compose it to account, but these problems are familiar and sometimes surmountable. Nations may be held to account even when some or all of the individuals who help to constitute them cannot justifiably be; so can corporations. There are sometimes ways of holding the supervening agent to account that does not harm the composite agents: we may dissolve the supervening agent, for instance. I do not deny that there are very hard problems that may arise, but these are problems we face in other cases. They are real problems, I claim: they arise only *because* agency can be composed of other agents, rather than always being dependent on the boundaries defined by skin.[8]

It is worth emphasizing that it may happen that *both* the supervening agent *and* the individuals who compose it exemplify moderate reasons responsiveness. That might be the case in some of the iterations of the Four-Case Argument, as Pereboom (2001, 2014) presents it. In some of those cases, the following three propositions may all be true: (1) the supervening agent may be appropriately reasons responsive; (2) some or all the manipulating neuroscientists are themselves reasons responsive, grasping the nature of the action they cause Plum to engage in; and (3) Plum himself is not moderately reasons responsive. This kind of case presents us with practical problems, once again, but not with any particular theoretical difficulties. The supervening agent may in such a case be held to account and so can some, but not others, of the individuals who compose it. Again, there may be closely analogous cases involving nations or corporations, since some individuals who compose them possess more power and more information with regard to the goals of such composite entities than others. Such corporate agents may be required to offer recompense or apology. They may be capable of the expression of guilt or shame, or analogues thereof; they may be fined or we may refuse to cooperate with them (Björnsson and Hess 2017). In addition, we may expect the individuals who partially constitute them, or who benefit from their wrongdoing, to feel shame or guilt.

In the preceding pages, I have offered a (very sketchy) hint as to how we might respond to well-known thought experiments in the philosophy of agency, with a view to attempting to shake the hold that the exclusively individualist conception of agents has on us. While I have suggested, with my asides about nations and corporations, that these hints may have real-world implications, it may be that there are few composite entities in the world that actually exemplify the rich set of agential powers required by accounts like that of Fischer. Very often, individuals act together while failing to constitute a supervening agent. While that fact entails that, in these cases, there is no collective entity that is the bearer of moral responsibility, the social institutions that distribute powers and resources to individuals—amorphous and inchoate as they may be— often constitute the external scaffolding on which *individual* powers depend. We cannot understand individual agency unless we understand these institutions and how they confer both powers and limitations on the individuals who are embedded within them.

Indeed, the cases in which individuals owe their powers to institutions that are not sufficiently integrated or appropriately structured to themselves be responsible collective entities are especially interesting, for the following reasons: In those cases in which it is true that, *had* these institutions possessed sufficient structure and feedback mechanisms to appropriately be held to account, we would blame them and not the individuals who are embedded in, or dependent on, them, those individuals are themselves blameless. The lack of responsible agency at the collective level does not bring it about that individuals possess it. If an organization is so structured that the individuals who partially constitute it lack access to sufficient information about their options or the effects of their choices to be morally responsible as individuals (and they are not responsible for their lack of knowledge), then they are blameless regardless of whether there is some other entity that can be blamed appropriately.

Consider, for example, the persistence of racism in Western nations. There is no doubt that the racist attitudes of individuals (conscious and unconscious) play an important role in the sustaining of systematic inequality and injustices. But structural and institutional racism may be as, or more, important than racist attitudes in producing harms, and these kinds of racism do not depend on the persistence of racist attitudes (Haslanger 2004; Glasgow 2009). Nevertheless, institutions are maintained in existence by the actions of individuals. Nonracist individuals may sustain racist institutions, when (for instance) they do not possess sufficient information to grasp the systematic effects of their actions. University admission offices, for example, might apply criteria that seem "color blind," without realizing that they filter admissions in ways that favor those people who possess superior (that is, preferred, for arbitrary reasons) cultural capital, rather than superior ability or knowledge. Even the blameworthy racist individual may not be blameworthy for the systematic effects of the institutions they help to sustain: being blameworthy for a token racist action need not entail being blameworthy for the pattern of actions that it helps to constitute.

More generally, I hope that by shaking the grip of the individualist view of agency, I thereby make readers more sensitive to other ways in which agency may be deeply dependent on external scaffolding. It is with this mind that I turn from a consideration of the control condition to the epistemic condition. Knowledge and the capacities to acquire it are themselves socially distributed, and the institutions (causally or morally) responsible for this distribution are appropriate loci of responses that ensure that it is better distributed and that significant truths come to be known. Further, the institutions responsible for individual-level failures of the epistemic condition may themselves constitute genuinely supra-individual agents.

3 The Epistemic Condition beyond Individualism

Moral responsibility requires the satisfaction of an epistemic condition: agents who exercise control over their behavior may be excused in virtue of the fact that they are (nonculpably) ignorant of important facts concerning that behavior. For instance, until recently physicians failed to treat peptic ulcers with antibiotics, and thereby may have failed to avoid significant harms to many of their patients. But very plausibly they were not blameworthy for doing so, because they acted in light of what they justifiably took to be medical knowledge at the time. It was not until Warren and Marshall established in the mid-1980s that peptic ulcers were caused by bacteria that it became reasonable to expect physicians to use antibiotics as a first-line treatment and (therefore) to blame them if they failed to do so.[9] Prior to the mid-1980s, physicians failed to be blameworthy for their actions when they caused avoidable harms to peptic ulcer patients, because they failed to satisfy the epistemic condition on moral responsibility.

Individual physicians are obligated to apply the knowledge that they have learned. They are very rarely in a position to test medical claims for themselves. They can collect data on treatment and patient outcomes, but for the most part this data is uninformative, for a number of reasons. First, general practitioners see too few patients with any particular condition to generate statistically significant results (given that differences between treatment types are anything short of spectacular). Second, there are too many confounds in clinical practice to easily generate useful data through this kind of process: patients who suffer from a condition may differ in too many ways for comparisons to be meaningful. Third, physicians cannot use placebo controls, and their close involvement with individual cases entails vulnerability to cognitive biases, like the confirmation bias. Researchers use double-blind procedures to avoid these biases, but physicians cannot use them.

These facts entail that for most knowledge claims, physicians find themselves at (or near) the end of chains of transmission for knowledge claims. They know very many of the things they know because they are the beneficiaries of testimony. In fact, almost everyone in science knows almost everything they know in very significant part in virtue of testimony. Consider the researchers who produce significant new knowledge. They use equipment designed by other researchers, which implement algorithms that they may be unable to understand. They use statistical techniques they could not have developed. They rely for the interpretation of their data on acquired knowledge they take for granted. Knowledge production in science is deeply distributed, with each scientist dependent on many others for their capacity to formulate hypotheses, test them, and interpret their data.

Even within a single laboratory and with regard to a single research finding, knowledge production may be deeply distributed. A single paper, for instance, is typically the work of multiple authors, each of whom has a different set of skills. Some may have no interest in the topic of the paper at all: they are involved nevertheless because of their expertise with the equipment used or with the paradigm employed or in statistical analysis. Science has depended on the distribution of cognitive labor since its inception, but today the trend is toward deeper and deeper distribution of labor. Medical research is often carried out today by multiple laboratories in many countries, to ensure that a sufficiently large number of sufficiently diverse patients are enrolled and a sufficiently great range of expertise is brought to bear on the problem. For cutting-edge physics, the distribution of cognitive labor is even deeper: the recent paper reporting the detection of the Higgs boson particle had more than five thousand authors (Castelvecchi 2015).

It is in part *because* science is a deeply distributed enterprise that it is the paradigm of successful knowledge production. Individuals alone are not especially impressive at generating knowledge, but together they may explore the space of potential hypotheses much more successfully and—under truth-conducive conditions—cancel out one another's biases (in particular, the disposition of each of us to seek evidence in favor of a hypothesis and overlook evidence that conflicts with it). Diversity in anything that causes people to entertain conflicting hypotheses will ensure that one agent's confirmation bias will be compensated for by another's; each will be motivated to defend their hypothesis, and therefore produce arguments that undermine the other hypotheses. Deeper diversity (of cultural background, gender, life experience, political orientation) may allow for the detection of or compensation for those biases correlated with sociocultural positioning. Whereas an all-male research group might overlook explanations of data that turn on women's agency, say, adding women to the research group may lead to a more thorough exploration of the space of hypotheses.[10]

The distribution of knowledge production is not a necessary evil, but rather the key to our cognitive success (Mercier and Sperber 2011). Indeed, there is evidence to suggest that the cultural distribution of cognitive labor is an evolutionary adaptation: that is how we are designed (by nature) to come to understand, and thereby intervene in, the world. It is not just now, in the complex society in which we live today, or just with regard to the difficult questions that contemporary science faces, that knowledge production must be deeply distributed to be successful. In fact, we have *always* engaged in distributed knowledge production. Culture is central to our success as animals, and culture is in very important part the embodiment of knowledge accumulated by many individuals over many generations.

I use "culture" in the manner defined by Richerson and Boyd (2005, 5): culture is information capable of affecting individuals' behavior that is acquired from other members of their species through mechanisms of social transmission like teaching and imitation. In human beings (perhaps alone), culture is cumulative: new generations add to the stock of transmitted information. Cumulative culture often embodies knowledge that is inaccessible to individuals. Consider the very many cultural techniques required for survival in a harsh environment, like the Arctic. The indigenous people flourished in this environment where well-prepared expeditions could not, despite the advantages of nineteenth-century science and the resources of one of the wealthiest empires ever known (Boyd, Richerson, and Henrich 2011). These expeditions were unable to acquire the knowledge needed for survival in this environment; it takes generations for such knowledge to accumulate, and its range once acquired exceeds the resources of any single individual, such that it must be distributed across many people (so not only is its acquisition dependent on the work of many people over many generations, but it can be maintained only if there are sufficient numbers of individuals to sustain it). Distributed knowledge acquisition is not just a fancy innovation that explains the relatively recent scientific takeoff; rather, it is one of the special tricks that explain human adaptive success (Richerson and Boyd 2005).[11]

Given that our epistemic success is and always has been dependent on the deep distribution of cognitive labor, it is often the case that agents—even agents understood as identical to skin-bound individuals—satisfy or fail to satisfy the epistemic condition in virtue of their place in such distributed networks. Whether they are in a position to know that an action is harmful, for instance, often depends on what testimony they have received, and the reception and assessment of testimony depend on social factors. Unsurprisingly (given that we are deeply cultural animals), human beings are disposed to accept the testimony of others. But our disposition to accept testimony is selective: we are sensitive to cues of lack of benevolence toward us and of incompetence in filtering testimony (Mascaro and Sperber 2009; Sperber et al. 2010). This disposition is obviously adaptive: the use of competence as a filter for reliability enables us to avoid acquiring false beliefs, while the use of lack of benevolence as a filter for reliability enables us to avoid exploitation by others. But cues for competence and for reliability are themselves dependent on social facts. We identify those to be trusted and mistrusted by reference to prevailing social norms, and we identify competence by reference to socially transmitted credentials. Our early, relatively promiscuous acceptance of testimony allows us to bootstrap our way to being appropriately selective in the testimony we accept: first we acquire, primarily from our caregivers, sensitivity to cues for reliability, and then subsequently we utilize those cues to acquire further testimony.

These facts entail that false claims, even obviously false claims, can come to be accepted by agents who might be said to believe virtuously. Cues to reliability are themselves socially distributed: we learn who counts as trustworthy and whose testimony is unreliable. We acquire this information in the first instance from those who *show* us that they are competent and trustworthy (caregivers, in the first instance, in most cases), but then we acquire them through mechanisms of social transmission like imitation, explicit teaching, and through subtle cues from those we trust (how they orient themselves in conversation, say, to whom they listen attentively, and whom they interrupt), as well as from the narratives with which we are surrounded. All too frequently, these cues are distributed so that many true claims are filtered out and false claims filtered in, for example when the true claims are promulgated by those who are denigrated as the source of testimony, such as women and minorities. When this happens, the speakers suffer epistemic injustice (Fricker 2007) at the hands of hearers who may be epistemically virtuous agents. They count as epistemically virtuous because they filter claims in response to the cues in a way that has the function of increasing reliability, and because they cannot reasonably expect to do better by ignoring testimony (again, we are all deeply reliant on testimony for almost all of our beliefs).

Consider, for illustration, Allen Buchanan's description of his lucky escape from the racism of the American South during the 1950s and '60s. Explicitly and by example, he was taught to regard black people as subhuman. Those he had trusted and relied on—family members, his pastor, his teachers, local government officials, were "sources of dangerous error, not truth." It was through the good fortune of leaving this environment that he came to be in a position to appreciate the falsehoods for what they were (Buchanan 2004, 95). Our epistemic capacities are designed (by evolution) to absorb local cultural knowledge, because we require such knowledge to cope with our natural and social environment. But when toxic falsehoods are promulgated alongside adaptive knowledge, we are apt to absorb those too. Filters on testimony are insensitive to the differences between truth and falsehood when both are culturally reinforced, and individual epistemic virtue is insufficient to avoid potential disaster. In cases like this, individuals may perpetrate racist acts but fail to be morally responsible for them: their epistemic bad luck entails that they do not satisfy the epistemic condition on moral responsibility.[12]

These considerations generalize broadly. Consider the politically charged issues that divide people within and across countries. Should taxation be higher than it currently is? Is climate change a serious challenge to humanity? Should coreligionists be accorded a higher moral value than nonbelievers and heretics? Each of these questions is one on which some people are recognized as experts and accorded socially mandated credentials (economists, climate scientists, political pundits, priests, and so on). The great mass of humanity has no special expertise on any of these topics, and no one is genuinely expert on more than a few. These are not questions that we can easily evaluate for ourselves.[13] In fact, the impression that many of us *do* evaluate these questions for ourselves is largely an illusion: we evaluate these questions using tools and biases (virtuous and vicious) that dispose us to take some sources of evidence seriously and dismiss others, and these tools and biases are socially produced and distributed. We must and should defer to others on these matters, except where we are capable of genuine expertise on them (where genuine expertise requires thousands of hours of learning). Epistemically virtuous believers come to have false beliefs on these topics through no fault of their own. They therefore nonculpably fail to satisfy the epistemic conditions on moral responsibility.

If we are justifiably to hold agents morally responsible for actions that are caused or enabled by false beliefs, they must be culpable for having those beliefs. Perhaps there are cases in which agents satisfy this condition, but there are very many significant cases in which they do not, and they do not because of the way in which knowledge claims are socially transmitted. Social animals like us, with cognitive faculties designed (by evolution) to utilize social cues for truth and falsity, are vulnerable to responsibility-undermining epistemic luck: when we are in an environment in which morally significant falsehoods are promulgated by those who count as epistemic authorities—that is, those individuals and institutions that pass the relevant tests for epistemic authority—we are unlikely to be able to come to understand that these claims are false. We lack a reasonable opportunity to come to better views: either these views are lacking from our environment, or they are advocated by individuals who fail the relevant tests for epistemic authority. Buchanan was the beneficiary of good epistemic luck, canceling out the bad epistemic luck of his having been socialized in an environment in which epistemic authorities promoted (vicious) falsehoods: he found himself in a new, and more truth-conducive, social environment.[14] In cases like these, there may be some individual agents who are blameworthy (perhaps agents who have deliberately brought it about that false claims would come to be accepted; see Oreskes and Conway [2010] for examples of individuals who may fit this description). However, the great mass of believers probably are not blameworthy (at most, they are due only a tiny fraction of the blame that might accrue to all of us insofar as we have a role in sustaining the institutions that distribute testimony and the cues of reliability that filter it). They believe virtuously, but their beliefs are false due to the way in which knowledge is socially sustained and distributed.

The mechanisms by which knowledge is socially produced, sustained, and transmitted often entail that individuals fail to satisfy the epistemic conditions on moral responsibility for false belief. When we acquire such beliefs via the virtuous utilization of mechanisms designed to equip us for lives in our culture, we often acquire widely shared false beliefs alongside genuine knowledge. When we act on these false beliefs, we will (at least often) fail to be morally responsible because we do not satisfy the epistemic conditions on moral responsibility. The explanation for our ignorance will essentially cite social and cultural practices, institutions, and norms.

It does not follow, of course, from the fact that we may fail as individuals to be morally responsible for our actions, due to a failure to satisfy the epistemic condition that is itself due to forces working at a supra-individual level, that there is some supra-individual entity that *does* satisfy the epistemic condition. In fact, it will at best rarely be the case that such an entity exists. My primary aim is to not to identify targets to hold to account, but to clear the way for better practices. Focusing on the individual abstracted from her structuring, scaffolding, and supporting context, as our preoccupation with individual-level responsibility encourages us to do, is an obstacle to responses that focus on restructuring the social environment (think, here, of how corporate resistance to common-sense measures to reduce sugar intake advocates that instead we take "personal responsibility" for our diets).[15] Recognizing that the individual is embedded in complex social networks that distribute knowledge paves the way for a focus on the redistribution of resources, and on moving beyond blame and searching for evidence-based solutions. Traditional theories of responsibility focus on the individual and her internal capacities (to control her actions, to regulate beliefs, to endorse her volitions, or what have you). More recent theories extend this concern to the collective and its powers to act and regulate itself. This leaves unexplored agents' embedding in social networks, in power relations, in culture: the ways in which the collective forms and sustains the individual. We cannot fully comprehend responsibility by dividing the territory into the individual, on the one hand, and the collective, on the other. We need as well to understand how the collective structures the individual. Identifying the social and cultural mechanisms responsible for our beliefs reduces the temptation to focus on individuals, and thereby enables us to focus our attention where it should be.

4 Conclusion

In the first half of this chapter, I focused on the control condition on moral responsibility. I suggested that if we utilize *agency* as a criterion for identifying *agents*, we will sometimes find that agents are not identical to individuals, where "individuals" are skin-bound bodies. Instead, agents sometimes extend beyond individuals and into the world. Extended agency is not always collective agency: the agent may owe her powers and capacities to other individuals and to institutions without coming to constitute a higher-level entity. Sometimes, the locus of agency dissociates from the person, without thereby becoming collective. In the second half of the chapter, I turned from the control condition to the epistemic condition. I argued that agents may fail to satisfy the epistemic condition on moral responsibility because of the way they are socially situated. They may exercise their epistemic faculties virtuously but acquire false beliefs because the socially produced cues to which these faculties are sensitive promote false beliefs and denigrate true ones. In this concluding section, I draw the two threads of this chapter together.

If the cues to reliability to which our testimonial mechanisms are sensitive dissociate from genuine reliability, whose fault is that? It may be no one's fault: very often there is no agent responsible for a state of affairs. But many widely accepted false claims (that global warming is not occurring, or is not human induced, or is not a serious problem, for instance) arise and are maintained largely because of the actions of individuals and of institutions that can reasonably be thought to possess and to exercise agency. I have already mentioned the "merchants of doubt" who may be individually responsible for knowingly promulgating false beliefs. But they could not have succeeded without the cooperation of institutions that fail to challenge them or are complicit in their behavior.

For a central instance, take the media. The media gives the merchant of doubt a voice. Some media institutions may be identical to merchants of doubt, but they would not be taken seriously if many others did not accord the skeptics a degree of respectability out of proportion to their epistemic standing, due to the widespread commitment to a norm of "balanced reporting." As this norm is often understood, reporting is balanced only if both sides are given an equal hearing. This is a norm that ought to be rejected or reinterpreted when we have good reason to think that one side is neither justified in its claims nor motivated by the search for truth or by a concern for the well-being of ordinary individuals. Of course, the media can no more assess the climate science than can other nonexperts. But it need not do so in order to develop a rubric for giving a hearing to the sides: it can refer to the scientific consensus and weight voices accordingly. There is a strong scientific consensus on the reality of anthropogenic global warming: many studies have found that approximately 97 percent of relevant experts hold that it is occurring, that it is human induced, and that it is a very serious problem (Cook et al. 2013; Carlton et al. 2015). Yet mainstream media organizations give both sides equal, or nearly equal, coverage (Boykoff and Boykoff 2004; Theel, Greenberg, and Robbins 2013). Other institutions—schools, universities, and parliaments, for instance—may be complicit in the fact that this situation goes without significant challenge.

There may be a case for holding that some or all of these institutions, perhaps together with some individuals, constitute genuine loci of agency that can be held responsible for the fact that many individuals fail to satisfy the epistemic condition. Someone may be to blame, or perhaps some*thing*; there may be genuine agents who ought to be held responsible and who have an obligation to correct the state of affairs, where these agents are not identical to any individuals.

Even if these institutions do not constitute agents who may justifiably be held responsible for the ignorance of so many, there is a strong case for thinking that they nevertheless play a significant role in the structuring of the agency of others—individuals and collectives—such that correcting the widespread ignorance will require reforming the institutions. The almost obsessive focus on the individual as the only locus not only of agency but also of responsibility has been counterproductive. It has focused our attention on arguing with one another, on identifying villains, and on denigrating those who come to hold false beliefs. If we set aside this obsession with individuals, the way may be clear for us to identify the agents who are the most important actors on this stage and then to play our individual and distributed parts in bringing them to play it better.[16]

Notes

1. Important exceptions to the individualistic consensus include Ciurria (2015), Doris (2015), and Vargas (2017). My own work also rejects the consensus: with a focus on (so-called) Frankfurt-style cases, I have argued that the mere presence or absence of other individuals can make a decisive difference to agents' moral responsibility (Levy 2008, 2015).
2. I am a moral responsibility skeptic (see Levy 2011). However, normative concerns other than concerns over blame and praise—concerns, for example, with who is capable of responding to reasons and for whom respect for agency requires the presentation of reasons—closely track necessary (though for me not sufficient) conditions for the ascription of moral responsibility. Throughout this chapter, I write as if agents could justifiably be held morally responsible for their actions, rather than allow my own views to obtrude. In so doing, I attempt to identify a set of conditions that are genuinely important for agency on my view and that ought to be held to be central for responsibility by those who are not skeptics.
3. There is a rich and growing literature on collective responsibility; see Sepinwall (2016) for a review, focused on the responsibility of corporations. This literature has significantly advanced our understanding of how collectives can exercise agency and the conditions under which the collective might be said to be culpable, but it is not intended to address my primary concern: how *individual* agency is dependent on its social context, including the way in which agents are embedded in collectives, and the extent to which individual powers of agency are dependent on, or even partially constituted by, this context.
4. The idea that agency may supervene on individuals plus things in the world builds on the extended mind hypothesis—the hypothesis that mind may extend beyond the skull and into the world; see Clark and Chalmers (1998). Clark and Chalmers argue that external artifacts sometimes play functional roles in cognition analogous (or even identical) to the functional role of brain mechanisms and therefore should be seen as partially constituting minds.

Agency, in turn, depends on cognition: action is guided by representations of the world. The view discussed here differs from the extended mind hypothesis not only in focusing on agency and not the mind, but also in focusing on how other individuals and social institutions—as well as or instead of artifacts—may constitute agency.

5. In Levy (2011), I argue that the control and epistemic conditions are not independent: rather, the epistemic condition is at least in important part a condition that must be satisfied in order for the agent to exercise control. It will do no harm to treat them as if they were independent in this context, however.

6. By building in these stipulations, Pereboom aims to ensure that Plum satisfies the conjunction of conditions on moral responsibility set down by a variety of leading theorists. The stipulation that Plum endorses the first-order desire on which he acts, for instance, ensures that he satisfies the conditions that Frankfurt (1971) influentially advances; the stipulation that Plum would respond and react to some reasons to do otherwise, including moral reasons, in counterfactual situations ensures that he satisfies Fischer and Ravizza's (1998) conditions for moral responsibility, and so forth.

7. Moderate reasons responsiveness also requires the satisfaction of an ownership condition for Fischer, because moral responsibility is intrinsically historical. I set that condition aside here.

8. There is a further difficulty that may arise in this context that does not arise with regard to nations and corporations: individuals like Plum and the neuroscientists might fail to constitute an aggregate agent across time. They may constitute a fleeting agent: by the time that anyone thinks to hold them to account, they may have dissolved. I grant that this may happen, but it has its individual-level analogue too (we may sometimes blame agents who are dead, for instance). A further worry is that the boundaries of the actual extra-individual agents who actually play an essential role in distributing powers to individuals are always shifting, making it hard to draw boundaries. This fact, too, may make it hard to identify an appropriate target to call to account. However, these barriers will not be encountered in every case. More centrally they should not distract us from the nonpunitive responses that are the most important: changes in policies, redistribution of resources, and alterations in social practices.

9. It is important to distinguish between medical researchers and general practitioners in making this claim. It is arguable that some medical researchers ought to have put the bacterial hypothesis to a more stringent test much earlier; in retrospect, at least, we can see that the evidence against the hypothesis was weaker than was widely thought (for discussion, see Zollman 2010). However, individual physicians cannot and should not be expected to test established medical claims, except in very rare cases; rather, they discharge their epistemic obligations when they keep up with the current state of medical knowledge.

10. Diversity is not sufficient on its own, of course. Groups may fail to outperform individuals at deliberation when dissenting individuals are unable to speak or be heard (Sunstein 2005). Too often, low-status individuals are unable to express their views, or their opinions may be given little credibility (Fricker 2007).

11. Kukla (2012) argues that there are deep problems with regard to contemporary science arising from the extent to which it is distributed across individuals. No one is in a position to understand or to take responsibility for the results of such research, she maintains. As a consequence, there is no one whom we can hold accountable for its truth claims. Kukla thinks that appeals to testimony cannot explain how such claims can be justified, because no one is in a position to test these claims for reliability. It may be that a shift in focus from individuals to collectives as loci not only of agency but also of knowledge may help to alleviate these concerns. It is worth emphasizing that the problem is not new (taboos, for example, may sometimes embody genuinely distributed knowledge that no individual is in a position to answer for or even to understand; Henrich and Henrich 2010), and that it has implications that extend well beyond concerns for the epistemic status of scientific claims. Distributed knowledge—justified for individuals or not—is central to our responsibility, including our individual responsibility. If no one can justifiably be held responsible when they cannot individually vouch for knowledge claims, there will be precious few cases in which anyone satisfies the epistemic conditions on responsibility.

12. Many philosophers argue that agents like Buchanan's counterpart, who did not have the good luck of escaping his toxic environment, would satisfy the epistemic condition because they

would (typically) be culpable *for* their ignorance (see, for example, Moody-Adams 1997; FitzPatrick 2008). Responding to these critics would take us too far afield. I have responded to their worries elsewhere (Levy 2003, 2009).

13. Despite the depth of our reliance on the distribution of cognitive labor, we tend to overvalue individual reasoning and undervalue group deliberation (see Mercier et al. 2015).

14. Note that these remarks do not commit me to denying that culpable ignorance is possible. Rather, they delimit the circumstances in which ignorance can be culpable: it is a necessary condition of culpable ignorance that the agent be presented with what she herself recognizes as a genuine opportunity to put her beliefs to the test. Culpable ignorance, on my view (owed to Smith 1983) requires a "benighting act"; such an act occurs when the agent culpably passes up such an opportunity.

15. One example among literally thousands: "Americans need to be more active and take greater responsibility for their diets," according to the CEO of Coca-Cola (Kent 2009).

16. I am extremely grateful to Katrina Hutchison, Catriona Mackenzie, and Marina Oshana for extensive comments on this chapter; every page and every argument are substantially better for their input. I am also grateful to Wendy Carlton for capable copyediting and advice. Work leading up to this chapter was supported by the Oxford Martin School and the Wellcome Trust (WT104848/Z/14/Z).

References

Björnsson, G., and K. Hess. 2017. "Corporate Crocodile Tears? On the Reactive Attitudes of Corporate Agents." *Philosophy and Phenomenological Research* 92 (2): 273–298.

Boyd, R., P. J. Richerson, and J. Henrich. 2011. "The Cultural Niche: Why Social Learning Is Essential for Human Adaptation." *Proceedings of the National Academy of Sciences* 108 (26): 10918–10925.

Boykoff, M. T., and J. M. Boykoff. 2004. "Balance as Bias: Global Warming and the US Prestige Press." *Global Environmental Change* 14 (2): 125–136.

Buchanan, A. 2004. "Political Liberalism and Social Epistemology." *Philosophy and Public Affairs* 32 (2): 95–130.

Carlton, J. S., R. Perry-Hill, M. Huber, and L. S. Prokopy. 2015. "The Climate Consensus Extends Beyond Climate Scientists." *Environmental Research Letters* 10: 094025.

Castelvecchi, D. 2015. "Physics Paper Sets Record with More than 5,000 Authors." *Nature*, May 15. http://www.nature.com/news/physics-paper-sets-record-with-more-than-5-000-authors-1.17567.

Ciurria, M. 2015. "Moral Responsibility Ain't Just in the Head." *Journal of the American Philosophical Association* 1 (4): 601–616.

Clark, A., and D. Chalmers. 1998. "The Extended Mind." *Analysis* 58 (1): 7–19.

Clarke, R. 2003. *Libertarian Accounts of Free Will*. New York: Oxford University Press.

Cole, D. 2014. "The Chinese Room Argument." *The Stanford Encyclopedia of Philosophy*, E. N. Zalta (ed.), URL = < http://plato.stanford.edu/entries/chinese-room/ >

Cook, J., D. Nuccitelli, S. A. Green, M. Richardson, B. Winkler, R. Painting, R. Way, P. Jacobs, and A. Skuce. 2013. "Quantifying the Consensus on Anthropogenic Global Warming in the Scientific Literature." *Environmental Research Letters* 8 (2): 1–7.

Doris, J. M. 2015. *Talking to Our Selves: Reflection, Ignorance, and Agency*. Oxford: Oxford University Press.

Fischer, J. M. 2006. *My Way*. New York: Oxford University Press.

Fischer, J. M., and M. Ravizza. 1998. *Responsibility and Control: An Essay on Moral Responsibility*. Cambridge: Cambridge University Press.

FitzPatrick, W. J. 2008. "Moral Responsibility and Normative Ignorance: Answering a New Skeptical Challenge." *Ethics* 118 (4): 589–613.

Frankfurt, H. 1971. "Freedom of the Will and the Concept of a Person." *Journal of Philosophy* 68 (1): 5–20.

Fricker, M. 2007. *Epistemic Injustice.* Oxford: Oxford University Press.

Glasgow, J. 2009. "Racism as Disrespect." *Ethics* 120 (1): 64–93.

Hackman, D. A., M. J. Farah, and M. J. Meaney. 2010. "Socioeconomic Status and the Brain: Mechanistic Insights from Human and Animal Research." *Nature Reviews Neuroscience* 11 (9): 651–659.

Haslanger, S. 2004. "Oppressions: Racial and Other." In *Racism in Mind,* edited by M. P. Levine and T. Pataki, 97–123. Ithaca, NY: Cornell University Press.

Henrich, J., and N. Henrich. 2010. "The Evolution of Cultural Adaptations: Fijian Food Taboos Protect against Dangerous Marine Toxins." *Proceedings of the Royal Society B: Biological Sciences* 277 (1701): 3715–3724.

Kane, R. 1996. *The Significance of Free Will.* New York: Oxford University Press.

Kent, M. 2009. "Coke Didn't Make American Fat." *Wall Street Journal,* October 7.

Kukla, R. 2012. "Author TBD: Radical Collaboration in Contemporary Biomedical Research." *Philosophy of Science* 79 (5): 845–858.

Levy, N. 2003. "Cultural Membership and Moral Responsibility." *The Monist* 86 (2): 145–163.

Levy, N. 2008. "Counterfactual Intervention and Agents' Capacities." *Journal of Philosophy* 105 (5): 223–239.

Levy, N. 2009. "Culpable Ignorance and Moral Responsibility: A Reply to FitzPatrick." *Ethics* 119 (4): 729–741.

Levy, N. 2011. *Hard Luck: How Luck Undermines Free Will and Moral Responsibility.* New York: Oxford University Press.

Levy, N. 2015. "Frankfurt in Fake Barn Country." In *The Philosophy of Luck,* edited by D. Pritchard and L. Whittington, 79–92. Hoboken: Wiley.

Mascaro, O., and D. Sperber. 2009. "The Moral, Epistemic, and Mindreading Components of Children's Vigilance Towards Deception." *Cognition* 112 (3): 367–380.

McKenna, M. 2008. "A Hard-Line Reply to Pereboom's Four-Case Manipulation Argument." *Philosophy and Phenomenological Research* 77 (1): 142–159.

Mele, A. 2006. *Free Will and Luck.* Oxford: Oxford University Press.

Mercier, H., and D. Sperber. 2011. "Why Do Humans Reason? Arguments for an Argumentative Theory." *Behavioral and Brain Sciences* 34 (2): 57–111.

Mercier, H., E. Trouche, H. Yama, C. Heintz, and V. Girotto. 2015. "Experts and Laymen Grossly Underestimate the Benefits of Argumentation for Reasoning." *Thinking and Reasoning* 21 (3): 341–355.

Moody-Adams, M. M. 1997. *Fieldwork in Familiar Places: Morality, Culture, and Philosophy.* Cambridge, MA: Harvard University Press.

Oreskes, N., and E. M. Conway. 2010. *Merchants of Doubt.* London: Bloomsbury Press.

Pereboom, D. 2001. *Living without Free Will.* Cambridge: Cambridge University Press.

Pereboom, D. 2014. *Free Will, Agency, and Meaning in Life.* New York: Oxford University Press.

Richerson, P. J., and R. Boyd. 2005. *Not by Genes Alone.* Chicago: University of Chicago Press.

Rovane, C. 1998. *The Bounds of Agency.* Princeton, NJ: Princeton University Press.

Searle, J. 1980. "Minds, Brains and Programs." *Behavioral and Brain Sciences* 3 (3): 417–457.

Searle, J. 1990. "Is the Brain's Mind a Computer Program?" *Scientific American* 262 (1): 26–31.

Sepinwall, A. J. 2016. "Corporate Moral Responsibility." *Philosophy Compass* 11 (1): 3–13.

Smith, H. 1983. "Culpable Ignorance." *Philosophical Review* 92 (4): 543–571.

Sperber, D., F. Clément, C. Heintz, O. Mascaro, H. Mercier, G. Origgi, and D. Wilson. 2010. "Epistemic Vigilance." *Mind & Language* 25 (4): 359–393.

Steward, H. 2012. *A Metaphysics for Freedom.* Oxford: Oxford University Press.

Sunstein, C. R. 2005. "Group Judgments: Statistical Means, Deliberation, and Information Markets." *New York University Law Review* 80 (3): 962–1049.

Theel, S., M. Greenberg, and D. Robbins. 2013. "Media Sowed Doubt in Coverage of UN Climate Report." Media Matters for America. Uploaded October 10. http://mediamatters.org/research/2013/10/10/study-media-sowed-doubt-in-coverage-of-un-clima/196387.

Vargas, M. 2017. "Implicit Bias, Responsibility, and Moral Ecology." In *Oxford Studies in Agency and Responsibility, Vol. 4*, edited by D. Shoemaker, 219–247. Oxford: Oxford University Press.

Vihvelin, K. 2013. *Causes, Laws, and Free Will: Why Determinism Doesn't Matter*. Oxford: Oxford University Press.

Zollman, K. J. S. 2010. "The Epistemic Benefit of Transient Diversity." *Erkenntnis* 72 (1): 17–35.

8

Moral Responsibility, Respect, and Social Identity

KATRINA HUTCHISON

1 Introduction

In "Freedom and Resentment" (1962), P. F. Strawson distinguished the participant stance that we take toward those we regard as fully functioning moral agents
from the objective stance we take toward those who cannot properly respond to
moral demands, and who must be managed rather than engaged with. According
to Strawson, we can learn much about the conditions of moral responsibility
by attending to which individuals we treat as participants and which we treat
as objects. Which of these two stances we take toward someone is responsive
to their capacities, and it is *these* capacities—the ones we intuitively track when
engaging with others in ordinary interactions—that underpin moral agency.

In this chapter, I focus on the participant and objective stances and their
role in oppressive moral responsibility practices. In section 2, I give a detailed
account of morally reactive exchanges as understood by Strawson, and the participant stance that parties to these exchanges take toward one another. I also
discuss the objective stance, in which someone who lacks the relevant capacities
is treated as an object to be managed, rather than a participant. This distinction
between the objective and the participant stance fits some cases well. However
many of our real interactions with others do not manifest either attitude straightforwardly. In view of this, I expand upon Strawson's concession that many cases
"straddle" the participant and objective stance (1962, 204), and I argue that the
capacities involved in being a moral agent can be possessed in greater or lesser
degrees by individuals. It follows that individuals can be participants to a greater
or lesser degree.

In section 3, I develop a further point, one that has been less often attended
to: namely, that both the participant stance and the objective stance, as presented

by Strawson, involve respect for the dignity of the target. However, the type of respect each involves is different. The objective stance involves a compassionate recognition of the limitations of individuals who cannot successfully participate in normal morally reactive exchanges. The dignity of these individuals is respected insofar as they are *spared* the sting of resentment. This respect, which is extended to individuals despite their limited capacities, is a form of what is sometimes called "status" or "recognition" respect. The participant stance involves a different sort of respect, a form of "achievement" or "appraisal" respect that recognizes individuals' agential capacities.

Correspondingly, the two stances are each associated with a distinctive negative aspect. The decision to take the objective stance amounts to a negative appraisal of the target's agential capacities. However, this negative aspect is idle. It does not license any sort of reprimand or response. The participant stance, in contrast, is inherently respectful of the agency of the target. But when an agent seriously violates the shared standards, that person's action (or character, or judgment) is negatively evaluated. This negative aspect is not idle: it occurs precisely because the target could have—and should have—done better. It can license various sorts of reprimand or response—punishment and blame, for example.

In section 4, I introduce some difficult cases. These cases involve encounters between Indigenous Australian women in custody, and prison officers, police, and health professionals. The cases appear to be marginal insofar as the reactions of other members of the moral community toward the women do not involve a purely participant or purely objective stance. What is striking about these cases, however, is how badly the women are treated. This bad treatment seems to invoke stereotypes about Indigenous women that are pervasive within the community. As such, it is difficult to regard the cases as isolated. In fact, they may represent systematically corrupted moral practices of responding to Indigenous women within the Australian community.

Strawsonian approaches have been criticized for looking to our practices to identify the capacities relevant to moral responsibility, precisely due to the risk that our practices may be systemically biased or wrong. Commentators have been concerned that Strawson ignored the complexity of our practices and ignored the fact that many of our reactions to one another are contingent on factors that we would not want to incorporate into an account of moral responsibility (e.g., Watson 1987, 282–283; McKenna and Russell 2008, 10). In this chapter I do not provide a full response to these concerns. However, drawing on my analysis of the types of respect involved in the participant and objective stance, I argue that these particular cases do not pose a problem for Strawsonians. In these cases, the appropriate attitudes of respect have come apart from the participant and objective stances. The women, I argue, are not treated with the compassion or recognition respect associated with the objective stance. But nor does there seem to be appraisal respect for their agency. Furthermore, the negative attitudes and actions of the authority figures who hold them in custody do not seem to connect in any plausible way with the act that they are in custody for: this treatment is not easily interpreted as a part of any punishment or blame for an identifiable wrongdoing.

Thus, however widespread the underlying negative attitudes toward Indigenous women are, Strawsonians have resources for criticizing the behavior of police, prison officers, and health workers who disregard their welfare. Such disregard cannot be understood as reflecting a "shared value" of the moral community. In addition to illuminating the cases discussed, these observations about the connection between respect and holding responsible may apply to other situations in which biases and stereotypes that are widely held within a community lead to systemic, discriminatory moral responsibility practices.

2 Morally Reactive Exchanges and the Participant Stance

In 2010, Australian Olympic swimmer Stephanie Rice posted a homophobic comment on Twitter. Taunting the South African rugby union team on a loss to Australia, she tweeted, "Suck on that, faggots!" Among many others, retired rugby league star Ian Roberts, who is gay, publicly condemned the tweet, saying, "She is an idiot . . . and anyone who continues to endorse her as an athlete is an idiot as well" (*Herald Sun* 2010). Rice was widely criticized for her comment, particularly in the wake of Roberts's response, and at least one of her sponsors— Jaguar—terminated her contract. Several days after posting the tweet, as the public fallout continued, Rice apologized to a packed media conference, saying, "I owe it to those who I have offended to publicly say, I am sorry" (White 2010).

This scenario can be understood as a three-way morally reactive exchange between an agent who acts (Rice), another agent who is directly harmed or helped by the act and responds with reactive attitudes such as resentment (Roberts), and third parties who are not directly harmed or helped, but who respond with moral approbation or disapprobation (Jaguar/the media). In "Freedom and Resentment" (1962), P. F. Strawson foregrounded such exchanges, developing an approach to moral responsibility based on the social practice of holding responsible that such exchanges reflect.

One feature Strawson highlighted is the "participant stance" we take toward one another in these exchanges. It involves engaging with someone else as a fellow subject, rather than an object to be managed. It includes caring about that person's intentions, expecting that she or he will respond in particular ways to moral demands, and expecting reciprocation. In contrast, when we do not regard someone as a full participant in ordinary human relationships, we take an objective stance:

> What I want to contrast is the attitude (or range of attitudes) of involvement or participation in a human relationship, on the one hand, and what might be called the objective attitude (or range of attitudes) to another human being, on the other. . . . To adopt the objective attitude to another human being is to see him, perhaps, as an object of social policy; as something certainly to be taken account, perhaps precautionary account, of; to be managed or handled or cured or trained. (Strawson 1962, 194)

Strawson does not explore examples of the objective stance in any detail. For him, the point is that we have a practice of tracking who is a moral agent and who isn't, and this practice is revealed in our ability to take the objective stance—to sometimes treat some individuals as objects to be managed rather than persons to be engaged with.

If the example involving Rice's homophobic tweet is a typical case of the participant stance, what would be a clear example of the objective stance? Strawson mentions several reasons we might take the objective stance, including when a person is psychologically abnormal, morally undeveloped, warped or deranged, neurotic, just a child, compulsive in behavior, or peculiarly unfortunate in formative circumstances (Strawson 1962, 194–195). Using these suggestions, it is possible to think of a case that represents the features of the objective stance as he describes it. Imagine, for example, a toddler who has a tantrum in a park after disagreeing with another child about the swing. In her rage, she pushes the other child. Her parent, who immediately intervenes, picks up the toddler and carries her to a grassy area where she is safe and cannot harm others, then lets her rage until the tantrum passes.

Like Rice, the toddler has caused others harm. However, it is not appropriate to ask the toddler to account for her behavior, or to seek a moral response from her. This is because, unlike Rice, the toddler lacks several capacities involved in the successful participation in a morally reactive exchange. First, her grasp of language and conversational conventions is limited. Second and more importantly, her understanding of the concepts and demands involved is limited. She is not yet able to understand the requirement that she treat others well, so she cannot respond as an adult would to the moral content of any reprimand. If she were asked, "Why did you hurt the other child?" her answer is likely to be focused on the desired outcome (i.e., "because I wanted the swing"). If she were prompted to apologize, the apology would be empty of the other-regarding content that gives real apologies their meaning. For these reasons, the parent manages the toddler's behavior to limit further harms, by removing her from other children and play equipment. In this case, the management minimizes the risks while remaining compassionate toward the toddler.

The reason Strawson drew attention to our ability to switch between a participant stance and an objective stance was its potential to reveal the conditions of moral responsibility. His view was that we already do track moral agency: we usually take the participant stance toward morally responsible agents, and the objective stance toward those who are not.[1]

Of course, there are idiosyncrasies in the stances particular individuals take toward one another. Sometimes the moral demands we make of others are unreasonable, or our reactive attitudes are insensitive to factors that should give pause. To avoid relativizing the conditions of moral responsibility to particular individuals requires a collective with shared practices, including shared norms for identifying who is an agent. Strawson refers to this as "the moral community" (1962, 202). The example at the beginning of this section is useful to illustrate: Roberts treated Rice as a participant when he responded to her tweet with resentment. But in addition to his response, others, including many who were not directly offended by the content of the tweet, echoed his stance. Given how widespread the condemnation was, it seems the wider moral community agreed with Roberts both in his decision to take the participant stance toward Rice, and in his assessment that her tweet violated a shared moral standard. Insofar as the conditions of moral responsibility can be ascertained from our practices, it is the stance accepted by the community, rather than the stance taken by individuals, that matters.[2]

Strawson leaves the boundaries of the moral community, and the identification of the norms of inclusion, ambiguous in "Freedom and Resentment." He does, however, note two different sorts of challenges to identifying these. One is cultural relativity: "One factor of comparatively minor importance is an increased historical and anthropological awareness of the great variety of forms which these human attitudes may take at different times and in different cultures" (Strawson 1962, 209). Given cultural differences, there is a question about how "local" a moral community is, and when, whether, and how it can accommodate significant value differences.

The other issue Strawson notes is the susceptibility of our practices to bias. He says, "A quite different factor of greater importance is that psychological studies have made us rightly mistrustful of many particular manifestations of the attitudes I have spoken of. They are a prime realm of self-deception, of the ambiguous and the shady, of guilt-transference, unconscious sadism and the rest" (1962, 210). Although he doesn't use this term, we might now include 'implicit biases' in the list. There is increasing awareness that many of our explicit views—in favor of gender and racial equity, for example—are undercut by unconscious associations (Greenwald and Marzarin 1995, 15). These unconscious associations explain why racist, sexist, or homophobic behavior persists even in those who explicitly disavow these attitudes. Like self-deception and other factors listed in this quote by Strawson, implicit bias is likely to influence the manifestation of attitudes such as resentment. As such, implicit bias might influence toward whom and under what conditions we take the participant stance. Furthermore, the unconscious influence of some factors—such as stereotypes—can be pervasive in a moral community, such that they are incorporated into the shared norms and not very susceptible to being challenged.

The two examples—Stephanie Rice and the toddler throwing a tantrum—seem to be clear cases of the participant stance and the objective stance respectively. However, many cases do not neatly fit either category. Strawson acknowledges this. In fact, he refers to his own distinction between the objective and the participant stance as "a crude opposition of phrase where we have a great intricacy of phenomena," and he notes that many cases "straddle these contrasted kinds of attitude" (Strawson 1962, 204).

Strawson is surely right that the participant and objective stance should not be thought of as a simple opposition. In my view, it makes more sense to think of the completely objective and completely participant stances as existing at either end of a spectrum. But if this is the case, then it is unclear how our judgments about moral agency should engage with cases in the middle of the spectrum. In order to understand the difficulties with cases that do not involve a purely participant or purely objective stance, it is useful to have an example to contrast with the Rice and toddler examples.

A recent high-profile Australian case manifests some of these ambiguities. In 2014, Ashlee Polkinghorne was sentenced to a minimum of four years and nine months in prison for the manslaughter of her daughter, four-year-old Chloe Valentine (Founten and Hancock 2014). Chloe died in 2012 as a result of injuries from multiple falls from a motorbike. She had been forced to get on the motorbike over and over again by her mother's boyfriend, only to crash while her mother and the boyfriend watched and recorded footage using their mobile phones. Chloe suffered widespread bruising, and in the following days she complained of pain, struggled to sleep, and eventually became unconscious. The mother and boyfriend did not seek medical help until Chloe stopped breathing, by which time it was too late. The sentencing remarks and public debate surrounding Polkinghorne's crime and sentence reveal ambivalence about her moral agency.

Chloe's death was not an isolated instance of parental neglect. Ashlee Polkinghorne, who gave birth to Chloe at sixteen, had been involved with the government agency Families South Australia (SA) since she was pregnant. She was known to be a drug user, her living situation was unstable with periods of homelessness, and for a period she was in a live-in relationship with a child sex offender. Between Chloe's birth and death, there had been more than twenty notifications made to the authorities by family and friends who were concerned about Chloe's safety. An inquest into the handling of Chloe's case, including these notifications, heard from Families SA staff, friends, family, and workers from other agencies (Johns 2015). Their evidence painted a grim picture of Polkinghorne's parenting.

In the report of the inquest, the remarks of the judge who sentenced Polkinghorne, and the public commentary around the case, there was considerable ambivalence regarding Polkinghorne's capacity and status as a responsible agent. In the sentencing remarks, Justice Trish Kelly repeatedly drew attention to what many would regard as moral failings of Polkinghorne in the care of her daughter. For example, she is quoted as saying, "You were Chloe's mother. . . . [Y]ou were the one who was closest to her yet you gave her no medication, you didn't take her to a doctor, even after you knew something was gravely wrong" (ABC News Online 2015).

These remarks were addressed directly to Polkinghorne, involve a moral demand, and seem to call (however rhetorically given the context in which they are delivered) for an answer. Justice Kelly apparently takes the participant stance toward Polkinghorne in this exchange. Further indication that Polkinghorne is regarded as a participant include the appeal by the director of public prosecutions against her sentence as "manifestly inadequate" (Marcus 2014). Comments by members of the public who attended the sentencing hearing for Polkinghorne and her boyfriend reinforce this interpretation. When the sentences were read, one observer called out, "Now you know how Chloe felt," and another said to reporters afterward, "They didn't look remorseful to me, not one bit" (Akerman 2014).

However, other features of the case give reason to question whether Polkinghorne is properly regarded as a participant. Unlike Rice, whose apology indicated that she understood and was able to play her "role" in a co-reactive exchange, Polkinghorne either never sought or was not given the opportunity to respond. Her history of drug use, interactions with Families SA and details of how she behaved during and after the incidents leading to the death of her daughter suggest that she lacked some of the capacities that would lead us to treat her as a full participant. Testimony at the inquest called into question her ability to parent, with one witness describing her as "simply incapable of understanding her role as a parent" (Johns 2015, 103).

The details of this case are difficult to reconcile with a hard and fast distinction between the objective and participant stance. The ambivalence regarding Polkinghorne's capacities that is reflected in the different reactions towards her suggest that she had a degree of capacity—enough to bear some responsibility for her daughter's death and to be treated as a participant to a corresponding extent. After all, her daughter was injured, and eventually unconscious, and there is evidence that Polkinghorne was aware of this. She was sufficiently aware to use the Internet to look up what to do with an unconscious person, for example (Johns 2015, 2). It seems that she knew she needed to do something to respond to her daughter's injury, and it is not a stretch to believe that she knew she should call an ambulance, but was afraid of the consequences and hoped the injury would resolve itself. That she is not incapacitated for moral address is suggested by her apparent suffering as a consequence of her daughter's death—her lawyer, Brian Deegan, described her as "suicidal" with suffering over the incident (Fewster 2014), which presumably indicates grief for Chloe and guilt regarding what happened. The idea that Polkinghorne has at least some of the capacities required for moral agency, albeit underdeveloped, is indicated by Deegan's comment that she has "learned, personally, an enormous lesson" from what happened to Chloe (Fewster 2014).

It seems plausible that Polkinghorne, despite her apparently underdeveloped moral capacities, nevertheless had sufficient ability to engage in moral dialogue, understand the requirement to treat others with basic regard, and recognize her own behavior as falling below acceptable standards *in the context of what happened to her daughter*. It does not seem that this particular situation required a sophisticated grasp of these matters. Many individuals, including children whose capacities are emerging, seem to fall on a spectrum. They are not full participants, but the objective attitude is not appropriate either.

In the next section, I give an account of another feature of the objective and participant attitudes—the sort of respect implicit in each. This helps, I think, to further illuminate cases that fall somewhere in the middle of the spectrum, like the case of Ashlee Polkinghorne.

3 Respect and Compassion in the Participant and Objective Stances

Several Strawsonians have noted that the participant stance inherently respects the personhood or agency of those toward whom it is directed. Victoria McGeer, for example, claims that when we hold people responsible,

> It says to the recipients of our reactive attitudes that we do not despair of them as moral agents; that we don't view them objectively—that is, as individuals to be managed or treated or somehow worked around; indeed, that we hold them accountable to an ideal of moral agency because we think them capable of living up to that ideal. So reactive

attitudes communicate a positive message even in their most negative guise—even in the guise of anger, resentment, or indignation. The fact that we express them says to the recipients that we see them as individuals who are capable of understanding and living up to the norms that make for moral community. (2012, 303)

If the participant stance conveys respect for the moral capacities of those toward whom it is taken, what about the objective stance? In a discussion of people with difficult formative circumstances, Angela Smith expresses concern about exempting them from our normal moral responsibility practices. This, she argues, "would require us to regard some agents as the passive victims of their faulty judgments," and she goes on to say that this "is a dangerously patronizing and disrespectful stance to take toward another human being, one that we should be very reluctant to resort to in practice" (2008, 390). I agree with McGeer and Smith that holding responsible and taking the participant stance can confer respect, whereas taking the objective stance can be disrespectful in at least some situations. However, philosophers distinguish different notions of respect, and it is important to ask what notion of respect is involved.

A key distinction in the literature is between respect owed to all persons *as persons*, irrespective of merit, and respect that is responsive to merit. The former applies to everyone, and it does not come in degrees. In contrast, the merit-tracking type of respect is domain specific and is only extended toward those who have the relevant skills or capacities. In addition, it comes in degrees—I can have more respect for one doctor's diagnosis than another's. Although a distinction along these lines is widely accepted, there is less agreement on exactly how to characterize each type of respect.

Perhaps the most widely accepted version of the distinction is due to Stephen Darwall (1977). He distinguished "recognition respect," which involves "giving appropriate consideration or recognition" to its object, from "appraisal respect," which "consists in an attitude of positive appraisal of that person either as a person or as engaged in some particular pursuit" (1977, 38). Respect for persons as persons is a form of recognition respect. According to Darwall, "To say that persons as such are entitled to respect is to say that they are entitled to have other persons take seriously and weigh appropriately the fact that they are persons in deliberating about what to do" (38).

Thus respecting persons as such involves regarding the fact that they are persons as reason giving: as something that must be factored in when deciding what to do.[3] According to Darwall's analysis, there are also other forms of recognition respect. Respect for the law, for example, is a form of recognition respect because it involves giving appropriate weight to the law in our deliberations. However, in what follows "recognition respect," will refer to recognition respect for persons as persons.

My remarks in the previous sections are consistent with regarding the respect involved in the participant stance as a form of appraisal respect. The participant stance is not extended to everyone, but only to those with the relevant capacities. Furthermore, the capacities relevant to moral responsibility seem to come in degrees. Appraisal respect (but not recognition respect) discriminates between those with the respect-worthy quality and those who lack it, and it is sensitive to degrees of achievement.

However, this picture is not consistent with Darwall's own view about the sort of respect involved in the participant stance. He thinks that the participant stance involves recognition respect rather than appraisal respect. This is partly because his conception of recognition respect is quite restrictive. Following Kant, Darwall thinks that being a person involves capacities that are arguably lacking in those we take the objective stance toward; specifically, it requires rational capacities.[4] This means it is not obvious that very young children, those with significant cognitive impairments, or those suffering from advanced dementia are persons. In fact, in Darwall's recent work (2004, 2006), he is committed to an even more restrictive account of recognition respect, according to which it requires not only rational capacities but also the ability to participate in specific kinds of relationships. He now regards being able to make and respond to direct person-to-person demands as a feature of recognition respect, and a central feature of the participant stance. He states, "I believe that recognition respect for someone as a person is also second-personal. It is an acknowledgment of someone's standing to address and be addressed second-personal reasons rooted in the dignity of persons" (2006, 126).

Darwall argues that second-personal demands—those actually addressed to us by other people—give us distinctive types of reasons for acting. These reasons differ from the reasons that arise from awareness of others' capacity to suffer, or awareness of their pain or discomfort. Rather than a one-sided decision to do the right thing for a suffering creature, responding to a person-to-person demand is two-sided. In exploring the precise character of this relationship, Darwall talks about the mutual vulnerability involved in making second-personal demands. Doing so does not only involve rational, cognitive, and communicative skills, but also a kind of emotional sensibility:

> To return someone's address and look back at him is to establish a second-personal relationship and acknowledge the other's second-personal authority. To look someone in the eye is to make oneself and ones' eyes, the "windows" of one's soul, vulnerable to him, and in both directions. One gives the other a window on one's responses to

him but also makes oneself vulnerable to his attitudes and responses. (2006, 142)

Being a person, then, if it involves all this, is quite an achievement. Perhaps because he sets the bar for recognition respect so high, Darwall also thinks that it (and not appraisal respect) is the type of respect involved in the participant stance. For several reasons, Darwall's (2004, 2006) conception of recognition respect seems a good fit with the participant stance and with other features of several recent Strawsonian theories of moral responsibility. The emphasis on the ability to make and respond to second-personal demands resonates with features of recent interlocutive or conversational theories, such as those advanced by Oshana (1997, 2004), McKenna (2012), and McGeer (2012). It is also consistent with another feature of Strawson's approach—his view that the participant stance unites a range of different types of interpersonal interactions. In addition to moral responsibility interactions, this includes "the sort of love which two adults can sometimes be said to feel reciprocally" (1962, 194–195). These sorts of interpersonal interactions are characterized by the parties making second-personal demands of one another. As Gary Watson has observed, we are prone to "a vivid sense of mutual expectations as spouses and sisters and co-workers" (2014, 29). Although Watson doesn't describe it in terms of recognition respect, he too thinks that being able to address second-personal demands to others and having them addressed to us are central features of the participant stance, features that unify it across different domains of our lives (e.g., our loving relationships, moral relationships, and collegial relationships).

There is much that is plausible in Darwall's account of the participant stance and its connection to the sort of interpersonal demands we can make of one another. However, it is less plausible that the capacities involved in being a person and the capacities involved in being a morally responsible agent are the same.[5] We ordinarily think that there are some individuals who are persons, but who are not fully morally responsible agents. A ten-year-old child is surely a person, but equally surely not a fully morally responsible agent. Likewise, most of us would regard someone in a schizophrenic psychosis as a person, but not a morally responsible agent.

The key to understanding this puzzle is to disambiguate between two different senses of 'having a capacity', one of which arguably applies to all persons, the other only to morally responsible agents. Paul Formosa and Catriona Mackenzie clearly identify the ambiguity with the following example:

Mary cannot speak a word of Finnish. In the context of comparing Mary to a native Finnish speaker, it would be true to say that he has the capacity to speak Finnish but that Mary does not. In contrast, in the context of comparing Mary to a dog, it would be true to say that Mary has the capacity to speak Finnish but the dog does not. (2014, 884)

The native Finnish speaker has the capacity *here and now* to speak Finnish, whereas Mary does not. However, Mary has the capacity to learn to speak Finnish; thus she "could" speak Finnish *should she choose to learn*, whereas the dog could not speak Finnish even in this hypothetical sense.

The same distinction can be applied here. The ten-year-old child and the person in a schizophrenic psychosis do not have occurrent capacities for moral responsibility—they do not have these capacities *here and now*. However, with time and under the right conditions (which might include medication or other forms of psychiatric support for the schizophrenic), they could. It is much more plausible to think that *personhood* only requires these capacities in the hypothetical sense that includes the child and the schizophrenic, whereas morally responsible agency requires these capacities here and now. This modification, however, undermines the close connection Darwall develops between recognition respect and the participant stance. Recognition respect tracks personhood, and personhood only requires the hypothetical capacity for person-to-person demands. In contrast, the participant stance (and our moral responsibility ascriptions) track occurrent capacities—that is, they track *mastery* of the associated skills, rather than the bare capacity to master them.

If this is correct, then it is more appropriate to regard the sort of respect involved in the participant stance as a form of appraisal or achievement respect. It is respect for the person's developed capacities for moral responsibility, rather than respect for the potential to develop these capacities. If this is right, then having the developed or "here and now" capacities required for moral responsibility can be a matter of degree, consistent with my analysis of the Polkinghorne case.

At the beginning of this section, I claimed that the objective stance can be "disrespectful." According to my analysis, what is absent in the objective stance is achievement respect, and this is absent because the individuals in question lack the occurrent capacities for moral responsibility. To conclude this section, I argue that the objective stance nevertheless involves recognition respect for those toward whom it is taken.

First, it is worth noting that while we naturally treat objects as objects, it does not make sense to talk about "*taking* the objective *stance*" toward them. In contrast, children and the cognitively impaired are similar enough to morally responsible agents that the idea of *adopting* a particular *stance* toward them— of either treating them as a participant or not—is meaningful. Thus (and at the risk of stating the obvious) both the objective stance and the participant stance are ways of treating people (and not things). Michelle Mason makes this same point:

> [T]aking the objective attitude toward another is consistent with relating to his or her will in a way that affords it a certain *weight* in our deliberations concerning how we respond to him or her. We are not, then, reduced to relating to those with respect to whom we adopt the objective attitude as if relating to a thing or force of nature. After all, a person who is incompetent with respect to second-personal reasons may nonetheless have preferences about the treatment that she and others receive. In taking the objective attitude toward a person, we in no way commit ourselves to ignoring this fact. (2014, 150–151)

Furthermore, at several points in "Freedom and Resentment," Strawson implies that taking the objective stance is not something we do simply because it is useful for us. Rather, it is something we do because it is an appropriate way of treating the individual. Identifying that someone does not (here and now) have the capacities for moral responsibility, Strawson says at one point, "tends to promote, *at least in the civilized*, objective attitudes" (1962, 195; my italics). It is civilized to take the objective attitude toward these individuals because, presumably, it would be unfair to take the participant stance. It would be unfair to demand that they answer for their behavior: they lack the capacity to understand the demand or to provide an answer (or both). Furthermore, the emotional content of the demand—particularly the "sting" of resentment—is not something it would be fair to inflict on someone who lacks these capacities.

The feeling that we must be "civilized" toward these individuals indicates that they are entitled to a type of respect or regard. However, they are not entitled to the appraisal respect that is extended to those who have mastered the capacities relevant to moral responsibility. Rather, the respect involved is recognition respect. It is the status of these individuals as persons—albeit persons with limited capacities—that gives rise to the question about what stance to take toward them, and underpins our decision to take the appropriate—that is, the objective—stance. The objective stance, when adopted because it is a fitting way of engaging with the individual (given his or her capacities), is thus respectful and compassionate.

There are two caveats to this. The first is that even for those who have a fairly inclusive notion of personhood, some human beings may not be regarded as persons. Thus Formosa and Mackenzie note that both Kant's more restrictive account of personhood and Martha Nussbaum's more inclusive account exclude anencephalic infants and those in persistent vegetative states (2014, 885). This means that insofar as recognition respect tracks personhood, there may be some individuals for whom we do not have recognition respect. Whether we still take the objective stance toward these individuals (whose capacity for "action" may be quite limited) is unclear. The second caveat is that, as Strawson notes, the objective stance is not solely used for those who lack the capacity for moral reasoning. We can also adopt the objective stance toward someone we do recognize as a moral agent "for reasons of policy or self-protection" or as "a relief from the strains of involvement" (Strawson 1962, 197–198).[6] Although I agree with Strawson that this can occur, my analysis of the relationship between the objective stance and respect ignores such cases. I take it that in these cases the adoption of the objective stance is *despite* rather than *because of* the capacities of the individual involved. Thus, in such cases, the stance we take does not reveal anything about the sort of respect the agent is entitled to.

What I have argued is that the objective stance and the participant stance each involve respect for the agent. The objective stance involves recognition respect for the individual's status as a person. But it does not involve achievement respect for his or her capacities as a moral agent. In contrast, the participant stance does involve respect for the individual's agential capacities. This respect comes in degrees. Thus someone like Polkinghorne is entitled to recognition respect as well as some degree of achievement respect. In holding Polkinghorne morally responsible for the death of her daughter, members of her moral community judged that despite her ongoing problems with drugs and alcohol, she did have sufficient capacity to recognize and respond to her daughter's suffering. Evidence presented during her trial supports this. For example, during the final hours of Chloe's life, Polkinghorne conducted Internet searches for advice on what to do with an unconscious person, which suggests that she had recognized the need to respond to the injuries (Johns 2015, 2). Statements by Polkinghorne's lawyer, Brian Deegan, at an appeal of her sentence also suggest that she is responsive to moral considerations. For example, in addition to drawing attention to Polkinghorne's difficult history—"impregnated when she was 15, a child herself" (Fewster 2014)—Deegan also describes her as having learned from the tragedy, an apparent affirmation of her moral capacity. "'What greater deterrence for her than to lose her only child in tragic circumstances?' he [Deegan] said. 'It would be trite to suggest she has not learned, personally, an enormous lesson'" (Fewster 2014).

To be complete, it is also important to note that both the recognition respect involved in the objective stance and the appraisal respect involved in the participant stance have a negative aspect. The decision to take the objective stance amounts to a negative appraisal of the individual's capacities. The person who is treated with a wholly objective stance is given no esteem for being a morally responsible agent. However, this negative evaluation does not license any corresponding response toward the individual. It is not appropriate to punish or berate someone for the immaturity or loss of their moral capacities.

The participant stance, in contrast, reflects the degree to which an agent's capacities for moral responsibility are functioning. But when an agent who has these capacities seriously violates the shared standards of the moral community, that person's action (or character or judgment) is subject to a negative appraisal. The appraisal is not merely an expression of disappointment for the harm caused. It centrally involves the fact that the agent did not do better even though she or he could have. Unlike the negative aspect of the objective stance, such judgments are not idle. They license a response—punishment or blame, for example. We usually expect such responses to be fitting both to the degree of capacity of the individual, and the nature and seriousness of the act. For some sorts of transgressions, the criminal law codifies aspects of a community's moral response. But many moral transgressions are not criminal (as when someone forgets a birthday, or utters a hurtful remark). In such cases, the response is sensitive to the individuals involved, the nature of their relationship, the wider ramifications of the act (e.g., inciting or frightening others), and so on.

Sometimes, the punishment an agent incurs for violating the shared standards of the moral community can involve (legitimately) treating that person in a way that would otherwise be inconsistent with recognition respect—imprisonment, for example. In order to be consistent with the requirement of recognition respect, punishment must be able to convey its intended meaning as a response to an action for which the agent is being held morally responsible. Thus, while it may be necessary to manage those who lack capacity in order to ensure their own safety and that of others, the management should be respectful of their status as persons, and it would ideally involve a degree of compassion that is absent in punishment. The balance can be difficult to get right in marginal cases such as Polkinghorne's, but the assessment of whether imprisonment (understood as a punishment) is acceptable should be responsive, roughly, to whether she has the capacity to understand its meaning as a response to her action.

4 Failures of Respect in the Deaths of Indigenous Australian Women in Custody

The case of Ashlee Polkinghorne illustrated how an agent can have the capacities relevant to moral responsibility to some degree but not fully. In this section, I explore several other cases that are arguably somewhere in the middle of the spectrum. But unlike the Polkinghorne case, in which the community's reactions were approximately right, in these cases the responses seem inappropriate. The stories I tell in this section all involve deaths of Indigenous Australian women in custody. These cases seem to be characterized by the sort of ambivalence that is evident in the Polkinghorne case: there is evidence that many of these women are alcoholics or drug addicts, factors that may impact on their capacities. Nevertheless, they are arrested and taken into custody, actions that imply a degree of capacity. And as the examples show, these women also remained able to speak for themselves and to make moral demands of others, even while suffering serious medical problems. This, I take it, is further evidence that they have the capacities required for moral agency, at least to some degree.

The 1991 Royal Commission into Aboriginal Deaths in Custody in Australia investigated the deaths of ten women and one teenaged girl (alongside the deaths of almost ninety men). All the women were in custody for minor offences at the time of their death, more than half for public drunkenness. Nine of the ten women were in police custody (i.e., being held temporarily in cells following arrest) rather than serving court-issued sentences. The tenth was a sentenced prisoner serving six months for driving unlicensed and under the influence of alcohol. The girl was a ward of the state, who died in a fire she lit while trying to escape from a Children's Home (Kerley and Cunneen 1995). Kerley and Cunneen note that "[i]n other jurisdictions, and indeed for other women in the same jurisdiction, the conduct [for which the women were in custody] might have been treated as a health issue rather than a criminal problem" (547).

The fact that these women were arrested and, apparently, punished might imply that police took the participant stance toward them. However, an analysis of several examples does not align with the accounts of either the objective or the participant stance as I have described them above. Rather, there is striking evidence that these women were denied both the appraisal respect associated with the participant stance, and the recognition respect associated with the objective stance.

For example, Muriel Binks, thirty-eight-years old and a mother of two, died in police custody in Innisfail, Queensland in 1989 from pneumonia. She had been arrested for public drunkenness and remained in custody due to an unpaid fine of thirty dollars. In the report, the commissioner was scathing of the medical assistance she received, citing as factors that contributed to her death "inadequate screening procedures, infrequent, neglectful and insensitive supervision, poor training, and ingrained and misconceived attitudes concerning the behavior and management of the severely intoxicated" (Kerley and Cunneen 1995, 543).

Other women whose deaths were examined by the commission also died from neglect of their urgent medical needs. Nita Blankett died of an asthma attack that went untreated until it was too late, despite staff at the center where she was serving a sentence being aware of her severe chronic asthma. She was distressed, appeared ill, and requested a doctor. In Darwall's terms, she made second-personal demands of the custodial officers, but they failed to recognize her authority to do so.

According to the analysis I presented above, it is sometimes consistent with the participant stance to expect an agent to submit to treatment that would otherwise be inconsistent with her status as a person, as a punishment for her moral transgression. However, in the case of Muriel Binks, it is implausible that the failure of those responsible for her supervision to provide medical care is a legitimate aspect of her punishment for a small, unpaid fine. Likewise, in the case of Nita Blankett, who was serving six months in prison (three months each for driving under the influence of alcohol and driving without a license), the failure of those responsible for her care to seek medical assistance for her asthma cannot be regarded as a legitimate aspect of her punishment.

The deaths investigated in the Royal Commission occurred more than twenty years ago, but recent, similar cases suggest that the same failures of respect persist. In 2014, Ms. Dhu was arrested in Port Headland, Western Australia for not paying fines (Langton 2016; Burton-Bradley 2016).[7] During the three days that she was in custody before her death, she repeatedly asked for medical assistance, crying with pain, vomiting, asking for help, and complaining of symptoms including numbness in her legs and mouth. She was taken to the hospital three times during this period, but medical staff failed to diagnose the conditions that eventually killed her: pneumonia, and septicemia from untreated broken ribs. In an article for *The Monthly*, Marcia Langton quotes from media reports on the death, according to which police officers responsible for Dhu's supervision called her a "fucking junkie" and told medical staff that she was faking her illness (Langton 2016). These findings were corroborated by the findings of a coronial inquest into the death by West Australian coroner Ros Fogliani (Burton-Bradley 2016). Langton's article also notes that medical personnel assessed her as having behavioral issues, while failing to accurately diagnose her serious medical conditions. In addition to their disregard for her demands and her basic health and safety, prison officers also showed disrespect for Dhu in their handling of her physical person. On her final trip to the hospital, where she would die,

> Ms. Dhu told them that she could not walk, and there being no wheelchair or stretcher available, Constable Matier took hold of Ms. Dhu under the arms, dragged her to the cell door and then with the assistance of Senior Constable Burgess picking up Ms. Dhu's legs, they carried her to the back of a police van. (Langton 2016)

Dhu, like Blankett, was unable to make successful second-personal demands of those responsible for her supervision, and she died as a result of their failures to respond to her demands.

Again, as in the cases of Binks and Blankett, it is not plausible to regard Dhu's treatment as a legitimate aspect of her punishment. None of these three cases can be understood as legitimate examples of punishment from within the participant stance. Nor can they be regarded as instances of the objective stance—as examples of the compassionate management of someone who lacks the capacities relevant to morally responsible agency. Insofar as police officers were apparently concerned that Dhu might be a heroin addict, there is no evidence that this suspicion modified their morally reactive attitudes toward her, or increased their compassion. Rather, this fact was used to justify a decision to question the legitimacy of her request for medical help.[8]

Several reports from the 1990s found evidence of chronic underpolicing of domestic violence, rape, and even murder of Indigenous women in Australia (Cunneen 2001, 161–162). That is, they found evidence that police were slower to respond and less likely to intervene satisfactorily in reports of domestic violence, rape, and murder if Indigenous women were the victims. This context of systemic failures of police to heed and respond to the second-personal claims of Indigenous women for help—even when they were the victims of serious crime—places the treatment of women such as Binks, Blankett, and Dhu in a context that makes it difficult to dismiss their treatment as isolated. In this context, the coroner's finding that Ms. Dhu "did not make a complaint to police" (Fogliani 2016, 44) regarding the domestic violence incident in which her ribs were fractured is particularly upsetting. There may be many reasons Dhu did not speak out, including factors internal to the relationship. However, it is tragic that while she was in prison for a minor offence—failure to pay fines—the police dismissed her serious illness because they considered that she was "faking it" (84), and that meanwhile she had been unwilling for whatever reason to report serious and—the coroner concluded, ongoing—domestic violence of which she was a victim (10).

In their exploration of gender differences in Aboriginal deaths in custody in Australia, Kerley and Cunneen discuss the positive light in which some justices regarded the imprisonment of Indigenous women for minor crimes:

> [O]ne justice in Western Australia stated that he sentenced Aboriginal and Torres Strait Islander Women to terms of imprisonment [for minor offences] for "welfare" reasons. "Sometimes I sentence them to imprisonment to help them. . . . To protect their welfare I put them inside for seven days. They get cleaned up and fed then." (1995, 538)

This example suggests that the judge lacks appraisal respect for Indigenous women on the basis of a stereotype rather than the particulars of their individual circumstances. In my discussion of the toddler example (section 2), I noted that the parent removes the toddler from the situation in a manner that is compassionate—the parent's focus is on ensuring that both the toddler and others are safe. The remark of the judge in this instance is reminiscent of the parent's attitude toward the toddler. He wants to ensure the "welfare" of the women, to ensure that they are "cleaned up and fed." However, insofar as the conditions that the women encounter in custody are like those encountered by Binks, Blankett, and Dhu, it is not safe to assume that their welfare will be protected while they are imprisoned. Furthermore, given that this is a general remark about Indigenous women rather than a comment about the details of the case of a particular individual, it reveals that the judge stereotypes Indigenous women as needing protection and lacking the capacity to keep themselves clean and fed. Insofar as he responds to particular individuals on the basis of this stereotype rather than the details of their own situation and capacities, it is likely that he will make errors in his assessment of their capacities.

The treatment of Binks, Blankett and Dhu involved failures of respect —their treatment was not consistent with the respect required in either the objective stance or the participant stance. Furthermore, unlike the Polkinghorne case, there is no way to understand the treatment of these women as appropriately reflecting their marginal status as morally responsible agents who only have the relevant capacities to a limited degree. Rather, their treatment involves failures of respect that can be identified and criticized from within a Strawsonian approach to moral responsibility.

Amanda Roth (2010) has identified features common to Darwall's (2004, 2006) and Sarah Buss's (1999) accounts of respect for persons that indicate why respect is fragile and can fail, particularly toward those who are viewed negatively due to their social identity. According to Roth, both Darwall and Buss incorporate an *experiential* dimension into their accounts of recognition respect. Darwall emphasizes the experience of mutual vulnerability involved in making second-personal demands saying, "To look someone in the eye is to make oneself and ones' eyes, the 'windows' of one's soul, vulnerable to him, and in both directions" (2006, 142). Buss, on the other hand, emphasizes the experience of shame:

> [O]ur belief that we owe one another respect must ultimately be based on our *actual relations* with one another. Here is where shame enters the story. Shame is one of the ways we directly apprehend one another. Though it is an attitude we take toward *ourselves*, it is, at the same time, an attitude toward another person—a perception of this other as something that transcends the limits of our own personal perspectives. (1999, 537)

Neither Darwall nor Buss believes or requires that we must experience shame or mutual vulnerability in our interactions with a given individual in order to respect him or her. Nevertheless, they both emphasize the importance of our susceptibility to these experiences. If negative identity stereotypes make us less susceptible to shame or mutual vulnerability with individuals from certain social groups then they undermine the foundation upon which respect for individuals in that group is built.

Roth's analysis of Darwall and Buss is useful because it explains how failures of recognition respect can erroneously occur, and are likely to systematically occur toward those who are negatively stereotyped due to their social identity. Identity group membership is likely to influence experiences of shame and mutual vulnerability, just as it influences judgments about people's CVs and whether they are carrying a gun (Steinpreis, Anders, and Ritzke 1999; Correll, Urland, and Ito 2006). So, too, therefore, it is likely to influence our practices of holding one another accountable, by influencing when and toward whom we take the participant stance, as well as the extent to which the participant and objective stances involve appropriate respect for their targets.

Roth offers several examples of how the making and receiving of demands for respect can be distorted by hierarchies between social groups. A demand for respect can be jarring when it is made by members of groups who are not experienced as respect-worthy. Drawing on material from Jason Sokol's *There Goes My Everything: White Southerners in the Age of Civil Rights* (2006), Roth says,

> Sokol describes how white southern moderates were often shocked at the developments of the civil rights movement: specifically, they had never thought that civil rights would arise due to the actions of African-Americans. These sympathizers had assumed that it would be whites who would "give" civil rights to African-Americans. . . . [T]hey failed to recognize the second-personal authority of African-Americans; it simply never occurred to them that civil rights weren't theirs to give because African-Americans already had a legitimate claim to them. (2010, 319)

The examples involving Indigenous Australian women discussed in this section resonate with Sokol's reflections on the Civil Rights movement. Just as the white sympathizers failed to recognize the African-Americans' second-personal authority to claim civil rights, the officers responsible for Nita Blankett, for example, failed to recognize her second-personal authority to demand medical assistance and relief of her asthma.

5 Conclusion

In this chapter, my focus has been on exploring the type of respect involved in the participant and objective stances. I argued that the objective stance involves recognition respect for persons, while the participant stance involves appraisal respect. This appraisal respect is responsive to the extent of functioning of the agent's capacities for moral responsibility. I then made use of this analysis to better understand what was going wrong in several cases involving Indigenous Australian women in custody. In these cases, it appears that police and prison officers' treatment of the women is affected by negative stereotypes of Indigenous women. The police and prison officers' interactions with the women display neither the recognition respect that would be appropriate if they were taking the objective stance, nor the appraisal respect that would be appropriate if they were taking the participant stance. Nor can their treatment of the women be understood as a successful blending of the two perspectives as might be involved in a marginal case. On this basis, the way the police and prison officers treat the Indigenous women can be criticized from within the Strawsonian framework.

I hope that, in addition to illuminating what has gone wrong in the cases I discussed, this analysis might be useful as part of a response to a more general concern for Strawsonian approaches to moral responsibility. Strawson illustrated his account of moral responsibility and our adoption of the participant and objective stances with examples that emphasize the strengths of the approach rather than its limitations. It seems highly plausible that we take the objective stance toward those who are acting under a psychosis, as he claims. Similarly, it seems true, as he claims, that most of the time we take the participant stance toward those with whom we share our most important interpersonal relationships: for example, a spouse or romantic partner, friends, or colleagues at work.

However, commentators have pointed out that these sympathetic examples obscure both the complexity of our practices and the fact that many of our reactions to one another depend on factors that we would not want to incorporate into an account of moral responsibility (e.g., Watson 1987, 282–283; McKenna and Russell 2008, 10). They ask whether it is really a good idea to trust our ordinary interactions to reveal anything about the capacities relevant to moral responsibility. There is, I take it, a concern that our utilization of the participant and objective stances might track social status or other irrelevant factors.

One way of engaging with this problem is to consider an example. If it turned out that within a particular moral community almost everyone took the objective stance toward Indigenous women, would a Strawsonian be committed to the view that Indigenous women were thereby not morally responsible agents? I do not think so, because the practice of taking the objective stance toward Indigenous women—no matter how widespread or recalcitrant—does not track a capacity. Neither being Indigenous nor being a woman is a capacity. Such practices might, however, track prejudicial stereotypes about incapacity—for example, that Indigenous Australians don't know when to stop drinking or don't have a strong sense of right and wrong (Marjoribanks and Jordan 1986). Such stereotypes can lead to mistaken and biased assessments of the capacity of individuals. This can be exacerbated when the individual has only partially developed capacities for moral responsibility, because it might be hard to tell whether assessments of *how much* capacity they have are due to irrelevant indicators such as negative stereotypes or relevant factors such as their actual capacity for moral dialogue. The analysis I provide in this chapter is not likely to prevent mistakes from occurring. However, by highlighting the complex interaction between actual capacities and bias in marginal cases, it does show that there is a need to take particular care when making ascriptions of moral responsibility in such cases.

Furthermore, I have argued that certain kinds of treatment are altogether precluded by both the participant and the objective stance (or any combination of the two). Specifically, treatment that is inconsistent with recognition respect for the person is never acceptable from within the objective stance. Moreover, it is only acceptable within the participant stance when it is a legitimate part of a punishment for a moral transgression. Thus the consequences of being mistaken about an individual's capacities should never result in treating that individual in the way that Muriel Binks, Nita Blankett, and Ms Dhu were treated. I have restricted my discussion to cases of discrimination against Indigenous Australian women in custody, but it is possible that this analysis can help explain what has gone wrong in other oppressive moral responsibility practices.[9]

Notes

1. Strawson also notes that we sometimes make use of the objective stance to avoid the "strains of involvement" (1962, 198) in cases involving individuals we would normally treat as participants. This seems right, but I do not focus on such cases in this chapter.
2. In contrast, in another recent Australian example, Indigenous Australian Football League (AFL) star Adam Goodes reacted to a thirteen-year-old spectator who called him an "ape" during a 2013 AFL match. At the time, shocked by the slur, he pointed the girl out to security who escorted her from the grounds. Goodes later clarified his response, saying, "[S]he's 13, she's still so innocent, I don't put any blame on her" (Crawford 2013). These comments reflected the wider view in the community: while most people accepted that the racial slur fell well below the standard normally expected of members of the moral community—thus they accepted or affirmed Goodes's assessment of the standards—there was considerable debate over her blameworthiness given her age (Crawford 2013; Davey 2015). Of course, the views of the moral community can also change over time. It is unclear whether Rice's comments would have attracted the same response two decades earlier, at a time when Ian Roberts was a closeted National Rugby League (NRL) star, counseled by his coach to avoid the gay bars on Sydney's Oxford Street to avoid damage to his reputation, and regularly taunted by fans and opposing players who had heard rumors about his sexuality (Webster 2017; Skene 2015).
3. However, appraisal respect can also be respect for persons as such, Darwall argues, insofar as it involves appraising their *excellence* as persons, specifically, an appraisal of moral character.
4. The secondary literature on Kant's conceptions of dignity and respect (and what it is to be a person) is of course significant, and there is no single agreed-upon interpretation of his position. What I say here, due to limits of space, does not engage with the intricacies of this debate.

However, further down in this section, I acknowledge some of these matters insofar as they are relevant to my argument.

5. The connection between personhood and moral responsibility has been made before. Harry Frankfurt, for example, applied his hierarchical conception of the person to free will and moral responsibility (Frankfurt 1971).

6. For a helpful discussion of the strategic use of the objective stance, see Mason 2014.

7. Ms. Dhu's first name is omitted for cultural reasons.

8. Presumably on the basis of the stereotype of heroin addicts as dishonest and likely to engage in drug seeking in medical contexts (Baldacchino et al. 2010; Merrill et al. 2002).

9. Thanks to my coeditors, Catriona Mackenzie and Marina Oshana, for their feedback on several versions of this chapter, and to Bob Simpson, for comments on an early draft. Thanks also to audiences at the Australian National University, University of Melbourne, University of New South Wales, and Macquarie University, who heard and gave feedback on earlier versions of the chapter.

References

ABC News Online. 2015. "Chloe Valentine Inquest: A Timeline of What Unfolded after the 4yo Girl's Death." *ABC News Online*. July 13. http://www.abc.net.au/news/2015-02-27/chloe-valentine-timeline/6262464.

Akerman, Tessa. 2014. "Ashlee Polkinghorne and Ben McPartland Receive Four-Year Minimum Jail Term for Motorbike Death of Four-year-old Chloe Valentine." *Advertiser*, April 3.

Baldacchino, Alex, Gail Gilchrist, Rod Fleming, and Jonathan Bannister. 2010. "Guilty until Proven Innocent: A Qualitative Study of the Management of Chronic Non-Cancer Pain among Patients with a History of Substance Abuse." *Addictive Behaviors* 35 (3): 270–272.

Burton-Bradley, Robert. 2016. "Coroner: Ms. Dhu's Death Preventable, Police 'Unprofessional and Inhumane.'" NITV Online, December 16. http://www.sbs.com.au/nitv/nitv-news/article/2016/12/16/coroner-ms-dhus-death-preventable-police-unprofessional-and-inhumane.

Buss, Sarah. 1999. "Respect for Persons." *Canadian Journal of Philosophy* 29 (4): 517–550.

Correll, Joshua, Geoffrey R. Urland, and Tiffany A. Ito. 2006. "Event-Related Potentials and the Decision to Shoot: The Role of Threat Perception and Cognitive Control." *Journal of Experimental Social Psychology* 42 (1): 120–128.

Crawford, Adrian. 2013. "Adam Goodes 'Gutted' by Racial Slur but Wants AFL Fan Educated." ABC News Online, May 27. http://www.abc.net.au/news/2013-05-25/goodes-gutted-but-places-no-blame/4712772.

Cunneen, Chris. 2001. "Policing Indigenous Women." In *Conflict, Politics and Crime: Aboriginal Communities and the Police*, edited by Chris Cunneen, 157–179. Sydney: Allen & Unwin.

Darwall, Stephen L. 1977. "Two Kinds of Respect." *Ethics* 88 (1): 36–49.

Darwall, Stephen L. 2004. "Respect and the Second-Person Standpoint." *Proceedings and Addresses of the American Philosophical Association* 78 (2): 43–59.

Darwall, Stephen L. 2006. *The Second-Person Standpoint: Morality, Respect, and Accountability*. Cambridge, MA: Harvard University Press.

Davey, Melissa. 2015. "Adam Goodes Should Apologise, Says Mother of Girl Who Called Him an Ape." *Guardian*, Australian edition, July 30. https://www.theguardian.com/sport/2015/jul/30/adam-goodes-should-apologise-says-mother-of-girl-who-called-him-an-ape.

Fewster, Sean. 2014. "SA DPP Adam Kimber Asks Court to Increase Sentences of Neglectful Couple Who Killed Chloe Valentine." news.com.au, May 22. http://www.news.com.au/national/south-australia/sa-dpp-adam-kimber-asks-court-to-increase-sentences-of-neglectful-couple-who-killed-chloe-valentine/news-story/99dea922a0f504826b76c789c7441a2b.

Fogliani, R. V. C. State Coroner of Western Australia. 2016. "Record of Investigation into Death (of Ms. Dhu)." Report. December 15. http://www.coronerscourt.wa.gov.au/_files/Dhu%20finding.pdf.

Formosa, Paul, and Catriona Mackenzie. 2014. "Nussbaum, Kant, and the Capabilities Approach to Dignity." *Ethical Theory and Moral Practice* 17 (5): 875–892.

Founten, Loukas, and James Hancock. 2014. "Couple Jailed Over 4yo's Death from Backyard Motorbike Crashes." ABC News Online, April 3. http://www.abc.net.au/news/2014-04-02/couple-jailed-girl-motorbike-death/5361036.

Frankfurt, Harry. 1971. "Freedom of the Will and the Concept of a Person." *Journal of Philosophy* 68 (1): 5–20.

Greenwald, Anthony G., and Mahzarin R. Banaji. 1995. "Implicit Social Cognition: Attitudes, Self-Esteem, and Stereotypes." *Psychological Review* 102 (1): 4–27.

Herald Sun. 2010. "Ian Roberts Slams Stephanie Rice's Anti-Gay Twitter Comment." September 6. http://www.heraldsun.com.au/archive/entertainment/ian-roberts-slams-stephanie-rices-anti-gay-twitter-comment/news-story/37635c5c23da47c06843cf552c7f5ba5.

Johns, Mark. State Coroner of South Australia. 2015. "Inquest into the Death of Chloe Lee Valentine." Report. Adelaide, SA: State Coroner, South Australia. April 9. http://www.courts.sa.gov.au/CoronersFindings/Lists/Coroners%20Findings/Attachments/613/VALENTINE%20Chloe%20Lee.pdf.

Kerley, Kate, and Chris Cunneen. 1995. "Deaths in Custody in Australia: The Untold Story of Aboriginal and Torres Strait Islander Women." *Canadian Journal of Women and the Law* 8 (2): 531–551.

Langton, Marcia. 2016. "Two Victims, No Justice: Ms. Dhu, Lynette Daley and the Alarming Rates of Violence against Indigenous Women." *The Monthly*, 124 (July): 36–39.

McGeer, Victoria. 2012. "Co-Reactive Attitudes and the Making of Moral Community." In *Emotions, Imagination and Moral Reasoning*, edited by Robyn Langdon and Catriona Mackenzie, 299–326. New York: Psychology Press.

McKenna, Michael. 2012. *Conversation and Responsibility*. New York: Oxford University Press.

McKenna, Michael, and Paul Russell. 2008. "Perspectives on P. F. Strawson's 'Freedom and Resentment.'" In *Free Will and Reactive Attitudes*, edited by Michael McKenna and Paul Russell, 1–17. Farnham, UK: Ashgate Publishing Limited.

Marjoribanks, Kevin, and Deirdre F. Jordan. 1986. "Stereotyping among Aboriginal and Anglo-Australians: The Uniformity, Intensity, Direction and Quality of Auto- and Heterostereotypes." *Journal of Cross-Cultural Psychology* 17 (1): 17–28.

Marcus, Candice. 2014. "Chloe Valentine Manslaughter Sentence Appeal: Jailed Mother Cites 'Trauma' for Missing Court." ABC News Online, May 22. http://www.abc.net.au/news/2014-05-22/mother-not-in-court-as-chloe-valentine-appeal-case-starts/5470296.

Mason, Michelle. 2014. "Reactivity and Refuge." In *Oxford Studies in Agency and Responsibility, Vol. 2, "Freedom and Resentment" at 50*, edited by David Shoemaker and Neil Tognazzini, 143–162. Oxford: Oxford University Press.

Merrill, Joseph O., Lorna A. Rhodes, Richard A. Deyo, G. Alan Marlatt, and Katharine A. Bradley. 2002. "Mutual Mistrust in the Medical Care of Drug Users." *Journal of General Internal Medicine* 17 (5): 327–333.

Oshana, Marina. 1997. "Ascriptions of Responsibility." *American Philosophical Quarterly* 34 (1): 71–83.

Oshana, Marina. 2004. "Moral Accountability." *Philosophical Topics* 32 (1–2): 255–274.

Roth, Amanda. 2010. "Second-Personal Respect, the Experiential Aspect of Respect, and Feminist Philosophy." *Hypatia* 25 (2): 316–333.

Skene, Patrick. 2015. "The Courageous Journey of Ian Roberts, Rugby League's First Openly Gay Player." *Guardian*, Australian edition, August 18. https://www.theguardian.com/sport/blog/2015/aug/18/the-courageous-journey-of-ian-roberts-rugby-leagues-first-openly-gay-player.

Smith, Angela M. 2008. "Control, Responsibility, and Moral Assessment." *Philosophical Studies* 138 (3): 367–392.

Sokol, Jason. 2006. *There Goes My Everything: White Southerners in the Age of Civil Rights, 1945–1975*. New York: Vintage Books.

Steinpreis, Rhea E., Katie A. Anders, and Dawn Ritzke. 1999. "The Impact of Gender on the Review of the Curricula Vitae of Job Applicants and Tenure Candidates: A National Empirical Study." *Sex Roles* 41 (7–8): 509–528.

Strawson, Peter F. 1962. "Freedom and Resentment." *Proceedings of the British Academy* 48: 187–211.

Watson, Gary. 1987. "Responsibility and the Limits of Evil: Variations on a Strawsonian Theme." In *Responsibility, Character, and the Emotions*, edited by Ferdinand Schoeman, 256–286. New York: Cambridge University Press.

Watson, Gary. 2014. "Peter Strawson on Responsibility and Sociality." In *Oxford Studies in Agency and Responsibility, Vol. 2, "Freedom and Resentment" at 50*, edited by David Shoemaker and Neil Tognazzini, 15–32. Oxford: Oxford University Press.

Webster, Andrew. 2017. "Ian Roberts to Lead the NRL Float at the Gay and Lesbian Mardi Gras 2017." *Sydney Morning Herald*, March 4. http://www.smh.com.au/rugby-league/ian-roberts-to-lead-the-nrl-float-at-the-gay-and-lesbian-mardi-gras-2017-20170303-gupw3f.html.

White, James. 2010. "Homophobic Twitter Rant Costs Tearful Australian Olympic Swimmer Lucrative Sponsorship Contract." *Daily Mail*, September 9. http://www.dailymail.co.uk/news/article-1310063/Australian-swimmer-Stephanie-Rice-apologises-homophobic-Twitter-slur.html.

9

Answerability

A Condition of Autonomy or Moral Responsibility (or Both)?

NATALIE STOLJAR

1 Introduction

One of the controversial cases discussed by autonomy theorists is that of Jehovah's Witnesses who were imprisoned in concentration camps as conscientious objectors. Jehovah's Witnesses did not seem to experience the extreme psychic disintegration and disorientation about their self-worth that was typical of other inmates (Bettelheim 1960, 122–123). On the contrary, they steadfastly continued to live according to their religious convictions: they continued to attempt to make converts; they had exemplary work habits; they never resorted to abuse of other prisoners; and although they were favored by the SS officers because of their compliant behavior, they never "misused their closeness with the SS officers to gain positions of privilege" (Bettelheim 1960, 123). This remarkable resilience raises the question of whether the Jehovah's Witnesses were autonomous despite the traumatic imprisonment to which they were subjected. They seemed to continue to live an *authentic* moral life. Their agential perspective remained integrated, and they experienced no alienation in their self-conception or practical identity. On one conception of autonomy—an *internalist* conception—such people are capable of full autonomy despite the external conditions. If they lack autonomy, it is because they lack some internal or psychological condition required for autonomy, such as rationality. For instance, Bernard Berofsky argues that the Jehovah's Witnesses were heteronomous due to the very steadfastness of their religious conviction; such "subjective certainty" interfered with taking an appropriately critical perspective on the truth of their situation (Berofsky 1995, 117).

On a contrasting conception of autonomy—the *externalist* conception— it is impossible for people in severely constraining external conditions, or for whom all aspects of their lives are under another's control, to retain personal autonomy. Marina Oshana calls the Jehovah's Witnesses a "textbook example of persons whose moral autonomy is intact while their personal autonomy is compromised" (Oshana 2006, 10).[1] The Jehovah's Witnesses retain some form of moral agency because they continue to govern themselves in accordance with their own moral code. But on the externalist conception of autonomy, the fact that they are imprisoned, forced into a servile position, and subjected to the continuous domination of the SS officers, generates a paradigm case of non-autonomy *by definition*. On this picture, even if the Jehovah's Witnesses were rational and managed to retain both their psychic integrity and moral conviction, their autonomy is undermined due to social conditions that are themselves inherently incompatible with autonomy.

The conception of autonomy on which external social and interpersonal conditions are included in the "defining conditions" of autonomy has been called "constitutively relational" (e.g., Christman 2009, 166). My aim in this chapter is to defend the externalist, constitutively relational conception through an examination of an alternative (also constitutively relational) approach that has been developed recently by Andrea Westlund (2009). Despite being constitutively relational, her approach has more in common with internalist than externalist conceptions of autonomy. The key condition of autonomy on her view is a psychological disposition (or "readiness") to answer for oneself in the face of external requests for justification of one's commitments. This disposition is a necessary component of the authentic agential perspective that in turn is required for autonomous agency. As Westlund puts it, "[T]he internal psychological condition of the autonomous agent [points] beyond itself, to the position the agent occupies as one reflective, responsible self among many" (2009, 35–36). Hence she is offering a constitutively relational test of autonomy because its defining conditions include interpersonal conditions.

Westlund develops her approach in response to a common objection to externalist, constitutively relational theories that has been raised by feminist discussions of oppression. The oppressed are often not literally imprisoned, but they are caged in a metaphorical sense by the social conditions to which they are subjected (Frye 1983). They have degrading norms and stereotypes applied to them; they are forced by institutional constraints or lack of options into servile positions; and they are often subjected to arbitrary interference in their daily lives. Moreover, the oppressed can come to internalize oppressive ideologies and therefore themselves develop preferences for social roles and norms that are oppressive to them. This internalization of oppression helps to perpetuate and entrench oppression because it can be mistaken for the "legitimate [expression] of individual differences in taste, when in reality it is the result of the oppression itself" (Cudd 2006, 183). It is important therefore to acknowledge the role of patriarchal and other structures of oppression in impeding autonomy. On the other hand, it has been argued that the claim that women and other oppressed agents lack autonomy *in virtue* of being oppressed compounds the problem of oppression. It seems to deny them the possibility of agency in the face of oppression and undermine their status as agents worthy of respect. This criticism has gained particular currency in the context of women living in non-Western societies who seem to embrace non-egalitarian, hierarchical social roles and norms. It has been claimed that externalist conceptions of autonomy that treat agents who embrace such norms as non-autonomous risk disrespecting these women and overlooking the myriad ways in which they exercise genuine agency (e.g., Narayan 2002).

I call the problem just described the "agency dilemma" (cf. Khader 2011, 30; Mackenzie 2015). Simply put, the dilemma arises because, on the one hand, oppression undermines autonomy; on the other, claiming that people are non-autonomous just in virtue of oppression erases their agency and disrespects their evaluative commitments. In section 2, I outline Westlund's argument in detail to show that her notion of answerability is offered as a solution to the agency dilemma. On Westlund's view, we should not presume that oppression per se undermines autonomy. Rather, we must recognize that the oppressed are not psychologically homogeneous and that some oppressed agents authentically embrace oppressive social roles and norms. Only those who are not *answerable*—only those who are "impervious to critical challenge"—do not have the authentic agential perspective required for autonomy. In section 3, I evaluate whether answerability is necessary and sufficient for several interrelated aspects of agency: autonomy, authentic agential perspective, and moral responsibility. I first point out that resolving the agency dilemma requires Westlund to claim that answerability is sufficient as well as necessary for autonomy. I then attempt to disentangle answerability from other features of agents that are relevant to their authentic perspective and moral responsibility. It is notable, for instance, that the notion of answerability that is centrally important for moral responsibility is *not* answerability in Westlund's sense but that of "intelligible" answerability (Smith 2005, 2012; Shoemaker 2011).[2] In section 4, I return to the Jehovah's Witnesses example and the agency dilemma in the light of the different dimensions of agency identified in section 3. I also respond to a further objection to externalist conceptions of autonomy. Whereas the agency dilemma focuses on agents who *endorse* their own oppression, this additional objection asks us to consider activists whose life is dedicated to resistance. It is claimed that by being a "resister," someone who repudiates both the structures and the norms of oppression, an activist is engaged in self-rule despite the external impediments to which she is subjected (e.g., Noggle 2011).[3] I argue that both this objection and the agency dilemma wrongly assume that denying autonomy implies erasing the agency of people who are oppressed. Once it is recognized that autonomy does not always overlap with authentic agential perspective or moral responsibility, and that there are categories of evaluative appraisal that correspond to the latter two dimensions of agency, the objections lose their force.

2 Westlund and the Agency Dilemma

In her paper "Rethinking Relational Autonomy," Westlund proposes a condition of autonomy that she calls "dialogical answerability" (e.g., 2009, 35). Her explicit aim is to provide an alternative to externalist conceptions of autonomy that characterize severely constraining social conditions—such as those experienced in concentration camps—as incompatible with autonomy by definition. Critics of externalist conceptions claim that they are not only externalist but also morally substantive; moral constraints are included in the articulation of autonomy either implicitly or explicitly (e.g., Christman 2009, 170). This means that, on externalist conceptions, agents can be deemed non-autonomous just in virtue of external conditions even if the morality or conception of the good that they voluntarily accept coincides with the morality inherent in the external conditions. John Christman claims that externalist theories imply a version of "perfectionism" that permits overriding people's voluntarily formed conceptions of the good in the name of promoting their autonomy (Christman 2009, 170–173). Such an implication is inappropriate and disrespectful.[4]

Westlund develops a version of Christman's objection:

> If a fundamentalist woman does freely and authentically accept a condition of social and personal subordination, it seems . . . problematic to assume that her condition as subordinate, in and of itself, undermines her status as a self-governing agent. . . . We should not assume that all individuals who willingly embrace subordinate roles will be psychologically similar to each other . . . to treat her as non-autonomous even *as she speaks on behalf* of her self-subordinating commitments is to refuse to take the possibility of such dialogue with her at face value: not only does this woman lack authority over her social circumstances, our treatment implies, she lacks authority over her own voice, and this flies in the face of the evidence she gives of such authority. (Westlund 2009, 29)

In other words, denying self-government would amount to disrespecting the woman by denying that she has "authority over her own voice." Westlund is articulating one premise of the agency dilemma: characterizing someone as non-autonomous erases her moral agency and undermines her status as an agent worthy of full respect and moral consideration.

On the other hand, there are many examples that generate the second premise of the dilemma, the idea that oppression threatens autonomy even when, or *especially* when, agents seem to endorse the oppressive norms that apply to them. Consider the well-known example of the "Angel in the House": "She was intensely sympathetic. She was immensely charming. She excelled in the difficult arts of family life. She sacrificed herself daily. If there was chicken, she took the leg, if there was a draught, she sat in it" (Woolf 1942, 59; cf. Hill 1991; Westlund 2003). Although admittedly this is a caricature, the norms of deference that the Angel adopts are not far from those associated with traditional forms of femininity in which wives are expected to cater to their husband's needs in a way that is almost indistinguishable from servility. Another example, mentioned by Serene Khader in recent work (2011, 78), is that of South East Asian women who malnourish themselves to ensure that their husbands and male offspring get enough food. Although these women's underlying motivations are complicated, it looks as if the needs and desires *of others* are driving their decisions. The preference to always prioritize others' needs and desires above one's own seems contrary to the preferences the women (as rational agents) would be expected to have in the absence of the patriarchal hierarchy in which they are systematically attributed second-class status. This suggests that although agents who endorse norms of oppression or self-subordination may appear to be forming preferences that are "their own," this is not really the case. Rather, their preferences for second-class status are the result of adaptation to the circumstances of oppression (cf. Stoljar 2014).

Westlund offers the notion of dialogical answerability to steer a middle course between externalist theories that claim that the Angel or the South-East Asian women are non-autonomous due to their oppression and well-known internalist theories that imply that agents are often fully autonomous despite their oppression.[5] She argues that the criteria of authenticity offered by internalist theories—in particular, those of Harry Frankfurt and Michael Bratman—do not adequately differentiate between oppressed agents who are autonomous and non-autonomous oppressed agents—those who are so "deeply deferential" or so deeply embedded in their situation of oppression that they accept it uncritically. She thinks that the internalist theories adopt the right *methodological* approach: they correctly grasp that providing the conditions for authentic agential perspective requires that we differentiate between influences that "grip" the agent from without and hence are inauthentic, and influences that are fully incorporated by the agent into her self.[6] However, although correct methodologically, such theories are incorrect in their characterizations of what is required for authentic agential perspective.

Consider Harry Frankfurt's (1988) influential account, in which an agent constitutes her authentic agency through second-order "identification" with her first-order desires. Even if the first-order desires correspond to preferences to be deferential, or preferences for self-subordination, the agent will be autonomous with respect to these preferences if they are endorsed at the second order. As many have pointed out, Frankfurt's account does not adequately differentiate between acts of identification at higher-order levels that are authentic or genuinely the agent's own and those that are the product of external factors such as socialization, particularly oppressive socialization. Frankfurt's account therefore leads to a regress. Michael Bratman's alternative approach tries to block the regress while retaining a hierarchical theory of autonomy. It introduces the notion of being satisfied with a "higher-order policy" that governs practical reasoning (Bratman 2003). A higher-order policy blocks the regress because it is partly constitutive of the agent's cross-temporal identity and may be said to "speak for" the agent (Westlund 2009, 32). Bratman notices that higher-order policies could themselves be formed by potentially autonomy-undermining conditions, such as depression: consider someone who has a policy of going to the gym every morning only because she is depressed and dissatisfied with her bodily appearance (Westlund 2009, 32; Bratman 2007, 211). Although Bratman himself is prepared to accept this consequence, Westlund thinks that "[e]ven if the depressed agent's self-governing policies do contribute to the organization of her agency over time, it is still, plausibly, a further question as to whether they do so in a way that renders her self-governing" (Westlund 2009, 32). In other words, she argues that Bratman's criterion of satisfaction with a higher-order policy is not sufficient for autonomous or self-governing agency.

Westlund advances a conception of authentic agential perspective as a disposition to dialogical answerability: "to count as governing one's practical reasoning, rather than being in the grip of the considerations that drive it, one must be open to engagement with the critical perspectives of others" (2009, 35). She writes,

> An agent who lacks the disposition to answer for herself may be reflectively satisfied with her commitments, but her practical reasoning will be strangely disconnected from, and insensitive to, any justificatory pressures to which she, the agent, is subject. Being impervious to critical challenge in this way is an excellent candidate for what it is to be gripped by an action-guiding commitment or bit of practical reasoning as opposed to governing it, which is precisely the distinction of which we need our account of autonomy to make sense. (34)

Westlund's criterion is psychological, but—unlike Frankfurt's—it does not offer a volitional test of autonomy. "Being impervious to critical challenge" and hence lacking the disposition—or conversely, being responsive to critical challenge and having the disposition—can be a characteristic of agents independently of volitional activity on their part. Further, although the disposition is psychological, it is dialogical and relational. It is defined partly by "the position the agent occupies as one reflective, responsible self among many" (Westlund 2009, 35–36). It is also important that dialogical answerability is "formal" or content-neutral; that is, all preferences, no matter their content, are in principle compatible with authenticity and autonomous agency. Dialogical answerability therefore can be employed to reject a potentially problematic claim that feminist theorists of oppression sometimes defend, namely that the internalization of norms of oppression per se is incompatible with autonomy. Since dialogical answerability provides a content-neutral test of autonomy, people who have internalized norms of oppression are *not* inauthentic simply due to the content of their preferences.

Two examples further elaborate Westlund's view. Consider first a patient in a clinical setting, Betty, who refuses life-saving medical treatment but "could not be drawn into direct discussion of her refusal, but instead simply shut down when pressed to give reasons" (Westlund 2009, 37). Betty seemed to reject as "unreasonable the very demand that she *give* reasons for her decision" (37). Westlund speculates that Betty's refusal to discuss her decision was the product of a habitual and life-long resistance to cooperating with authority figures like medical professionals. She suggests that Betty's decision *could* be autonomous, because answerability is not "a disposition to defend one's choices and actions to all comers, but to respond (in one of a range of appropriate ways) to *legitimate* challenges," namely those who satisfy both "relational situatedness" and "context-sensitivity" (39). "Relational situatedness" is being situated in a "sense-giving relationship" (40). Agents do not have to be ready to cite their reasons on demand to anyone, for instance telemarketers or proselytizers who turn up at the front door (40). Moreover, Westlund suggests that if some agents do not have the intellectual ability or education to cite reasons *at all*, they can display a readiness to engage in justificatory dialogue in alternative ways. Demands for justification must be sensitive to such contextual factors. Betty's initial refusal to give reasons for her rejection of life-saving treatment therefore does not automatically rule out that she has the dialogical answerability required for autonomy. But if further discussion with Betty that is sensitive to both her intellectual capabilities and her antagonism to authority figures cannot elicit some kind of justificatory response, then it must be concluded from Westlund's view that Betty's decision to reject life-saving treatment is non-autonomous.

A second example is that of Paul Benson's "invisible man" (2005, 111–113).[7] Benson argues that "taking ownership" is a necessary condition of self-governing agency and that the "distinctive authority involved in taking ownership does not depend on the authorization of agents' wills in relation to their reflective identities. Rather, it concerns agents' position to speak for their actions in the face of potential criticisms" (2005, 102). Hence, taking ownership corresponds to dialogical answerability.[8] Benson employs the notion of taking ownership to show, not that people who endorse their oppression can be autonomous, but rather that practices of oppression can *undermine* the answerability required for autonomy. He notices that aspects of the social and discursive environment—such as those due to racist oppression—can lead to the internalization of a picture of oneself that is inimical to taking ownership. The invisible man has internalized a sense of social invisibility because of the objectification inherent in racist institutions such as Jim Crow or slavery. Martin Luther King Jr. powerfully captures this possibility when he speaks of a "degenerating sense of 'nobodiness' "experienced by African-Americans under Jim Crow (King 2010, 92). Benson argues that the " 'invisible man's' autonomy has been damaged because, suffering serious doubt about his own personhood, he does not regard himself as worthy to answer for what he does by the normative standards that he accepts" (Benson 2005, 113).

The examples of Betty and the invisible man illustrate that for Westlund (and Benson) dialogical answerability is necessary for autonomy. If even relationally situated and context-sensitive requests to Betty do not elicit a response, we can conclude that she does not have the disposition and hence is not autonomous. The invisible man does not have the disposition because he correctly identifies the social context as one that would be hostile to seeing him as an interlocutor who is expected to provide a justification of his attitudes and commitments. Both therefore lack autonomy with respect to their decisions in the relevant normative domains. Dialogical answerability can be used to differentiate among agents who are oppressed and to solve the agency dilemma: people who take ownership over their actions and commitments by holding themselves ready to answer challenges *can* be autonomous *despite* living under (and endorsing their) oppression.

3 Answerability, Authenticity, and Moral Responsibility

In this section, I accept for the sake of argument that dialogical answerability is necessary for autonomy and turn to the question of whether Westlund's theory implies that it is also sufficient. I first point out that dialogical answerability must be treated as sufficient (all things being equal) for Westlund's solution to the agency dilemma to succeed. I also attempt to disentangle the necessary and sufficient conditions of autonomy from those of authentic agential perspective and moral responsibility. Westlund herself is tentative about whether dialogical answerability is sufficient for autonomy: "whether it is sufficient is a question on which I remain neutral here" (2009, 46n27). Indeed, it is initially plausible that Westlund's theory could remain neutral on the question of whether answerability is sufficient for autonomy. Many theories of autonomy distinguish between *competency* and *authenticity* conditions of autonomy (Christman 2009; Mackenzie 2008). Competency requires that agents' capacities of critical reflection are intact and includes conditions such as "procedural independence" (Dworkin 1988, 18) or "competence to form effective intentions" (Christman 2009, 155). For instance, people under the influence of alcohol or drugs might retain a disposition to answer justificatory challenges, but their competence for critical reflection will be severely diminished. It is certainly plausible therefore that dialogical answerability is not sufficient for autonomy.

It is not plausible, however, that the focus of the agency dilemma is on agents who lack competence. Recall the women in circumstances of oppression who "freely and authentically accept a condition of social and personal subordination." On Westlund's account, the feature that distinguishes these women from similarly situated women who are non-autonomous is precisely that they are reflective and disposed to provide a justification of their commitment to oppressive norms. It is implicit in the articulation of the agency dilemma that we cannot suppose that oppression *itself* undermines procedural independence or competence. Therefore, these women must be presumed to be competent, and Westlund's argument must be committed to the position that (all things being equal) answerability is sufficient for autonomy.

I come back to the question of whether dialogical answerability is sufficient for autonomy in section 4. For now, I turn to disentangling the necessary and sufficient conditions of autonomy, authentic agential perspective, and moral responsibility. The assumption that these conditions coincide is inherited from Frankfurt's influential work "Freedom of the Will and the Concept of a Person" (1988). On Frankfurt's account, authentic self-constitution is a process through which an agent delineates herself as a separate or "autonomous" agent from forces that are external to her: "the person by making a decision by which he identifies with a desire *constitutes himself*. The pertinent desire is no longer in any way external to him" (170; my italics). In so doing, agents such as the willing addict acquire a dimension of freedom of the will or autonomy: "[b]ut when he [the willing addict] takes the drug, he takes it freely and of his own free will. . . . His will is outside his control, but by his second-order desire that his desire for the drug should be effective, *he has made this will his own*" (24–25; my italics). Moreover, this process renders the willing addict morally responsible for taking the drug despite the fact that due to the addiction he would have taken the drug even if he had been unwilling at the second-order level to do so; that is, despite causal overdetermination. In contrast to Frankfurt's proposal that identification simultaneously constitutes an authentic perspective and renders the agent free and morally responsible, I suggest that these are distinct concepts that do not always apply to the same cases. If I am right, it is possible in principle that agents who are non-autonomous could nevertheless retain authentic agency and moral responsibility.

First let us examine whether dialogical answerability is necessary or sufficient for authentic agential perspective. Consider, for example, an agent with obsessive-compulsive disorder (OCD). As Angela Smith points out, OCD "is a psychological condition that deeply affects an agent's motives and attitudes in normative domains. An agent who suffers from this condition often cannot have normal relationships with others, for she is constantly obsessed with keeping clean or checking over and over again to make sure she has completed certain tasks" (2012, 584). An agent with OCD seems to be gripped by her condition. On either Frankfurt's or Bratman's account, however, the agent could in principle make the preferences that arise due to the OCD *her own* through an act of volition. She might identify with those preferences or adopt a higher-order policy with which she is satisfied such as "To avoid contamination, never visit friends in hospital."[9] Westlund argues that this in-principle possibility reveals a failing of these theories: despite the fact that a person with OCD seems to be in the grip of forces external to her, these theories allow that she could be authentic and hence, in principle, autonomous.

Notice, however, that Westlund's own notion of dialogical answerability may be subject to a parallel criticism. Suppose the person with OCD fails to visit a friend in hospital due to his fear of contamination. He may be articulate and disposed to engage in dialogue with interlocutors to provide reasons for why he failed to live up to an obligation of friendship. He may feel remorse and hold himself responsible because he perceives his inability to conquer his fear to be a moral failing. Westlund's objection to Bratman is that a higher-order policy with which one is satisfied could itself be produced by external influences such as depression or OCD that are incompatible with an authentic agential perspective. Similarly, if the condition of OCD itself is what inclines the agent to offer justificatory answers in the relevant normative domain, the disposition does not represent an authentic perspective in that domain.[10] The failure to visit the friend, as well as any attempt to justify it, would correspond to "the OCD speaking," not to an authentic or autonomous agential perspective (cf. Westlund 2009, 33).

Moreover, a person with OCD could have a disposition to dialogical answerability in normative domains that are affected by the condition for reasons that are unrelated to the condition. That is, even if autonomy-distorting factors do not themselves cause the answerability disposition, the latter could coexist with an agential perspective that is not authentic. There are numerous psychological and social factors that influence whether or not agents have a disposition to hold themselves answerable, including self-confidence in one's ability to be articulate, reticence or other aspects of character, or the attitudes of interlocutors that for instance might have the effect of either fostering the disposition or causing it to wither.[11] The invisible man does not have the disposition because he recognizes that others do not see him as a worthy interlocutor. Similarly, the gendered expectations of interlocutors about how people should express themselves in public might deter the development of the disposition in girls, but promote it in boys. Boys are more likely to be encouraged to debate their points of view and adopt an attitude of "authority over their own voice." Such psychological and social factors may be enough to cause a person with OCD to hold himself answerable for being a bad friend when in fact not visiting his friend is a direct result of being gripped by the OCD and hence, on Westlund's view, does not reveal his authentic agential perspective. It is thus possible that dialogical answerability and *inauthenticity* could coexist in a particular domain;[12] therefore the disposition is not sufficient for authentic agential perspective or for autonomy, assuming authenticity is the key to autonomy.

Is dialogical answerability *necessary* for authentic agential perspective? The invisible man example suggests that it is not. If Benson is right, the invisible man does not take ownership of his evaluative commitments because he sees himself as a social nonperson. Notice however that he *has* evaluative commitments. David Shoemaker points out that attitudes that disclose my evaluative commitments are "obviously mine . . . , they reflect on me, on my deep self, and in particular on who I am as an agent in the world" (2011, 611; cf. Watson 1996). Thus, the invisible man has an authentic evaluative perspective in the relevant normative domain although he lacks dialogical answerability. As Shoemaker observes, there are other examples in which authentic agential perspective exists without answerability. As a matter of fact, people do not hold themselves ready to answer requests for justification of attitudes that express deep emotional commitments. For instance, I am not disposed to provide a justificatory response to "Why do you continue to visit your father despite his being cantankerous and ungrateful?" because my commitment to love and care for my father is based on an emotional commitment rather than a judgment that is responsive to reasons. Similarly, Huckleberry Finn appears to have an authentic agential perspective for which he is not answerable (Shoemaker 2011, 614).[13] Huck's good moral character is revealed through his attitude to Jim, a runaway slave he has befriended and finds himself unable to turn in (Arpaly and Schroeder 1999, 163; Shoemaker 2011, 614). But Huck is unable to justify his attitude to Jim and indeed sees himself as a kind of moral failure because he cannot respond appropriately to what he considers to be the relevant justificatory challenges.

Shoemaker notices that agents can be subject to "aretaic" appraisals on the basis of their authentic agential perspective. I can be appraised as "generous" or "loyal" for visiting my father every day or "ungenerous" and "selfish" for not doing so. Huck is the proper subject of aretaic appraisals such as "kind," "brave," and "honorable" (Shoemaker 2011, 614). Aretaic appraisal is a broader category of evaluative appraisal than core moral appraisal that employs praise and blame. Is dialogical answerability necessary or sufficient for moral responsibility and moral appraisal? Many scholars of moral responsibility hold that answerability is key to moral responsibility (Scanlon 1998; Shoemaker 2011; Smith 2005, 2012). For instance, Smith writes, "To say that an agent is morally responsible for some thing is to say that the agent is open, in principle, to demands for justification regarding that thing. . . . [I]t only makes sense to direct these forms of moral response to an agent on the basis of things that reflect her evaluative judgments" (2012, 577–578). Like Westlund, Smith proposes a notion of answerability that is both relational—because it requires that the agent be thought of as open to interpersonal demands for justification—and nonvolitional. She argues that agents can be answerable and morally responsible even for nonvolitional attitudes and activities such as failing to notice, forgetting, or spontaneous action. For instance, agents who are persistently "tone-deaf" with respect to the needs and happiness of their family or intimate friends manifest an evaluative perspective for which it is appropriate to hold them answerable (Smith 2005, 242–243). Smith offers a "rational relations" view of answerability, for which the key question is "whether it is appropriate, in principle, to ask a person to give a rational defense of her attitudes" (269).[14] It does not make sense to demand justification from a person for physical states such as height or having a headache (cf. 257). In such cases, one can ask for an explanation, but not for a justification.

Westlund's notion of dialogical answerability does not correspond to the intelligible answerability that is required for moral responsibility under Smith's rational relations view. The former is a subjective readiness to hold oneself answerable, whereas the latter does not require this.[15] For instance, people can be answerable and potentially blameworthy even when their characters or their evaluative judgments themselves block the development of the disposition to hold themselves answerable. Recall Betty, for whom the demand to give reasons for her decision to refuse life-saving treatment is itself unreasonable. Although she is not answerable in the subjective sense required by Westlund, she could be morally responsible for the decision to refuse treatment as long as it was based on her evaluative judgments. This situation may not be uncommon; for instance, narcissists believe that other people's views are worthless because others are in effect instruments to be used for their own advancement. It is unlikely that they will hold themselves ready to answer others' critical perspectives except perhaps in so far as doing so might get them what they want.[16] But such agents have made evaluative judgments about the worth of other human beings for which it is appropriate to hold them answerable and morally responsible. Thus, it seems that dialogical answerability—understood as a subjective readiness to hold oneself answerable—is not necessary for moral responsibility. Neither is it sufficient, for reasons that we have already outlined in the above discussion of the person with OCD. Even if the agent with OCD has a subjective disposition to answer for his failure to visit his friend, he is not answerable (or morally responsible) because the failure by hypothesis does not bear the appropriate relation to his evaluative judgments.

A question that remains unresolved in the moral responsibility literature is whether intelligible answerability is both necessary and sufficient for moral responsibility or whether it is only sufficient. As was already observed, Shoemaker argues that people have evaluative commitments and authentic agential perspectives for which they are not answerable. It does not make sense, for example, to demand justification of the care we have for parents and children. Nevertheless, such commitments are attributable to us, and we are proper targets of aretaic appraisal in virtue of such commitments. Although Shoemaker acknowledges that answerability picks out the core cases of moral responsibility—for which blame and praise are appropriate evaluations—he argues that there is a distinct additional sense of moral responsibility, "responsibility as attributability," that applies in cases in which answerability does not obtain (Shoemaker 2011). If he is right, answerability is sufficient but not necessary for moral responsibility. Smith (2012) disagrees, arguing that agents are not in fact *morally* responsible for all the authentic perspectives that may be attributable to them. I do not take a side on this dispute here.[17]

Let me summarize what has been established in this section. (1) For the sake of argument, I agreed that dialogical answerability is necessary for autonomy; (2) I argued that dialogical answerability is neither sufficient nor necessary for authentic agential perspective; (3) I distinguished between dialogical answerability—a subjective readiness to hold oneself answerable—and intelligible answerability, and I explained that philosophers of moral responsibility agree that intelligible answerability is sufficient for moral responsibility even if it is not necessary; (4) I suggested that dialogical answerability is neither necessary nor sufficient for moral responsibility; and (5) I made clear that attributions of authentic agential perspective and moral responsibility go hand in hand with certain categories of appraisal: aretaic appraisal and moral appraisal, respectively.

4 Defending Externalist Conceptions of Autonomy

The points established in the previous section show that authentic agential perspective, moral responsibility, and autonomous agency do not always overlap.

In this section, I use this insight to respond to the main objections to externalist theories of autonomy. I also suggest that dialogical answerability is not sufficient for autonomy. My argument will be twofold. First, I propose that the best explanation of the Jehovah's Witnesses example is the externalist thesis that they are heteronomous in virtue of the external, social conditions imposed in the camps. Since the Jehovah's Witnesses are also answerable (and mentally competent in other respects), it follows that answerability is not sufficient for autonomy. Second, I argue that there is no explanatory loss in attributing non-autonomy to people just in virtue of their circumstances. I address two difficult cases, those of *resisters* and *endorsers*. It has been urged that it is implausible that social activists whose lives are committed to resisting the oppression to which they were subjected lack autonomy just in virtue of their circumstances. On the contrary, they are moral exemplars and paradigms of how to lead an autonomous life (Noggle 2011; cf. Oshana 2015). Further, as we saw in section 2, Westlund and others argue that attributing non-autonomy in the face of agents' *own* authorization of the values inherent in the external circumstances is particularly problematic. I argue that denying that either "resisters" or "endorsers" are self-governing is not tantamount to denying agency tout court. Many dimensions of agency, as well as accompanying dimensions of evaluative appraisal, survive even if autonomous agency does not.

Were the Jehovah's Witnesses in concentration camps heteronomous or autonomous? In his psychological study of inmates in concentration camps, Bruno Bettelheim describes what the inmates had to endure: they were "torn away from . . . family, friends and occupation and then deprived of . . . civil rights and locked into a prison," and they experienced "trauma of subjection to extraordinary abuse" (1960, 119).[18] However, he also notes the psychological differences among inmates: Jehovah's Witnesses, political prisoners, and criminals were significantly more resilient than nonpolitical, middle-class prisoners, who were likely to experience severe disorientation and psychic breakdown. The Jehovah's Witnesses in particular retained a high degree of psychic integrity, instrumental rationality, mental competence, and even trustworthiness, all of which made them favorites for the positions of household servants to the SS officers. However, it is only if we conflate moral responsibility or authentic agential perspective with autonomy that we would be tempted to explain their situation in the camps as autonomous despite the conditions. Once we recognize the distinctions outlined in section 3, a better explanation is that the Jehovah's Witnesses were heteronomous—though not necessarily lacking in authentic agency or moral responsibility—due to the conditions in the camps. Indeed, these conditions are clearly incompatible with the necessary conditions of autonomy offered by prominent externalist accounts. For instance, Joseph Raz argues that autonomy requires "adequate" external options, options that are both nontrivial and of sufficient variety (1986, 373–374).[19] It is obvious that the options available to inmates in the camps were woefully inadequate: they were "short-term and negligible" (372), and they lacked variety especially because inmates were overwhelmed by having to navigate and attempt to survive the abuse meted out by the SS officers.

If we accept that the Jehovah's Witnesses were heteronomous, this shows that dialogical answerability is not *sufficient* for autonomy. The Jehovah's Witnesses had a disposition to respond to challenges—such as "Why are you proselytizing in the concentration camp?" or "Why don't you attempt to escape when you have the chance?"—by employing their moral code to provide a justification of their actions. Indeed, Bettelheim mentions that the Jehovah's Witnesses became argumentative only "when someone questioned their religious beliefs" (1960, 123). The Jehovah's Witnesses also retained an authentic agential perspective—their self-conception disclosed their evaluative commitments—and on this basis they are appropriate subjects of aretaic appraisal: they were courageous, admirable, upstanding, and loyal. Further, they were answerable in the sense required for moral responsibility. It would have been appropriate to ask them to provide a justification of many of their activities—such as the attempt to make converts, and the decision not to escape even when they had opportunities to do so—because these actions were justifiable on the basis of their evaluative judgments. The Jehovah's Witnesses therefore are appropriate subjects of praise and blame.

The conclusion that dialogical answerability is not sufficient for autonomy is problematic for Westlund's argument because, as we saw in section 3, her theory must be committed to the sufficiency thesis if it is to provide a solution to the agency dilemma. Westlund may respond that there is a difference between the Jehovah's Witnesses and the women who embrace social roles and norms that are oppressive to them. The Jehovah's Witnesses embraced their own moral code but did not endorse the ideology of the camps itself. Perhaps what is important for autonomy is that people are self-authorizing with respect to the morality inherent in their circumstances. Before addressing this possible response, I examine the "resisters" objection to externalist conceptions of autonomy. This example is closer to that of the Jehovah's Witnesses because resisters also do not endorse the ideology of their external circumstances. There are many examples of social activists and reformers whose life projects are dedicated to resisting the institutions and norms of subordination that are applied to them: Martin Luther King Jr., Nelson Mandela, Mahatma Ghandi, and Harriet Tubman (Noggle 2011; Oshana 2015, 8–13). It has been urged that such resisters are paradigms of self-governing, autonomous agents. Hence, theories claiming that resisters are non-autonomous just in virtue of their external circumstances must be false.

Oshana provides one possible externalist response to this objection. She acknowledges that King, because of his charisma and public recognition, could have eked out limited autonomy despite living under Jim Crow. She proposes that this makes him an "outlier," an exception to the externalist picture rather than typical of it:

> Like every other American descendant of enslaved Africans, King lacked many of the *de jure* rights of autonomy granted his white brethren. On a daily basis, he had to navigate a minefield of indiscriminate constraints and interferences that were calculated to prevent him from realizing his goals. . . . It consisted not simply of social hindrances but of systemic obstacles that were socioeconomically, politically, and legally reinforced. If we couple this with a risible paucity of options and the fact that King functioned in a climate that was the very antithesis of secure and in which the probability of interference was high . . . King's having met the threshold for *de facto* autonomy is nothing short of extraordinary. (2015, 11)

Once we separate different aspects of agency, however, there is no need to accommodate the objection by treating resisters as "the exceptions to the rule" within externalist theories. On an externalist conception, resisters like King are non-autonomous just in virtue of their circumstances. Despite this, they are the proper subjects of both aretaic and moral appraisal. King was admirable, courageous, a moral exemplar, a person with integrity, and a person to be esteemed and respected. He was also morally responsible for his activism because his activism was "rationally related" to his evaluative judgments. There is no explanatory loss, therefore, in denying King's autonomy. We do not thereby remove the possibility of appropriate evaluative appraisal. It is true that King was answerable (in both senses), but it does not follow that he was autonomous.

Finally, I return to the agency dilemma to consider the case of "endorsers." For Westlund, it is especially problematic to deny that agents are self-governing in cases in which they embrace the very ideology that is constraining them. Notice first that examples of endorsers are not uncommon and are not limited to circumstances of oppression. Oshana's externalist view treats as non-autonomous members of religious orders (nuns or monks) who voluntarily adopt an externally directed daily routine and submit themselves to the will of the head of the order and ultimately to the will of God (Oshana 1998, 92). In voluntarily submitting to an external will that directs their daily lives, such people relinquish their autonomy. The fundamentalist women (including converts) described by Westlund who "willingly assume subordinate roles" are similar: they embrace a regimented daily life that is directed by others and a value system in which men have superior status and control what women can do in the public realm. Westlund argues that the externalist conception that characterizes such agents as non-autonomous is problematic both because it assumes psychological homogeneity and because externalist theories in effect claim that such agents lack authority over their own voice and lack moral standing as agents worthy of respect. She writes that "substantive ideals of independence, egalitarianism, and the like [can] be rejected by autonomous agents. . . . [W]e ought to proceed by treating their detractors as autonomous interlocutors. . . . The disrespectful nature of any other treatment has, in effect, been roundly recognized within the global feminist literature" (2009, 42).

Do externalist theories really have the problematic consequences implicit in the agency dilemma and in Westlund's critique? If we employ the insights of section 3 to unpack different dimensions of agency, we see that many dimensions of agency survive constraining external circumstances or even voluntarily submitting to another's rule. Externalist conceptions of autonomy are committed neither to psychological homogeneity nor to permitting the disrespectful treatment of non-autonomous agents. The criticism implied in the agency dilemma is that denying autonomy is disrespectful because it is tantamount to erasing agency. To respond to this criticism, it will be useful to recall P. F. Strawson's (1962) distinction between the "reactive" stance and the "objective" stance. Strawson observes that our practices of holding people morally responsible track categories of moral appraisal. Holding people morally responsible corresponds to taking a "reactive" stance within which certain attitudes toward agents are appropriate, such as attitudes of resentment, blame, and so forth. Having an appropriate reactive stance implies engaging appropriately in all categories of evaluative appraisal, not just moral appraisal. Aretaic appraisal linked to authentic agential perspective is also a component of the reactive stance. When evaluative appraisal is not appropriate, however—for instance, with respect to actions that are the direct result of conditions like OCD—we adopt an objective rather than a reactive stance. A moral attitude of resentment or an aretaic judgment 'disloyal' would make no more sense directed to someone with OCD who does not visit a friend in hospital due to a fear of contamination than would evaluative appraisal of her height or of her having a headache.[20] Therefore, attributions of *agency* are crucially linked to the appropriateness of taking a reactive rather than an objective stance. I have already shown that evaluative appraisal is appropriate even when agents are heteronomous; hence attributions of non-autonomy do not imply the erasure of agency, or disrespect on that basis.

5 Conclusion

This chapter has defended externalist conceptions of autonomy by examining Westlund's conception of autonomy as dialogical answerability. Although I agreed for the sake of argument that dialogical answerability—or "taking ownership"—is necessary for autonomy, I argued that it is not sufficient. We see from examples such as that of the Jehovah's Witnesses that dialogical answerability survives in situations of heteronomy. Moreover, I claimed that externalist conceptions that characterize certain agents as non-autonomous due to social conditions are not in principle disrespectful to these agents. Judging someone as non-autonomous is compatible with a wide variety of appropriate evaluative appraisals that in turn imply the attribution of agency and the possibility of an attitude of respect. Externalist theories *do* imply that people can be mistaken about what is conducive to their own autonomy. Conceptions of the good are misguided if they imply that autonomy is compatible with hierarchical social structures in which people are subordinate and under others' effective control.[21] However, since autonomy is not the only value, externalist theories allow that conceptions of the good that endorse hierarchical social structures might promote other important values, such as those related to identity, culture, and social cohesion.

I have not had time in this chapter to explore the social nature of dialogical answerability in any detail. As Benson (2005) points out, the answerability disposition can be damaged due to interpersonal circumstances in which people see themselves as socially invisible. This raises the question of whether the disposition would be damaged also in less extreme situations that do not correspond to internalized social invisibility, for instance, those in which an agent's testimony is systematically subject to what Miranda Fricker calls a "credibility deficit" due to prejudice against the group in which she is a member (1997, 17). Women are particularly subject to credibility deficits. Therefore, there is an interesting further issue that Westlund will have to address if she continues to defend the notion of dialogical answerability as a test for autonomy. This is the effect of the circumstances of oppression themselves on women's ability to cultivate answerability.[22]

Notes

1. For the purposes of this chapter, I speak of externalist conceptions of autonomy in a general sense. It should be noted that there are different externalist positions. For example, Joseph Raz (1986) argues that adequate external options are necessary for autonomy, and Marina Oshana (2006) offers a social-relational account in which severely constraining external conditions undermine the "practical control" required for autonomy. I would add that there can be another kind of externalist position—a Kantian position—on which autonomy requires that agents adopt or endorse external, morally correct reasons as their action-guiding commitments.
2. See Oshana (2002) for a different argument distinguishing autonomy from moral responsibility.
3. Oshana also responds to this objection as well as to objections to externalist theories of autonomy in general in Oshana 2015.

4. For the purposes of this chapter, I leave aside discussion of Christman's perfectionism argument against externalist conceptions of autonomy. In 'Relational Autonomy and Perfectionism' (2017), I question whether externalist conceptions of autonomy do in fact imply problematic forms of perfectionism. I argue against Christman's perfectionism argument and antiperfectionism in general.

5. Note that not all internalist theories have this failing. For example, Diana T. Meyers (1989) and John Christman (2009) propose theories of autonomy that are internalist, but they explicitly acknowledge that the internalist conditions that they require can be adversely affected by the circumstances of oppression, e.g., when lack of adequate education or gender-differentiated expectations lead girls not to hone the internal and psychological competencies required for autonomy.

6. For the origin of the metaphor of being "gripped" by external influences, see Westlund 2009, 46n18.

7. As Benson notes, the example is based on Ralph Ellison's novel *Invisible Man* (1952).

8. Catriona Mackenzie calls this the "self-authorization" condition of autonomy. Notice, however, that both Westlund and Benson claim that self-authorization is necessary for self-government, whereas Mackenzie argues that self-authorization is a separate "dimension" of autonomy from that of self-government (Mackenzie 2014). I will not discuss here potential differences between Benson's and Westlund's notions of self-authorization, for instance that his is "weakly substantive," whereas hers is "formal." For an explanation, see Stoljar 2013.

9. Angela Smith considers the example of failing to visit a friend in hospital in Smith 2012, 585n14.

10. Marina Oshana helped me clarify this point.

11. I am grateful to Catriona Mackenzie for this observation.

12. Another possible example—suggested by Marina Oshana—in which answerability might coexist with inauthenticity is of someone who holds herself answerable in a way that reflects back or mimics the stereotypical expectations of particular interlocutors or society in general. This would be disingenuous or inauthentic answerability in which a person's justificatory responses are not really her own but rather the products of the oppressive norms to which she is subjected.

13. In this context, saying that Huck is not answerable does not imply either a normative claim that he rightly can refuse to answer or an empirical claim that he lacks the rational capacity to respond to justificatory challenges. Rather, it implies an alternative empirical claim: Huck is not answerable because he does not consider his commitment to Jim to be based on reasons to which he is (subjectively) committed. He cannot articulate a justification of his commitment to Jim because he does not as a matter of fact have reasons of his own that justify this commitment. For more on the relationship between answerability and rational capacity, see note 15. I am grateful to Marina Oshana for urging me to clarify these points.

14. Smith's analysis of moral responsibility as (intelligible) answerability is both more inclusive and less inclusive than Frankfurt's. It is the former because it allows that one can be morally responsible for aspects of character and patterns of behavior that are nonvolitional. It is the latter because certain agents might not be morally responsible on Smith's account when they would be on Frankfurt's. For example, on Smith's account, the moral responsibility of the willing addict is an open question. It will not be intelligible to ask the willing addict to justify desires that arise from the addiction despite a higher-order identification with her first-order desire unless the act of identification itself bears a rational relation to the agent's evaluative judgments.

15. David Shoemaker observes that "a demand for justification presupposes that the agent as he is is capable of offering a reason-based account of his actions or attitudes" (2011, 614n30). In other words, for a person to be answerable, he must actually be rationally *capable* of being answerable. Although having the capacity will often be displayed through dialogical answerability—the subjective readiness to hold oneself answerable—dialogical answerability need not be always present even for people who have the capacity. It would seem that a narcissist could have the intellectual capacity but nevertheless not have the disposition.

16. If we think the narcissist is autonomous, the case of the narcissist may seem problematic for the claim that dialogical answerability is *necessary* for autonomy. On Westlund's view, the narcissist cannot be self-governing if he does not have dialogical answerability.

17. I also do not discuss David Shoemaker's (2011, 615–630) argument that there is a third sense of moral responsibility called "responsibility as accountability." See Catriona Mackenzie's chapter in this volume for a discussion of Shoemaker's tripartite account of moral responsibility. In response to Shoemaker, Angela Smith proposes a "unified" account—namely that answerability is necessary and sufficient for moral responsibility. She thinks that responsibility in the attributability sense is not genuine moral responsibility and responsibility in the accountability sense presupposes responsibility as answerability (Smith 2012). Accountability is connected to *holding* responsible. In her chapter in this volume, Andrea Westlund explores the relationship between holding responsible and blaming. She argues that in some cases—especially in therapeutic cases—it is helpful to hold someone responsible without blame.

18. Oshana discusses another example in which a person is stripped of her civil rights, in particular of opportunities to pursue the profession for which she was trained. Shirin Ebadi was a lawyer and became the first woman judge in Iran. In 1979, after the Iranian Revolution, she and other female lawyers were removed from their positions and given clerical duties instead. Their situation was improved to some extent when they were appointed as "experts" in the Justice Department, but Ebadi nevertheless found this unacceptable. She retired and was "housebound" until she was allowed to practice law again in 1992 (Oshana 2015, 16–17). On an externalist conception of autonomy, the social-relational conditions under which Ebadi was not allowed to practice her profession and effectively became housebound rendered her non-autonomous.

19. Raz used the examples of The Man in the Pit and The Hounded Woman to make these points (1986, 373–374). The Man in the Pit can make choices such as when to move around in the pit, what time to wake up and go to sleep, and so forth. But these are trivial. The Hounded Woman is on a desert island with a carnivorous wild animal that is hunting her down. She has a range of options, including nontrivial ones, but she is consumed by the need to protect herself from the beast. This latter picture is close to the situation of inmates in concentration camps.

20. As Catriona Mackenzie notes, conditions such as OCD do not completely undermine a person's capacities for social relationships or effective agency, so in many normative domains, an objective stance directed toward a person with OCD would be inappropriate. I am restricting myself here to situations (such as not visiting a friend in hospital due to fears of contamination) where the action is the direct result of the condition. In such a case, evaluative appraisal—the reactive stance—would be inappropriate.

21. It is important to notice that disagreeing with someone's conception of the good does not imply disrespecting *the person* who holds this conception of the good; see my discussion of respect as a process-related value in Stoljar 2017.

22. An early version of this chapter was presented at the Centre for Agency, Values and Ethics, Macquarie University, Sydney, at a workshop on "Social Dimensions of Moral Responsibility" in November 2014. I am grateful to the organizers of the workshop and to the audience for their comments on that occasion. I am also indebted to the editors of this volume, particularly Catriona Mackenzie and Katrina Hutchison, for extensive comments on a previous draft.

References

Arpaly, N., and T. Schroeder. 1999. "Praise, Blame and the Whole Self." *Philosophical Studies* 93 (2): 161–188.

Benson, P. 2005. "Taking Ownership: Authority and Voice in Autonomous Agency." In *Autonomy and the Challenges to Liberalism: New Essays*, edited by J. Christman and J. Anderson, 101–126. Cambridge: Cambridge University Press.

Berofsky, B. 1995. *Liberation from Self: A Theory of Personal Autonomy.* New York: Cambridge University Press.

Bettelheim, B. 1960. *The Informed Heart: Autonomy in a Mass Age.* New York: The Free Press.

Bratman, M. 2003. "Autonomy and Hierarchy." *Social Philosophy and Policy* 20 (2): 156–176.

Bratman, M. 2007. "Planning Agency, Autonomous Agency." In *Structures of Agency*, 195–221. New York: Oxford University Press.

Christman, J. 2009. *The Politics of Persons: Individual Autonomy and Socio-Historical Selves.* Cambridge: Cambridge University Press.

Cudd, A. E. 2006. *Analyzing Oppression.* Oxford: Oxford University Press.

Dworkin, G. 1988. *The Theory and Practice of Autonomy.* Cambridge: Cambridge University Press.

Ellison, R. 1952. *Invisible Man.* New York: Random House.

Frankfurt, H. 1988. "Freedom of the Will and the Concept of a Person." In *The Importance of What We Care About*, 11–25. New York: Cambridge University Press.

Fricker, M. 1997. *Epistemic Injustice: Power and the Ethics of Knowing.* Oxford: Clarendon Press.

Frye, M. 1983. *The Politics of Reality: Essays in Feminist Theory.* Trumansburg, NY: Crossing Press.

Hill, T. 1991. *Autonomy and Self-Respect.* Cambridge: Cambridge University Press.

Khader, S. 2011. *Adaptive Preferences and Women's Empowerment.* New York: Oxford University Press.

King, M. L., Jr. 2010. "Letter from a Birmingham Jail." In *Why We Can't Wait (The King Legacy)*, Introduction by Dorothy Cotton, 85–109. Boston: Beacon Press.

Mackenzie, C. 2008. "Relational Autonomy, Normative Authority and Perfectionism." *Journal of Social Philosophy* 39 (4): 512–533.

Mackenzie, C. 2014. "Three Dimensions of Autonomy: A Relational Analysis." In *Autonomy, Oppression, and Gender*, edited by A. Veltman and M. Piper, 15–41. New York: Oxford University Press.

Mackenzie, C. 2015. "Responding to the Agency Dilemma: Autonomy, Adaptive Preferences, and Internalized Oppression." In *Personal Autonomy and Social Oppression: Philosophical Perspectives*, edited by M. Oshana, 48–67. New York: Routledge.

Meyers, D. T. 1989. *Self, Society, and Personal Choice.* New York: Columbia University Press.

Narayan, U. 2002. "Minds of Their Own: Choices, Autonomy, Cultural Practices and Other Women." In *A Mind of One's Own: Feminist Essays on Reason and Objectivity*, edited by L. Antony and C. Witt, 418–432. Boulder, CO: Westview.

Noggle, R. 2011. Review of *Personal Autonomy in Society*, by Marina Oshana. *Journal of Value Inquiry* 45 (2): 233–238.

Oshana, M. 1998. "Personal Autonomy and Society." *Journal of Social Philosophy* 29 (1): 81–102.

Oshana, M. 2002. "The Misguided Marriage of Responsibility and Autonomy." *The Journal of Ethics* 6 (3): 261–280.

Oshana, M. 2006. *Personal Autonomy in Society.* Aldershot: Ashgate Publishing.

Oshana, M. 2015. "Is Social-Relational Autonomy a Plausible Ideal?" In *Personal Autonomy and Social Oppression: Philosophical Perspectives*, edited by M. Oshana, 3–24. New York: Routledge.

Raz, J. 1986. *The Morality of Freedom.* Oxford: Oxford University Press.

Scanlon, T. M. 1998. *What We Owe to Each Other.* Cambridge, MA: Harvard University Press.

Shoemaker, D. 2011. "Attributability, Answerability, and Accountability: Toward a Wider Theory of Moral Responsibiltiy." *Ethics* 121 (3): 602–632.

Smith, A. 2005. "Responsibility for Attitudes: Activity and Passivity in Mental Life." *Ethics* 115 (2): 236–271.

Smith, A. 2012. "Attributability, Answerability, and Accountability: In Defense of a Unified Account." *Ethics* 122 (3): 575–589.

Stoljar, N. 2013. "Feminist Perspectives on Autonomy." *The Stanford Encyclopedia of Philosophy* (Summer 2013 Edition), E. N. Zalta (ed.), URL = http://plato.stanford.edu/archives/sum2013/entries/feminism-autonomy/.

Stoljar, N. 2014. "Autonomy and Adaptive Preference Formation." In *Autonomy, Oppression, and Gender*, edited by A. Veltman and M. Piper, 227–254. New York: Oxford University Press.

Stoljar, N. 2017. "Relational Autonomy and Perfectionism." *Moral Philosophy and Politics* 4 (1): 27–41.

Strawson, P. F. 1962. "Freedom and Resentment." *Proceedings of the British Academy* 48: 1–25.

Watson, G. 1996. "Two Faces of Responsibility." *Philosophical Topics* 24 (2): 227–248.

Westlund, A. 2003. "Selflessness and Responsibility for Self: Is Deference Compatible with Autonomy?" *Philosophical Review* 112 (4): 37–77.

Westlund, A. 2009. "Rethinking Relational Autonomy." *Hypatia* 24 (4): 26–49.

Woolf, V. (1942) 1979. "Professions for Women." In *Women and Writing*, edited and with an introduction by M. Barrett, 57–63. New York: Harcourt Brace Jovanovich.

10

Answerability without Blame?

ANDREA C. WESTLUND

1 Introduction

Blame has many defenders these days. George Sher, in his book *In Praise of Blame* (2007), treats blame as inseparable from morality and as called for in response to the violation of moral principles we endorse. R. Jay Wallace takes blame to be a form of "deep moral assessment" (2008, 179) that is intimately connected to the practice of holding people to moral expectations. Macalester Bell, similarly, takes blame to be crucial to our responsibility practices and considers the standing to blame to be inalienable—it is of such central importance to our status as valuers, she argues, that we cannot be stripped of it in virtue of hypocrisy, complicity, or other such failings. Blame is not the preserve of the morally pure but an important exercise of moral agency for all valuers (Bell 2013).

A quick survey of the titles of popular self-help books about blame tells a different story. Take, for example, the particularly colorful *Beyond Blame: Freeing Yourself from the Most Toxic Emotional Bullsh*t* (Alasko 2011). This book, like others in its genre, treats blame as an entirely destructive emotional phenomenon. According to its author, to blame is to *find fault* with others (using criticism, accusation, punishment, or humiliation) and to *shift responsibility* for one's own behaviors on to others, in order to avoid being seen as wrong or bad oneself. The latter tactic is presented as a defensive maneuver, and it is not hard to see why it is supposed to be toxic: insofar as blaming someone else is just a sneaky way of avoiding accountability for oneself, there's not much to be said in its favor. It is not clear, however, why we should suppose that blame is always or even typically misdirected in this way—and if this presupposition does not hold up, the reach of the responsibility-shifting critique will be limited.[1]

The critique of "fault-finding," by contrast, does not rely on assumptions about the (mis-)assignment of responsibility. Carl Alasko, in the above-cited text, claims that the hostile and accusatory attitudes associated with blame are always destructive, and that blame damages relationships by representing other persons as flawed or defective in virtue of the fault. On these points, the concerns of self-help writers like Alasko are shared by at least some philosophers. Martha Nussbaum, for example, has recently argued that anger, as a response to wrongdoing, is nearly always irrational and deeply destructive; she recommends replacing it with forward-looking attitudes of unconditional love and generosity (2016, 348–349). Glen Pettigrove is similarly suspicious of emotions in the anger family, and argues that "meek" responses to wrongdoing have significant epistemic and moral advantages (2012). Although these arguments are focused on negative emotions associated with blame, rather than on blame itself, they clearly share the view that harshly critical, accusatory, or vilifying reactions to wrongdoers are ethically flawed and do more harm than good.

While I do not myself endorse a thoroughgoing rejection of anger, related concerns about the destructiveness of blame nonetheless strike me as containing a kernel of truth.[2] I want to push against the grain of recent defenses of blame just far enough to articulate what this popular line of critique gets right. In this chapter, I distinguish between blame as a reactive attitude and blaming as a speech act; I argue that some disagreement over the value of blame can be explained by the fact that blaming, as a speech act, takes several distinct forms. The critique of fault-finding, I suggest, properly targets what we might call judgmental or strongly verdictive blaming, the sort of blaming that passes judgment on the wrongdoer him- or herself, and treats him or her as deserving of the blamer's hostile or "punishing" reactions. This kind of blaming, I argue, tends to foreclose engagement in further moral dialogue with wrongdoers, and such dialogue is something that we ought to care about for a variety of reasons—not least because of the way in which it underwrites and supports agents' capacity to hold themselves and others answerable.

The problems with strongly verdictive blaming are perhaps most visible in therapeutic or pedagogical contexts, where passing judgment on a wrongdoer runs counter to the aim of encouraging her to hold herself answerable and take responsibility for her actions. I therefore begin, in section 2, by considering Hannah Pickard's recent account of responsibility without blame in therapeutic settings. In section 3, I build on her account by distinguishing between blame (the attitude) and blaming (the speech act), and explain what I mean by 'strongly verdictive' blaming. I argue that strongly verdictive blaming clearly runs counter to the therapeutic aims identified by Pickard, but that we can hold others answerable, and even be angry with others, without blaming them in this sense.

In section 4, I challenge the idea (taken for granted by some neo-Strawsonians) that there is a sharp dividing line between therapeutic and non-therapeutic responses, or between objective and participant-reactive attitudes, toward wrongdoers. "Holding answerable," I suggest, is a dialogical response that may have a therapeutic or pedagogical dimension without thereby objectifying its target. In section 5, I extend the model of holding answerable without judgmental blame to several other cases, in which appropriate reactions range from quasi-therapeutic, to pedagogical, to dialogical. Finally, in section 6, I recapitulate the sense in which our responsibility practices involve the exercise of normative powers, and I argue that nonjudgmental answerability has an important role to play in supporting these practices. To hold another answerable in a nonjudgmental mode is to treat her as a moral peer and partner in moral dialogue. Such treatment expresses a genuine commitment both to moral norms and to others' standing as members of the moral community, and it can support the development and exercise of key normative powers in a way that judgmental blame often cannot.

2 Blame in Therapeutic Contexts

In her paper "Responsibility without Blame" (2011), Hannah Pickard argues that in certain clinical contexts it is crucial that service providers treat service users as responsible without subjecting them to blame. Pickard's focus is on the case of effective treatment of personality disorder (henceforth, PD). Service users with PD are responsible, she argues, in the sense that they are generally consciously aware of what they are doing and exercise choice in doing it. In other words, they meet basic epistemic and control conditions for responsible agency. Responding to these service users as if they were *not* responsible—treating them, for example, as passive victims of their troubled personal histories—is counterproductive with respect to therapeutic goals, which include the goals of getting the service users to *take* responsibility for their behaviors and to choose to act differently, and more constructively, in the future. But responding to these service users with blaming attitudes and behaviors is also known to be disruptive of these therapeutic goals. Pickard takes on the challenge of articulating a stance that avoids both pitfalls, rescue and blame, a stance to which she refers as "responsibility without blame."

What accounts for blame's interference with therapeutic goals, according to Pickard, is its characteristic "sting"—"[e]ffective treatment," she observes, "is not possible if the service user feels judged, shamed, berated, attacked, or hurt" (2011, 216). Pickard describes blame as a "punishing" mental state (219), which may be expressed through actual punishment but which "can also be manifest in berating, attacking, humiliating, writing off, rejecting, shunning, abandoning, and criticizing" (218), among other things. There is a striking similarity between this list of behaviors and that put forth by Alasko (2011) in the critique of fault-finding mentioned above. But Pickard makes a further, insightful point about the structure of blame, namely that it is not just a collection of negative attitudes and dispositions to behave, but a mental state in which these attitudes and dispositions are united by the feeling that one is *entitled* to feel them toward the offender, in response to the offenders' behavior, and that one's hostile emotional reactions are deserved by the wrongdoer.

In recommending responsibility without blame, Pickard is in effect recommending a kind of blame that is stripped of this sense of entitlement—or, at least, a kind of blame in which the tendency to act on one's sense of entitlement has been tamped down. The model Pickard has in mind is the stance of a service provider who judges a service user to be responsible—and, indeed, *morally* responsible and thus blameworthy—for problematic behavior, without actually blaming them in the hurtful, affective sense. Pickard argues that providers who take this stance hold users responsible (indeed, hold them blameworthy) without having, as she puts it, "a feeling of entitlement to any negative reactive attitudes and emotions one might experience, no matter what the service user has done" (2011, 219). Their blame is detached: it includes a judgment of blameworthiness, but no corresponding feeling of entitlement to the attitudes and emotions characteristic of affective blame.[3] Without that feeling of entitlement guiding one's reactions, Pickard argues, one can allow compassionate consideration of the service user's troubled background to moderate one's anger or resentment, keeping it in check while one holds the user accountable in more constructive ways.

Pickard paints a compelling picture of what it might be to hold responsible without what she calls affective blame. There is, however, a puzzle at the heart of this picture. "We judge a person to be blameworthy," Pickard tells us, "when they are responsible for harm, and have no excuse" (2011, 215). This tells us the conditions under which we rightly judge a person to be worthy of blame, but not yet what it is that such a person is judged to be worthy *of*. What exactly is it, of which one is judged worthy, when they meet these conditions? Surely it must, on pain of vicious circularity, be the attitudes and emotions involved in affective blame. (If what one were judged worthy of, in detached blame, were blame in the detached sense, then we wouldn't yet have said anything substantive at all about what it is of which one is worthy.) But if one judges that an offender is worthy of affective blame (in other words, that affective blame would be "fitting" with respect to such an offender), then the feeling of entitlement that is part and parcel of affective blame would be fitting as well—one would be every bit as entitled to one's anger and resentment as one felt. And, if that feeling of entitlement would be fitting, it appears that it would take a bit of self-hoodwinkery to convince oneself one ought not to feel it.

In the case of PD, there are, of course, reasons for not allowing oneself to feel the sense of entitlement characteristic of affective blame, or at least not allowing oneself to express or act on the various negative emotions to which one feels entitled: as we've already seen, it would be better, from the point of view of clinicians' therapeutic aims, *not* to feel it (or at least not to express it), because then one is able to engage the service user more effectively in interactions that will encourage her to take responsibility for problematic behavior and to refrain from such behavior in the future.[4] But are these instrumental reasons the *right kind of reasons* for not feeling or expressing affective blame? Do we not, in virtue of treating the user compassionately for therapeutic reasons, slip out of the participant-reactive stance altogether, and into what Strawson calls the objective stance, and thus in the end fail to treat her as responsible after all? The power of the example of PD resides in the convincingness of the claim that individuals with PD are responsible, so it would be a theoretical loss to have to retreat to a stance on which we merely pretend to react to them as such (engaging in "as if" behavior), while in fact stepping outside the realm of genuinely participant-reactive attitudes.

I think Pickard is right that service providers can in principle (and properly speaking) hold service users responsible without blaming them in the problematic, hurtful sense. They are not simply treating service users as forces of nature, to be managed rather than reasoned with. But the appeal to detached blame—which, if I am right, is just an appraisal concerning the fittingness of affective blame—does not give us all the tools we need to understand their stance. In the next section, I suggest that we must distinguish not only between affective and detached blame, but also between blame as a reactive attitude and blaming as an expressive act. We will then be in position to consider various forms that blaming may take, as well as the aspects of our responsibility practices that are supported (or undermined) by these forms.

3   Blaming as a Speech Act

Blame, understood as a reactive attitude, is closely associated with the speech act of *blaming*—an act that is sometimes explicitly performed through utterances such as "I blame you," but is sometimes instead implicitly expressed through acts of criticism, censure, and the like. I propose that focusing on the uses of blame, instead of on the attitudes felt by blamers, may help us move forward. Blame in the speech-act sense makes several (brief) appearances in J. L. Austin's (1962) classic text *How to Do Things with Words*. Most prominently, it is offered as an example of a behabitive—or in other words, of a performative that exhibits, as opposed to merely describing, attitudes and feelings (Austin 1962, 83).[5] In classifying blame as a behabitive, Austin places it in what he describes as "a very miscellaneous group, . . . [having] to do with attitudes and *social behavior*"

(88; italics in original). But Austin later notes that blame also has verdictive and exercitive uses. What do these add to the behabitive use?

Verdictives, according to Austin, involve the giving of a verdict or the delivering of a finding with respect to matters that require the exercise of judgment. In official contexts, verdictives are delivered by judges or others in positions of authority, and many of Austin's examples are drawn from the realm of law. But he also suggests that informal blaming has a verdictive sense, which he takes to be equivalent to holding responsible (1962, 155).[6]

Exercitives, by contrast, involve the exercise of "powers, rights, or influence" (Austin 1962, 151). I take this to mean that they involve the exercise of what many philosophers now refer to as normative or moral powers—powers to make claims, give reasons, impose obligations, or otherwise alter the normative landscape just through expressing an intention to do so. (Austin's initial list of examples clearly falls in this category: "appointing, voting, ordering, urging, advising, & c" [151].) According to Austin, an exercitive "is a sentence rather than a verdict" (151). He does not explicitly argue that blame has an exercitive use, but he clearly implies that it does when he gives what he describes as "non-exercitive" uses of blame as an example of a behabitive (160).

When considering blame as a speech act, it is important to notice that the term as we commonly use it is ambiguous between its verdictive, exercitive, and behabitive senses. When one takes into consideration the possibility that these three uses may in practice overlap and be combined in various different ways, the prevalence of sharp disagreement over the value and significance of blame begins to seem much less surprising (and, indeed, much less intractable). Defenders and critics may well be focusing on different senses, and different uses, of blame.

Let us return to the case of PD and ask ourselves what it is to which service users are responding when they are blamed in a way that makes them feel "judged, shamed, berated, attacked, or hurt" (Pickard 2011, 216). The fact that they feel *judged* strongly suggests that they are reacting to blame in its verdictive sense—a verdict has been passed, and it is not a favorable one. The fact that they at the same time feel shamed, berated, attacked, and hurt suggests that the verdict has been accompanied by the targeted expression of "punishing" attitudes, as if an implicit sentence has been carried out through the expression of blame itself. One experiencing these reactions experiences herself as (metaphorically) having been convicted, sentenced, and punished all at once: the blamer acts as judge, jury, and executioner. It is not hard to see why blame in this sense—blame that is at once verdictive, exercitive, and behabitive—is contrary to therapeutic goals. This blame—to which I'll refer as 'strongly verdictive'—is judgmental and punitive, and implicitly puts the blamer in a position of authority over the one blamed. One might, of course, contest such blame, but it is not the sort of thing that naturally draws one into moral dialogue. In the face of such an onslaught, it may be less emotionally costly to disengage than to defend oneself.

Let's consider, by contrast, how service providers (as described by Pickard) regard and respond to service users, and how service users with PD respond to the overtures of their service providers, when all goes well. We are given the impression that in such cases, service providers hold service users responsible, and service users respond by coming to hold *themselves* (increasingly) responsible for their actions, a stance that allows them to make different and better choices in the future. Such an outcome must, presumably, proceed from a shared sense that current or past behavior has been problematic. But the passing of a verdict seems not to be central to the point of this interaction. (Certainly, the point is not to pass a verdict on the *person* as defective or faulty in light of her behavior, which is the kind of maneuver that self-help writers find so destructive.) Service users begin from a position of imperfect self-responsibility, but insofar as they are responsive to therapeutic interventions, they manifest the capacity to hold themselves responsible with the right sorts of promptings from others—and service providers interact constructively with them by proceeding on the assumption that this capacity is indeed in place, and not irredeemably faulty.

Agents with PD thus appear to lie at the margins (but, importantly, not outside the margins) of our responsibility practices, insofar as these practices presuppose the capacity to hold oneself and others responsible. The point of engaging service users in the way that service providers do is to draw them in, from the margins, somewhere closer to the center. Reacting with the trifecta of verdictive, exercitive, and behabitive blame does not support these agents' incipient responsibility competence, but *holding them answerable* does. So what is it to hold someone answerable, and how is it different from (or related to) blaming them?

Holding answerable, like blaming, is both an attitude and an act. In the act sense, holding another answerable involves some aspects of blaming behavior but not others. First of all, it seems clearly to be exercitive: it involves exercising a moral power to demand a response from another, and puts them under a (defeasible) obligation to respond. It is not, however, punitive, and thus differs even in its exercitive dimension from strongly verdicitve blame: as an exercitive, holding answerable is akin not to a sentencing (at least as that term is commonly understood), but to a summons to moral dialogue.

As such, holding answerable may seem to presuppose something like verdictive blame, at least in the sense of a pro tanto finding of wrongdoing. This seems right, but, again, it is important to note that holding answerable is nonetheless not *strongly* verdictive in the sense outlined above. The prospect of dialogue highlights the pro tanto nature of the accompanying verdict, and makes it defeasible in practice and not merely in principle. The meaning or significance of an action is typically subject to competing interpretations, particularly in morally complex situations. Currents of answerability run in more than one direction, and may lead to mutual moral insight and growth—as well as, in some cases, the sharing of associated moral burdens or costs. Holding another answerable, in other words, is not just a way of checking whether a person is indeed blameworthy by scanning her answers for considerations that might excuse or justify. In holding another answerable, one invites her into an alternative perspective on her action, and opens up the possibility of coming to a constructive shared response.

The dialogical structure of holding answerable in the exercitive sense also casts any accompanying behabitives in a different interpretive frame: even the exhibition of negative emotions such as anger may be read as demanding and engaging rather than as punitive and vilifying (more on this below). In holding another answerable, one implicitly treats her as a moral peer, or at least as one who *can* be a moral peer, rather than shaming, humiliating, or otherwise downgrading her in virtue of a moral fault.

In sum, holding answerable (in the act sense) shares some key elements with blaming behavior: it typically involves a pro tanto judgment of wrongdoing and the subjection of the other to moral claims or demands, and it often also involves the exhibition of associated attitudes or emotions such as anger. In light of this overlap, one might reasonably describe holding answerable as a *form* of blaming—albeit a form that is not strongly verdictive in the sense outlined above. I suspect that defenders of blame are at least in some cases using the term 'blame' in a non-strongly verdictive way that is roughly synonymous with 'holding answerable.' As long as we are clear about the details, these uses should not be problematic. In some contexts, though, it may be more helpful to reserve 'blaming' for its more strongly verdictive uses, which seem to be presupposed by its critics, and use 'holding answerable' to describe the more dialogically oriented speech acts I've been describing here. I'm not sure there is a single right way of proceeding, particularly since, unlike 'blame' and 'blaming,' 'holding answerable' is not a term that has very extensive presence in everyday language.

This brings us to the attitudinal side of holding answerable. To hold a person answerable is to take a practical, affective stance toward her, and indeed, it seems to count as having a reactive attitude. Lucy Allais helpfully defines a reactive attitude as "an affective way of regarding a person, which involves being disposed to have a range of feelings toward her in a range of circumstances. It involves seeing her in a certain way, being disposed to have characteristic patterns of attention, interpretation and expectation with respect to her actions" (2008, 7). It is not hard to see that treating someone as answerable involves certain patterns of attention, interpretation, and expectation with respect both to her dialogical responsiveness and to her future decision-making and action. One will attend to her responsiveness or lack thereof to one's challenges and suggestions, will interpret her replies or evasions as the replies or evasions of one who can be held to relevant normative standards (not as a force of nature), and will be disposed to hold her to expectations regarding how she carries the result of such dialogue over into her future decision-making and action.[7]

It might be more difficult to establish what feelings are central to the attitude of holding answerable. I would argue that while anger is not required for holding answerable, it has a proper place here: I take anger to be an affective appraisal of wrongdoing that demands (or is such as to demand) a response from the wrongdoer. Those who take anger always to be destructive tend to argue that it conceptually includes a desire for payback (Nussbaum 2016) or a desire to lash out (Pettigrove 2012). I don't think these punitive desires are essentially connected to anger, but I will not try to settle that issue here. Whether or not one takes anger to have a proper place in holding answerable, one will feel other emotions—disappointment, gratification, frustration, or hope, for example—depending on how one's interactions with the agent go, and one may certainly experience friction or harmony with the other and be motivated to change tack or tone as appropriate in light of such experiences. Holding answerable as a practical stance, or reactive attitude, will indeed include a disposition to engage in corresponding speech acts of holding answerable—the attitude and the act, though not inseparable, tend to go hand in hand in our everyday responsibility practices.

In centering the attitudes and speech acts involved in holding answerable, my reading of interactions with agents with PD supports a variation on a communicative approach to responsibility. Defenders of communicative accounts of responsibility argue that meeting the control condition on responsible agency depends in part on the responsible agent's having the capacity to hold herself and others responsible. On Michael McKenna's (2012) view, for example, the morally responsible agent is analogous to a competent speaker of a natural language—a speaker, that is, who is conversationally adept in that language. Much as a competent speaker's speaking skills are enmeshed with her interpretive skills (that is, with her ability to interpret and understand what other speakers of the language are saying, and to allow relevant norms of meaning to guide her own conversational forays), a morally responsible agent's competence as a responsible actor is enmeshed with her competence as an interpreter of the actions of others. One's ability to appreciate the significance of what others do, insofar as it manifests the quality of their will, is entwined with one's own ability coherently to manifest the quality of one's own will in one's own actions. One who is at sea in this system of "agent meaning" is not fully morally responsible, in a manner analogous to that in which a speaker who is at sea with respect to a language she cannot competently speak is not fully linguistically responsible for what she says or fails to say. On McKenna's model, an act performed by a morally responsible agent is analogous to an opening gambit in a conversation—a gambit to which others respond with further moves, which themselves invite yet further responses. Competent moral agents know their way around complex practices of praising, blaming, excusing, repenting, apologizing, forgiving, and so on and so forth.

What the PD cases suggest is that it is of even more fundamental importance that competent moral agents know their way around practices of holding and being held answerable—or, at least, that they are capable of finding their way around these practices with the right sort of support, guidance, or prompting from others. Agents who "shut down" in the face of strongly verdictive blame may still be responsible, and appropriately *held* responsible, insofar as they are competent (enough) participants in our answerability practices.

4 Answerability and Moral (Dis)Fluency

One thing the example of PD reveals, in my view, is that there isn't really any very sharp or clear line between those who are capable of holding themselves and others responsible and those who are not.[8] There are, to be sure, those who cannot be drawn into our responsibility practices, just as there are those who cannot be drawn into linguistic practices, because they lack underlying cognitive and (perhaps) emotional capacities. And perhaps (though I find it less likely) there are those who are perfectly fluent. But then there are the rest of us: the large majority of people who exhibit varying degrees of fluency or disfluency in both kinds of practice, in ways that fluctuate across the span of a life, and vary across different local subpractices or "idiolects." Moreover, the systems of meaning within which we maneuver are not themselves fixed, but instead morph and shift over time, and require the constant growth and development of interpretive and expressive skills. Individuals with PD may indeed be marginal, as far as their competence within the relevant practices goes, but they are not unreachable, and the form that therapeutic intervention takes with such individuals bears out this important point. The practice of *holding* them responsible would make no sense were it not for the fact that these service users are at least incipiently capable of holding others—and, importantly, themselves—responsible as well.

The forms of regard and reaction that are characteristic of strongly verdictive blaming do not seem fitting as default responses to those who manifest a significant degree of disfluency in the relevant responsibility practices—not because there is nothing to be done but shift to an "objective" (nonconversational) stance, but because further moral dialogue is therapeutically necessary, and, as noted above, strongly verdictive blaming is not at all likely to be a way forward in this particular kind of conversation. It is more likely to be received as a threatening show of power (or perhaps as mere irrational "upset"), and to shut conversation down. Avoiding confrontation with strongly verdictive blamers (and the kind of humiliating abasement they often seem to demand) may understandably take priority over reflection on and adjustment of one's own attitudes, responses, and future behaviors.

It is worth noting that strongly verdictive blame often has similar effects even on those who are highly fluent in the relevant responsibility practices. One might wonder, then, whether it is ever a fitting response. Fully exploring this question would take me beyond the bounds of this chapter, but I think the answer will turn at least in part on whether strongly verdictive blaming can have a morally defensible function even where it does obstruct constructive dialogue with wrongdoers. Such blame communicates a vilifying and even ostracizing message, one that arguably underscores the importance of the moral boundaries that have been crossed by a wrongdoer. It sends this message not just to the one blamed him- or herself, but often also to a wider community. It tends to discourage sympathetic responses to wrongdoers, instead encouraging the community to see wrongdoers primarily through the prism of their wrongdoing. In some cases, sending and reinforcing such a message may be appropriate or even morally required—perhaps most especially in cases in which the seriousness of the wrong, and the harm done to victims, is otherwise at risk of being overlooked or downplayed.[9] But in therapeutic cases—and, I suggest, in a range of cases that fall somewhere along the therapeutic/pedagogical continuum—the aims of constructive moral dialogue with a wrongdoer coexist with and place limits on the pursuit of wider communicative aims, such that strongly verdictive responses may be out of place.

In sum, I suggest that responses to those performing morally criticizable acts ought to be attuned to apparent levels of fluency or disfluency in relevant responsibility practices. Moreover (it is worth noting), they should also manifest sensitivity to would-be blamers' own relative fluency in unfamiliar or unusually complicated situations, and to their own contributions to conditions that impede fluency for others. (This last point becomes important in the next section, in my discussion of "self-defeating" destruction.) The point, again, is not that signs of disfluency should prompt us to shift out of the participant-reactive mode and opt for an objective stance. Rather, the point is that the contrast between situations calling for therapeutic and nontherapeutic stances is not as clear and sharp as it has been made out to be, and that the therapeutic stance should not be defined in *opposition* to the participant-reactive stance. In morally engaging one another, imperfectly responsible agents attempt to elicit, from one another and themselves, *more* perfectly responsible behavior. Responsible agency is always to some degree a work in progress, and responses that strike us as therapeutic, insofar as they contribute to such progress, may nonetheless be fully participatory, insofar as they operate by engaging others *as practitioners* (at least in prospect) from within the practices in question.

5 "Affluenza," Deference, and "Self-Defeating" Destruction

Let us consider some further examples that lend support to the above ideas.

5.1 Case 1: "Affluenza"

A few years ago, an unusual criminal defense hit the news with the case of Ethan Couch, the so-called Affluenza Teen. At age sixteen, an intoxicated Couch lost control of the pickup truck he was driving and caused a horrific accident that killed four pedestrians. His attorney, Scott Brown, argued that the blame should be placed not with Couch himself, but with his parents, who subjected him to very few limits and little discipline and repeatedly used their wealth to help him avoid consequences for his actions. All of this, Brown argued, left Couch unable to take laws and rules seriously. He required treatment, not punishment, for his actions. Couch initially received no prison sentence, but instead ten years of probation and a requirement to serve in an expensive rehabilitation center in California.[10]

The so-called affluenza defense has been widely derided, and the irony of the fact that Couch's parents' affluence (manifested here in their ability to pay for a pricey rehab program) again shielded him from consequences has not gone unnoticed.[11] There is something clearly unfair about the fact that wealthy and well-represented youth have such options available to them when others don't. But the attorney's argument does point to a familiar conundrum about blame and the limits of responsibility in cases of what is more commonly called a "deprived" upbringing.

Obviously, Couch's upbringing was not materially deprived (indeed, affluence was supposed to have been part of the problem). But the term "affluenza" is something of a misnomer for the background conditions to which Brown pointed in his defense. What was really at issue was an upbringing lacking in stability, reasonable discipline, and, generally, decent parenting. Couch was caught in the crossfire of an acrimonious divorce, manipulated for his parents' own ends, and generally left without any constructive guidance or limits in his tumultuous teen years. "No wonder!" one might well exclaim, upon reading the rather appalling details of the parental neglect he experienced.[12] We are susceptible to such sympathetic responses in cases of even more serious crimes (such as the case of Robert Harris, which was influentially discussed by Gary Watson in "Responsibility and the Limits of Evil" [2004].)[13] When we hold the pertinent background facts in view, we tend to struggle with the question of whether Harris (and, I suggest, Couch) are apt targets of blame, despite their terrible deeds.

Couch is not as extreme a case as Harris. (Harris, by all accounts, had a far worse childhood, and also appears to have been far more marginal in terms of his ability to hold himself responsible.) Couch is likely also less marginal than the service users discussed by Pickard. He does not, so far as I know, have PD or any other diagnosable disorder (I'm assuming here that "affluenza" is not truly a diagnosable disorder, which seems to be the consensus of the psychiatric community). Still, it is plausible that, given the facts about his upbringing, he was to some degree compromised in his ability to navigate responsibility practices. At the same time, though, it seems highly problematic to regard him as "not responsible" at all. Like those with PD, he is consciously aware of what he is doing and exercises choice in doing it (intoxication notwithstanding). Also like those with PD, he strikes us as someone who can and should be *held* responsible. Indeed, around the time of his initial sentencing in 2013, the media exploded with negative reactions to what many perceived as an inexcusable *failure* to hold Couch responsible for his actions. What sort of stance toward Couch would capture these various intuitions?

A stance that is, to some degree, therapeutic might in fact be morally defensible.[14] If I'm right, taking a more "therapeutic" approach to offenders who have difficulty in holding themselves answerable is not necessarily incompatible with holding them responsible. One might coherently reserve strongly verdictive blame for Couch's parents, while at the same time continuing to hold Couch himself responsible by holding him answerable for what he has done and attempting to draw him further into our shared responsibility practices, rather than effectively shunning, censuring, or punishing him.

I hope it is apparent that I am abstracting, here, from the very serious problem of differential treatment being accorded to offenders with wealth and privilege. Those with similar stories but no affluence to fall back on are done a serious injustice insofar as they are systematically treated more harshly and more dismissively for their offenses. If answerability without blame is appropriate for Couch, it is appropriate for many others as well.[15] Nor do I mean to be commenting directly on what consequences would be appropriate for Couch's crimes. Though such questions are of course related to questions about blame and answerability, they are not exactly the *same* questions. As Pickard also points out in her discussion of PD, holding responsible without blame might still involve the imposition of consequences, and it is an open question what those consequences should be.

5.2 Case 2: Deference

The second case I'll discuss is drawn from Carol Gilligan's *A Different Voice* (1982). My discussion here differs from that of other cases considered in this chapter, in that I will not be focusing on choices that are prima facie morally criticizable—except, perhaps, insofar as they manifest an undue amount of self-sacrifice on the part of those who make them.[16] In her chapter on abortion decisions, Gilligan interviews a number of troubled girls and women who seem to have difficulty taking responsibility for their decisions and actions. They feel helplessly constrained by their understanding of what others want from them and often describe themselves as "having no choice" about what to do when faced with a moral dilemma. For these women, any course of action other than the self-sacrificing one feels unthinkable, and their "chosen" course of action feels not so much chosen as inevitable. Gilligan points out that, while the feeling of powerlessness is very real for these women, it stems in large part from a confused abdication of responsibility for their own responses to their situations. Instead of seeing themselves as agents with a decision to make, they feel pushed and pulled by the demands of others and can assert themselves in only relatively inchoate ways. They do not see themselves as *choosing* what to do.

One of Gilligan's central themes in *In a Different Voice* is that socialization into gendered norms of deference deters women from taking ownership of their choices, putting culturally normative femininity at odds with the requirements of moral adulthood. Reaching moral maturity, on her view, requires overcoming certain aspects of feminine socialization. Agents who have deeply internalized norms of feminine deference do not in fact hold themselves answerable for their choices, but consistently defer responsibility to putatively authoritative others. Would strongly verdictive blame be an appropriate response to such agents, were they to engage in wrongdoing through an excess of deference?

Laurie Zoloth (2004) warns against the perils of regarding women who abdicate responsibility for morally bad choices simply as victims of patriarchy.[17] She emphasizes the fact that, however confused they may be about it, such women do exercise choice and ought to be held responsible for it. I agree. Like PD sufferers, "Affluenza Teen," and other recipients of notably flawed moral educations, women deeply socialized into deference may have limited resources for participating in our responsibility practices. Like these others, however, they are also consciously aware of what they are doing, and (despite their own confusion over the matter) they do exercise choice in doing it. From the fact that they do not now hold themselves answerable, we need not draw the conclusion that they lack the capacity to do so. It seems at least as natural in such cases as it does in the case of "Affluenza Teen" to respond to such agents by holding them answerable, and to aspire in so doing to *elicit* a greater degree of self-answerability in future deliberation and choice-making. But it also seems at least as counterproductive, in relation to this latter aim, to subject agents who are confused about the reach of their own agency to strongly verdictive blame. A message of condemnation or vilification is of little use to an agent who feels (however confusedly) that she had no choice but to do as she did.

As Gilligan aptly puts it, "The essence of moral decision is the exercise of choice and the willingness to accept responsibility for that choice" (1982, 67). Our responsibility practices include practices of holding answerable precisely in part to support and promote the willingness to exercise choice and accept responsibility for doing so—not just for agents with clinically diagnosable conditions, but for a great many agents who have been shaped, in one way or another, by incomplete or flawed moral educations or by adverse socialization. This is not a nonstandard or deviant use of our responsibility practices, but rather, something that is central to their very point. I return to this idea in the final section of the chapter.

5.3 Case 3: "Self-Defeating" Destruction

The third and final case I'll consider has a rather different moral, though not, as I'll try to show, an unrelated one. Many philosophical discussions of blame and blameworthiness proceed by taking for granted an epistemically privileged position in which the would-be blamer is assumed to be fully fluent in relevant responsibility practices, and in a position to assess the evidence, identify unjustified wrongdoing, and respond appropriately without significant moral education. This assumption neglects the possibility that the would-be blamer's own moral fluency might be compromised in ways of which she is unaware, and that in some cases it may be incumbent upon the blamer to withhold affective blame and hold *herself* answerable to external, critical perspectives on the choices and actions in question.

Perhaps the following case will serve as an illustrative example. In April of 2015, after the death of Freddie Gray in police custody, the city of Baltimore erupted in what has been variously described as riots, protests, an uprising, or quite simply, unrest (Blake 2016). In the course of ensuing events, arson and looting were reported, and a neighborhood CVS store was burned down. The latter incident was heavily covered by the media and became the cause of much public consternation. The mayor of Baltimore lamented the fact that the looters and arsonists were depriving neighborhood residents of their only place to fill prescriptions. President Obama urged a halt to what he described as "senseless violence and destruction" (Hyman 2015), and countless contributors to online comment sections wondered how "they" (the arsonists) could do such a thing to their own neighborhood, why anyone would engage in such irrational, self-defeating, short-sighted destruction.

This emphasis on the apparent senselessness, irrationality, and self-destructiveness of the acts in question frames the incident in familiar, but constraining terms: we are encouraged to see the perpetrators as having committed an unjustified wrong against innocent property owners and (indirectly) against members of their own community. Within these terms, the perpetrators are at best thought not to speak for the community but to be "bad actors" who ought to be called out and held responsible. If one rejects this narrative, one might be drawn in the opposite direction to argue that these so-called bad actors are in fact victims of their bleak circumstances, which have driven them to senseless acts of violence, and not to be held responsible after all. Neither response seems adequate. What neither allows is that the destructive acts might themselves have an expressive dimension, and constitute a move within (or at the margins of) our "conversational" responsibility practices.

Consider, for example, a dissenting conclusion drawn by a commentator for the online political opinion forum *Daily Kos*, upon reflecting on the disproportionate outrage of white Americans against those involved in the "unrest," as opposed to those responsible for police brutality against black Americans:

> As a white male, I don't particularly care for looting and rioting. I wouldn't like to be one of the store or property owners who will have to replace or rebuild. *But I'm forced to recognize this destruction as the final option for a group of people so systematically disenfranchised that their voices have not been heard.* And I have to ask myself a difficult question— who is the worse moral monster: The young man whose hopelessness leads him to jump on the hood of a cop car, or me, a person who has acquiesced to a system that creates justified hopelessness among young people in places like Baltimore? (DuBose 2015; my italics)

This sort of critical self-reflectiveness requires willingness to allow oneself to entertain counternarratives that cast apparently senseless acts in a different light. It requires opening oneself to the possibility that the acts in question are *not* senseless after all, but instead convey a message—and then making a concerted effort to hold *oneself* answerable to their implicit challenge. Strongly verdictive blame can, of course, be countered and overcome—but the attitudes that underlie such blame are not themselves characteristic of self-critical reflection. Openness to self-criticism requires a kind of humility about one's judgments and a willingness to summon or be summoned into dialogue rather than a sense of entitlement to inflict punishing attitudes on others.

Holding answerable while withholding (strongly verdictive) blame permits reflection on background conditions against which apparently senseless acts take on meaning and call for response. The claim is not that apparently unjustified acts will turn out to be either excused or justified in light of such reflection. DuBose, in the remarks cited above, does not seem to be suggesting that burning down a CVS is itself either justified or excused (though he is, clearly, arguing that the anger *expressed* by that act is justified). The claim is, instead, that a sense of entitlement to moral anger, resentment, and other "punishing" emotions (to use Pickard's evocative phrase) toward the perpetrator(s), will, at least for some respondents, turn out to be inapt—as will a sense of entitlement to dismiss the anger expressed by the offending act itself. DuBose's remarks suggest that, for him and other white Americans, verdictive blame would be an unfitting and counterproductive response—unfitting because unfair, in light of white America's complicity in the exclusions that undermine the ordinary exercise of normative powers for black citizens of Baltimore, and counterproductive because of the way in which such blame reinforces the very exclusions against which the act protests. In such cases, overcoming barriers to full participation in responsibility practices requires those who have been complicit (knowingly or not) to hold *themselves* answerable, a response that verdictive blame tends to crowd out.

6 Responsibility and the Exercise of Normative Powers

Of the cases considered in section 5, the first two are continuous in important ways with the case of PD considered by Pickard, insofar as all involve a degree of moral disfluency that is located on the side of the agent in question and concerns her inner, psychological states and self-relations. The third differs in that the "disfluency" of the agents engaging in apparently self-defeating destruction is (as I read it) both a product and expression of their exclusion from responsibility practices that *should* allow them to make moral claims and hold others answerable but do not. This inability is social in a more straightforward sense than the first two, although social factors are implicated in all three. What is it that binds the above cases together and makes them all variations on one theme?

I propose that all are cases in which the ability to exercise important normative powers is relationally compromised in one way or another (but not precluded by, for example, a lack of necessary cognitive or psychological capacities). One way of being incapacitated, with respect to one's ability to exercise such powers, is through having one's own ability to hold oneself and others answerable compromised: through lack of moral education (as in the case of Affluenza Teen), or through adverse socialization (as in the case of Gilligan's subjects), or through traumatizing experiences that leave one with a diagnosable disorder (as in the case of individuals with PD). But another way of being incapacitated,

with respect to the exercise of normative powers within our responsibility practices, is socio-relational: one may be excluded from those practices by a lack of
uptake for one's attempts to hold others responsible and make claims on one's
own behalf. How could protest over systematic exclusion possibly take the form
of an ordinary conversational move, when the problem is that no one is listening
in the first place?

To refrain from strongly verdictive blame is, I think, an appropriate response to
all three kinds of disfluency. With respect to agents whose upbringing or personal
history has left them indisposed to hold themselves answerable, acting as "judge,
jury, and executioner" conveys a censorious message *to* the wrongdoer (or to other
members of the community) at the expense of facilitating moral engagement *with*
the wrongdoer. Holding answerable without (strongly verdictive) blame reverses
this sense of priority, and, to borrow a phrase from Victoria McGeer, allows one
to "scaffold the moral agency of others" (2012, 9). In cases like the CVS arson and
others, where questions of *standing* to blame arise, tendencies toward strongly
verdictive blame again reveal a misplaced sense of moral priority, given one's own
complicity or hypocrisy, and an underlying sort of motivated ignorance of the
expressive value of a supposedly senseless act. But loss of standing to blame in
the strongly verdictive sense does *not* undermine one's standing to hold answerable. Engaging in moral dialogue in such cases (as opposed to retreating to the
objective stance) has the potential to at one and the same time strengthen one's
own disposition to hold oneself answerable, while improving one's uptake for the
claims and challenges of others. Holding others answerable in a dialogical mode
requires one to give uptake to their conversational moves; that is, it requires one
to hold oneself answerable to *their* perspectives as well.

One might object that, in the case of serious wrongdoing, only strongly verdictive blame (and the "punishing" anger or resentment it carries) actually expresses
our commitment to and investment in moral values that have been violated.
I agree that anger and resentment do sometimes express a deep commitment
to and investment in moral values, and, when we have been directly wronged, in
our own moral worth. Unfortunately, however, they sometimes instead manifest
a kind of defensiveness or insecurity about one's own standing—a defensiveness
that comes out in the sense of entitlement identified by Pickard. A feeling of
entitlement to subject another to punishing attitudes tends to set the other up
as one's adversary or, worse yet, one's target, rather than as a potential partner in
moral dialogue. Blame can in this way undermine not just compassion but also
mutual answerability.

Recent philosophical defenses of blame are a useful corrective to the idea that
blame is *never* a fitting response, and that it lacks any moral value. But blame's
lingering bad reputation, I would argue, is not entirely undeserved—in some
cases in which it is appropriate to hold others answerable, and even to be angry,

there is nonetheless a sense in which blame is *not* an appropriate response to their wrongdoing. Some disagreement over blame's moral value can, I've suggested, be explained by the fact that "blame" is not just one thing. The term may refer either to an attitude or a speech act, and, indeed, it may refer to speech acts of various different sorts. I have used the term 'strongly verdictive' to pick out the sort of blaming that passes judgment on the wrongdoer as morally flawed or defective, and treats him or her as deserving of the blamer's hostile or "punishing" reactions in virtue of this fault. This kind of blaming, I have argued, tends to discourage or even preclude engagement in further moral dialogue with wrongdoers, and is particularly destructive in cases in which such dialogue would serve legitimate therapeutic or pedagogical purposes. But it may be destructive more generally, as well. Moral life is, after all, to a large degree constituted by moral dialogue—and we have reason to be wary of practices that subordinate the facilitation of such dialogue to other moral aims. To hold one another answerable in a nonjudgmental mode is to refuse to give up on one another as responsible moral interlocutors. Holding answerable without strongly verdictive blame can express a serious, nonsuperficial commitment to moral values. But more to the point, perhaps, it also expresses a commitment directly to those we address—a commitment to engage with them as co-inhabitants of one and the same moral community, regardless of the myriad ways in which they (and we) undoubtedly fall short of its governing ideals.[18]

Notes

1. The responsibility-shifting critique rests on the background presumption that blamers are rarely (if ever) *justified* in assigning responsibility to the others—a presumption that is clearly questionable, and potentially pernicious, since it may serve to silence or dismiss the expression of legitimate concerns and claims by those who have been wronged.

2. I will say more about the relationship between anger and blame below. I explore reasons for disagreeing with Nussbaum's assessment of anger in my review of *Anger and Forgiveness: Resentment, Generosity, Justice* (Westlund 2017).

3. Cold blame, as Wallace (2008) and others construe it, seems to me compatible with feeling entitled to the negative emotions involved in affective blame, but just not feeling those emotions themselves. So I take it to be a slightly different attitude from the one Pickard describes as detached blame.

4. Pickard discusses various techniques that service providers might employ—including focusing one's attention on the service user's past history—to tamp down counterproductive impulses.

5. Strictly speaking, Austin treats blame as "half descriptive" rather than purely performative. Blame's purely performative counterparts, in the passage under discussion, are criticism and censure (Austin 1962, 83).

6. I would quibble with this equivalence, since I think 'holding,' especially as it figures in the phrases 'holding responsible' and 'holding answerable,' itself has nonverdictive senses. I use these phrases in a nonverdictive sense myself in what follows.

7. Wallace (2008) argues that holding another or oneself to a moral expectation must itself be understood in terms of dispositions to respond with blame (and corresponding attitudes such as guilt). On my view, holding to an expectation does require dispositions to respond in a way

that marks unwillingness simply to "let go" of the behavior in question, but I think there are ways of refusing to let go that do not involve the anger or resentment characteristic of blame.

8. Strawson himself acknowledges that a "simple opposition" between the participant-reactive and objective stances is too crude, and he observes that there will be cases that straddle the two kinds of attitude. He discusses parents' attitudes toward children in this regard, as well as therapists' attitudes toward their patients. In the case of children, he describes parents' attitudes as a compromise, shifting back and forth "between objectivity of attitude and developed human attitudes" (2003, 88). In the case of the therapist, he says, "*His* objectivity of attitude, *his* suspension of the ordinary moral reactive attitudes, is profoundly modified by the fact that the aim of the enterprise is to make such suspension unnecessary or less necessary" (88). What Strawson describes in these passages still seems to involve more of a *suspension* of participant-reactivity than I have in mind. I will argue that some modes of participant-reactivity themselves have a therapeutic or quasi-therapeutic dimension, such that one is not shifting back and forth between attitudes but adopting an attitude that combines features of both.

9. I am thinking, here, of the now-infamous "Stanford rape case," in which the relatively light sentence imposed on the convicted assailant (a celebrated student athlete whose Olympic dreams were dashed by his crime) struck many as reflecting precisely this sort of imbalance. See Koren (2016) for one account of the case.

10. Couch later broke the terms of his probation and has since been sentenced to two years in prison.

11. See, for example, Rosenberg 2013; Zurcher 2013.

12. See Mooney 2015.

13. Watson (2004) discusses the ambivalence we are likely to feel toward Harris, who was sentenced to death for the brutal murder of two teenaged boys in 1978. The utter callousness with which Harris committed his crime tends to make him an "'archetypical candidate' for blame" (Watson 2004, 238), while his sister's heartbreaking description of the abuse he suffered as a child nonetheless tends to elicit compassion, and a sense that it is "no wonder" he turned out as he did (243). Sarah Buss also considers cases of disadvantaged upbringing in her paper "Justified Wrongdoing" (1997).

14. I say "might," both because I recognize this is a controversial case, and because we now know that Couch did not in fact respond well to therapeutic intervention.

15. In one way, the Couch case is a refreshing corrective to the idea that *materially* disadvantaged upbringings are likely to be the *morally* disadvantaged ones. If nothing else, the Couch case demonstrates that material privilege is no safeguard against disastrously bad moral education. That Couch should be treated more leniently by the justice system than similarly affected children of materially disadvantaged parents is, of course, unfair. But at least one commentator suggested that the lesson to be drawn is not that all offending children should be thrown on what he calls the "trash heap" of the Texas prison system, but that the state should find a way of doing better by all of them (Schutze 2013).

16. The remainder of this paragraph is a slightly modified version of a passage from my earlier paper "Autonomy and Self-Care" (Westlund 2014).

17. It should be noted that Zoloth's focus is on women who commit violent crimes, whereas Gilligan's focus is on the personal choice either to terminate or carry a pregnancy to term. Gilligan does not imply that any of her subjects are making morally wrong (much less criminal) choices, whereas there is no doubt in Zoloth's cases that the choices in question are both criminal and morally horrific.

18. I would like to thank Katrina Hutchison, Catriona Mackenzie, and Marina Oshana for their insightful comments on an earlier draft of this chapter. I also benefitted from discussion of the chapter at the 2016 meeting of the North American Society for Social Philosophy in Ottawa, and am grateful to the UW-Milwaukee Graduate School for supporting my travel to that conference. I am especially grateful to the members of the workshop Milwaukee-Area Women in Philosophy for an extremely helpful and constructive discussion in fall of 2016, which prompted me to reformulate some of the chapter's central ideas in important ways. I also received very helpful feedback at the Northwestern Society for Theory of Ethics and Politics conference in the spring of 2017, and I would like to thank Mihailis Diamantis and Per-Erik Milam for their detailed written comments on the version of the chapter I presented there.

References

Alasko, Carl. 2011. *Beyond Blame: Freeing Yourself from the Most Toxic Form of Emotional Bullsh*t*. New York: Tarcher/Penguin.

Allais, Lucy. 2008. "Dissolving Reactive Attitudes: Forgiving and Understanding." *South African Journal of Philosophy* 27 (3): 1–23.

Austin, John L. 1962. *How to Do Things with Words*. 2nd ed. Edited by J. O. Urmson and Marina Sbisa. Cambridge, MA: Harvard University Press.

Bell, Macalester. 2013. *Hard Feelings: The Moral Psychology of Contempt*. Oxford: Oxford University Press.

Blake, John. 2016. "Baltimore Faces Its Original Sin a Year after Riots." CNN, April 25. http://www.cnn.com/2016/04/22/us/baltimore-future/.

Buss, Sarah. 1997. "Justified Wrongdoing." *Nous* 31 (3): 337–369.

DuBose, William ("Grizzard"). 2015. "The Dominant White Response to Baltimore Shows Why Black Residents Are Justified in Their Anger." *Daily Kos*, April 28. https://www.dailykos.com/stories/2015/4/28/1380944/-The-Dominant-White-Response-to-Baltimore-Shows-Why-Black-Residents-are-Justified-in-their-Anger.

Gilligan, Carol. 1982. *In a Different Voice*. Cambridge, MA: Harvard University Press.

Hyman, Louis. 2015. "Why the CVS Burned." *Slate*, May 1. http://www.slate.com/articles/news_and_politics/crime/2015/05/baltimore_riots_it_wasn_t_thugs_looting_for_profit_it_was_a_protest_against.html.

Koren, Marina. 2016. "Telling the Story of the Stanford Rape Case." *Atlantic*, June 6. http://www.theatlantic.com/news/archive/2016/06/stanford-sexual-assault-letters/485837/.

McGeer, Victoria. 2012. "Co-reactive Attitudes and the Making of Moral Community." In *Emotions, Imagination, and Moral Reasoning*, edited by R. Langdon and C. Mackenzie, 299–326. New York: Psychology Press.

McKenna, Michael. 2012. *Conversation and Responsibility*. Oxford: Oxford University Press.

Mooney, Michael J. 2015. "The Worst Parents Ever." *D Magazine*, May. http://www.dmagazine.com/publications/d-magazine/2015/may/affluenza-the-worst-parents-ever-ethan-couch?single=1.

Nussbaum, Martha. 2016. *Anger and Forgiveness: Resentment, Generosity, Justice*. Oxford: Oxford University Press, 2016.

Pettigrove, Glen. 2012. "Meekness and 'Moral' Anger." *Ethics* 122 (2): 341–370.

Pickard, Hannah. 2011. "Responsibility without Blame: Empathy and the Effective Treatment of Personality Disorder." *Philosophy, Psychiatry, & Psychology* 13 (3): 209–224.

Rosenberg, Robin S. 2013. "There's No Defense for Affluenza." *Slate*, December 17. http://www.slate.com/articles/health_and_science/medical_examiner/2013/12/ethan_couch_affluenza_defense_critique_of_the_psychology_of_no_consequences.html.

Schutze, Jim. 2013. "Ethan Couch Should Have Gone to Prison, but Justice? There's No Justice for Texas Kids." *Dallas Observer*, December 13. http://www.dallasobserver.com/news/ethan-couch-should-have-gone-to-prison-but-justice-theres-no-justice-for-texas-kids-7105977.

Sher, George. 2007. *In Praise of Blame*. Oxford: Oxford University Press.

Strawson, Peter F. 2003. "Freedom and Resentment." In *Free Will*, edited by Gary Watson, 72–93. Oxford: Oxford University Press.

Wallace, R. Jay. 2008. "Emotions, Expectations, and Responsibility." In *Free Will and Reactive Attitudes: Perspectives on P. F. Strawson's "Freedom and Resentment,"* edited by Michael McKenna and Paul Russell, 157–185. Surrey, UK: Ashgate Publishing Company.

Watson, Gary. 2004. "Responsibility and the Limits of Evil: Variations on a Strawsonian Theme." In *Agency and Answerability: Selected Essays*, 219–259. Oxford: Oxford University Press.

Westlund, Andrea. 2014. "Autonomy and Self-Care." In *Autonomy, Oppression, and Gender*, edited by Andrea Veltman and Mark Piper, 181–198. Oxford: Oxford University Press.

Westlund, Andrea. 2017. Review of *Anger and Forgiveness: Resentment, Generosity, Justice*, by Martha Nussbaum. *Ethics* 127 (3): 797–802.

Zoloth, Laurie. 2004. "Into the Woods: Killer Mothers, Feminist Ethics, and the Problem of Evil." In *Women and Gender in Jewish Philosophy*, edited by Hava Tirosh-Samuelson, 204–233. Bloomington: Indiana University Press.

Zurcher, Anthony. 2013. "'Affluenza Defense': Rich, Privileged, and Unaccountable." *Echo Chambers* (blog), BBC, December 13. http://www.bbc.com/news/blogs-echochambers-25374458.

11

Personal Relationships and Blame

Scanlon and the Reactive Attitudes

BENNETT W. HELM

1 Introduction

Traditionally, responsibility has been understood to be a feature of a particular agent—deriving from the structure of her desires or from her capacity for contra-causal freedom, for example. Consequently, it is appropriate for others to *hold* someone responsible (by praising or blaming her, for example) only if she already *is* responsible. Strawsonian accounts of responsibility reverse this priority, understanding our practices of holding each other responsible to be primary, and understanding what it is to be responsible in terms of those practices. One might well think that at issue in the Strawsonian alternative is not simply our actual practices of holding each other responsible that might be found in a given community, practices that might well treat certain subgroups unjustly. Rather, what matter are the conditions of the *appropriateness* of holding others responsible, so that the distinctive Strawsonian move is to understand such conditions independently of and prior to the agent's *being* responsible (Wallace 1994).[1]

To make sense of the conditions of the appropriateness of holding someone responsible, Strawsonians appeal primarily (or even exclusively) to the *reactive attitudes.* The reactive attitudes are emotions like resentment, indignation, and guilt, as well as their positive counterparts, gratitude, approbation, and self-approbation—emotions in terms of which, in the context of normal human relationships, we praise or blame each other and so hold each other responsible. One way to criticize such Strawsonian accounts of responsibility, therefore, is to question whether the reactive attitudes are adequate to the job. In effect, this is Tim Scanlon's strategy in calling into question reactive attitude accounts of blame.[2] Central to Scanlon's discussion is his appeal to the variability of blame: "different reactions [to a wrong] are appropriate, depending on one's relation to the person who fails to show the concern demanded" (2008, 128), so that some people, in certain relationships with a wrongdoer, can appropriately blame the wrongdoer in ways that others of us cannot. Consequently, he concludes, blame is deeply personal: "the content of *blame* depends on the significance, for the person doing the blaming, of the agent and of what he has done" (145). I shall argue that this is a mistake: in order to account for the appropriateness of blame, the significance of the wrongdoing relevant to blame is fundamentally the significance to members of a particular community such that the relevant relationship is not primarily a personal relationship but rather a communal relationship. Nonetheless, as I shall argue, there is still room within a broadly Strawsonian account to accommodate the evident variability of blame to which Scanlon rightly points us.

2   Scanlon on Blame

Consider the following example that motivates much of Scanlon's account of blame (Scanlon 2008, 129–130). Your close friend, Joe, betrays you by revealing to others at a party embarrassing secrets about you behind your back. Although Joe feels remorse for what he has done and likely will not do it again, you nonetheless are faced with the question of how to respond. Scanlon thinks such a response might involve three separable elements: (1) a possible judgment about the significance to you of what Joe has done and what this reveals about his attitude toward your relationship; (2) possibly revised attitudes toward Joe in light of this judgment; and (3) possible actions you might take toward Joe, such as confronting him. The first of these, Scanlon claims, is a *judgment of blameworthiness*, and the second is the *blaming*. Thus he says,

> [T]o claim that a person is *blameworthy* for an action is to claim that the action shows something about the agent's attitudes toward others that impairs the relations that others can have with him or her. To *blame* a person is to judge him or her to be blameworthy and to take your relationship with him or her to be modified in a way that this judgment of impaired relations holds to be appropriate. (128–129)[3]

In clarifying this basic account, Scanlon provides some details about what he means by a "relationship" and by "impairments" to such relationships:

> A relationship is constituted by certain attitudes and dispositions. Central among these are intentions and expectations about how the parties will act toward one another. But relationships also include

intentions and expectations about the feelings that the parties have for one another, and the considerations that they are disposed to respond to and see as reasons. (131–132)

Just what sorts of attitudes, dispositions, and expectations serve to define relationships is something Scanlon leaves open, presumably so as to be able to accommodate the wide variety of possible relationships we might have. Concerning impairments of these relationships, Scanlon says,

> Impairment of the kind I refer to occurs when one party, while stand-ing in the relevant relation to another person, holds attitudes toward that person that are ruled out by the standards of that relationship, thus making it appropriate for the other party to have attitudes other than those that the relationship normally involves. (2008, 135)

Again, Scanlon leaves open just how one party's attitudes make appropriate pos-sible changes in the other's attitudes, which once again might seem reasonable given the variety of possible relationships.

Nonetheless, this openness is frustrating. Presumably not just any type of relationship is going to be relevant to understanding blame and its appropriate-ness. To take an easy case, the mere fact that I believe you are more than one meter tall and am disposed to say so to your face when asked, together with your expectation that I have this attitude and disposition, is presumably not enough for us to have the sort of relationship for which questions of blame are at issue; indeed, these attitudes, dispositions, and expectations seem to be utterly irrel-evant to blame. Another problematic case would be that of my "relationship" with my arch-rival, a relationship in which we each intend, and expect the other to intend, to despise and harm the other. Is this sort of relationship relevant to blame? Why or why not? What about the more realistic and more problematic relationship of domination between abusive and abused spouses within which the abused spouse acquiesces to her subordinate position as reason for certain kinds of abusive treatment: would violating the mutual expectations and atti-tudes defining this relationship, thereby impairing that relationship, be for that reason blameworthy? The problem is that Scanlon has not provided a principled reason for a particular delineation of which relationships, defined by which atti-tudes, and so on, are relevant to blame as he understands it.[4]

This lack of clarity in the notion of a relationship results in similar lack of clarity concerning the nature of the sort of impairment relevant to blame. When my arch-rival does me a good turn for my sake, thereby acting in ways ruled out by the standards of our "relationship" and violating the expectations I have for his conduct (as well as his standing intention to harm me), has he impaired our "relationship" in a way that is blameworthy? Do I have reason to resent him and, as part of holding a grudge against him, refrain from further wronging him— from continuing to act in accordance with the terms of our relationship—until that relationship can be repaired? Of course, Scanlon notes that there can be relationships that are not morally defensible, so that one would not be genuinely blameworthy for violating the standards of such relationships, and that may well be the case here—and certainly is in the case of the abusive spouse. Yet even if true, this does not avoid the criticism insofar as it brings to bear considerations outside the relationship itself, whereas my questions are focused on the way violations of the standards of this particular relationship can provide pro tanto reasons for blame. In the case of my "relationship" with my arch-rival, the norms of that "relationship"—the attitudes and behaviors we each expect of the other—are apparently not standards in the relevant sense. The same goes for relationships of domination and abuse. Once again, Scanlon has failed to provide a principled way of understanding this notion of a standard or how violations of such standards can make blame appropriate.

Setting these worries aside for the moment, Scanlon's claim is that his understanding of blame and blameworthiness can make sense of the way in which the appropriateness of blame varies depending on one's relationship to the wrongdoer. Return to the example of your friend Joe's betrayal of you: it is because Joe has harmed *your* relationship with him that it is appropriate for you to blame him. Perhaps I as another of Joe's friends would also be in a position to blame him, for his actions with regard to you may reveal something about his attitudes toward friends quite generally and, in particular, toward *me*, attitudes that would make appropriate revisions in my attitude toward him—my blaming him. Even so, the ways in which it is appropriate for you to blame Joe—the adjustments to your attitudes and intentions toward him— will almost certainly be different from the ways in which it is appropriate for me to blame him, for he has not impaired our relationship in the way he has impaired yours. Furthermore, a complete stranger would not be in a position to blame Joe at all: "A third party can judge that the action of betrayal has this meaning for you [of impairing the relationship], but because he is not a participant in the relationship to begin with, he is not in a position to adjust his attitudes towards the guilty party in the relevant way" (Scanlon 2008, 137). To a certain extent, this seems right: not just anyone has the appropriate standing to blame, and whether one does or not depends in some sense on the relationship one has with the wrongdoer.

Nonetheless, Scanlon seems to misinterpret his own insight. Thus he says,

> A judgment of blameworthiness is one that anyone can make, however
> distant he or she may be from the relevant agent and action. But the

content of *blame* depends on the significance, for the person doing the blaming, of the agent and of what he has done. . . . Blame has the most substantial content for people who interact with the agent in some way, as friends or family members, or as neighbors or coworkers or fellow citizens. (145)[5]

By the 'content of blame', Scanlon seems to mean not merely that, for example, one finds the wrongdoer to be responsible for a certain type of offense; after all, that would seem to be a judgment of blameworthiness rather than blame itself. Rather, the content of blame must include not simply such an evaluation but also the revised attitudes the blamer comes to have toward the wrongdoer—revised attitudes that themselves "depend on the [blamer's] exact relation to the blameworthy action and the attitudes it reveals" (146). This means, Scanlon thinks, that the actions of a person who lived long ago can have "mainly vicarious significance" for us. Thus he claims that a judgment of blameworthiness is

> a judgment about how it would have been appropriate for those closer to the agent to understand their relations with him. . . . But the idea that we ourselves *blame* him for what he did can sound somewhat odd. As our distance from a person increases, blame becomes simply a negative evaluation, or attitude of disapproval, and even this evaluative element can seem pointless grading unless we have some particular reason to be concerned with what the person in question was like. (146)

This seems wrong: I may not merely judge that President James Buchanan is blameworthy for his cowardly acquiescence to slavery, which was a contributing cause of the US Civil War; I may also *feel* indignation and disapprobation directed at him as my attitude toward him changes upon learning of his actions, policies, and attitudes with regard to slavery and states rights. To blame President Buchanan in this way and not merely to judge him blameworthy seems fully appropriate, even though his actions and attitudes apparently have no direct personal significance for me.

The underlying problem, I argue, is that, by wrongly emphasizing the *personal* significance the wrongdoing has for oneself and, where it exists, one's own *personal* relationship with the wrongdoer, Scanlon's understanding of blame is unacceptably egocentric. Rather, as I shall argue, the sort of significance relevant for blame is more generally a significance those actions and attitudes have *for us* members of a community. Thus, I shall argue, the sort of *relationship* relevant to blame is that of co-membership in a certain form of community, and the relevant sort of *impairment* of such relationships is one that affects not just the wrongdoer and the blamer but in addition the whole community. For, as I shall argue, it is only in this way that we can properly explain—what Scanlon does not—why particular changes in one's attitudes toward the wrongdoer are justified. Moreover, I shall argue, we should give an account of blame in terms of the reactive attitudes.

On a basic reactive attitude account of blame, to be blameworthy is to be an appropriate target of negative reactive attitudes, and to blame someone is to take up one or another negative reactive attitude toward her. Scanlon, while praising such accounts for accommodating the variability of blame as dependent on the relevant relationships, criticizes them for failing to accommodate the variety of ways in which blame involves modifications in one's relationship with the wrongdoer: merely feeling a reactive emotion like resentment is not enough.

> I do not deny that these attitudinal responses can be appropriate, and that they are elements of blame. But an account of blame that focused only on these elements would be too thin. Blame also involves other modifications of our attitudes toward a person, including changes in our readiness to interact with him or her in specific ways . . . [such as] refus[ing] to make agreements with that person or to enter into other specific relations that involve trust and reliance. (Scanlon 2008, 143)

Scanlon's remarks here are surely right: if we are to understand blame, we need to think about the role it plays within particular human relationships, and the basic reactive attitude account of blame fails to do this. Indeed, Scanlon's attention to this point is a substantial advance in our understanding of blame. Does this imply that any account that focuses only on the reactive attitudes must be too thin?

As I shall argue, the answer is no; rather, what is too thin is Scanlon's understanding of the reactive attitudes. As I have long argued (see for example Helm 2001) and sketch again in section 3, emotions play a central role in constituting a subject's caring about things, and the reactive attitudes in particular constitute not only respect (in something like Darwall's sense of "recognition respect" [2006]), as a distinctive kind of caring, but also a distinctive kind of community, which I shall call a "community of respect." It is such respect that, as I argue in sections 4, 5, 6, and 7, can provide a principled account of the sorts of relationships and impairments of relationships to which Scanlon rightly directs us in our thinking about blame; yet the way such respect is essentially embedded within communities reveals a dimension to our understanding of blame and relationships not found in Scanlon's work and that can overcome the egocentrism of his account.

3 Emotions, Caring, and the Reactive Attitudes

To care about something, to find it to have worth or "import" to you, is to have a kind of concern for its well-being that involves both a vigilance for things that happen to it and a preparedness to act on its behalf. Such vigilance and preparedness, and hence the caring itself, are intelligible in terms of rational patterns of emotions.[6]

Emotions have several different kinds of objects. Most obvious is their *target*: that which an emotion is directed at and which gets evaluated by the emotion in some way. Each type of emotion evaluates its target in a distinctive way—in light of that emotion type's *formal object*. Thus, fear evaluates its targets as dangerous, and anger evaluates them as offensive, and so danger and offensiveness are the formal objects of fear and anger, respectively. We must also consider why in having an emotion we evaluate the target in this way: what is it that, for example, makes the kids playing baseball in the street be something that, in fearing them, I find to be dangerous? Here we must consider a third object of emotions, their *focus*: the background object (1) that one cares about and (2) that in the circumstances normally makes intelligible why the target is appropriately evaluated in terms of the formal object. Thus, my fear of the kids might be focused on my car, which the kids may well damage by playing baseball, and so it is the import of my car that explains why I evaluate the kids here and now as dangerous.

In this example, my fear of the kids is part of my vigilance for the well-being of my car, and it also disposes me to act in various ways to protect my car: to ask the kids to move their game or to move my car out of danger. As such, it is plain that my fear is rationally connected to other emotions and desires with the same focus. Most obviously, my fear of the kids—a forward-looking emotion—rationally ought to become anger at them—a backward-looking emotion—when they break my windshield with an errant fly ball. These rational interconnections extend to emotions with a common focus but different targets: I ought also to feel fear when a hailstorm approaches, upset and annoyed when a large tree branch falls on my car, and angry when I discover that my car has been stolen. For each emotion is, in effect, a commitment to the import of its focus and so to having other emotions with that same focus when otherwise warranted. In this way, emotions essentially form projectible, rational patterns. My claim, which I cannot defend here (see Helm 2001, especially chapters 2–4 for detailed arguments), is that by constituting our vigilance for, and preparedness to act on behalf of, its focus, such a pattern of emotions—as well as corresponding desires and evaluative judgments—constitutes my *caring* about that focus.

Given this account of emotions and caring, we can define different classes of emotions in terms of their potential to share a common focus and to join together in such rational patterns. Indeed, distinctive classes of emotions constitute distinctive kinds of caring. Thus, the common emotions I have been discussing so far—hope, fear, satisfaction, disappointment, etc.—form patterns that constitute a basic sort of caring, roughly finding something worth pursuing or preserving. I have elsewhere identified what I call "person-focused emotions"—emotions like pride, shame, and certain forms of anxiety and self-confidence—as a distinctive class that forms rational patterns constitutive of our *valuing* things (finding them to be a part of the kind of life worth one's living) and *loving* people (Helm 2010). As I shall suggest now, the reactive attitudes themselves form a distinctive pattern of emotions with a common focus, constitutive of our *respecting* members of a community as a part of *revering* the community itself.

The reactive attitudes are emotions responding to the good or ill will of others (or oneself) in such a way as to hold them responsible (or oneself to take responsibility) for upholding or failing to uphold particular norms. Peter F. Strawson (1962), who introduced the notion of a reactive attitude, identifies three types: the *personal reactive attitudes*, like gratitude and resentment, are responses to the good or ill will someone shows to you; the *vicarious reactive attitudes*, like approbation and indignation, are responses to the good or ill will someone shows to a third party; and the *self reactive attitudes*, like self-approbation and guilt, are responses to the good or ill will you show to another.

Like other emotions, the reactive attitudes exhibit intrapersonal rational interconnections: other things being equal, if I resent you for harming me, I ought also to feel gratitude toward you when you benefit me; likewise, if I resent you for doing something to me, I ought also resent others for doing the same thing to me, and I ought to feel indignation (or guilt) when I find one person (possibly myself) doing that same thing to someone else. Yet part of what is especially interesting about the reactive attitudes is that their rational interconnections are essentially interpersonal: one person's reactive attitudes are rationally tied to those of others, *addressing* them and *calling* on them for a response (see, for example, Watson 2008, 122–123). Thus, if you resent me for harming you, then (other things being equal) I ought to feel guilty and others ought to feel disapprobation or indignation directed at me. The rational interconnections here are among the personal reactive attitudes of one person (the "victim," as I shall say), the self-reactive attitudes of another (the "perpetrator," who is the target of the victim's personal reactive attitudes), and the vicarious reactive attitudes of still others (the "witnesses").[7] In this way, the reactive attitudes form interpersonal rational patterns.

Since Strawson, philosophers have understood reactive attitudes to be backward-looking emotions, responsive to a notable upholding or violation of a norm that has already happened. As I have argued elsewhere, we should also recognize trust and distrust to be forward-looking reactive attitudes (Helm 2014b). After all, what makes a particular type of emotion (such as resentment) belong to a certain class of emotions (such as the reactive attitudes) is that it joins together with other emotions in that class to form rational patterns constitutive of a distinctive form of caring. Trust and distrust fit the bill: they are rationally connected to other reactive attitudes, as when personal reactive trust ought to transition to resentment when one's trust is betrayed or to gratitude when it is upheld; the same goes for self-reactive trust transitioning to guilt or self-approbation or vicarious reactive trust transitioning to indignation or approbation, as well as, mutatis mutandis, for distrust. Thus, trust and distrust are forward-looking reactive attitudes. (This will be important for my account of the role of personal relationships in blame.)

If the reactive attitudes form such interpersonal rational patterns, what is their common focus and what distinctive form of caring do these patterns constitute? As I have argued elsewhere (Helm 2014a, 2015), the reactive attitudes are focused on, and so involve a complex concern for, both particular people and particular norms, all as part of a particular community. In part, we do not feel the reactive attitudes toward just anyone who notably upholds or violates a particular norm; the norm must be the norm of a community to which the target of our reactive attitudes belongs. After all, it is only members of my family whom I hold responsible to the norms of my family; outsiders, not bound by its norms, are not proper targets of the reactive attitudes. In this way, having a reactive attitude involves recognizing the *standing* of the target, the perpetrator, as bound by the norm and so as a member of the community. In addition, one's reactive attitude calls on the perpetrator to feel self-approbation or guilt and thereby to hold herself responsible; in this way, one's reactive attitude also involves recognizing her *authority* to hold not only herself but also others responsible to the community's norms. Moreover, this "call" of the reactive attitudes extends to other members of the community—the witnesses—to hold the perpetrator responsible as well, and so it involves recognizing their standing and authority as members of the community.

In short, particular reactive attitudes involve a commitment to and recognition of the import both of the perpetrator and witnesses as having standing and authority within the community and of the norms of that community, all as a part of an overall commitment to the import of the community itself. To be a *witness*, then, is not simply to be one who observes the wrongdoing but is rather to be a member of the community who has the relevant agential and epistemic authority to *bear witness* to the wrongdoing and thereby to hold the wrongdoer responsible. Such a commitment to and recognition of the standing and authority of others just is, I submit, what Stephen Darwall has called *recognition respect*: a recognition of someone's *dignity*—of a kind of "worth without price"—she has as a member of the community (2006, 119). Likewise, the commitment to and recognition of the norms of that community amount to a kind of respect for those norms. And because such recognition respect for fellow members and respect for the norms are a part of an overall commitment to the community itself, I shall say that we respect the members and norms as a part of *revering* the community itself. Thus, to exhibit a rational pattern of reactive attitudes focused on the community and subfocused on its members and norms constitutes our respect for those members and norms and our reverence for the community. Such a community is a *community of respect.*

As I argued above, part of what is distinctive of the reactive attitudes is the way their rational interconnections—and so the rational patterns they form—are interpersonal. This means that *my* reactive attitudes focused on a particular community are only a part of the overall pattern that constitutes reverence and respect. Consequently, the proper subject of this reverence and respect is not each of us individually but all of us jointly: it is *we* who revere this community and its defining practices and who respect each other and its norms. Indeed, other things being equal, I as a member of this community rationally ought to revere it and respect its members and norms insofar as I am one of us.

4 Blame and Relationships: First Pass

I return now to my central question concerning the nature of blame and the relevance of relationships. Recall that on a basic reactive attitude account, to be blameworthy is to be an appropriate target of the reactive attitudes, and to blame someone is to take up one or another (negative, factive) reactive attitude toward her. Scanlon's complaint against such an account is that it is too thin: to blame someone is not merely to feel a particular reactive attitude like resentment but rather to modify your overall attitude and behavior toward her in ways that depend on the specific sort of impairment of your relationship at issue. One of my central criticisms of Scanlon concerned the vagueness of his account of the relevant types of relationships, of the relevant types of impairments to those relationships, as well as of how such impairments make appropriate certain (which?) changes in attitude toward the wrongdoer. Of course, blameworthy behavior affects relationships and attitudes, and of course to blame is to have a different attitude toward the perpetrator, but we need to understand in detail how these are related, something that Scanlon fails adequately to address.

Given all of this, how does my overall account of the reactive attitudes and communities of respect enable me both to respond to Scanlon's criticisms about the thinness of a reactive attitude account of blame and to fill in the deficiencies

I have identified in his own account? What do I add to the basic reactive attitude account that enables me to do better?

Scanlon's appeal to relationships is meant in part to help us understand who has the appropriate standing to blame the perpetrator (rather than simply make judgments of blameworthiness): those not in the relevant sort of relationship with the perpetrator lack such standing. The account I have just offered of communities of respect in terms of interpersonal rational patterns of reactive attitudes can help clarify this: to have the relevant standing to blame just is to be a member of the appropriate community of respect and so to be someone whose reactive attitudes are appropriately rationally connected to those of her fellow members—someone who is appropriately addressed by the call of their reactive attitudes—by virtue of being someone whom they ought to respect both as accountable to the norms and as having the authority to hold them accountable. That is, the relevant *relationship* in terms of which we can understand the appropriateness of blame just is that of co-membership in the community of respect whose norms have been violated. Consequently, the relevant sort of *impairment* of that relationship can be understood (at least initially[8]) in terms of the violation of communal norms—in terms of the way the perpetrator's attitudes or behavior manifest a lack of respect for one or more fellow members, for the community's norms, or both.

How does this understanding of the sort of relationship (and impairment thereof) relevant to blame handle some of the problem cases I presented for Scanlon's account? Consider first the case of my arch-rival, with whom I have a "relationship" in which we consistently harm each other. It is most natural to assume that such a "relationship" is not a communal relationship, grounded in the norms of a community of respect, so that the expectations we have for how each other will behave are nonnormative in character, merely a matter of prediction rather than a precursor to holding someone responsible to a norm. Consequently, were he to do me a good turn for my sake, I have grounds to praise him, in spite of his violation of the expectations we each have for how the other typically behaves in our "relationship," because he has upheld the norms of some community, perhaps the moral community, of which we are fellow members. Likewise, were he to harm me out of malice, I have grounds to blame him because he has violated those norms, in spite of his upholding my expectations for how he tends to behave in our "relationship": blame would be appropriate even in such a context in which the (nonnormative) expectations of a personal relationship have been upheld. In short, the sort of relationship relevant to blame must involve such normative expectations, the potential for holding someone responsible to certain norms within a community of respect. The same goes for the relationship of domination between the abusive and abused spouse: even when the abused spouse acquiesces to her being abused and dominated by her spouse, such acquiescence does not involve the mutual recognition of each as having the standing and authority to hold the other responsible to the norms of a community of respect.

Now consider the second case of my blaming President Buchanan for long-past wrongs. It might seem that my account cannot handle such a case. For although we might say that he was a member of the same community of respect I am—a community of American citizens, say—it might seem that he no longer *is* a fellow member for exactly the reasons Scanlon provides: I would seem to have no meaningful relationship with a man who died almost 150 years ago, and his actions and attitudes would seem to have no personal significance for me now. Consequently, it might seem, although I might judge that a feeling of indignation would be appropriate, this is merely a claim of blameworthiness rather than actual blame, and actually to feel indignation would be otiose. Nonetheless, this is mistaken. It should be clear that what is at stake in blame is not merely a response to a particular person on a particular occasion, but rather the import the community of respect has for us and so the import not only members but also communal norms have for us. My indignation, therefore, is not otiose; it is, rather, the manifestation of the proper respect I as a community member ought to have for its norms—which, as I have just learned, was previously and egregiously violated by a community member. Of course, that President Buchanan's misdeeds are long past may modulate their "severity"—the degree to which they bear on the well-being of objects of one's concern—but in some cases (as, I would suggest, in this one), the magnitude of the wrong as an affront to the norms and the community is itself enough to warrant indignation.

An objection is looming. Part of what is interesting and important about Scanlon's understanding of blame is the way he weaves it into an understanding of individual persons and, where they exist, particular relationships with the perpetrator. One of Scanlon's central concerns is to explain "the evident variability of blame, and its clear dependence on particular relationships" (2008, 212). He rightly insists that just how one can appropriately blame someone and so what alterations to one's relationship are justified depend on other, more local facts about one's relationship to the perpetrator: the victim (or close friends or relatives of the victim), for example, can often blame the perpetrator in a way that would not be appropriate for others. Thus, the parents of a child killed by an inattentive driver may justly feel that their relationship with the driver has been irrevocably altered in significant ways, whereas the rest of us may not thereby have our relationships with the driver altered in the same way or to the same degree. In such cases, to put the point in my terms, the import an offense has to the victim may well be properly different from the import it has to other fellow members: different in a way that (somehow) explains the different effects this has on their respective relationships. This is behind Scanlon's insistence that the significance that matters in blame is the significance of the actions and attitudes of the perpetrator *for the blamer*, that the relationship that matters for thinking about blame is the *particular* relationship between the perpetrator and the blamer.

This gives rise to the following objection. I earlier complained that Scanlon's appeal to the significance for the blamer and the particular relationship between the blamer and the perpetrator is too egocentric, and that the concern at issue behind the blame is not a personal concern but rather our joint concern for the community of respect, the norms of that community, and our fellow members. On my account, then, it is not the blamer's particular relationship with the perpetrator that grounds and justifies the blame but rather their *communal* relationship—as, for example, fellow members of the moral community of respect. Nonetheless, it may seem that I am missing something here about the importance of particular relationships. Indeed, one might object that the account I have offered wrongly implies that other fellow members will have their relationships to the perpetrator altered in the same way and to the same degree as the victim. This is, of course, what Scanlon (rightly) denies. Given my focus on overall communities rather than individuals or particular relationships, am I not simply ignoring Scanlon's central insight? As I shall argue, the answer depends on understanding how particular relationships (and, indeed, particular individuals) fit into and are affected by the communities to which they belong; this is a dimension of human relationships that Scanlon does not consider.

5 Latitude

Thus far, I have emphasized the relative homogeneity of the interpersonal patterns of reactive attitudes constituting communities of respect. Nonetheless, there are several sources of individual differences in what reactive attitudes different people might have in the same circumstances. One such source lies in the considerable *latitude* for which emotions an individual is warranted in feeling in a given situation. In the case of nonreactive emotions, both fear and hope can be warranted in the face of the same risks involving something one cares about—the prospects of one's candidate winning the election, for example. In the case of the reactive attitudes, we find similar latitude: in some cases, it might be reasonable to feel either trust or distrust; in other cases, it might be appropriate either to continue to feel resentment or to stop feeling it or even to forgive. There are several sources for such latitude. One lies in individual temperament and mood: optimists and pessimists will tend to respond with hope and fear—or trust and distrust—respectively. Another lies in the indeterminacy of interpretation: one person may interpret the perpetrator as just self-absorbed and oblivious to the slight he unintentionally inflicted on another, a slight that therefore warrants little or no reactive response, whereas someone else might interpret the slight as the consequence of unconscious racism worthy of considerable indignation. Moreover, in particular cases it may be that, with all the facts in, neither interpretation is clearly better than the other, and both reactive responses would be equally warranted. That is, there can be genuine indeterminacy in what the perpetrator's actions, motives, and attitudes actually were, so that how individuals interpret the perpetrator in responding reactively may justly depend on particular details of their personal relationship and past history with the perpetrator.

That we have such latitude means that in some cases how we respond emotionally can be a matter of decision and will be based on considerations other than simply the warrant of the emotion. One might successfully decide to be brave and so confront a danger without fear. Or one might, given one's past experiences with being burned by trusting too much, decide that a pessimistic interpretation of someone's motives is best and so decide to distrust rather trust him, even though trust would have been reasonable as well (on deciding to trust, see, for example, Holton 1994). Or one might, given one's generous nature and desire to heal one's impaired relationship with someone, decide that a charitable (but still reasonable) interpretation of her attitudes and motives is best and so adopt a more forgiving attitude. Hence, such latitude provides room for individual differences to play an important role in what sort of blaming response one makes—differences including, as Scanlon rightly notes, one's sense of one's personal relationship with the perpetrator or victim.[9]

Nonetheless, this appeal to latitude on its own cannot explain the variability of blame with which Scanlon is rightly concerned. Part of Scanlon's claim is that it would in general be inappropriate for witnesses to blame the wrongdoer in the same way and to the same degree as the victim, a claim that seems to run contrary to my appeal to such latitude. To accommodate this insight, a second and ultimately more important source of individual differences relevant to blame can be found in the kinds of *excuses* we have for having or failing to have certain reactions to wrongdoers.

6 Excuses

Whether someone is subject to praise or blame for his actions or attitudes, whether he should be held responsible for particular upholdings or violations of communal norms, depends in part on whether he has a valid excuse. If our community has a norm against stepping on the toes of others, and someone steps on your toes by accident—because he tripped or was pushed, for example—he is ordinarily not to blame for doing so: his tripping or being pushed ordinarily excuses him from such blame. In particular, the presence of such an excuse undercuts the warrant of subsequent reactive attitudes, such as your resentment or others' disapprobation or his guilt. Likewise, when I am dismissive of you, thus violating our community's norms against rudeness, I may be partially excused because I have been so overworked and stressed that I am not really myself.

In the simplest cases, such as the one just described, the excuse arises from what looks to be a lack of agency. Thus, being pushed is not something he did, and although tripping is something he in some sense did (albeit not intentionally) in the course of walking (which was intentional), one might wonder to what extent his agency is really involved in the consequences of that behavior (if it is involved at all). (Here, of course, questions of negligence are relevant for determining responsibility and whether he has an excuse, but I shall set these aside.) Likewise, we might think that my rudeness is not (or not fully) expressive of my own agency given the stress I am experiencing. Yet more interesting for the purposes of understanding the relationship between individuals and the community are cases in which the excuse arises from a clear exercise of agency. For example, I might skip out on my obligation to my local community garden cooperative (of which I am a member)—an obligation to join with others in preparing the gardens for spring planting this weekend—because of other professional obligations (to travel to give a talk, say) or personal obligations (to attend my son's clarinet recital). In these cases, I am making a choice to violate the communal norm, a choice grounded in my sense that my professional or personal obligations are, here and now, more important than my communal obligations, and the nature of my excuse lies somewhere in the grounds for this choice. Clearly cases like this raise the question of the relationship between a community of respect (and its norms) and an individual member of that community (and his commitments to personal values or to other communities of respect). How exactly do excuses work in such cases?

To understand this more clearly, consider first cases in which we are forced to choose between two conflicting personal values. For example, my value of being a father and my value of being in good shape might come into conflict when I learn, just as I am about to begin my exercise routine, that my daughter has been taken to the hospital. In these circumstances, assume that I find being with my daughter more important than getting exercise; that is, I find my daughter to have greater relative degree of import here and now than my getting exercise. It is this greater relative degree of import that provides me with a reason here and now to go to the hospital and skip getting exercise today, even though in valuing being in good shape I think I ought to exercise every day. For while in valuing something I find it to be a part of the kind of life worth my living, my ultimate concern is for how best to live, and in these circumstances setting aside my value of exercise and going to be with my daughter just is my living the sort of life I think I ought. How is this notion of degree of import to be understood?

The basic idea is this (for more details, see Helm 2001, chap. 4). If import is constituted by rational patterns of emotions, so too is the relative degree of import. In part, the idea is that *degree of import* should be understood in terms of the patterns in the strength of emotions focused on it: the *stronger* such emotional responses—including not merely the *intensity* of an emotion but also its *persistence* or how long it lasts—the more import something has to us, other things being equal. (In part, other things will not be equal when severity differs: my emotional response to my daughter's breaking her leg ought to be stronger than my response when she gets a paper cut precisely because the severity of the former circumstance is greater than that of the latter. Consequently, the rational structure of emotional strength partly constitutive of degree of import is modulo severity.) In addition, the degree of import that one thing has to me relative to the import something else has to me—*relative degree of import*—is constituted by rational patterns of relationships among the emotions constituting my caring about these things. For example, in particular circumstances, my fear for my daughter's well-being may simply trump my dismay at missing a meeting with you or my joy at having just gotten a paper accepted. In such cases, my fear *dampens* or *suppresses* my dismay and my joy, such that, we might say, I am "excused" from feeling the normal dismay or joy I am otherwise rationally required to feel. The structure of dampening or suppression relations is a rational structure: if my fear dampens my joy in this case, then it ought to do so in other cases, other things being equal. (Once again, other things are not always equal. My joy at receiving a fellowship ought not be dampened by my concern for my daughter when she gets a paper cut. So again this rational structure of dampening or suppression relations is modulo severity.) My claim is that the rational structure of dampening and suppression relations across patterns of emotions with different focuses constitutes the relative degree of import of those focuses, other things being equal.

How does this apply to conflicts that might arise between the norms of a community of respect of which I am a member and my personal values? As a member of a community of respect, I revere the community as one of us: I find it to have import to us jointly and therefore to me insofar as I am one of us. This implies that the import of the community is a source of reasons for how we should act and respond and, in particular since I am one of us, for how *I* should act and respond. Yet my personal commitments or other commitments I might have as a member of other communities of respect might provide me with reasons that here and now outweigh the reasons I have grounded in the import of this community, so that I have reason, all things considered, to act in violation of this community's norms. Assume that this is the case for the conflict between my son's clarinet recital and my helping the community garden cooperative this weekend: all things considered, given the greater importance my son's clarinet recital has in my life, I have reason to attend to it rather than to help others in the garden cooperative, and so I thereby have reason to violate a norm of that community. Such a reason provides me with what looks to be an excuse to violate the communal norm.

Whether what looks to be an excuse from the individual's perspective really is a valid excuse depends on more than the individual; it depends as well on whether it is accepted as an excuse by others in the community. After all, claiming that I need to dust my pet rock collection that weekend likely would not be accepted as an excuse for skipping out on the work of getting the gardens ready, and I would be subject to blame for doing so for this reason: *we* do not find that to be an important enough reason for me to fail to uphold my obligation to the community. For us to *accept* an excuse is for us generally to find negative reactive attitudes (guilt, disapprobation, indignation, and so on) in response to a fellow member's conduct to be unwarranted in a particular case and so is for us to find her actions to be not blameworthy from the perspective of the community. This means not merely that we do not in fact feel such reactive attitudes but also that we criticize those who do as, for example, unfairly laying a guilt trip on her, and we potentially adopt further reactive attitudes toward them if they persist, as when we feel disapprobation toward someone for his heartless rigidity. Moreover, we refuse to find the norm violation to be grounds for an assessment of her as untrustworthy and so as providing reason for subsequent distrust.

I have argued elsewhere that our communal norms structure the practices or way of life that partly defines this community as the community it is, and that our understanding of our community and what we stand for is at least in part implicit in the interpersonal, rational patterns of reactive attitudes we display (Helm 2014a). Yet these practices are further structured by what we accept as an excuse for which norm violations, and this contributes to the members' at least tacit understanding of the community itself. For at stake in our acceptance or rejection of an excuse is our shared sense of the place reverence for the community in general, and respect for one or more of its norms in particular, can permissibly have as a part of the individual lives of its members. To reject my excuse of needing to dust my pet rock collection is in effect to blame me for not revering the community highly enough. Likewise, to blame someone who rejects what the rest of us find to be a valid excuse as heartlessly rigid is to blame him for a failure properly to understand the import this community can have in its relation to individual lives: that is why he is heartlessly rigid.

It is important, therefore, to distinguish between the import the community has to us jointly and the import it has to us individually insofar as we are each one of us. Thus whether the community is more or less important *to us* depends on the extent to which we are willing to accept excuses from members to violate its norms and instead act on behalf of other things that have import in their lives. By contrast, whether the community is more or less important *to me* as a member depends on the place it has within a rough system of priorities relative to other things that are important to me.[10] Conflicts between what is required by adhering to communal norms and what is required by upholding personal values can be resolved by my finding the community, here and now, to be more or less important to me than the relevant personal values. However, that such resolutions do not accord with our joint sense of the importance the community has to us in particular cases, so that we refuse to accept my excuses for violating communal norms, does not on its own imply that I am being irrational for such violations. It can be rational for me, all things considered, to violate a communal norm even when the community itself rationally ought to blame me for doing so. Nonetheless, such cases must be the exception, or the community would not have a viable understanding of its own importance in the lives of its members.

7 Blame and Relationships (Again)

What can all of this tell us about the nature of blame and, in particular, the variability of blame with which Scanlon is rightly concerned?

As just indicated, while a particular norm violation might have a certain degree of import to the community, this does not mean that it has the same degree of import to each member of that community. In virtue of the relationship she has to the perpetrator or to the victim, for example, a particular member might find that norm violation to have greater import to her and so to provide her with excuses for acting or responding toward the perpetrator in ways that normally would violate our communal norms. For example, if my violating a communal norm in a way that victimizes you has a relatively high degree of import to you, your resentment ought to be relatively strong not merely in the sense that it is relatively intense but also in that it can persist for some time afterwards. If, several days later, I extend my hand to you in greeting, you can be justified in giving me the cold shoulder, thereby refusing properly to acknowledge my greeting. The wrong I did to you, let us assume, still has in these circumstances greater import than acknowledging my greeting, so that your resentment of my wrongdoing suppresses your ordinary desire politely to recognize and respond to me insofar as that suppression itself is a way for you to express your resentment and so to continue to hold me responsible for my past transgression. In effect, this is to dampen your ordinary recognition respect for me, and your excuse for the failure of recognition respect in this case is grounded in and justified by the greater degree of import to which you respond in blaming me (a response that manifests, in a different way, your recognition respect of me as a fellow member meriting blame).

Of course, whether your resentment properly suppresses your subsequent acknowledgment in this case depends on how significant my wronging of you is. If the slight were minor, such as the clueless and unapologetic jostling of you as I go about my business, it may not have sufficiently greater relative degree of import in these circumstances than your later reciprocating my greeting, and so you would fail to have an excuse. But if my slight were more major (such as premeditated and slanderous acts that aim to undermine your reputation), its relative degree of import may be high and lasting, providing excuses for a long time. Once again, what degree of import my wrongdoing has is not simply up to you; it depends on the rational pattern of *our* reactive attitudes. In particular, others' reactive attitudes ought, other things being equal, to line up with yours: your continued resentment of me thereby calls on others to respond accordingly and so to continue to feel indignation toward me or at least to fail to feel disapprobation toward you and thereby accept your excuse for giving me the cold shoulder. Our doing so is not guaranteed, and the interpersonal rational pattern in our reactive attitudes may instead constitute my wrongdoing as having much less significance than you took it to have and so as not providing an excuse for your subsequent response.

My claim so far has been that blame involves the excused dampening of ordinary recognition respect; yet its effects go further than this. Central to blame, as I have said, is the degree of import the wrongdoing has relative to other things that have import to the blamer or to us in the community. Such relative degree of import may dampen or suppress other responses. Included here are reactive desires to help the wrongdoer or to respond favorably to the call of her reactive attitudes. Here it should be noted that the relative degree of import a wrongdoing has can vary depending on particular details about the communal relationship the blamer has with the wrongdoer, such as the prospects for future interactions with her. This implies that there will be situations in which a witness will justly feel more and longer-lasting indignation than the victim feels resentment. For example, assume that you invite Mary, a promising young philosopher, to give a highly technical talk to your department. Afterwards, as you are talking to Mary, you both overhear one of your colleagues dismissing her talk out of hand: "it was so boring and pointless!" Mary might feel mildly insulted and resentful and yet shrug it off, confident in her own abilities, knowing your colleague's reputation as close-minded and opinionated, and knowing that she is unlikely to encounter him the future. On the other hand, you might have reason to feel considerable indignation, more so than Mary's resentment even though you are merely a witness, given that you will have to put up with his close-mindedness and its repercussions on a weekly basis.

In addition, blame's effects extend to subsequent trust or distrust and can ramify widely from there. Most obvious is that the wrongdoing blame recognizes is defeasible evidence for the diminished trustworthiness of the wrongdoer, which may well play out in terms of diminished trust and so diminished willingness to cooperate or enter into agreements with the wrongdoer, as Scanlon rightly points out. Less obvious is the way one's recognition of the import of the wrongdoing and of diminished trustworthiness affect one's willingness to trust rather than distrust and one's willingness to interpret the wrongdoer's subsequent actions and motives charitably. That is, blame can alter the way one exercises one's latitude in responding to the wrongdoer. Consequently, the effects of blame can persist well into the future and in circumstances that may seem to have little to do with the original wrongdoing.

In all these ways, then, a wrongdoer's actions alter the normal communal relationships fellow members have with him by providing them with excuses to respond or fail to respond in ways that otherwise would violate the norms defining those communal relationships. As we have seen, the alteration of this relationship can depend on facts about the individuals involved and their personal commitments or commitments to other communities of respect—on your being the victim of my wrongdoing or being the friend or colleague of the victim, for example; it can depend on personal details about the way one's communal relationship with the wrongdoer plays out; and it can depend on the latitude the blamer has to interpret the wrongdoing as significant or minor and to use this as a basis for increasing distrust of the wrongdoer and thereby allow the wrongdoing to alter their relationship. Consequently, my account can accommodate Scanlon's insight about the variability of blame: the import an offense has to the victim, for example, may well be different from the import it has to other fellow members in a way that explains the different effects this has on their respective communal relationships—the different excuses each can have for violating the norms of that relationship. Given this, we can see that the sort of *impairment* to a relationship relevant to blame lies in precisely this sort of alteration in the normal communal relationships fellow members have with the wrongdoer, an alteration that excuses their dampened recognition respect for and diminished trust in the wrongdoer. Such an impairment harms not only the particular relationship between the blamer and the wrongdoer; it also harms the community, for it alters our reactive responses to failures of recognition respect in a way that potentially undermines the community itself were blame (and such altered reactive responses) to become widespread.

In short, *blame* is the normally rational reactive response to the import of communal norm violations by which one holds the perpetrator responsible to the violated norms. This response may (but need not) involve the excused dampening or suppressing of one's ordinary recognition respect for the perpetrator, which thereby alters one's willingness to respond to the call of her reactive attitudes, one's reactive desires to help her, one's willingness to trust her or to interpret her subsequent actions and motives charitably, and so on. The effect of this possible excused dampening of ordinary recognition respect is to alter one's normal communal relationship with the perpetrator in a way that harms both one's particular relationship and potentially the community itself. This is fundamentally a reactive attitude account of blame, though the details of my account of the reactive attitudes and their connection to community involves extending the basic reactive attitude account in a way that can accommodate Scanlon's insights into the importance of relationships in blame.

Scanlon is therefore right to understand blame in general to involve the impairment of relationships, but my account differs from his in important ways by providing an explicit—and explicitly normative—account of the relevant sort of relationships and impairments to these relationships. In part, on my account, the impairment of the relationship is a typical rational *consequence* of the blame, not a part of its content, as Scanlon claims. Indeed, we should not overemphasize the place such impairment has in understanding blame itself, inasmuch as minor norm violations for which we may blame someone need not lead to any such impairment given that such violations may well fail to dampen or suppress one's ordinary recognition respect. Crucially, on my account the relationship between the blamer and the wrongdoer is at its root a *communal* relationship that as such is defined in terms of interpersonal, rational connections to others within the community in terms of which we can make sense of the authority one has to blame others. Likewise, the impairment to this relationship must be understood in part in terms of the community as well, even though Scanlon is right to emphasize how blame properly varies depending on the details of the blamer's particular instantiation of that communal relationship with the wrongdoer. Scanlon's account of blame in its focus on personal relationships, then, is egocentric precisely because it ignores the important role of communities of respect and the interpersonal, rational interconnections among reactive attitudes within such communities.

8 Conclusion

I have argued that we can account for many of Scanlon's insights concerning blame and personal relationships by appealing to the reactive attitudes and the way in which interpersonal patterns of reactive attitudes constitute communities of respect. In doing so, I have tried to present a clearer account than Scanlon of the sort of relationships and impairments of relationships relevant to blame. Thus, I have argued, the relationships relevant for blame are grounded in being fellow members of a community of respect, for it is our standing and authority in the community as meriting recognition respect that explains why we (but not outsiders) can properly blame fellow members for their violations of communal norms. This means that some third parties—other fellow members of the community—*are* (contra Scanlon) participants in the same relationship and so are in a position to adjust their attitudes toward the perpetrator in relevant ways.

I also suggested provisionally in section 4 that the impairment of such a relationship relevant to blame consists in the way the wrongdoing manifests a lack of respect for one or more fellow members, the community's norms, or both. We can now refine this in light of my account of the role of excuses in blame. The relationships we have with other fellow members of the community (and not just the perpetrator or victim) are impaired by virtue of the way the perpetrator's wrongdoing gives rise to certain excuses, in which we accept certain failures of our recognition respect of the perpetrator to be appropriate, all things considered. Although I have acknowledged the way in which personal relationships are impaired as well (insofar as the resulting structure of excuses alters the relationship, at least temporarily, in a way that deviates from the norm), this is a consequence rather than a part of blame, and such personal impairments cannot be separated from the impairment to the community.

Throughout I have acknowledged that Scanlon is right to point us to particular relationships as central to blame, though I claimed that his understanding of the importance of particular relationships gives us an account of blame that is too egocentric insofar as he thinks that what is relevant for understanding the content of blame is the significance the wrongdoing has for the blamer. As I have argued, the significance blame has for the particular relationship between the blamer and the perpetrator is not the only significance that is relevant to blame. For even when personal considerations come into the picture in providing excuses, it is we members of the community, by virtue of our interpersonally and rationally interconnected reactive attitudes, who make such excuses possible and define the conditions of their appropriateness. So although Scanlon is right to distinguish the attitude of blame from judgments of blameworthiness, and although this attitude has consequences for one's (possible) personal relationship with the perpetrator, the content and justification of blame are to be understood in terms of the communal significance of the wrongdoing: blame is to be understood in terms of a response to the import that wrongdoing has for *us*. This essential communal aspect of blame is something Scanlon does not acknowledge.

If this is right, it has important implications for understanding the nature of forgiveness. Forgiveness is not merely, as Strawson says following Joseph Butler (1726), the forswearing of resentment but also as the forswearing of excuses in a way that aims at a restoration of trust and the quality of one's former relationship.

In other words, to *forgive* is to commit oneself to finding, both in judgment and reactive attitude, that the wrongdoing no longer has a greater relative degree of import to one than one's normal relationship with the perpetrator and therefore that it no longer grounds the excuses that constitute the impairment not only in one's personal relationship but also in the broader community of respect. Consequently, forgiveness is not something we can accomplish merely by saying the words, "I forgive you," but rather may well require significant work to overcome one's tendencies not only to feel continued resentment but also to respond, in reactive emotion, motivation, and action, to the perpetrator. Moreover, although one may have some latitude, perhaps grounded in the relative degree of import things have to one as an individual, for when it is appropriate to forgive, it is clear that this latitude is constrained by our shared understanding of the importance our reverence for the community and respect for its members can have in an individual life. In terms of such constraints, we can make sense of people as either forgiving not readily enough (and thereby persisting in actions and attitudes we no longer find excusable by the relative degree of import of the wrongdoing) or forgiving too readily (and thereby failing properly to recognize the relative degree of import the wrongdoing really has).[11]

Notes

1. See, for example, Wallace 1994. While I agree with Strawsonians that we cannot understand what it is to be responsible except in terms of our practices of holding others responsible, I think the Strawsonian reversal of priority is a mistake as well. For, I believe, we cannot make sense of the conditions of appropriateness for holding someone responsible except in terms of the target's being responsible. Hence I reject both that (appropriate) holding responsible is prior to being responsible and that being responsible is prior to (appropriate) holding responsible. Hints of this no-priority view can be found in section 3, below; for more careful arguments, see Helm 2012, 217–232; 2015, 189–212; 2017. Nonetheless, I set this point aside here.

2. Others question the adequacy of Strawson's appeal to the reactive attitudes by questioning whether there are ways of holding others responsible or accountable that do not involve blame at all. See, for example, Watson 2008; Westlund, chapter 10, this volume. While I agree with Watson and Westlund that there are important cases in which we ought to hold others responsible for wrongdoing even while refraining from blaming them, it is not clear to me that our holding others responsible in such cases does not involve the reactive attitudes, as Watson (but not Westlund) seems to suggest. Much depends here on how we understand what the reactive attitudes are and how we conceive the relationship between our emotions and our judgments. I discuss these issues at length in *Communities of Respect* (Helm 2017).

3. Scanlon (2008, 131) notes that blaming someone may involve not a modification of your relationship but a confirmation of it instead.

4. Scanlon does clarify things a bit in the moral case, claiming that a moral relation is "the relation of 'fellow rational beings'" (2008, 140), a relation that requires attitudes of "mutual regard and forbearance" and a "concern with the justifiability of his or her actions" (141). Yet these claims depend on our intuitions about morality rather than a principled account of the relevant relationships, and so it remains unclear how these features of moral relationships can be generalized to make sense of what other sorts of relationships are relevant to blame.

5. See also Scanlon 2008, 146: "the content of blame depends in this way on the significance of the agent and the agents' faults for the person doing the blaming."
6. While I focus here on the emotions, it should be acknowledged that the relevant rational patterns include desires and evaluative judgments as well. I omit these here to keep things simple.
7. This language of "victim" and "perpetrator" most clearly fits the negative reactive attitudes, though I shall use it in the positive cases as well: I as the "victim" of your kindness feel gratitude toward you, the "perpetrator" of that kindness.
8. I have more to say about such impairment section 7.
9. This appeal to the latitude we have for feeling (or not feeling) various reactive attitudes might seem to be problematic on my account. For I have said that part of what is distinctive of the reactive attitudes is that they involve interpersonal rational interconnections: the victim's resentment calls on the perpetrator to feel guilt and witnesses to feel indignation or disapprobation, such that the failure of the perpetrator or witnesses to feel the corresponding self or vicarious reactive attitudes provides the victim grounds for further resentment. Yet my claim that we have latitude in what reactive attitudes we feel may seem to be inconsistent with this understanding of the rational interconnections: if I as a witness have the latitude not to feel indignation, then what right does the victim have to resent *me* for failing to hold the perpetrator responsible? Likewise, it might seem, my trust in someone thereby calls on others to trust her, which again seems inconsistent with my claim that we have latitude to trust or distrust.

   In response, it should be clear that this latitude is not total. For backward-looking reactive attitudes, some cases are clear-cut and warrant further reactive response, as when the victim feels resentment toward a witness who feels approbation toward the perpetrator for his wrongdoing or who fails for no good reason to feel indignation toward a severe wrong. Other cases may clearly involve this sort of latitude, permitting but not requiring reactive attitudes, as when I choose to ignore a minor wrong I witness, but another witness who is more compassionate toward the victim may feel (and express) disapprobation. Still other cases may be borderline. For forward-looking reactive attitudes like trust and distrust, it should be clear that this latitude is considerably greater (though it still cannot be in complete disregard for the evidence of the target's trustworthiness). Nonetheless, it is not an implication of my account that my trust in someone calls on others to trust her as well. For in every case, reactive attitudes call on others to respond to the import the circumstances have to us, and so in particular to respond appropriately to both the target of trust and the relevant norms as worthy of respect. Yet trust and distrust may be equally responses to others as meriting respect, and so the fact that you distrust the person I trust does not on its own reveal any failure of coherence within the overall pattern of our reactive attitudes. (I return to this issue section 7.)
10. I do not, of course, mean to imply that such a system of priorities will be well worked out or even that we can always prioritize one value over another across all situations. For details, see Helm 2001.
11. This chapter was written through the support of a grant from the John Templeton Foundation and fellowships from the Princeton Center for Human Values and the National Endowment for the Humanities, whose support is gratefully acknowledged. (Of course, the views expressed here do not necessarily reflect those of these funding agencies.) For discussions of earlier versions of this chapter, thanks to Matthew Ratcliffe and the audience at Durham University, as well as to Andrew Franklin-Hall, Katie Gasdaglis, Agnieszka Jaworska, Alex Madva, Jeffrey Seidman, and Julie Tannenbaum at the Vassar College Workshop on Love and Human Agency. Finally, thanks to the editors of this volume for insightful comments on the final draft.

References

Butler, Joseph. 1726. *Fifteen Sermons Preached at Rolls Chapel*. London: James and Johnz Knapton.
Darwall, Stephen L. 2006. *The Second-Person Standpoint: Morality, Respect, and Accountability*. Cambridge, MA: Harvard University Press.

Helm, Bennett W. 2001. *Emotional Reason: Deliberation, Motivation, and the Nature of Value.* Cambridge: Cambridge University Press.

Helm, Bennett W. 2010. *Love, Friendship, and the Self: Intimacy, Identification, and the Social Nature of Persons.* Oxford: Oxford University Press.

Helm, Bennett W. 2012. "Accountability and Some Social Dimensions of Human Agency." *Philosophical Issues* 22 (1): 217–232.

Helm, Bennett W. 2014a. "Emotional Communities of Respect." In *Collective Emotions*, edited by Christian von Sheve and Mikko Salmela, 47–60. Oxford: Oxford University Press.

Helm, Bennett W. 2014b. "Trust as a Reactive Attitude." In *Oxford Studies in Agency and Responsibility, Vol. 2, "Freedom and Resentment" at Fifty*, edited by David Shoemaker and Neal Tognazzini, 187–215. Oxford: Oxford University Press.

Helm, Bennett W. 2015. "Rationality, Authority, and Bindingness: An Account of Communal Norms." In *Oxford Studies in Agency and Responsibility, Vol. 3*, edited by David Shoemaker, 189–212. Oxford: Oxford University Press.

Helm, Bennett W. 2017. *Communities of Respect: Persons, Dignity, and the Reactive Attitudes.* Oxford: Oxford University Press.

Holton, Richard. 1994. "Deciding to Trust, Coming to Believe." *Australasian Journal of Philosophy* 72 (1): 63–76.

Scanlon, Thomas M. 2008. *Moral Dimensions: Permissibility, Meaning, Blame.* Cambridge, MA: Belknap Press of Harvard University Press.

Strawson, Peter F. 1962. "Freedom and Resentment." *Proceedings of the British Academy* 48: 187–211.

Wallace, R. Jay. 1994. *Responsibility and the Moral Sentiments.* Cambridge, MA: Harvard University Press.

Watson, Gary. 2008. "Responsibility and the Limits of Evil: Variations on a Strawsonian Theme." In *Free Will and Reactive Attitudes: Perspectives on P. F. Strawson's "Freedom and Resentment,"* edited by Michael McKenna and Paul Russell, 115–141. Burlington, VT: Ashgate.

12

Sharing Responsibility

The Importance of Tokens of Appraisal to Our Moral Practices

MAUREEN SIE

1 Introduction

The starting point for discussions of moral responsibility in contemporary philosophy is our practice of holding one another morally responsible for what we do. This practice consists of, among other things, responding with the moral sentiments, and reactive attitudes such as resentment and blame for someone's wrongdoing. The philosophical discussion of moral responsibility is concerned with the questions of when and toward whom it is legitimate to respond in this way.[1] Often, that discussion is connected to the legitimacy of, for example, punishing people for their wrongdoings, imprisoning them, and holding them accountable in the legal sense. At the foreground of this discussion, the thesis of causal determinism tends to loom large. It is this thesis that, according to many, undermines the legitimacy of our practices of moral responsibility.

There is also another way to look at our practices of moral responsibility, and that is from the point of view of their social function. In this chapter, I explore the benefits of approaching moral responsibility in this way, which, I argue, leads us to reflect on *why* it is legitimate to respond with the moral sentiments. From this point of view, what is striking about the moral sentiments is that they serve important communicative and coordinative functions. Suppose, for example, we witness an accident caused by a teenager texting her friend while crossing a schoolyard on her skateboard and we respond with resentment (as her parents or the victim) or moral indignation (as onlookers). Besides the question of whether the teenager does or does not deserve our resentment and indignation in the sense of asking whether she is a proper or fitting subject of these sentiments, we could also discuss what purposes these sentiments serve and evaluate them in light of these purposes. In this case, for example, our sentimental responses communicate to the teenager that we do not accept her behavior—that we think it wrong of her not to pay attention to what she is doing when in traffic. And it might well be that we believe that response to be appropriate even though we do not believe that the teenager deserves punishment of any sort, or that her behavior should, for example, be legally forbidden. Considered from this perspective, the moral sentiments organize and coordinate our practices *alongside*, and sometimes (fundamentally) as separate from, measures such as punishment, imprisonment, or holding accountable in the legal sense.[2]

We could say that this approach focuses on the more basic or less strict ways in which we respond to one another's transgressions. "More basic" and "less strict" because these responses are not necessarily connected with the kind of wrongdoing we regard as in need of regulation, punishment, or imprisonment. There are many domains in which we respond to one another in this more basic and less strict sense; think, for example, about sports, but also politics. When watching a soccer game, we see players resent, be grateful, blame, praise, and be indignant a lot of the time. And the same holds for politics. We can discuss whether the subjects targeted by these responses are deserving of them, and these discussions might influence the exchange of moral sentiments at the "playing field," but we can also discuss them from the point of view of their social function.

One of the claims that I argue for in this chapter is that things that we respond to, and are able to regulate, with frowns, blame, indignation, and resentment, are often typically not the kind of things we need to arrange through protocols and laws. Moreover, and this is a second claim, being responded to in such a manner might be key to our developing certain ways of acting and the capacities required for those ways of acting (cf. Vargas 2013; McGeer 2010, 2015).[3] I regard this as an empirical claim, which, if correct, has some important normative implications. If this is the case, parents, peers, as well as the larger community of which the teenager is a part share at least some responsibility for the wrongdoing of the teenager. Had they frowned at, blamed, and resented the teenager for her inattentive behavior from an early age onward, she might not have developed into a teenager causing an accident later in life. Hence, it is in this sense that we can evaluate and justify moral sentiments with an eye to the social functions they serve. Let us contrast and distinguish this approach from the approach that is dominant in contemporary discussions of moral responsibility and that we could call the "ontological-desert-oriented" approach.[4]

The ontological-desert-oriented approach looks to our moral practices primarily from the point of view of individual desert. According to this approach, it is not fair to expose people to (often negative) sentiments if they do not deserve it. The thought here is that if someone does something that is considered to be really wrong, you should only hold that person responsible when she or he deserves it. That is, you should only hold people morally responsible under certain conditions that determine whether this person is an agent in the proper sense, because it is unfair to blame or resent, let alone punish, people for things they cannot help or cannot control.

The bulk of the philosophical discussion about moral responsibility focuses on the conditions under which people can reasonably be held morally responsible for what they do. I take this to be a difficult, important, and interesting discussion, but it is one I do not want to address in this chapter.[5] I think the focus on this issue, and the argumentative dynamic that results from taking this issue as our starting point, obscures some important features of our practices of moral responsibility. These features are related to the communicative and coordinative purposes our practices serve and the way in which they serve it. As I argue, it is by interacting with one another that we figure out (1) who is responsible and who is not and (2) what norms and values should regulate our everyday interactions.

It is important to stress that I am not developing an alternative theory of moral responsibility in the sense of proposing a different set of conditions. Rather I want to make clear that philosophical efforts and attempts to articulate such conditions obscure the degree to which, and the importance of the fact that, we figure out in practice who is responsible for what, and to what extent, by simply engaging with one another as responsible beings. To be sure, for beings like us, this engagement is bound to get tangled up with all kinds of sophisticated justificatory issues as they are addressed in the ontological-desert-oriented approach, but keeping those issues out of the picture helps us to fully grasp the social dimension of moral responsibility. At least that is what I argue.

In the following section, I set out a view of human agency, which I have advanced elsewhere (Sie 2014), to explain why we are in many respects like the texting teenager in our example. I offer a view of why we need other people's moral responses to our behavior to become moral agents—to develop a way of responding and relating to the world that is regulated by norms and values. In section 3, I elaborate on what it means to claim that holding people responsible serves communicative purposes and facilitates coordination of a shared practice. I explain how it is that holding one another morally responsible enables us to determine, consolidate, and fine-tune our normative expectations of one another. In section 4, I explain what light my elaborations shed on the ontological-desert-oriented approach. I argue that in order to fully capture the social dimension of our practices of moral responsibility, it pays to resist defining or identifying what capabilities are required for us to be morally responsible and emphasize instead that there is an important sense in which we figure out who is morally responsible for what as we go along. In section 5, I illustrate that idea with some brief remarks on contemporary discussions of implicit bias. Insofar as harmful stereotyping and prejudiced behavior serve to further entrench and perpetrate implicit biases, we need to figure out how to improve our practices. I argue that we can figure this out only by holding one another morally responsible even when implicit bias is a causal factor in the behavior in question (cf. Calhoun 1989).[6] Although my remarks will be brief, I hope they show how the topics hotly debated in the contemporary discussion on our responsibility for implicit bias can be addressed in a more natural and less contrived way than when addressed from the ontological-desert-oriented approach. I also hope to explain why changing our practices, if we want to make them less biased, is bound to be a difficult, painstaking, and, above all, collective enterprise.

2 Morality, Values, Identity, and Practices

I regard the view of human agency and morality that I am about to set forth as philosophically uncontroversial because its basic philosophical assumptions are minimal. Moreover, the assumptions that it does make are in line with many of the empirical findings in the cognitive, behavioral, and neuroscientific literature of the past couple of decades.[7] These findings show, as I have argued elsewhere (Sie 2014), that we often do not know exactly why we act, choose, and judge as we do, and for what reasons. According to this view, humans are emotionally and motivationally complex beings who tend to act from a plethora of motives, beliefs, and circumstances. On many occasions, a whole set of diverse considerations and overarching aims come into play—partly implicitly—and their complex combination makes us respond in the way we do. I call this set of considerations and overarching aims "motivational frameworks": they make up the basic underlying structure against the background of which we act. These motivational frameworks include roles such as student, parent, and employee, but also characteristics such as restlessness, honesty, caring, and our existence as psychological, emotional, and bodily beings. As a caring parent, for example, it might be part of our motivational framework to respond to our children's needs, but also to take care of our home so they have a safe and pleasant place to grow up in. What exactly the phrases 'respond to our children's needs' and 'take care of our home' imply depends upon context, our interpretation of the situation, and the other motivational frameworks that guide our actions. Annoying noises wake us up (the alarm clock goes off), our children need to go to school, we have a meeting, we feel energetic and want to get active, we have promised a colleague we would see her at work, and so on. Why do we get up? Because the alarm clock woke us up, because we love our job, because we are responsible parents, because we keep our promises? Most of the time, the adequate answer will consist of a combination of considerations only a few of which we are aware of and/or care to mention when asked. We are not fully aware of, and do not think about and reflect on, all the overarching motivational frameworks that make sense of the myriad triggers we respond to (alarm clocks, promises), things we do (arising, taking the children school), and projects we pursue (becoming a philosopher, becoming an attentive and relaxed parent). Many of the overarching frameworks are taken as given and legitimate. It is when conflicts or tensions mount or when we are confronted with explicit moral demands or evaluations that we (attempt to) articulate our moral reasons or principles in response.[8] In many of these cases, we articulate the reasons without much prior thought as well, repeating the reasons we have learned to be, or think are, appropriate for the occasion. Often in adult life, we just go through the motions of apologizing, excusing, and explaining how important certain things are to us, that is, without really examining or reflecting upon them.[9] In a split second, we judge that a situation calls for exactly such and such reply, response, or mixture of apology, excuse, and reply, and we are able to provide it instantly. I return to this in section 3.2.

We are, in other words, thoroughly embedded beings from the moment we are born. We are raised and act in a specific social and cultural setting, surrounded by devices and artifacts, involved in all kinds of institutions, personal relationships, and activities, many of which we did not choose or decide upon but which constitute our lives nevertheless. In a very similar manner, our evaluations, values, and normative expectations are not neatly organized, thought through, or clearly articulated at one point in time. As a result, we are often not aware of what moral considerations, values, and principles matter to us and make us act as we do; we might even be mistaken with regard to them.

Note that I am not denying that we are self-governing beings who are partly or sometimes guided by our values, ideals, views, or "higher-order self-governing policies," as Bratman (2007, 83) calls them. Surely we sometimes plan, decide, and intend to do things, and manage to act in accordance with those plans, decisions, and intentions.[10] However, those plans, decisions, and intentions originate within larger motivational frameworks and those frameworks we did not choose or decide upon; moreover, the motivational framework seldom is part of our deliberative horizon. Take, for example, such things as the fact that we are healthy, that we live in a rich (or poor) society, that there are things and people we care for, that the people we care for and the society we live in accept or even appreciate who we are and what we do, and so on. For human beings, the world they grow up in is a meaningful and morally organized one. That is to say, it is not the case that each and every one of us individually endows it with meaning after long and careful deliberation, though our individual histories might make it the case that we are very aware of the importance of certain things such as our family or health.

Moreover, with respect to many moral matters what it means to value things, endorse principles, and take certain considerations as moral reasons becomes clear and vivid in our everyday interactions only when we have to put our money where our mouths are—that is, when we have to "translate" abstract concepts such as honesty, attentiveness, conscientiousness, and so on into specific actions or behaviors that warrant those labels in particular situations and conditions. You might have believed your whole life that honesty matters more to you than anything else, until you face a situation in which honesty would cost you your job, relationship, or something else that is of vital importance to you. Or vice versa, you might discover (or make it the case) that honesty matters more to you than your job or relationship only when faced with a situation in which you have to choose. In other words, we often do not know exactly what we value in the sense that we often do not know exactly what we stand for and are willing to stand for until we are tested by a situation. Hence, taking all of this into account, an important manner in which we learn to apply, really understand, and grasp values and morality more generally is in interactions and dialogue with other people, most notably those by whom we are raised and those with whom we interact on a regular basis in life.

Elsewhere, I refer to this view of moral agency as "the traffic participation view of human agency" (TPV) (Sie 2014).[11] The way in which we are and become moral agents bears a strong resemblance to what it means to be and how we become proficient traffic participants who navigate shared practices within our community. As traffic participants, we allow room for the attentive aspects of our interactions (e.g., what we deliberately aim at, the destination we are trying to get to, and so on) as well as the more automatic (unconscious) aspects of our interactions (e.g., the motivational background that steers us without our being aware of it, the manner in which we find our way around, and so on). As said, I do not regard this philosophical view as particularly controversial because its philosophical assumptions are minimal. When discussing moral agency, practical philosophers, at least in the analytic tradition, tend to be concerned with ideal typical examples of (moral) agency—hence examples in which the above described "fuzzy" character of our moral agency is not at the center of attention.[12]

We human beings are mammals and as such are born completely dependent on others to take care of us in the first years of our lives. The way in which those caregivers take care of us in our early years determines how we function as agents later in life.[13] This seems true to me not only at the level of the capacities that we develop to interact with others, but also at the level of the specific normative considerations that provide us with the maps along which we navigate our shared practices. It is again in interaction and dialogue with others that we fine-tune, discover, and develop our more individual moral profiles and identities. If the TPV is right, then it would be very bad if we gave up on (expressing) the moral sentiments. Now let us turn to why exactly that is the case.

3 Sharing Moral Responsibility

3.1 Communication and Coordination

Let us start with a very basic example in which people have to work together and need a way to coordinate their behavior.[14] Let us bear in mind what was said in the previous section: we often do not know exactly what we value in the sense that we often do not know exactly what we stand for and are willing to stand for. Besides these individual uncertainties, people involved in a shared project often differ in their wishes and ideas about how to carry out the project and their capacities to contribute to it. As a consequence, they need to communicate with each other during the project and practice dividing the labor. If we want to build a house, we need to meet several technical requirements (e.g., stable construction), and we need to reach an agreement on the design of the house and the division of duties. Different people engaged in building the house will have different capacities (one might be good at laying bricks, another at painting), but also different interests (one needs the money, another will be the owner). Hence, they will also have different expectations about what is required for a good house, how much time and energy everyone should invest, and so on.

The coordination of shared practices has two important, but distinct, aspects. First, we must decide what is to be done (the plan of the house and the way to build it) and what is expected from the different people involved. I shall call this the "design aspect" of our shared practices to capture the fact that how exactly we regulate our shared interactions in the future is something that we fine-tune and determine (design) together. I shall call the expectations about how people should behave "normative expectations," that is, expectations about what should be done by whom, why, and when (and sometimes also about what should *not* be done). Second, it must be ensured that people behave as expected, that they keep up their end of the deal, so to speak. Let us call these aspects in which we hold people to the normative expectations the "process aspects" of our shared practices. The design and process aspects are closely intertwined, and I explain them more elaborately in the course of this chapter.

Several practices (obedience to authority, tradition, voting procedures) help us realize those two aspects. One important way to ensure that people do what is expected of them is to make clear to them what is expected. It is an important aspect of our Western society that making clear to people what is expected of them, and explaining why, suffices to get them to behave accordingly.[15] Other ways to get people to behave in ways we would like them to is through conditioning and manipulation. When people fail to do what is expected, we can punish them, or we can reward them for doing (or exceeding) what is expected. The moral sentiments of blame, praise, resentment, gratitude, and moral indignation often function as rewards and punishment. We are thoroughly social beings, and it matters greatly to us to be regarded as moral beings.[16] Both punishment and reward function as part of the conditioning processes, although in different ways (cf. McGeer 2015, 2647). However, it is common in our Western society that we put great trust in people's ability to figure out what is expected of them in a variety of situations. We rely on their willingness and ability to do what is expected because they want to and without the need to take recourse to institutional force, violence, manipulation, or other measures.

This means that when normative expectations differ, ideally we try to bring them into line by discussing which expectations are reasonable.[17] Out of such discussions evolves, again in the ideal case, what we might call a space of reasons: interconnected views of what we should do (and not do) in what situations and under what conditions.[18] Although the moral sentiments certainly have conditioning and manipulating effects, they also function as an intermediary between the space of reasons, our normative expectations, and our actions. When we blame someone, or communicate that we think her or his action is blameworthy, this is often taken as an invitation to explain and justify ourselves.[19] Peter F. Strawson succeeded in making the moral sentiments so influential in discussions of responsibility because he disclosed this communicative feature of our practices. He makes clear that holding someone morally responsible is not an isolated activity we sometimes undertake with respect to some people, but is completely intertwined with our interpersonal relationships (Strawson [1962] 1982, 78). It is responding to one another with, among other things, the moral sentiments that make our everyday practices *moral* practices. According to Strawson, criticism and adjustments, as well as pessimism and optimism about moral responsibility are only possible from within these practices. As we will see in the next section, many philosophers have repeated, elaborated, and criticized his claim. A central claim of this chapter is that our moral practices are indeed, as suggested by Strawson and others, shaped by the dynamics of our responsibility practices. However, the moral sentiments expressed in our interactions with each other serve important dual functions. Tokens of appraisal, such as frowns and compliments, blame and praise, and resentment and gratitude, not only encourage us to behave in morally acceptable ways in specific situations, but also enable us to contribute to determining what these acceptable ways are. Let us discuss an example to illustrate more precisely how this practice, the dynamics of responsibility, is supposed to work and why I think the moral sentiments serve dual functions pertaining to what I have called the process and design aspects of our practices.

> Some time ago, my colleague, Arno, left his bicycle pump in the corner of the pub where he had lunch. He wanted to have his hands free on his after-lunch walk, and the barman of the pub promised to keep an eye

on the pump. When Arno came back, the pump had disappeared. Upon asking the barman where his pump had gone, the barman shrugged his shoulders; he could not remember (and was busy anyway). In response to this attitude, Arno blamed the barman for being inattentive; did he not ask him explicitly to keep an eye on it? The barman, feeling guilty now, tried to remember what happened to the pump and realized he might have allowed a customer who often visits the pub to use the pump. He vaguely remembers her entering the pub looking for someone to help her with a punctured tire. He now realizes she must have forgotten to bring it back after using it. The barman promises Arno to call her to account at her next visit. A week later, a friendly young woman rang at Arno's door, handed over his pump, and apologized for having taken it. She had assumed that the owner of the pump had forgotten it and would not miss it. Also, she had assumed that the barman, whom she knows from her regular visits to the pub, meant her to take it home when he said that she "could take it." Hence, she had taken the pump on the road to pump up her punctured tire a second time on her way home. It was only after the barman asked her whether she took the pump and why, that she realized that the owner did miss the pump and that the barman had not intended to allow her to take it as her own.[20]

This example illustrates the occasions when we blame, the immediate function of blaming, and its effects. We blame people when they do not behave as we think or feel they should. In the resulting exchange, both parties explain how they think the blamed behavior fits into a shared space of reasons, and they might come to share a common view of what happened, what should have been done, and the proper response. Arno expected the barman to take care of the pump and blamed him because it seemed to him that he did not fulfill that expectation. The barman initially did not really perceive that he had done anything wrong, but as a response to Arno's blame, realized his mistake, figured out what happened, and explained his behavior. He concludes that in his view he did nothing wrong; he let someone use the pump with the expectation that she would bring it back. If anyone is to be blamed, it is the woman. Arno accepted the barman's interpretation and his explanation and, subsequently, changed his view of what the barman should have done, and accepted his offer to call the woman to account. In the exchange between the woman and the barman, it is the blamed person who changes her interpretation of what happened, agrees that she should not have taken the pump, and offers to return it. Finally, in the exchange between Arno and the woman, Arno changes his view of what happened again and accepts that the woman is not to blame for theft, but for having a wrong view of what one can do with objects one has permission to use.

To be sure, this is a rather cerebral and idealized reconstruction of what happened, but it is necessary to make clear how to understand the dynamic of responsibility from the perspective developed in this chapter. In everyday situations, much of what is articulated in this reconstruction might remain unarticulated. Now let me turn to why, according to this understanding of the dynamic of responsibility, expressing our tokens of appraisal is indispensable.

3.2 Why Tokens of Appraisal Are Indispensable

What is illustrated by the pump example is that we constantly have to figure out ways to live together and align all our different normative expectations against the background of our individual motivational profiles, the projects we pursue, and so on. This is an ongoing and continuous process even in cases where we agree on the basic values that should regulate our shared practices. It is crucial to the dynamics of responsibility ascriptions, as explained at the beginning of this section, that it allows for differences between individuals, differences in capacities, interests, and degrees of participation.[21] It is by way of the moral sentiments and subsequent exchange of reasons that we fine-tune our mutual normative expectations and that we figure out what can be expected when, from whom, and why. This is what I referred to as the "design aspects" of our shared practices. It is this aspect that becomes more noticeable when we attend to why it is legitimate to respond with the moral sentiments viewed from the perspective of their social function.

Part of this process of fine-tuning our *mutual* normative expectations is that the moral sentiments are also vital for each individual to develop something like a moral identity. As explained in the previous section, what we care about, what values matter to us, and how we weigh these against, for example, other wishes, interests, and desires only becomes clear when we are held to normative expectations in particular situations. This interaction might prompt the barman, for example, to pay closer attention whenever someone asks him to borrow something or, alternatively, he might no longer be prepared to fulfill such requests, discovering that he is not able to do so properly and will be resented when something goes wrong. That he is not able to do so properly might be because he is too busy, decides these kinds of requests are not part of his job description, or because, for example, he is too easily distracted to keep track of other people's property. Arno and the woman might have learned similar lessons. Note that in this fine-tuning of our reciprocal normative expectations, as in the building of a house example, it is taken into account that not all individuals possess equal capacities. We allow for many individual differences and estimates in what it seems "reasonable to expect" from someone in a particular situation.

I have discussed a very mundane example, but it is good to keep in mind that situations might be and often are much more complicated than the example suggests and more difficult to assess and observe from a third-person perspective. We respond to one another with the moral sentiments from a very young age. By the time we reach adulthood, we have developed a way of responding to the world that is heavily infused by our culture, our caretakers, and our peers. By 'heavily infused,' I mean that what we value and care for bears the mark of those prior interactions and our ways of responding. 'Heavily infused' also implies that what we value and care for and how we respond to others might, to a certain extent, be hidden from view. Situations might "push our buttons" without it being completely clear to us why, and this might happen for the right or wrong reasons. That is, sometimes we realize that our initial moral response was exactly the right one even though, at the time, we did not understand exactly why. On the other hand, sometimes our moral gut responses might lead us astray. If only for that reason—the fact that it is not always clear to us what pushes our buttons— it pays to hold one another morally responsible for transgressions of our normative expectations. For, holding one another responsible in the basic and less strict ways of these examples creates opportunities to reflect on, articulate, and discuss with one another what we did and why. This includes a discussion of the appropriateness of our moral reactive responses. Often when someone blames or resents us, part of the discussion that follows is the appropriateness of these sentiments or the degree to which they are felt or expressed. The outcome of such a discussion might change the way in which we continue to interact with one another. Also, they make us aware of what others expect of us and encourage us to take those expectations into consideration in the future. On this point I am in complete agreement with so-called scaffolding views of moral responsibility (e.g., McGeer 2010, 2015; Holroyd, chapter 5, this volume).[22] I return to this point in the next section.

To the above, let me add that we should not only evaluate others critically, but ourselves as well. This includes taking other people's moral responses to our own behavior seriously even though what we are reproached for does not fit our self-understanding. It is important to be open to the possibility that our motives may be other than we believe them to be and therefore that our behavior may be less defensible than we initially believe it to be.[23] Therefore, the moral sentiments also have a role to play in the development of our moral identity and our ability to act in accordance with the things we value and believe to be important.

Not all exchanges in which the moral sentiments are involved have the character just set out. In many cases, the moral sentiments function rather as a kind of social glue, ways to smooth and steer our interactions with one another, but with no need for significant reflection. This too is understandable on the basis of the communicative and coordinative function that holding one another

responsible usually serves. Often our frowns, small tokens of blame and resentment, the standard apologetic gestures, and excuses function as the signs that
we are aware of navigating the same moral and social space. In such cases, the
moral sentiments function to ensure the process aspect of our shared practices.
As already noted, when someone is late, accidentally hurts or insults you, acts
inattentively, or causes you some trouble, that person might apologize, provide
some reason, make up for her or his behavior before you even so much as frown.
If that does not happen, some frowning, comments, or reproaches will evoke
the desired response. On such occasions, we are going through the motions pre-
scripted by our shared practices. In these rituals, all those involved affirm to one
another that they agree on the norms and values transgressed and on what is
required to remedy the situation.

In other situations, such as in the example above, the moral sentiments
introduce reflective moments in the flow of interactions. These moments can
offer occasions to adjust one's normative expectations of one another slightly,
but they might also occasion much more radical and important changes with
respect to one's moral identity. The opposite seems very likely as well; if such
occasions do not occur, we might never come round to question our values and
ways of responding (cf. Calhoun 1989).[24] Perhaps this dynamic might partly
explain why in certain circles (e.g., bankers, professional sportsmen) behavior
that would be considered immoral in other contexts (e.g., deception, cheating),
can become the rule rather than the exception.

Before concluding this section, let me come back to the design and process
aspects of our shared coordinated practices, to the fact that they are so closely
intertwined. As our example illustrates, the moral sentiments, ideally, open up
a space of reasons in which to fine-tune our reciprocal normative expectations.
When this happens, each individual participant participates in designing our
shared moral practice, contributing to coconstituting its shape. The moral sentiments also function as social glue to make sure that we continue to act in accordance with widely shared normative expectations. These features are intertwined,
because when you are not engaged with as a morally responsible individual, you
are not able to leave your mark on the shared practice. Suppose, for example,
that Arno had not blamed the barman for inattentiveness when he shrugged his
shoulders, causing Arno to infer that, for whatever reason, the barman was not
someone to be taken seriously. In that case, the barman would not have been
blamed, but also would never have been put in the position to take a stance on
the matter either. As a result of the latter, the barman would not have left his
mark on which normative expectations regulate their interactions in subsequent
encounters. It is in this sense that the process and the design aspects of our moral
practices are closely intertwined. Those who are regarded as full-blown, equal
participants in our shared practice are held morally responsible for their actions

(process-aspect) and, as a result, are able to take part in the activity of fine-tuning these reciprocal normative expectations or changing them (design-aspect).

To be sure, it is not the case that the social aspects of our everyday practices elaborated on in this section have gone unnoticed in contemporary discussions of our practices of moral responsibility. Following Strawson's lead, many philosophers have developed accounts that capture its social dimension at least partly. Those philosophers accept what Jules Holroyd refers to as the "social thesis," the idea that holding one another morally responsible is constituted by our moral reactive responses to one another and does not rely on "any metaphysically deep notion antecedent to our social relations" (Holroyd, chapter 5, this volume). Jay Wallace, for example, defends a reactive account of moral responsibility where holding someone morally responsible is understood as "holding that person to expectations," which is a thoroughly social notion. "Holding a person to expectations" he subsequently understands as the "susceptibility to a range of reactive attitudes and emotions" with regard to that individual (Wallace 1994, 21).[25] Wallace's account is compatible with the view I have proposed in this section. However, like other compatibilist accounts, he does not capture sufficiently the thoroughly social dimension of moral responsibility practices, due to his focus on the justificatory issue characteristic of the ontological-desert-oriented approach, as I explain in the next section.

4 Disadvantages of the Ontological-Desert-Oriented Approach

Wallace and some other Strawsonian compatibilist philosophers fear that accepting the social thesis does not suffice to block incompatibilist worries (Wallace 1994, 104; Wolf 1990, 21). As a response to this fear, they examine what kind of capacities agents should have to make it fair to hold them morally responsible. Their answer, broadly speaking, is that it is our reasons-responsive nature that makes us a proper subject of the reactive attitudes and emotions (see also, e.g., Fischer 1994; Smith and Pettit 1996; Vargas 2013).[26] By articulating this answer, they explain why we can accept not only the social thesis, but also what Victoria McGeer refers to as Strawson's "metaphysical non-commitment thesis." This thesis is that "the concepts and practices of responsibility, as embodied in our reactive exchanges, do not presuppose anything so metaphysically demanding as libertarian (or contra-causal) free will" (McGeer 2010, 302; cf. also Wallace 1994, 102). We can accept the metaphysical non-commitment thesis because we hold people morally responsible only when they are reasons responsive and only in conditions that do not interfere with this reasons responsiveness. And this reasons responsiveness is a metaphysically undemanding notion.

Incompatibilists, as might be expected, have countered this claim from various directions (e.g., Pereboom 2013; Strawson 2013).[27]

When we, as I have done in this chapter, steer clear of the question of whether or not we deserve to be held morally responsible, we see that not to be subjected to the moral sentiments is to be excluded from the collective enterprise of figuring out how to get along with one another.[28] Although we can exclude some people, on some occasions, we cannot steer clear of this enterprise altogether, because social animals like ourselves have to get along with one another for a variety of reasons and purposes. Hence, we need to communicate and coordinate our actions and behavior and, as described in the previous section, the moral sentiments are vital to this process. Why this is the case is disclosed when we focus on the more basic and less strict ways in which we respond to one another's transgressions. It is by holding one another morally responsible that we figure out what we can expect from one another and what we stand for and are willing to stand for ourselves; it is also only after we enter that dynamic that the issue can arise of who deserves to be held responsible and under what conditions.[29]

Does this mean that we can do without research into and a discussion of certain cognitive, volitional, and emotional incapacities that impair what McGeer (2010) has called our "co-reactivity" or what compatibilist philosophers have called our reasons responsiveness? I think that is not the case. Such research is important to our moral practices and the dynamic that I have described in the previous section, but not because it enables us to decide whom to hold responsible under what conditions. Uncovering and identifying conditions that have an impact on how we understand, communicate, and interact with one another is in many respects vital, for example, to figuring out ways in which to extend the circle of people able to participate in our practices and which actions not to take (too) seriously.[30] Discovering sources of miscommunication and misunderstanding is often the first step in working toward a more inclusive and reasonable practice, as I argue in the next section of this chapter. However, the conditions of responsibility articulated in the debate should not be understood as conditions that we could apply prior to engaging with people in shared enterprises or practices. They do not allow us to determine who the equal participants to this practice are and with whom we should fine-tune our reciprocal normative expectations of one another. To be sure, it is not part of the "reasons responsive"-compatibilist argument, or the argument of McGeer, that conditions of responsibility can be identified prior to our practices. Indeed, it was a crucial part of Strawson's argument to point out that they cannot. However, once we start discussing which capacities make us proper subjects of the moral sentiments, several questions naturally arise. First, what is it about any specific capacity that makes someone an appropriate subjects of moral sentiments? Second,

under what conditions can we differentiate between deserving and undeserv-
ing recipients of our responses? These questions lead us down the ontological-
desert-oriented path. I have already argued that this approach may obscure the
communicative and coordinating functions of the moral sentiments in the context of responsibility practices. To prevent these misunderstandings, it pays to
resist taking the ontological-desert-oriented approach to our practices of moral
responsibility, and to focus on spelling out the communicative and coordinative
purposes of these practices.

Let me summarize. To adequately grasp the social dimension of our practices of moral responsibility, it pays to direct our attention away from the justificatory issues central in the dominant ontological-desert-oriented approach
to moral responsibility. Even though compatibilist views such as Wallace's and
more recent ones, such as Vargas's and McGeer's, already articulate many of the
insights central in this chapter, restricting our attention to the social function of
our moral practices highlights how basic and indispensable the communicative
and coordinative purposes of holding one another morally responsible actually
are. Viewed from this perspective, articulating ever-more sophisticated conditions for moral responsibility is a waste of conceptual effort. Rather, we should
pay more attention to the many ways in which, and the different reasons why, the
moral sentiments can be detrimental or conducive to the communicative and
coordinative purposes they tend to serve.[31]

To conclude, let me illustrate how, from the perspective developed in this
chapter, we can bring together several issues that are discussed in contemporary debates about our responsibility for stereotypes, prejudices, and implicit
biases.

5 Responsibility for Stereotypes, Prejudices,
and Implicit Bias

In contemporary societies, our everyday interactions with one another require
us to process enormous amounts of information. Stereotypes and prejudices are
important shortcuts to get this done. Very probably the reason why they are efficient as shortcuts is the involvement of something like implicit biases (hereafter,
IBs). IBs influence our actions automatically and without our being aware of
it; hence they save us cognitive energy in comparison to applying stereotypes
and prejudices reflectively.[32] What fascinates philosophers and scientists in the
wealth of literature on IBs of the past decades is the finding that IBs seem to operate regardless of and sometimes even contrary to our explicit attitudes.[33] If this
the case, the existence of IBs might explain the persistence of harmful stereotyping and prejudiced behavior in the domain of social cognition in self-declared

"egalitarian" societies.[34] It might explain why, even when we claim to truly reject certain stereotypes and prejudices, our behavior is difficult to change.[35]

From the ontological-desert-oriented approach, the primary question is whether it is fair to blame the individual involved in harmful stereotyping and prejudiced behavior when IBs are (at least partly) the cause of that behavior.[36] After all, if we are not aware of acting in stereotyping or prejudiced ways, and even object to such ways of behaving, how can it be fair to blame us? By now, that question is hotly debated (e.g., Kelly and Roeder 2008, 532; Saul 2013; Holroyd 2012). From the perspective developed in this chapter, IBs are problematic because they interfere with the social dynamic of our practices of moral responsibility, not because they make us act in ways we reject at a deliberative level. Moreover, from this perspective, the literature on IBs gives us cause to wonder whether we can claim to be true egalitarians in the domain of social cognition. Let me explain each of these points.

It is important to keep in mind, as many in the discussion on IBs have pointed out, that the kind of harm we are concerned with when discussing IBs can be very serious, even when the wrongdoing that causes it is not. Behavior that is trivial at the individual level can add up to an environment that systematically puts certain groups at a disadvantage. Those trivial actions are also called a "micro-inequities" (cf. Brennan 2016). From the perspective developed in this chapter, it is easy to take that observation on board. Some stereotypes and prejudices are harmful because they interfere with the ability of some to contribute equally to the design of our moral practices. IBs aggravate that harm because they obstruct or slow down the process of changing these stereotypes and prejudices.

Take, for example, a newly arrived student who addresses the only female assistant professor at a department of philosophy office as the secretary. This action is innocent enough. The student is just assuming what her experience has taught her: when in need of a secretary at a philosophy department, look for a female employee.[37] Hence, she is just making an understandable mistake. However, the young assistant professor is disadvantaged when virtually all of the time she is addressed or approached as a secretary or just as a "very special case" for being a female professor in a male-dominated field. The reason why she is disadvantaged is that she does not feel and is not regarded as an equal participant to the practice she participates in. As a result, she is unable to leave her mark on the practice in which she participates.

Note that in the above example the professor need not be suffering from any negative associations that go with her gender; it is the mere fact that she does not fit the stereotype that results in her being treated and approached in a different way than male professors.[38] It might even be the case that, in a sense, she also benefits as a result of not fitting the stereotype. For example, people might more easily remember her after a lecture because she was the only female in an all-male lineup; people might allow her a bit more space in determining office hours, assuming that she has parenting duties.[39] However, advantaged or not in this sense, the mere fact that she does not fit the stereotype of her professional community impacts her ability to participate equally in this community: she stands out as special (not fitting the stereotype), and her actions, behavior, and contributions to the practices are likely to be approached as such. To make this more concrete, when her classes are very interactive, chances are that that feature is associated with her as an individual, rather than with the discipline she is part of. Hence, her style of teaching will not impact what the students come to expect from philosophy or what her colleagues will take into consideration as an adequate way of teaching philosophy.

On top of that, due to implicit biases, those who stand out risk reinforcing existing stereotypes and prejudices rather than correcting them. For example, it has been suggested that we evaluate CVs, publications, and teaching performance of female professors differently than we do those of male professors (e.g., Moss-Racusin et al. 2012). If this is the case, this will reinforce the idea that female professors are not as suited for the profession as male professors.[40] As a result, stereotypes and prejudices are not likely to disappear simply as a result of our practices slowly becoming more diverse. It is in this sense that IBs aggravate the harm done by stereotypes and prejudices. These examples illustrate how stereotyping and IBs can affect people's abilities to codetermine the normative expectations that regulate their practices.

Let me now turn to question whether we fully understand and grasp what it means to declare oneself to be an egalitarian vis-à-vis the literature on implicit bias. In section 3, I illustrated in what sense we need one another's moral responses to become aware of, and be able to change, our behavior. It is these moral responses that introduce reflective moments in the everyday flow of our interactions. It is these responses that are able to make us aware of, in this case, the biased nature of our actions and that invite us to explain and justify ourselves and to determine our moral attitude with respect to what others expect of us and what our explicit egalitarian attitudes commit us to. Even though we might view ourselves as egalitarians, the question is whether we understand what that means exactly, prior to figuring this out in practice—that is, prior to attempts to interact with one another in ways undistorted by the stereotypes and prejudices that we want to get rid of. As explained in section 3, what we care about, what values matter to us, and how we weigh these against, for example, other wishes, interests, and desires only becomes clear in everyday situations where we have to translate these abstract values into specific actions. If only for this reason, the transition from explicit egalitarian commitments to a truly egalitarian practice is bound to take time, effort, and practice. It is only through particular occasions on which we address one another with respect to non-egalitarian manners and behavior, and hold one another morally responsible for these, that we are able to figure out new ways to interact with one another.

The above observation is unaffected when a considerable part of our stereotyping and prejudiced behavior is due to the role of implicit biases. However, if the "implicit bias" literature is correct, it identifies an important source of miscommunication between people. It explains why people might sincerely experience being, or believe themselves to be, wrongfully approached and reproached for stereotyping and prejudiced behavior, when their explicit commitments are egalitarian (cf. Saul 2013). This does not mean that we should cease to hold one another responsible for biased behavior that we believe harmful. Whether we should do so or not rather depends on the context and situation of that behavior (cf. Calhoun 1989). When a student refers to a female philosopher by her first name only in a presentation on this philosopher's work, this invites and requires a different response than when a senior professor does the same. Not because the senior professor should have known better, although that might also be the case, but because our responses with one of the moral sentiments serves a different communicative and coordinative purpose in each case.

To conclude, let me wrap up the argument of this section. From the perspective developed in this chapter, whether or not we can help harmful stereotyping and prejudiced behavior that runs counter to our explicit egalitarian attitudes is not such an important question. The simple fact is that we need one another to "change our ways" and to figure out what these ways should be. That is, we need one another to develop the capacities required to act in more egalitarian ways and to determine our attitude with respect to egalitarian values in specific settings. The question whether or not we *deserve to be held responsible as individuals* steers our attention away from this collective responsibility to make our practices more egalitarian. Rather, we need to respond to one another with the moral sentiments whenever we are bothered by its stereotyping or prejudiced nature and see how this response is answered. This is how we figure out how to make our practices more egalitarian, given the interactive dynamics of our responsibility practices sketched in this chapter. That is, we figure out what we want to change, in what way exactly, by "muddling through together." It might well be that the negative moral sentiments, in many cases, do not contribute to this collective enterprise, especially on occasions when it is not clear what is harmful about the behavior concerned. However, if we want to change our ways, addressing one another is the only way in which we can figure out ways to live together and align our different normative expectations against the background of our individual motivational profiles, the projects we pursue, and so on. This is an ongoing and continuous process even in cases where we agree on the basic values.

6 Conclusion

It is not the case that we are born as individuals with a fixed set of capacities that either make us morally responsible (able to fulfill normative expectations) or not. Rather, from the moment we are born, we are part of a community of people who respond to us as capable of fulfilling all kinds of normative expectations, which is why and how we develop the ability to do so. Of course, this is not to claim that we can develop any capacity whatsoever, provided that we are in the right social circumstances, but just to claim that our social circumstances play a crucial role in selecting and developing certain capacities. It is for this reason that we should not give up on holding one another morally responsible for transgressing normative expectations. We should not give up, first of all, because holding one another responsible for specific transgressions is what enables us to become responsible persons (process aspect) and secondly, because only holding one another responsible enables us to codetermine and influence which normative expectations will regulate our shared interactions in the future (design aspect). Many contemporary compatibilist accounts have articulated views that highlight the social dimensions of our moral practices elaborated in this chapter. However, caught up in the enterprise of justifying our moral practices against skeptical worries, many of them remain "in the business" of articulating necessary and sufficient conditions for moral responsibility. Once in this business, we seem to be able to distinguish between morally responsible and nonresponsible agents prior to interacting with them. However, as I hope to have made clear, in our everyday practices we determine who is responsible for what and why exactly and that we need to do so "as we go along." Hence, we do not need to invest so much energy and effort in figuring out and discussing in theory whether or not we can be held responsible for certain actions or behavior, for example, harmful, prejudiced, and stereotyping behavior caused by implicit bias. This only steers our attention away from our collective responsibility to make our practices more egalitarian and to figure out, while "muddling through together," how we can do so.[41]

Notes

1. Thanks to Katrina Hutchison for suggesting this formulation.
2. Which is not to say that the behavior we decide to regulate by our protocols and laws might not start out as behavior we frown upon, blame for, and resent.
3. Vargas (2013) and McGeer (2010, 2015) have both developed accounts in which such forward-looking aspects of our practices of moral responsibility play a crucial role. For a comparison between those views see Holroyd, chapter 5, this volume. I indicate in what sense my account differs from theirs in section 4.

4. The approach taken in this chapter could be referred to as the "pragmatist-sentimentalist" approach. However, since my main aim is to show what it is exactly that risks being overlooked when we approach moral responsibility from the ontological-desert-oriented approach, not to establish or explain in what sense the approach taken in this chapter is an alternative and novel approach, I restrict myself to positioning the claims endorsed in opposition to the onto-logical-desert-oriented approach.

5. I address this issue in Sie 2005.

6. Calhoun argues that, once we approach the issue of moral responsibility at the level of our social practice, there are reasons to blame people for wrongful behavior even when they are not to blame. The argument advanced in this chapter is not so much about behavior we *know* to be wrong, but about ways in which we come to agree on what is wrong. Thanks to Catriona Mackenzie for drawing my attention to this chapter. Also see note 24.

7. I refer to those findings that show that much of what we do is influenced in ways that we are unaware of, findings that are often subsumed under the heading of the "adaptive uncon-scious," although some people also refer to these findings under the heading of "dual-process theories" of human cognition.

8. I explain this view more elaborately in relation to the moral hypocrisy paradigm in psychol-ogy in Sie 2015. It is from this paper that this paragraph derives.

9. This is especially the case when we grow up in roughly the same cultural setting.

10. Moreover, as Bryce Huebner has convincingly argued, it is the fact that we are the kinds of agents who are able to plan and act *together* that provides us with a very special sort of freedom, the freedom to cooperatively imagine and create a different world (Huebner, forthcoming).

11. In Sie (2014), I elaborate this view in relation to the Social Intuitionist Model of Jonathan Haidt (2001) and the problem of free will understood as "conscious will."

12. The reason for this, as I understand it, is that they care to pinpoint what it is exactly that makes us full-blown agents, or makes us full-blown *moral* agents. That does not mean that they believe that we are such full-blown agents all the time or even occasionally. Nor does it mean that they believe we are born with the capacity to act as full-blown agents and only need the right ideal circumstances and conditions to do so. At least that is not the most charitable interpretation of their views.

13. One of the important insights that Barbara Herman (2012) puts center stage in her "Love and Morality (or Love's Complexities)" is that these first years of our lives and the dynamic between us and our caregivers might very well be crucial to the development of the capacities required for moral agency (Herman, 2012). For this, she partly draws on attachment theory in psychology.

14. The ideas elaborated in this section were originally developed together with Arno Wouters for a paper presented at a workshop on responsibility in 2010. Unfortunately, due to personal circumstances we failed to finish a joint version of that paper, but the ideas put forward in this section bear the marks of a joint enterprise. The first part of this section is an adapted version from section 1 of Sie 2013.

15. I emphasize 'Western' because I am not familiar with other cultures and can imagine that they might differ in this respect.

16. See Sie 2015. Actually "caring about morality," as Daniel Dennett has argued, might be very close to and/or developed from caring about appearing to be moral; see Dennett 2003, chapter 7.

17. To be sure, a lot can be/go wrong in these practices, for example, power imbalances within societies or between people can be (and often are) severely distorted. I think it is very impor-tant to be aware of what can be/go wrong, but for now I concentrate on elaborating on the general structure of these practices.

18. It might well be that the moral sentiments, or tokens of appraisals more generally speaking, are crucial elements to start off a process in which we are invited and required to "coopera-tively imagine and create a different world." See note 10 of this chapter.

19. Cf. McKenna's (2012) "conversational" account of moral responsibility.

20. This is an adapted version of an example that can be found in Wouters 2011. I also use it in Sie 2013.

21. For an example of how, return to the example with which we started this section. To be sure, this is not to claim that differences in capacities, interests, and degrees of participation cannot cause all kinds of misunderstandings and unproductive or unfair blame: unproductive because it fails to contribute to the communicative and coordinative purposes of this practice, or unfair because the agent is not a "fitting subject of these attitudes" in another respect.

22. Thanks to Katrina Hutchison for pointing this out to me.

23. I owe this formulation to Marina Oshana (personal communication).

24. Cheshire Calhoun argues that in some contexts blame or reproach is required even though the agent might not be blameworthy, because withholding those sentiments legitimizes behavior that is clearly wrong.

25. Wallace defends a tripartite account of holding people responsible to make room for the fact that we sometimes hold someone responsible without actually responding to that person with the moral sentiments. In his view, people can be said to hold someone morally responsible if a wrong—a transgression of a normative expectation—committed by this individual provokes (1) a reaction with one of the moral sentiments, or (2) the judgment that a reaction with one of the moral sentiments would be appropriate, or (3) both (1) and (2) (Wallace 1994, 21). Although I agree with him that we can hold someone responsible without actually responding to her or him with the moral sentiments, I also believe that in some cases the emotional component of these sentiments is required for its communicative and coordinative purposes.

26. Actually, Wallace refers to our capacity for "reflective self-control" (Wallace 1994, 1-2) but I regard his view and that of Wolf (1990, Chapter 4) as among the first ones to defend what is now commonly referred to as "reasons-responsiveness views."

27. Moreover, findings in the behavioral cognitive and neurosciences of the past decades have given us cause to reconsider how well we understand what it means to be reasons responsive (Sie and Wouters 2008, 2010).

28. In a sense, I argue that it is bad not to be held responsible. However, not because, for example, being held responsible enables us to become better beings, to "foster [a] valuable form of agency" (McGeer 2015, 2635; Vargas 2013) or because only by being held responsible are we addressed as moral persons (for example, Watson 1987; Darwall 2006; McKenna 2012).

29. I take it that this was the point that Strawson meant to establish in "Freedom and Resentment" ([1962] 1982). However, he also elaborately discusses which excuses and exemptions our current society accepts as mitigating our moral responsibility, thus steering our attention away again from the thoroughly social dimension I have highlighted in the previous section, and toward conditions that determine which individuals are to blame and when exactly.

30. Cf. Vargas (2013), who refines the notion of reasons responsiveness to take into account what the empirical sciences have taught us about the many ways in which it can be undermined. Also see the discussion of his "circumstantialism" by Jules Holroyd, chapter 5, this volume.

31. Although I have mainly focused on the many ways in which the moral sentiments are conducive to the communicative and coordinative purposes of our practices of moral responsibility, there is also ample reason to be suspicious of them. For example, a lot of attention these days is paid to what is called "outcome bias." When we perceive the outcome of a certain action or chain of actions as bad, unwanted, or extremely sad, we will judge the agent more harshly than we would if that exact same action or chain of actions would have had, in our eyes, a less bad, unwanted, or sad outcome. See, for example, Nadelhoffer 2008. Strawson was already quite aware of the "seamy side" of our moral sentiments and the importance of the findings in moral psychology, which, as he states, "have made us rightfully mistrustful of many particular manifestations of the attitudes I have spoken of" (Strawson [1962] 1982, 80).

32. See Sie and Voorst Vader-Bours (2016) for an elaboration of these points. Also see Huebner (2016) for an illuminating discussion of implicit bias in the domain of social cognition against the background of contemporary theories of the cognitive architecture that enables us to interact with our surroundings fluently.

33. See Saul and Brownstein (2016) for an excellent and much-needed overview of the philosophical questions and controversies surrounding implicit bias.

34. The topic of implicit bias is not restricted to the domain of social cognition. During the past decades, a variety of disciplines have identified many other influences on our evaluative and

decision-making capacities that escape awareness. As a result, philosophers and cognitive scientists also have raised general questions about our moral responsibility very similar to those raised in the domain of social cognition. I discuss these questions in Sie 2014.

35. By emphasizing that we "claim" to object to these ways of behaving, I do not mean to suggest that we do not actually object to them. However, as will become clear, I do think there is an important sense in which we do not fully grasp yet what it implies to object to those ways of behaving.

36. See, for example Zheng (2016, 69) for a reconstruction of the simple argument that leads to this question.

37. It is not my intention to suggest that stereotyping and prejudiced behavior are always the understandable results of a given practice, as the example just provided suggests. I take it that many stereotypes and prejudices we worry about in the domain of social cognition are ideological constructions reinforced by popular culture, advertisements, and so on.

38. However, there is reason to believe that peoples' self-conception and professional efficacy are affected negatively when they participate in a surrounding where they stand out as special (Dasgupta 2013).

39. I address the difficulty in identifying the harm done by stereotyping and prejudiced behavior more elaborately in Sie and van Voorst Vader-Bours 2016.

40. For research findings and arguments to the contrary, see Ceci and Williams 2011; for a critical discussion of those findings and arguments, see Lee 2016.

41. I am greatly indebted to Katrina Hutchison, Catriona Mackenzie, and Marina Oshana for their very constructive comments on earlier versions of this chapter. I also benefitted greatly from discussions with Arno Wouters, the fellows of the Einstein group on Consciousness, Emotions and Values at Humboldt University, Berlin and participants in the workshops organized by this group, Awee Prins, Jan Springintveld, and Nicole van Voorst Vader-Bours. I also thank Wendy Carlton for some important and very helpful editorial suggestions.

References

Bratman, M. 2007. *Structures of Agency*. Cambridge, MA: Harvard University Press.

Brennan, S. 2016. "The Moral Status of Micro-Inequities: In Favor of Institutional Solutions." In *Implicit Bias and Philosophy, Vol. 2, Moral Responsibility, Structural Injustice, and Ethics* edited by J. Saul and M. Brownstein, 235–253. Oxford: Oxford University Press.

Calhoun, C. 1989. "Responsibility and Reproach." *Ethics* 99 (2): 389–406.

Ceci, S. J., and W. M. Williams. 2011. "Social Sciences—Psychological and Cognitive Sciences: Understanding Current Causes of Women's Underrepresentation in Science." *Pnas* 108 (8): 3157–3162.

Darwall, S. L. 2006. *The Second-Person Standpoint: Morality, Respect, and Accountability.* Cambridge, MA: Harvard University Press.

Dasgupta, N. 2013. "Implicit Attitudes and Beliefs Adapt to Situations: A Decade of Research on the Malleability of Implicit Prejudice, Stereotypes, and the Self-Concept." *Advances in Experimental Social Psychology* 47: 233–279.

Dennett, D. 2003. *Freedom Evolves*. London: Penguin Putnam Inc.

Fischer, J. M. 1994. *The Metaphysics of Free Will*. Blackwell, Cambridge Mass USA.

Haidt, J. 2001, "The Emotional Dog and Its Rational Tail: A Social Intuitionist Approach to Moral Judgment." *Psychological Review* 108 (4): 814–834.

Herman, B. 2012, "Love and Morality (or Love's Complexities)." Paper delivered at Utrecht University, the Netherlands, September 18, 2012.

Holroyd, J. 2012. "Responsibility for Implicit Bias." *Journal of Social Philosophy* 43 (3): 274–306.

Huebner, B. 2016. "Implicit Bias, Reinforcement Learning, and Scaffolded Moral Cognition." In *Implicit Bias and Philosophy, Vol. 1, Metaphysics and Epistemology*, edited by M. Brownstein and J. Saul, 47–79. Oxford: Oxford University Press.

Huebner, B. Forthcoming. "Planning and Prefigurative Politics: The Nature of Freedom and the Possibility of Control." In *Engaging Daniel Dennett: Essays*, edited by B. Huebner, 47–79. New York: Oxford University Press.

Kelly, D., and E. Roedder. 2008. "Racial Cognition and the Ethics of Implicit Bias." *Philosophy Compass* 3 (3): 522–540.

Lee, C. K. 2016. "Revisiting Current Causes of Women's Underrepresentation in Science." In *Implicit Bias and Philosophy, Vol. 1*, edited by J. Saul and M. Brownstein, 265–282. Oxford: Oxford University Press.

McGeer, V. 2010. "Co-Reactive Attitudes and the Making of Moral Community." In *Emotions, Imagination and Moral Reasoning*, edited by C. MacKenzie and R. Langdon, 299–326. New York: Psychology Press.

McGeer, V. 2015. "Building a Better Theory of Responsibility." *Philosophical Studies* 172 (10): 2635–2649.

McKenna, M. S. 2012. *Conversation and Responsibility*. New York: Oxford University Press.

Moss-Racusin, C. A., J. F. Dovidio, V. L. Brescoll, M. J. Graham, and J. Handelsman. 2012. "Science Faculty's Subtle Gender Biases Favor Male Students." *Pnas* 109 (41): 16474–16479.

Nadelhoffer, T. 2008. "Bad Acts, Blameworthy Agents, and Intentional Actions: Some Problems for Juror Impartiality." In *Experimental Philosophy*, edited by J. Knobe and S. Nichols, 149–170. New York: Oxford University Press.

Pereboom, D. 2013. "Skepticism about Free Will." In *Exploring the Illusion of Free Will and Moral Responsibility*, edited by G. D. Caruso, 19–40. Plymouth, UK: Lexington Books.

Pettit, P., and M. Smith. 1996. "Freedom in Belief and Desire." *Journal of Philosophy* 93 (9): 429–449.

Saul, J. 2013. "Implicit Bias, Stereotype Threat, and Women in Philosophy." In *Women in Philosophy: What Needs to Change?*, edited by K. Hutchison and F. Jenkins, 21–38. Oxford: Oxford University Press.

Saul, J., and M. Brownstein, eds. 2016. *Implicit Bias and Philosophy, Vol. 1, Metaphysics and Epistemology and Vol. 2, Moral Responsibility, Structural Injustice, and Ethics*. Oxford: Oxford University Press.

Sie, M. 2005. *Justifying Blame: Why Free Will Matters and Why It Does Not*. Amsterdam: Rodopi.

Sie, M., and A. Wouters. 2008. "The Real Neuroscientific Challenge to Free Will." *Trends in Cognitive Science* 12 (1): 3–4.

Sie, M., and A. Wouters. 2010. "The BCN Challenge to Compatibilist Free Will and Personal Responsibility." *Neuroethics* 3: 121–133. doi:10.1007/s12152-009-9054-8.

Sie, M. 2013. "Free Will an Illusion? An Answer from a Pragmatic Sentimentalist Point of View." In *Exploring the Illusion of Free Will and Moral Responsibility*, edited by G. D. Caruso, 273–289. New York: Lexington Books.

Sie, M. 2014. "Self-Knowledge and the Minimal Conditions of Responsibility: A Traffic-Participation View on Human (Moral) Agency." *The Journal of Value Inquiry* 48 (2): 271–291.

Sie, M. 2015. "Moral Hypocrisy and Moral Reasons." *Ethical Theory and Moral Practice* 18 (2): 223–235.

Sie, M., and N. van Voorst Vader-Bours. 2016. "Stereotypes and Prejudices: Whose Responsibility? Indirect Personal Responsibility for Implicit Bias." In *Implicit Bias and Philosophy: Vol. 1, Metaphysics and Epistemology*, edited by M. Brownstein and J. Saul, 90–114. Oxford: Oxford University Press.

Strawson, G. 2013. "The Impossibility of Ultimate Responsibility?" In *Exploring the Illusion of Free Will and Moral Responsibility*, edited by G. Caruso, 41–52. Plymouth, UK: Lexington Books.

Strawson, P. F. (1962) 1982. "Freedom and Resentment." Reprinted in *Free Will*, edited by G. Watson, 59–81. Oxford: Oxford University Press.

Vargas, M. 2013. *Building Better Beings: A Theory of Moral Responsibility*. Oxford: Oxford University Press.

Wallace, R. J. 1994. *Responsibility and the Moral Sentiments*. Cambridge, MA: Harvard University Press.

Watson, G. 1987. "Responsibility and the Limits of Evil: Variations on a Strawsonian Theme." In *Responsibility, Character, and the Emotions*, edited by F. Schoeman, 256–286. New York: Cambridge University Press.

Wolf, S. 1990. *Freedom within Reason.* New York: Oxford University Press.

Wouters, A. 2011. "Vrije wil en verantwoordelijkheid in evolutionair perspectief." In *Hoezo Vrije Wil?*, edited by M. Sie, 190–209. Rotterdam: Lemniscaat.

Zheng, R. 2016. "Attributability, Accountability, and Implicit Bias." In *Implicit Bias and Philosophy, Vol. 2, Moral Responsibility, Structural Injustice, and Ethics,* edited by J. Saul and M. Brownstein, 62–89. Oxford: Oxford University Press.

INDEX

accountability, 5, 15, 22, 23, 54n2, 61–62, 66–75,
  78n14, n16, 84–86, 92, 103, 250n17. *See
  also* answerability; attributability; moral
  responsibility
actions
  intentional, 85, 112
  interpretation of, 40, 45–48, 51, 56n24, 69–71,
    260–62, 287–88, 294–95, 308
  responsibility for, 163–64, 180–81
  See also agency
Adams, Robert, 33n20, 181n9, 182n26
adaptive preferences, 11, 64–65, 132n4, 133n14
affluenza, 264–66, 269, 273, 274. *See also* class
agency, 103n4, 132n3, 167–68, 185–86, 199–201,
    233–34, 246–47, 303–5
  circumstances and, 7–9, 85, 112–17, 126,
    128–31, 132n8, 137, 141–43, 244, 247
  collective, 26–27, 185–86, 200, 201n3
  cultivation of, 24, 117–23, 158–59, 140
  dilemma, 28, 233–39, 246–47
  epistemic, 17, 19, 125
  individual vs extra-individual, 185–94, 202n8
  individualism about, 10, 24, 26–27, 59, 116,
    185–94, 199–201
  marginal, 15, 61, 207, 220, 224, 262, 265
  moral, 7–9, 28, 32n7, 52, 142, 210–13,
    232, 305
  morally responsible, 10, 13–14, 56n20, 59–62,
    75–76, 113, 140–54, 189–90
  self-governing, 10–14, 140, 147,
    236–37, 244–46
  situated, 117, 120, 123–27, 186, 200, 238
  the social constitution of, 24, 110–31
  See also actions; autonomy; rationality
Allais, Lucy, 260
Anderson, Elizabeth, 17
Anderson, Joel, 78n10
answerability, 6, 14–15, 28, 66–75, 78n14,
    233–48, 249n12–17, 253–71. *See also*

accountability; attributability; moral
  responsibility; reasons
Antony, Louise, 89–90, 92
appraisal
  aretaic, 62, 241–42, 243, 245–47 (*see also*
    attributability, character)
  evaluative, 28, 234, 242, 243, 246–47, 250n20
  moral, 30–31, 242, 246–47
  See also respect
Arpaly, Nomy, 11, 129, 181n4, 182n20, 241
attributability, 14–15, 20, 22, 62–66, 78n14,
    n16, 243, 250n17. *See also* accountability;
    answerability; appraisal, aretaic; character;
    moral responsibility
Austin, J. L., 29, 257–58, 271n5
authenticity, 10–12, 15, 77n8, 235, 238–45
autonomy, 1, 9–15, 28, 77n2, n8, 132n4, 231–48
  as capacity, 9–12
  externalist conceptions of, 28, 231–35, 243–48,
    249n4, 250n18
  internalist conceptions of, 231–32, 235, 249n5
  moral responsibility and, 10–15, 28, 231–48
  procedural theories of, 11–14, 77n8, 239
  relational conceptions of, 9–15, 28, 64–65,
    77n2, n8, 231–48
  as self-authorization, 14, 249n8, 250n16
  as self-determination, 14
  as self-governance, 10–12, 14, 15, 249n8
  as status, 10, 12, 234–35, 246
  substantive theories of, 12–13, 234, 247, 249n8
  See also agency, self-governing; authenticity
Ayer, A. J., 31n1

beliefs, false, 27, 64–65, 77n8, 168–69, 196–201
Bell, Macalester, 253
Bennett, Christopher, 128, 155
Benson, Paul, 13–14, 28, 65, 237–38, 241,
    248, 249n8

Strawson, P. F., 2–5, 27, 31n1, 32n2, n5,
38–39, 47, 55n10, 59, 139, 151, 155, 164,
206–11, 216, 218–19, 226, 227n1, 247,
257, 272n8, 282, 296, 297n2, 307, 312,
320n29, n31
Sunstein, Cass, 129, 131, 133n18, 202n10
Superson, Anita, 77n7, 103n10

Tadros, Victor, 126
Taylor, Charles, 10
Thaler, Richard, 129, 131, 133n18
Thompson, Morgan, 89
Tognazzini, Neil, 32n4

values
moral, 270–71
personal, 289–90, 292
social influences on, 110–14, 304–5
See also authenticity
Vargas, Manuel, 7–8, 12, 24–25, 31, 45,
56n25, 59–60, 75–76, 77n3, 78n16, 137,
138–43, 145, 147, 150–55, 157, 159n1–4,
160n5–6, n14, 182n25, 301, 312, 314,
318n3, 320n28, n30
violence, 16, 61, 97–102, 267–68
domestic, 223
systematic, 16, 61, 97–102

volitionism, 164, 166–67, 177, 181n4, 182n22–23,
236–37, 249n14

Walker, Margaret, 74, 82, 85
Wallace, R. Jay, 4, 253, 271n3, n7, 275, 297n1, 312,
314, 320n25–26
Washington, Natalie, 19, 20
Watson, Gary, 3–5, 7, 10, 14–15, 39, 45, 54n1–2,
61, 62, 103n6, 114, 116, 177, 207, 216, 226,
241, 265, 272n13, 282, 297n2, 320n28
Westlund, Andrea, 13–14, 28–29, 232–242, 245,
246–48, 249n8
will
bad, 165–75, 182n23
good, 21, 38–40, 45–48, 53, 155
implicit bias and, 166–68, 178
quality of, 21, 38–42, 45–54, 55n11, 60, 69–70,
77n3, 123–25, 139, 164–65, 181n1, 261, 282
Wolf, Susan, 32n9, n13, 55n6, 116, 182n26,
312, 320n26
women, 17, 19, 27, 42–43, 65, 73, 87–95, 104n13,
168–69, 174–75, 179–80, 207–8, 220–27,
233–35, 239, 245, 246, 248, 266, 272n17.
See also gender; sexism

Zheng, Robin, 19
Zoloth, Laurie, 266, 272n17